INVENTING

the

IT GIRL

ALSO BY HILARY A. HALLETT

Go West, Young Women! The Rise of Early Hollywood

INVENTING

the

IT GIRL

How Elinor Glyn
Created the Modern Romance
and Conquered Early Hollywood

HILARY A. HALLETT

Liveright Publishing Corporation
A Division of W. W. Norton & Company
Independent Publishers Since 1923

Frontispiece: *Elinor Glyn* by Philip de László (1914)

For information about permission to reproduce selections from this book,
write to Permissions, Liveright Publishing Corporation, a division of
W. W. Norton & Company, Inc., 500 Fifth Avenue, New York, NY 10110

For information about special discounts for bulk purchases, please contact
W. W. Norton Special Sales at specialsales@wwnorton.com or 800-233-4830

Manufacturing by Lakeside Book Company
Book design by Lisa Buckley
Production manager: Anna Oler

Library of Congress Cataloging-in-Publication Data

Names: Hallett, Hilary A., 1968– author.
Title: Inventing the it girl : how Elinor Glyn created the modern romance and conquered
    early Hollywood / Hilary A. Hallett.
Description: First edition. | New York : Liveright Publishing Corporation, [2022] |
    Includes bibliographical references and index.
Identifiers: LCCN 2022009212 | ISBN 9781631490699 (cloth) |
    ISBN 9781631490705 (epub)
Subjects: LCSH: Glyn, Elinor, 1864–1943. | Novelists, English—20th century—
    Biography. | Journalists—Great Britain—Biography. | Women travelers—Biography.
Classification: LCC PR6013.L8 Z655 2022 | DDC 823/.912 [B]—dc23/eng/20220301
LC record available at https://lccn.loc.gov/2022009212

Liveright Publishing Corporation, 500 Fifth Avenue, New York, N.Y. 10110
www.wwnorton.com

W. W. Norton & Company Ltd., 15 Carlisle Street, London W1D 3BS

1 2 3 4 5 6 7 8 9 0

For my boys, again, Jackson, Miles & Christopher

CONTENTS

INVENTING
the
IT GIRL

On Flappers
and Their Philosophers

It girl, *n. colloquial* (orig. *U.S.*). A woman who is very famous,
fashionable, or successful at a particular time, *esp.* (chiefly *U.S.*) a
glamorous, vivacious, or sexually attractive actress, model, etc., or
(chiefly *British*) a young, rich woman who has achieved celebrity because
of her socialite lifestyle. Originally (with *the*) referring to the U.S. actress
Clara Bow (1905–65), and her role in the silent film *It* (1927).

—*Oxford English Dictionary* (1927–)

This is an unconventional biography about an unconventional
British woman, the late Victorian romance writer and celebrity author Elinor Glyn (1864–1943) who midwifed much
of the sexual ethos of Anglo-American popular culture. When she
died peacefully in London, Glyn's obituaries called her "the founder
of the modern sex novel" and "originator of the popular term 'It.'"
They also recalled that the redheaded writer with cat-green eyes
who had "shocked the world of our grandmothers" had "led a life
as glamorous as anything in her novels," earning the friendship and
respect of the most powerful and creative personalities in Britain,
France, and America, through war and peace, over the half century
between 1890 and 1940.[1]

Elinor Glyn's life and legacy gives the lie to some of the most
enduring assumptions regarding the dynamics involved in the ascent
of mass culture. Most believe that the stories and images that took
flight in the imaginations of so many people more than a century
ago were man-made. Perhaps there is a vague awareness that women

readers—long the primary consumers of fiction—and writers like Jane Austen were central from the start to the fortunes of the novel in Anglo-America (arguably its first mass culture). But that is all.

Nowhere has this notion about the assumed maleness of the movers and shakers who created our cultural past been more pervasive—or wrong—than in what has been called the basic story about the founding of Hollywood. This story focuses either on the creative genius of directors D. W. Griffith, Cecil B. DeMille, and Mack Sennett, or the business smarts of the mostly immigrant Jewish men who built the Hollywood studio system. As is often the case, the victor writes the history, and in the evolution of how power and prestige got distributed in the American film industry white men obviously won out. But the reality of Hollywood's founding, as much recent work has shown, was far more complicated given that it was the least sex-segregated of America's major industries when Elinor Glyn arrived in Los Angeles in 1920. This startlingly unfamiliar landscape, in which many white women wielded considerable control, in part accounts for how Glyn managed "the paradox of bringing not only 'good taste' to the [movie] colony, but also 'sex appeal,'" as both Sir Cecil Beaton—perhaps the twentieth century's sharpest eye—and producer Samuel Goldwyn recognized.[2]

Yet the durable belief that a masculine cast of characters established the dreamscapes of mass culture has consigned the influence of women like Elinor Glyn—who wrote of some of the most popular novels of her day, reoriented the romance genre, and set the mold for a new kind of female celebrity author *and* how to represent heterosexual sex in Hollywood—to the status of trash.

To be clear: this biographer has no interest in engaging debates about the relative artistic merits of Glyn's many creative works. Rather, *Inventing the It Girl* restores the impossibly elegant, witty tastemaker and prolific author—of more than forty books, countless magazine articles, and twenty-seven stories that became films—to her rightful place at the fountainhead of mass culture. For it was there that this visionary lady with hedonistic leanings infused her fantasies and philosophies about sex, love, and marriage into the romantic aesthetic that shaped the desires of untold millions of her fans for generations to come.

This is not a typical literary or scholarly biography, then, nor is it an exhaustive, cradle-to-grave account of her life. Here, I have tried to track the unfolding of a woman bred only for a respectable marriage into one of the most notoriously influential cultural figures of her age.

This slice of Elinor Glyn's story begins in the privacy of her stepfather's library, where, like so many women who became writers in her day, she had unfettered access to the materials she would draw on to fashion her own ideas about how life and love should work. But her story gathers steam at the point where most romances have always ended: *after* her marriage up the social ladder in 1892 to Clayton Glyn, a member of the English gentry class who was far less well off than he appeared. The marriage proved a misalliance and she soon turned to her pen for escape and, later, the economic survival of her family, which included her two little girls, Margot and Juliet.

Here is the place—in the aftermath of an adult woman's reckoning with a difficult sexual and social adjustment to marriage—where Glyn would leave her mark as a writer. By 1901, she had become society's premiere chronicler before devising, at the age of forty-three, the erotically focused modern romance novel with her great success-de-scandal, *Three Weeks* (1907). The novel celebrated the titularly short, illicit affair of an older, unhappily married Slavic queen and the patrician young lover she selects and schools in erotic arts to conceive their love child. Perhaps the most widely denounced work of popular fiction published before World War I, Glyn's "free love" novel helped to splinter the genteel code in English literature years before D. H. Lawrence's more celebrated troubles with the censors. *Three Weeks* also reportedly sold more than 2 million copies in English by 1917, when republication in a cheaper "million-seller" edition produced an estimated 5 million copies. Translated into every major European language, it spawned a host of imitators, generating at least twelve adaptations in print and on stage, film, and television through 1977. By the 1920s, "if a director wanted to show that one of the characters in his film was leading a racy life, all he had to do was show her holding a copy of *Three Weeks* in her lap, just holding the book was enough to tag her as independent and modern," a silent-era film archivist observed decades later, explaining why Ohio censored a Disney cartoon in 1930 for showing Clarabelle the cow in a field reading Glyn's bad book.[3]

Although ostracized by much of British society, the popularity of her pro-sex tale purchased her a freedom of expression that the censors and the critics could not silence. Glyn rode her notoriety to unparalleled celebrity for a female author and, in the aftermath of her sudden rise to international fame, concocted a glamorous literary persona who blended her imposing stature as a very fashionable British lady with the seductiveness of her Tiger Queen heroine (so-called for the novel's most infamous sex-scene on a tiger skin). This persona smoothed the acceptance of her naughty book.

The fame Glyn accumulated first as a novelist, and then as a journalist in Paris writing on modern morals and the state of society during World War I, led to her remarkable third act. Movie producers invited her to Hollywood in 1920 at the age of fifty-six. In Los Angeles, she quickly established her leadership over the movie colony's young residents and taught Hollywood's first stars and directors how to express passion on the screen with a persuasiveness and finesse that delighted audiences and quieted the howls of the moral reformers during the Jazz Age. Glyn baked her approach to staging heterosexual sex into the visual style of mass culture. Rose petals, silken lingerie, long velvet gowns, and ropes of pearls have never gone out of fashion for signaling a woman's sexual self-possession. Smoldering looks, long kisses, lingering caresses, and embraces that contain a show of force became the stock-in-trade of the romance, whatever medium. She conceived all of these.

For it is no exaggeration to say that all modern romance falls under the shadow cast by her chic silhouette. Elinor Glyn's reorientation of the romance novel toward the "sex novel" focused on the essential, and often difficult, role that sexual passion played in love. This added the special ingredient that led the genre to outsell all others over the twentieth century (alongside detective stories).

If many don't know that today, Glyn's successors did. The well-born English novelist Barbara Cartland (reputedly the twentieth century's bestseller) was her protégée and later brought some of her mentor's books back into print in the 1970s, carefully expunging some of the steamiest eroticism first.[4] Novelist Catherine Cookson—

who never accepted the label of romance writer but sold more than a 100 million books in the genre—was an acolyte at a distance in the 1920s. The illegitimate daughter of an alcoholic, Cookson had almost no formal education and used the reading list Glyn prescribes for her heroine in *The Career of Katherine Bush* (1916) to become a writer. Glyn's lifelong touchstone—Lord Chesterfield's *Letters to His Son on the Fine Art of Becoming a Man of the World and a Gentleman* (1774)—became Cookson's: "With Lord Chesterfield I read my first mythology. I learned my first history and geography. With Lord Chesterfield I went travelling the world. I would fall asleep reading the letters and awake around three o'clock in the morning my mind deep in the fascination of this new world, where people conversed, not just talked." And where they made exquisite love, Glyn would have added with her imperious air.[5]

"A storm centre wherever she went," as the great fan from her last years, Cecil Beaton, recalled, "who possessed the talent of making friends easily," Glyn fascinated, frustrated and provoked some of the world's most interesting people across three continents. One of the challenges of this biography was not to let her many fascinating friends—and the many places they traveled—carry away the narrative for too long.[6]

If Glyn were to invite all of the most interesting people from the pages that follow to one of the dinner parties that she loved, the guest list would include almost equal parts aristocratic politicians and creative souls, with a sprinkling of newspapermen. At her right would sit her older sister, Lady Lucy Duff-Gordon, who got her start designing clothes for her beautiful little sister and became perhaps the most famous couturier of the Edwardian period. At her left would be Glyn's brilliant younger daughter, Juliet, Lady Rhys-Williams, who drew closer—not without friction—to her mother as she aged and became a self-taught economist and governor of the BBC. Close by, one would find her greatest inspiration, the French stage diva Sarah Bernhardt; her dearest friends, the English royal hostess par excellence of her era, "Daisy" Greville, Countess of Warwick, and the colonial administrator, Lord Alfred Milner, who waged the Boer War; her best confidant, the famed Swedish mystic and healer, Dr. Axel Munthe; her grandest love, Lord George Curzon, Marquess of Kedleston, Secretary of State for Foreign Affairs, traveler, and viceroy of India; and her favorite intellectual, English philosopher and fellow Spiritualist, F. H. Bradley. Arrayed farther away would be the many people who aided her professional feats over decades: the Romanov hostess, Grand Duchess Maria Pavlovna; newspaper tycoons Lord George Riddell and William Randolph Hearst; and the many younger colleagues in the movie colony with whom she worked and danced the night away, including Gloria Swanson, Mary Pickford, Charlie Chaplin, Rudolph Valentino, King Vidor, Cedric Gibbons, Marion Davies, Jesse Lasky, Samuel Goldwyn, Irving Thalberg, Louis B. Mayer, John Gilbert, Cecil B. DeMille and, of course, Clara Bow, the young woman she made into the first official "It Girl" and the flaming symbol of the roaring 1920s.

Although no other person could assemble such a remarkable party, almost all of her guests have received recognition far beyond their host, until now.[7]

The 1920s' most famous flapper, Clara Bow, recognized that the writer, herself, was the original model of a new kind of sexually emancipated, professionally independent, and spiritually brave woman who inspired so many. "Miss Bow always said Miss Glyn was the epitome of 'It,'" as the actress remarked when the "Famous Novelist" died in 1943. Elinor Glyn and the Tiger Queen she created, imitated, and then cast for MGM became a cultural touchstone for generations who wanted to imagine plunging into waters where women might frolic freely alongside men. Down into the 1950s, Ian Fleming—author of the James Bond spy novels and known as an irresistible ladies' man—presented women he wanted to seduce with books from his collection of French pornography and *Three Weeks*, hoping to give them the courage to act on their desires—and his.[8]

Certainly, courage was never in short supply in the life of the young redhead everyone called Nell or Nellie Sutherland when she began reading her way through her stepfather's library as an impressionable adolescent on Jersey, the island where she was born. Like the vast majority of women worldwide, Elinor Glyn did not have the same name over the course of her life; she also shared a first name with her mother. For simplicity's sake, she will go by Nell here, which was what those who knew the Tiger Queen best mostly called her anyway.

The title of this prologue alludes to a collection of stories, *Flappers and Philosophers* (1920), by F. Scott Fitzgerald who began (unsuccessfully) trying to scale MGM's gates not long before Glyn made her triumphant final exit in 1928. Widely honored as the premiere poet of the Jazz Age and the flapper, Fitzgerald's views on the period have been hailed as literary masterpieces and, all too often, taken to stand in for the whole. Relegated to the trash bin, the impress of Madame Glyn's much more successful romantic effusions—in terms of absolute numbers reached—have left only the faintest recognition of her authorship behind.

Interestingly, Fitzgerald recognized Glyn's position in the vanguard of projecting franker ideas about heterosexual passion—and particularly about the sexual desires of white women, which Fitzgerald himself seemed to fear and certainly never imagined from the inside out. A very young man in the 1920s, he mistakenly called Glyn, thirty-two years his senior, a contemporary. Fitzgerald was right because Elinor Glyn was, if nothing else, ever-forward looking, a woman ahead of her times.[9]

Nell Sutherland (Glyn) in the 1880s

Act I

BEAUTY

CHAPTER 1

In the Library, Jersey, the Channel Islands, 1880

Love is so physical, and so is reading.

—Virginia Woolf[1]

Nell Sutherland slipped into her stepfather's stone house by the back door and padded toward the library with the air of one of the tigers that later made her notorious.[2]

She and the collie had walked farther than usual, and Roy had collapsed just inside the gate. The two had wound their way along Colomberie Street past the Georgian townhouses and stately buildings like the Hotel de France near the old harbor and the stalls in the market square that marked St. Helier as the island's capital.

The tide had been out down at the cobblestone port and the harbor looked like some angry sea god had sucked it down to the muck. Turning west on a path that edged along the coast, they passed boats listing precariously in every direction as they languished on the bay's exposed bottom. Farmers struggled to haul their potato-laden carts across the silt, calling directions in Jèrriais, the dialect particular to this island perched within sight of Normandy. Near dusk, the waters would return with astonishing speed, righting the vessels and drowning the unwary. Ship captains would set sail, navigating the rocks and reefs that explained why Jersey had been for more than a thousand years the Channel Islands' shipwreck capital and a place dotted with imposing forts facing the sea. Despite the temperate climate and turquoise waters, it was not an easy place to visit, or to leave.

Inside the library, undetected, sixteen-year-old Nell reasonably

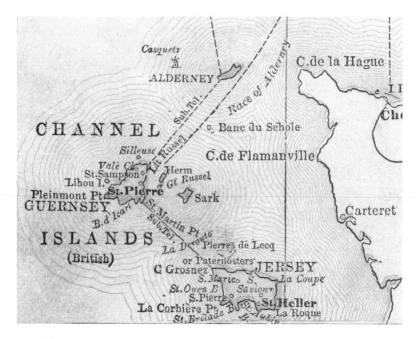

Textbook map from 1884 of the Channel Islands

hoped to escape notice until teatime. If luck went her way, she would return later with a candle and read deep into the night. When she finally left home, what she missed most was this "wilderness of books." Here, in her stepfather's library, like so many of the luckiest women who became writers later on, Nell had access to the books that allowed her to pursue an independent education in an era in which very few girls could claim such a privilege. Here, she found the materials to create her story as a modern woman whose novels would take the world by storm.[3]

The library's thick door silenced the coughing and complaining of her detested stepfather, David Kennedy. Elinor Sutherland Kennedy, Nell's mother and namesake, had been left a widow at twenty-three when her beloved husband of just four years, Douglas Sutherland, caught typhoid fever and died while working as an engineer on the Turin tunnel in Italy. The distraught woman promptly returned to her parents' Canadian farm in January of 1865, gave her two baby girls' care over to her mother, and retreated from the world. Nell was four months old, and her older sister, Lucy, not yet two.

Grandmamma Lucy Saunders rigorously trained her grand-daughters for finer things at Summer Hill, the home whose pillared portico looked down from a hilltop onto the growing outpost of Guelph (population 2,000), in Southwestern Ontario. The daughter of Sir Richard Wilcocks of Dublin, Lucy Anne had grown up principally in Paris where she met Thomas Saunders, whose French mother was said to have survived the Revolutionary Terror by hiding in the countryside. The Saunderses had moved to Canada by way of Pondicherry, India, in 1833. While they carved a farm from the wilderness, Lucy Anne bore eight daughters and one son, always quietly longing to return to France. After laboring all day, husband and wife dressed for dinner each night, often in the finery sent to the exiled couple by their wealthy French relations.

"A natural rebel," granddaughter Lucy "hated Grandmamma and her rules and teachings" and ran around with the boys whenever possible. Meanwhile, the "odd, vain, imaginative" Nell hid in quiet corners spinning fairy tales in which she always played the queen.[4]

Everyone at Summer Hill loved March best because it promised the end of another relentless gray winter and the arrival of *le tonneau bienvenu*, as they called the enormous plain wooden barrel their relations sent from Paris. The day the barrel's riot of color and textures spilled the pleasures of another world onto the kitchen floor was even better than Christmas, both sisters agreed. The profusion of plenty was the point: silk stockings as delicate as spider webs; bonnets dyed teal or magenta to match the birdwings on their trim; flouncy dresses in every garden shade; wigs dressed in the latest mode; yards of shimmering fabrics; bonbons; books; and even false teeth.[5]

The sisters' memories of their earliest years in Canada lingered most on Grandmamma's stern instruction in the code of noblesse oblige developed by the French aristocracy in the pre-Revolutionary ancien régime. The distance between society's orders was unbridgeable and ordained by God, they learned, but also that good breeding was as essential as good birth. Each day a housemaid ushered the two little girls into the parlor, where they sat before her imposing personage for five long minutes without making a movement or sound of any kind.

"Grandmamma's code," Nell recalled, "demanded that one should adjust oneself to all realities, preserving a cheerful and witty outlook upon life in the face of adversity and accepting the inevitable with calm. 'If your hand has been cut off,' she used to say, 'it is driveling and mawkish to meditate upon each drop of blood.'" Lucy remembered a more succinct version: "'Ladies must never show emotion or cry. The common people can find that relaxation.'"[6]

Everything changed for the two sisters when a well-off, well-traveled Scottish bachelor of sixty-four came to court the young widow with the cameo profile and auburn hair. David Kennedy "exerted a kind of fascination" that drew the withdrawn woman back into the world. Their mother felt "nothing but an exaggerated respect" for Mr. Kennedy, which had blossomed into "something more like terror" by the wedding. But marry she did to fulfill her husband's dying wish that his girls grow up in Britain rather than the Canadian wilds.[7]

Mr. Kennedy quickly kept his word, moving his new bride and two stepdaughters in 1871 to Balgreggan Castle, his ancestral home in the Mull of Galloway along the southern Scottish coast. Arriving at night in their "colonial clothes," the castle and its inhabitants at once enchanted the seven- and eight-year-old little girls, leaving an impression that permanently shaped both their aspirations. "Ushered by grand looking footmen into a spacious beautiful room with shaded lamps and filled with ladies and gentlemen in full evening dress," the sisters got their first view of the dazzling life hinted at in *le tonneau bienvenu*.[8]

A guest at the castle who had been the belle of the season that year in London took pity on the oddly dressed girls, letting them play in a bedroom whose cerise silk draperies still stretched vividly across Nell's imagination seventy years later. Thrilled by the elegant environment and the woman's glamorous clothes—a pink silk peignoir with matching satin slippers was a particular delight—Nell decided that her ambition was no longer to be a fairy queen, but a fashionable lady of the world.[9]

Lung problems quickly drove Mr. Kennedy and his new family

to the more temperate climate of Jersey, a tax-free, rigidly ordered island society of well-born younger sons and retired military officers stretching their bank accounts, where Norman farmers worked the land. They stayed first at Richelieu, a large manor house of some distinction in the countryside furnished with fine reproductions of notable figures from the seventeenth century. A portrait of Nell Gwynn—the actress and royal mistress of King Charles II— by the great court painter Sir Peter Lely that graced the drawing room became Nell's favorite. In 1874 they moved again, this time to the more modest stone house that Mr. Kennedy bought in town on Colomberie Street.

Consumed by tending her crusty, infirm, and miserly husband, Elinor Kennedy would raise two daughters whose mistrust of womanly submission ran deep. Victorian ideals of wifely duty, then particularly prevalent among the middle class, led their mother to make the satisfaction of Mr. Kennedy's incessant demands her main purpose. To both her daughters, she appeared "a perfect slave" to a man "selfish and domineering to the point of cruelty. . . . The reasons for actions and decisions were never explained. Obedience must be blind and instantaneous, and feeling did not count one way or another," Nell noted with still evident bitterness decades later of her notoriously flinty stepfather. "My rebellious tendencies naturally flourished under this regime, and gratitude and affection died away."[10]

Separated by little more than a year, "the Sutherland girls"— as everyone called them on Jersey—were "both exceeding clever," according to their closest friend, Ada Northcott, the daughter of Sir William, governor of Jersey. Both Lucy and Nell loved to draw and had imaginations capable of transforming their surroundings. A resolute tomboy with precocious dressmaking skills, Lucy's nimble fingers meant they always appeared well tended. "Although their old stepfather kept them very short of money, they were always the best dressed girls of all our society," Ada boasted of her friends.[11]

The sisters' mutual creative talents fed each other's determination to glitter in the world, but they possessed distinctly different temperaments. Impetuous Lucy "never knew the meaning of shyness" and "found it easy to make friends." While fastidious Nell was "very reserved," with an innate caution compounded by the family's repeated reshufflings and the self-doubt that went along with having bright red hair.[12]

A sign of perverse sexuality, bad temper, and religious heresy associated with Judas, Jews, and witches since the Middle Ages, the red hair explained why no one considered Nell pretty as a child, according to her friend Ada. "The prejudice against habitual silence," wrote an English novelist in 1884, "is almost as inveterate as the prejudice against red hair." Only Lucy, with her artist's eye, saw early on that her sister's pale green, almond shaped eyes, porcelain complexion, and symmetrical features marked her as a beauty-to-be. Lucy treated Nell as a life size doll from the start. Beneath Nell's prim expression lay a keen sense of humor and a talent for caricature vented in sketchbooks "with sententious remarks written beneath the pictures." But the girl with the spooky green eyes, brilliant red hair, and distant manner left all the other children "rather afraid," Ada admitted.[13]

At a party at Government House in 1878, the great Victorian beauty and Jersey's native daughter, Lillie Langtry, left an indelible impression about what an independent-minded woman might achieve if she followed her desires off the island. Five years before, Langtry had married and left on a yacht bound for London, where several Pre-Raphaelite painters immortalized her beauty. Famed for her severe black dresses and brandishing an irreverent wit, she became the Prince of Wales's consort before taking up the stage, horse racing, and a series of wellborn men.[14]

Langtry caught Nell, Lucy, and Ada hiding beneath the dressing table in the cloakroom the night she dined at Government House. "There were plenty of scandals whispered about the 'Jersey Lillie,'" Nell wrote later, "but my sister and I would never listen to anything but good of our heroine." A woman capable of capturing the public's attention faced a life in which scandal always lurked, the girls learned young.[15]

Fifteen-year-old Lucy left Jersey for a series of extended stays with various English relatives not long after their brush with Langtry. After years of butting heads, Mr. Kennedy and his willful eldest stepdaughter had had enough. No more depending on the cheap tyrant;

it was time to find her fortune in London, Lucy announced with a flourish Nell resented and admired in equal measure.[16]

Shortly after Lucy's departure, Ada's father got stationed off the island, and David Kennedy announced he would waste no more money on the education of one girl. Nell's only faithful companions became the family dog and the fictional characters who inhabited the library. Tucked in a corner on the ground floor, the simple room did not match its lofty name. But that did not lessen the care Nell invested in this wood-paneled room filled with many of the major historical, philosophical, and literary works published in English and French over the last two centuries.[17]

Nell would be forever insecure about her informal education. But her voracious and largely unsupervised reading in two languages allowed her to embark on a remarkable course of study for a girl of her time. Reading made it possible to question the "doctrines of the Church of the Victorian Age," which promised the luckiest women only marriage, motherhood, and wifely submission. The library nurtured Nell's sense of herself as a closet "heretic" who quietly rejected her parents' hypocritical teachings and "the prohibitions and repressions which they imposed." Into the library she crept, "secretly in rebellion against the whole series of Lawgivers from Moses to Zeus to Queen Victoria, and my stepfather, Mr. Kennedy."[18]

This period primed her imagination: to become a romance writer capable of venturing into foreign territory. Though not a "natural rebel" like her sister, Nell assembled her own pantheon of favorite authors whose views about life and love differed dramatically from those outside the door. Sent from Balgreggan Castle, the books carried Scottish dust. The inventive adolescent revisited the romantic novels of the Edinburgh native Sir Walter Scott. The "Wizard of the North" was the first Anglophone writer to gain an international following during his life; his intensive study of medieval tales and Scottish folklore made him historical fiction's originator. Scott's magic-infused, yet credible novels about the righteous quests of heroes like Robin Hood were the most popular romances of their day. He released the word "glamour" into English as a powerful dark magic that distorts reality. When a goblin ordered to find a book of spells finds the right one, he reads:

It has much of glamour might
Could make a ladye seem a knight
The cobwebs on a dungeon wall
Seem tapestry in lordly hall
And youth seem age, and age seem youth
All was delusion, nought was truth.

Nell reinterpreted glamour's transformative charms in the romances she wrote later, bending its power toward a reinvention that her heroines harness for their pleasure, liberation, and escape.[19]

Primed early by her grandparents to revere the monarchy, the royal past Nell selected to romanticize was the pleasure-minded, gender-bending reign of the Stuart monarch she called "Dear Good King" Charles II. Restored to the throne once the Puritans lost power in 1660, Charles II was an unpopular figure in Nell's time. His commitment to frivolity was the antithesis of the current Queen Victoria. Nell's devotion to this different noble acted as a kind of lifeline to her late father, said to have been the last descendant of a Scottish lord who lost his lands for supporting the Stuart line.

Charles II led her to the Restoration Era's great gadfly and bureaucrat, Samuel Pepys, who taught Nell early that writing and reading were the safest way to engage dangerous thoughts. Pepys rose from humble Puritan beginnings to professionalize the British Navy, offering an early model of a new kind of brilliant, self-made man. But it was the daily diary that he kept from 1660 until 1669 that secured his place in history. First published in 1825, an entirely uncensored version of his diary appeared only in 1970. (Nell began her own not long after and kept it under lock and key for the rest of her life.) Pepys gossiped about the private habits of public figures, recorded the decimation of London by plague and fire, and captured the outpouring of amusements after Charles II returned from exile, reopened the theaters, and allowed women to strut upon the English stage for the first time. Unlike most noblemen, Charles's "capacious heart" adored women of every class. Pepys condemned the king's hedonism even as he emulated his philandering, theatre-loving ways. Historians would echo Pepys's view down to Nell's time: here was a king whose good humor, libertinage, and laziness (about the political aspects of his job) made him impossible to hate or to respect.[20]

The embrace of such habits by the king and those who aspired to keep his company made possible the lionization of a new type of woman. Charles II's mistress Nell Gwynn—the actress whose Lely portrait Nell had so admired at Richelieu, their first home on Jersey—was an early notable British example of the type. Gwynn started on the streets, and in her mother's bawdyhouse, and rose to become the greatest comedic actress of the Restoration stage. Her personal glamour had allowed her to cut an individual path that grabbed the fancy of her times with a force that made her a folk heroine. "She is young, indiscreet, confident, wild and of an agreeable humour" and "acts her part with a good grace," said a court visitor of the king's latest official royal mistress.[21]

The cynical moral outlook of Charles II and his favorites exposed the impressionable young woman to a frank attitude toward sex and the sexes that was fundamentally out of step with the Victorian culture in which she lived. "In all ages it is unfortunately not the simple good women who have ruled the hearts of men," Nell's adulterous heroine kindly explains to her young lover in *Three Weeks*, which made her name synonymous with the scandal associated with the modern woman. "Immoral! It is so quaint a word," her heroine laughs. "Each one sees it how they will, if one remains the faithful beast of burden to one man, one is counted in the world a moral woman."[22]

The figures Nell grew to admire most on the library's shelves assumed, much as she would, that moral perfection did not exist either "among Gods or mortals." Such was the case with Nell's lifelong favorite author, the courtier Philip Stanhope, the 4th Earl of Chesterfield. The good earl's *Letters to His Son on the Art of Becoming a Man of the World and a Gentleman* sat next to her bed all her life and became a touchstone that emphasized the ultimate importance of style. When published after his death in 1773, the four hundred letters that Chesterfield wrote to his illegitimate son brought the word "etiquette" into English and, in a strange twist, made the earl the posthumous author of a popular conduct manual that taught middle-class strivers like Nell how to rise to new occasions. "I have

read them over and over again, and have found them more instructive than any other book," Nell had an aristocratic dowager advise
in another novel she would write, espousing a view she aired whenever the chance arose.[23]

Chesterfield taught Nell that birth was not destiny and that only
perpetual effort could produce the effortlessly attractive manner so
essential to getting ahead in modern life. "Any man of common
understanding may, by proper culture, care, attention, and labour,
make himself whatever he pleases except a good poet," he assured his
bastard son. "Style is the dress of thoughts; and let them be ever so
just. . . . It is not every understanding that can judge of matter; but
every ear can and does judge, more or less, of style." The approach
emphasized that the right key could permit saying the wrong thing,
a lesson that made possible the publication of Nell's steamy "sex
novel," *Three Weeks* (1907) and so much more.[24]

Nell also absorbed the prevailing view of women as weak in body
and mind from Lord Chesterfield, her stepfather, and virtually every
volume in his library. The emptiness of women's brains, the paucity
of their education, and the vanity behind their actions made them
merely "children of a larger growth," Chesterfield advised. "They
have an entertaining tattle, and sometimes wit; but for solid reason-
ing, good sense, I never knew in my life one who reasoned or acted
consequentially for four-and-twenty hours together," he cautioned.
"A man of sense only trifles with them, plays with them, humors
and flatters them, as he does with a sprightly, forward child; but he
neither consults them about, nor trusts them with serious matters."
For much of her adult life, she would struggle to overcome this prejudice against her sex and to prove herself a woman whose vision and
intellect could keep pace with any man's.[25]

What separated the feminine vanity Chesterfield bemoaned in
women from the self-confidence necessary to pursue a grand ambition in some great city beyond the reefs surrounding Jersey? And
what made the strivings of men less pathetic; the infernal stroking
their egos required, their incessant jockeying for position amongst
each other like a pack of sled dogs? What, after all, was calling out
vanity in woman but another of the many ways that men had of
keeping women from saying anything at all?

Energized by her long walk earlier out along the coast with the dog, sixteen-year-old Nell stayed in the library that particular night long past when the stars appeared, her nose deep in *Vanity Fair: A Novel without a Hero* (1847). William Thackeray's lengthy study of the troubled relationship between the self and society satirizes objects of conventional concern—hypocrisy, greed, social climbing, pretense, and moral blindness—in Britain's industrializing, empire-minded society. The subject fascinated many novelists of the age, but Thackeray's tone was grimmer, his moral harder to assess, than that of most Victorian narrators. "In *Vanity Fair*," protested one critic, "[Thackeray's] greatest work, how little there is to love! The people are all scamps, scoundrels, or humbugs." Doing well there—and who wants to fail?—often depends on appearances. "It is all vanity to be sure: But who will not own to liking a little of it?" Thackeray asks his readers. "I should like to know what well-constituted mind, merely because it is transitory, dislikes roast-beef? That is a vanity; but may every man who reads this, have a wholesome portion of it through life. . . . Yes, let us eat our fill of the vain thing, and be thankful thereof."[26]

With the last candle burned almost down to the quick, it was time to head upstairs, her thoughts circling around Thackeray's heroine, Becky Sharp. A roguish, ambitious country girl, Becky embraces the forces of free will and decides to make her own fate. Becky channels her artistic talent and smarts into crafting a witty self who charms her way to the king's court. Her adventures make the "delighted exercise in being alive" palpable, a quality that endeared her to readers like Nell ever since.[27]

But Thackeray also used Becky to expose the dangers associated with a shallowly rooted life in which an attractive mask might disguise a corrupted soul. "I defy anyone to say that our Becky, who certainly has some vices, has not been presented to the public in a perfectly genteel and inoffensive manner," Thackeray reproaches. "In describing this syren, singing and smiling, coaxing and cajoling . . . has he once forgotten the laws of politeness and showed the monster's hideous tail above the water? No!"[28]

Nell knew all about the sirens, the sea nymphs or birds (depending on the source) whose sweet voices tried to tempt men like

The Siren by John Waterhouse (1900)

Odysseus to their doom. She had struggled in the library to learn ancient Greek history, mythology, and philosophy when that pleasure was still one reserved only for boys because the pagan Greek's ideals were thought to challenge Victorian orthodoxies about religious authority and sex roles. (Recall all the naked and fornicating gods and the many powerful goddesses, just for starters.) But even without her passion for the "Old Greeks," it would have been hard to miss the sirens by the late Victorian era, when pre-Raphaelite painters often made their often unconventionally beautiful redheaded models into sirens who symbolized the danger of listening to women at all.[29]

Whatever her failings and follies, Becky Sharp likely also caught Nell's heart because she already knew the sin of vanity to be her worst vice. Nell would earn the right to portray vanity's classic symbol: either a female nude or, more recently, a bourgeois woman primping in front of her mirror. In truth, the care she took with her appearance—with how she dressed, spoke, walked, and smiled— would have made Lord Chesterfield proud. She grew into a woman willing to spend more than she had to make things look and feel just right.[30]

But all that lay ahead.

Once she reached her bedroom, Nell closed the door, put the candle on the bureau, and started to undress. Like Becky, Nell already understood the importance of not getting trapped in one place, of the wonderful tonic of changing scenes. Like Becky, "she would never stay where [she] was, or be content with an uneventful life." Becky knew the price of roast beef and paid it for making life so much sweeter. So would Nell. Like Becky, the price for her freedom would demand freeing the siren inside her no matter the cost—first on the page and then later in the flesh and on screens.[31]

She put the candlestick down on the bedside table and blew out the light.

CHAPTER 2

A Gentleman's Wife

Because she loves him is the only reason a woman should give her life to a man.

—Elinor Glyn, *The Point of View* (1913)

Nice feelings are for people who have money to live as they please.

—Elinor Glyn, *The Vicissitudes of Evangeline* (1905)

Clayton Glyn Jr. waited for his bride beneath an enormous painting of William Kent's *Last Supper* in St. George's Church, Hanover Square, on an unusually fine blue morning on April 27, 1892. The parish church of Mayfair, aristocratic London's heart, St. George's had been solemnizing fashionable weddings for two centuries. The church's intimate scale and plain ornamentation—minus Kent's oil at the front and the giant gold organ selected by George Handel at the rear—made the groom's height and broad shoulders loom larger.

Clayton had bright-blue eyes that crinkled with his thirty-five years, perfect teeth, and a head of silver hair so thick it might have been one of Lord Chesterfield's prize wigs. Or so his finicky bride liked to think. Just seven years older than his bride, he looked handsome enough, like Prince Charming, to satisfy Nell's need for a husband who could make her heart pick up its pace.

Friends called Clayton "a splendid shot" and considered him a generous man with an even disposition, dry wit, and an open, if uncurious, mind. After proposing to Nell in Monte Carlo two months earlier, the devoted hunter abruptly returned home to his Essex estate to "see about his young pheasants" to ensure a good shooting season in the fall. The two had hardly seen each other since. Though not one to linger over aesthetics, Clayton appreciated beautiful things like his wife-to-be. He had carefully selected her Cartier engagement ring and the diamond tiara perched atop her head.[1]

Nell had found a man who would never complain about her decorating and dressmaking bills, however high they piled, an essential quality in the husband of a lady of fashion. From a "fine, old Essex family," the Glyns were members of the parish gentry class of small landowners who regularly socialized with peers like their neighbor Lady "Daisy" Greville, Countess of Warwick, who quickly became Nell's closest friend. One of England's wealthiest counties, Essex remained a rolling green expanse left relatively untouched by the industrial revolution that had made Britain the world's workshop over the last century.[2]

Clayton had inherited the Glyn estate four years before, which included three properties near the small village of Harlow: Durrington House, the elegant Georgian mansion in which Clayton, his brother, and three sisters were raised; Sheering Hall, a pair of timber-framed medieval hall houses that had been roofed together with handmade red clay tiles; and Lamberts, a two-story cottage for the estate manager. A garden, meadow, and heather wood separated the main houses by a mile, which abutted acres of farmland worked by the tenants and day laborers who tended the woods, wheat, and animals, including a fine herd of Jersey cows.[3]

Before his death, the groom's father, Clayton Glyn Sr. Esquire, had acted as justice of the peace, prosecuting his neighbors for crimes like stealing donkeys and poaching game birds four times a year. He had also served on Essex's finance committee and helped to found a "Friends of Labour Society" to slow the creep of tensions between the men who worked the land and those who owned it. "One of a notable, but, alas, rapidly diminishing group of highly useful men," remarked his obituary in 1888; his son's different habits would prove the remark more than a platitude.[4]

Death took up residence at Durrington House the year Clayton succeeded his father as master of the estate. That fall a cart loaded with wheat overturned when a horse stumbled making the turn at Durrington Corner. The cart's shaft instantly crushed the skull of

William Brown, the sixteen-year-old lad riding there whom Clayton had loaned to a neighbor to help during harvest time. Clayton's mother met a slower end after an accident two months later. Riding into town, the carriage horses became spooked by a railroad engine drawing water from a canal in Harlow. The horses ran wild for several hundred yards before the brougham toppled over its embankment. The driver and footman were thrown from their seats, but Mrs. Glyn remained trapped inside, her arm pinned under the carriage. Taken home with a crushed hand, a doctor amputated her arm up to the elbow. Six days later she died.[5]

Clayton arranged for a new set of stained-glass windows to adorn the Norman church in Harlow in his mother's name and then left on an extended trip in 1889. Thirty-two, he was already a confirmed "bon-viveur," accustomed to managing polo matches and shooting parties, not the commonplace horrors associated with rural life. Over the next two years he indulged his taste for fine wines, rich food, and fast company that had first become apparent at Oxford, where he had gotten terribly into debt and came down early from studying law. On this trip, he became a familiar face at gaming tables and restaurants across Europe and the Near East.

Clayton tried to start afresh when he returned to Essex in 1890, almost two years after his mother's death. He rented Durrington House and moved into the more modest Sheering Hall. There he radiated a confidence born of being exceptionally well traveled even among the traveling classes. That quality above any other attracted his bride-to-be.

An English gentleman of the sporting type, Clayton shared a common culture with higher-ranked elites that began with their relationship to the land. Landed estates came with the tenants whose labor and rents funded the leisurely ideal at the center of their lives. The houses on these estates, all named like dear friends, were run by men and women whose constant work formed the self-effacing labor that made possible their occupants' matchless style.[6]

The sons of these estates increasingly attended Britain's "ancient" public (fee-paying) boarding schools, which had consolidated their role as institutions binding these boys together as a class over the nineteenth century. Clayton had gone to Eton at ten, where he learned a habit of absolute deference to precedence and authority through athletic competitions and the brutal enforcement of rules. After going up to university at Cambridge or Oxford, as Clayton did, an English gentleman shunned profitable employment—whether in trade, the professions, or commerce.

Instead, he might seek a position of governance locally or in Britain's expanding empire, which required large numbers to staff the military forces and bureaucracies enforcing its "civilizing missions" across the globe. During Britain's so-called long nineteenth century—from the Napoleonic Wars' end in 1815 until the Great War's start in 1914—its empire grew to encompass nearly 20 percent of the Earth's land mass and 400 million souls. In times of war, a gentleman was called to lead his countrymen and die with gallantry on the field. But such duties took place infrequently and in faraway places during this century of domestic peace, when Empire-made money flowed through London's banks and into the pockets of gentlemen and ladies who spent it on entertainment and goods as never before.[7]

This meant that a sporting gentleman who came of age in the 1880s like Clayton spent most of his time turning the wheels of society's "season." The season had developed in the eighteenth century as a means for the aristocrats and peers, who controlled the state, to marry off their children while carrying out the duties of Parliament in London. For those in this tiny circle, the season offered a means to transact politics and business while still social-izing close to home.

In the decades before Clayton took a wife, a shift in political power and economic resources had eroded the landed basis of society membership that had kept its season relatively simple. The "hundred great families," whom Winston Churchill fondly recalled as being firmly in control of the United Kingdom, confronted new faces in their circle. When the American Consuelo Vanderbilt became the Duchess of Marlborough in 1895, her husband instructed her to memorize the lineage and titles of an old guard of two hundred families. Such aristocrats may still have accepted only those at the very top, but a more generous definition of the English upper classes by the 1890s consisted of ten thousand people.[8]

By the time Clayton returned from his travels to take up the role of master of his estate, a global collapse in agricultural prices combined with tax reforms pressed by the rising discontent of those "below" cracked the old order's economic foundation. Capital and opportunities spread, and peerages regularly came to those with fortunes but no land. Between 1885 and 1914, businessmen represented a third of all new lords. Fresh claimants arrived in London with new sources of wealth from Europe, America, South Africa, and Australia. Society magazines like *The Queen* began to write about the "Upper 10,000 at Home and Abroad."[9]

The British aristocracy had long been comparatively cosmopolitan since primogeniture pressed younger children, who received relatively little from their families, into far-flung matches. Now it diversified further. Girls from the lesser gentry came out in London instead of at local balls. Those with special artistic or intellectual merit—long excluded from court like people "in trade"—came to regularly circulate along the margins of this enlarged society.

In response, the season had become longer and more elaborate: its orientation shifted from the transaction of politics to the display of wealth, the performance of distinctions, and an almost purist pursuit of fun among the most fashionable set. The dramatic growth of the press, the spread of photography, and a sensational style of "new journalism" that relied on sex, scandal, and interviews, all intensified interest in the most charismatic individuals in society circles.[10]

The modern season opened in April with the glittering "coming out" balls that announced the arrival of the greatest heiresses on the marriage market. Here, women wearing thirty-five pounds of clothes danced late into the night. Nell would come to love these balls and the garden parties, intimate musical soirees, and private theatricals that followed. There were trips to West End theaters, the opera, and along Hyde Park's Rotten Row between nine and eleven each morning to be "seen" walking or riding about. Dinner parties with eight- to seventeen-course meals stretched on for hours followed by cards and gambling, particularly for the men.[11]

From May 1 until the end of July, "dinners, balls, and parties succeeded one another without intermission," recalled Lady Churchill, and the most fashionable folk left London "only to attend the classic races—the Derby, Ascot and Goodwood." "For these months nobody is ever alone," a disgruntled politician complained, "it is talk—talk—talk; talk at luncheons and tea and dinner; talk at huge, undignified crowded receptions, . . . [and] talk at dances and at gatherings far into the night; with morning devoted to preparation for further talking in the day to come."[12]

"They would be called idlers now," Nell later admitted of the gentlemen who partnered her on this social whirl for years, and of the particular gentleman whom she married that fine blue day in April. "But they were not thought so then, and their unquestioned supremacy gave them that unconscious self-confidence which is the essence of charm."[13]

Nearly twenty-eight on her wedding day, Nell had reached the age at which her prospects for a good match, always hazardous, could only hope to make a steep decline. She had crossed the finish line in what can only be called the nick of time.

She had kept her head since coming of age, cultivating a style and flair for making a good impression, and a talent for friendship that would always serve well. With red hair, milk-white skin, green eyes, and a waist that looked small enough to snap in two, she had become the unusual beauty Lucy had predicted.

Like many ugly ducklings who blossom into swans, her exterior papered over a wobbly confidence further disguised by her skill as a flirt, sharpened to razorlike precision over ten years on the marriage market. Over that decade, Nell had crafted a bewitching manner that mixed provocative challenge with mysterious reserve. She learned when to remain silent, when to employ her storyteller's gift for shrewd observation to comic effect.

Under her sister's faultless eye, Nell mastered what the French called chic—a word some later credited Lucy with bringing into English. Chic demanded the appearance of doing almost nothing at all. "Dressed simply in quiet satin, with no jewellery and no makeup," her arrival had the capacity to make a "place suddenly brilliant and notable," one hostess of the era recalled. Chic's simplicity could also be more economical, a helpful quality, given the sisters' meager means. In the years before she met her groom, these qualities had made Nell magnetic to men and gave her cachet with hostesses ever in need of pretty, witty adornments for their tables.[14]

"In those days English society still existed in its old form," sighed Winston Churchill with a romanticism that came after the cataclysmic changes to British society that followed World War I. The "great families, who had governed England for so many generations and had seen her rise to the pinnacle of her glory, were interrelated to an enormous extent by marriage," he said of the world into which Nell now cautiously stepped: "The leading figures of Society were in many cases the leading statesmen in Parliament, and the leading sportsmen on the turf."

"The result was a pleasant informality," Nell agreed, before acknowledging it had "drawbacks for newcomers like myself" since no one in this tight circle ever bothered with introductions.[15]

Nell first gained entry to this intimidating social set when she went to stay with Lucy and her new husband in 1885 at a cottage that had been lent to them on the grounds of Cranford Park, a grand estate near Hounslow north of London. Determined never to live under her stepfather's roof again, Lucy had accepted the proposal of James Wallace almost on a whim after being jilted by her first love. Lucy was twenty and James, a wine merchant, more than twice her age. She cried herself to sleep the night before the wedding.

Afterward, she found the hot-tempered, hard-drinking, serial philanderer harder to please than their stepfather had been. Lucy's marriage provided Nell with new social opportunities, but a grim picture of wedlock. When Lucy gave birth within the year to a daughter, Esmé, her relationship with James Wallace deteriorated further and he spent long periods away from home in the company of other women.[16]

Still, Lucy's cottage on the grounds of Cranford Park offered Nell her first chance to study the patrician elite in their natural habitat; the connections she first made here would eventually lead her to Clayton, but only years later. James Wallace was a friend of Lord Francis William Berkeley, 2nd Baron FitzHardinge. Lord FitzHardinge and his wife, Lady Georgiana, presided over the estate with the panache of patricians who reserved their alarm for revolutions rather than well-bred social climbers like Nell. A former captain in the Royal Horse Guards, FitzHardinge was partial to tall hats with hedgehog quills sticking out of the crown. Friends called the tiny man "The Giant." Nell recalled Lady Georgiana as the largest person she ever saw outside a circus.

Almost sixty and childless, Lady FitzHardinge took an interest first in Lucy, and then in her unmarried, lovely younger sister; she began by trying to capture the hue of Nell's hair on canvas and ended by making her a companion, effectively launching her into society. Extremely wealthy, the FitzHardinges loved to host elaborate "Saturday to Monday" parties and valued entertainment as much as bloodlines. Nell endeared herself to the couple by making caricatures to amuse their guests, who always included a dashing young member of the Royal Horse Guards.[17]

But Lady FitzHardinge was no replacement for an ample dowry or a mother devoted to securing her daughter the right catch. A priceless asset, a good society mother instructed her daughter in the proper protocol, ordered her wardrobe, and presented her at Court. She kept one eye fixed on her daughter's chastity, acting as a chaperone to protect her reputation and vetting every introduction until the right man proposed. Competition for such men was fiercer than ever by the 1880s. The era of the American "Dollar Princesses" had begun, as industrial titans from the United States traded their millions to marry their daughters to men like the duke of Marlborough's son. (Winston Churchill's Brooklyn-born mother was one early example.) The chances were slim that a penniless woman like Nell, who possessed no dowry or maternal guidance, could catch a member of the increasingly cash-poor landed elite.[18]

Dollar princesses like Consuelo Vanderbilt gave the lie to Anglo-Americans' growing reputation for following their hearts down the aisle. The age of Queen Victoria was (rhetorically speaking) also an Age of Love: the first in which lovers' desires—not *only* parental preference and financial considerations—were at least officially touted as the best guide to the altar. "Gold is a paltry thing compared to love," warned the author of *Matrimony: Or, What Marriage Life Is, and How to Make the Best of It* (1866) when Nell was just two years old.[19]

The emphasis on a sentimental attachment between husbands and wives fueled the Victorians' experiment with creating what scholars now call companionate marriages. Such norms took hold throughout Western Europe and North America in the decades before Nell wed, but with particular force among the middle classes of the United States and British Isles, where the Evangelical religious revival was also strongest.

This new approach to imagining marriage began with the crash of falling in love, an experience celebrated with the tradition Queen Victoria invented in 1840 when she paraded down the aisle in a pure white gown, music wafting through the air. Bowled over by Albert's beauty, the two cousins had arranged their marriage themselves. It became one of the happiest and most successful in the history of the English royal family until Albert's early death in 1861 led Victoria into a mourning that lasted until her own in 1901.[20]

The queen's example further pressed the upper classes (at least publicly) to disavow *marriage a la mode* in favor of an outward commitment, particularly among women, to romantic love. A long-established tradition among elites, the fashionable approach viewed marriage in pecuniary and dynastic terms and pragmatically condoned partners' pursuit of their sexual preferences after the birth of "an heir and a spare." Victoria's union instead captured the increasingly modern expectation to make marriage the vital center of people's lives and married love the principal focus of their feelings, loyalties, and fulfillments.

Buffeted by such high and often contradictory expectations—locate a "good" catch who was also a love match—it's no wonder that penniless Nell had such a hard, confusing time finding the right husband.[21]

Elite women also modeled a kind of economic independence that set striving middle-class girls like Nell dreaming in other ways too. Making a good first marriage fully preoccupied this class; over the centuries 95 percent of such women married, more than any other. But elite families also increasingly put their daughters' sizable dowries into special legal trusts that protected them from total dependence on their husbands. By the 1890s, their dowries produced an average annual income of £1,000 a year, an amount equivalent to the salary supporting an upper-middle-class family of six at that time. Such trusts also allowed them to control any income, inheritance, and estates in their possession, thwarting the laws of coverture that completely erased women's legal identity before the passage of the Married Women's Property Act in 1882. This relative financial autonomy likely explained why so few joined the era's budding women's rights movement.[22]

Marrying up was Nell's only chance to join these charmed women's circle. She knew "her success or failure as a woman" depended upon accomplishing the near-impossible task of making "a rich alliance" in spite of her dowryless state. But the middle-class core that Nell always worked so hard to hide meant the desire for romantic love, as much as security and status, drove her search. Nell wanted a man who possessed charm and animal force as well as cash.

During her first two years husband-hunting in England, she rejected marriage proposals from two wealthy suitors she deemed too unpleasant and ugly to wed. Lord Henry Pelham-Clinton's title of Duke of Newcastle (and there were only twenty-two dukes in all the United Kingdom) failed to compensate for his "walrus moustache" and tendency to drone on about "the details of ecclesiastical apparel." A famously delicate man, Pelham-Clinton would bear no children after he married in 1889. When she turned down the proposal of her second serious suitor—a parvenu millionaire who had "all the qualities and faults of his type"—Lucy's husband, James, banished her back to her stepfather's home.[23]

Preoccupied by her elderly husband's failing health, Nell's mother sent her youngest daughter to Paris to stay with her well-off distant cousins, Margot and Auguste Fouquet Lemaître. Perhaps she would have better luck finding the right man in France.

Lucky Nell encountered Paris at the dawn of the Belle Époque, just as Gustave Eiffel's tower rose as the preeminent symbol of the modern age. Eiffel's efforts were part of the general rebuilding of Paris that had transformed the medieval city into an elegant, boulevard-sized metropolis during the previous two decades.

The resurrection had been required after the Prussian Army had surrounded and starved the city into a peace that its workers would not accept. The Paris Commune of 1871—three months of brutal class warfare—followed. Huge swaths of the city burned and tens of thousands of people died. The city was left bereft of horses (mostly eaten) and trees (burned for fuel) and covered in ashes and blood. Yet by the 1880s, the Third Empire was at peace and the city's cafés, theaters, galleries, and salons offered those with enough francs unrivaled displays of creativity. An impossibly long list of painters, writers, architects, actors, and musicians reemerged after the Commune to create a series of artistic movements that reimagined how to represent, and inhabit, the ever-more-urban conditions under which so many lived.[24]

Here Nell would learn a great deal more about the expression of sexual desire than most unmarried women, while of course guarding her chastity for the husband she had yet to catch. She had first learned about Parisians' bubbly (im)morality in her stepfather's library and from her single previous holiday to the city years before, when a friend visiting her mother had offered to interrupt her adolescent daughter's lonely days with a trip to the City of Light. This first visit had turned Nell's already well-rooted preference for French manners and styles into a passion for their more verbally expressive and steamy approach to romance.[25]

Under the less-than-watchful eye of her mother's friend Mademoiselle Duret, Nell had experienced how France's more liberal censorship laws had made Paris's popular culture much more erotically daring than anything found in London or New York. Material forbidden in the United Kingdom and United States made its way into French newspapers, books, and theatrical productions, which featured images and stories noted for their unusually frank presentation of sexual matters. A qualified tolerance for elegant, sophisticated women who transgressed sexual norms also distinguished French from Anglo-American popular culture, explaining how French theatre became a key location to question Victorian sexual roles as well as the popularity of the actresses who often defied them. The broad cultural equation between power and sexual seduction meant that women in France interested in claiming greater opportunities used a distinctly feminine glamour to smooth the acceptance of their version of the emancipated woman.[26]

Unaware of—or, more likely, misled about—the sixteen-year-old's mastery of French, Mademoiselle Duret brought Nell to see Sarah Bernhardt perform in *Théodora*, a tragedy about the Byzantine empress by Victor Sardou. The most famous actress of this theatre-crazy age in which half a million Parisians went to a show at least once a week, Bernhardt epitomized using glamour to get away with erotic misbehavior. "It would require some ingenuity to give an idea of the intensity, the ecstasy, the insanity as some people would say, of curiosity and enthusiasm provoked by Mlle. Bernhardt," observed Henry James.[27]

Nell's secret sexual mentor, Sarah Bernhardt performing as Théodora (1884)

On- and offstage, Bernhardt presented an entirely unsuitable role model for conventionally marriage-minded women. The "Divine Sarah" was reported to sleep in a coffin in her Paris apartment, where she also kept a private zoo. She wore dead bats on her hats, conducted a series of highly publicized love affairs, and flaunted the fruit of her virility—her illegitimate son, Maurice. "*Nothing* could ever convince you to behave like a lady," despaired one of her many lovers. Doctors warned that women's weaker brains could not safely handle exposure to such a woman.[28]

This iconoclastic publicity hound's performance in *Théodora* combined with the heady atmosphere of Paris in the Belle Époque to spark Nell's sexual awakening. "As [Bernhardt] moved & undulated over her Lover—strange thrills rushed through me," she later confided to her diary. "Although I analyzed nothing in those days I know now I had suddenly found my group, the group of the Syrens, the weird fierce passionate caressing & cruel group." "Obsessed" with the performance, the teenage Nell played at being Bernhardt, being Théodora. That night she recited "long sentences of her love words . . . before the dim glass in the little dark room in the rue de la Borde."[29]

Left with a vision of "a new and undreamt of kind of love" of "a rather wicked, tigerish, variety," Nell embarked on her first love affair with a handsome Frenchman she had met in Jersey the month before. As the two wandered around the Jardin des Plantes, he "contrived to make love to me in English," which Mademoiselle Duret barely understood. "*Belle Tigresse*," he kept whispering into her ear, beginning her lifelong devotion to this imperial symbol of male authority that underscored the importance she would place on following animal instincts in the search for true romantic love.[30]

Unsurprisingly then, Nell was "wild with joy at the idea of seeing my dear Paris again" when she set sail in June of 1888. "Paris the adored! Paris the gay! Paris the land of moral champagne!" she exulted in her diary on the boat across the Channel. Her cousins the Fouquet Lemaîtres kept a chateau in Poissy, just north of Paris, and an elegant townhouse on the Champs-Élysées, offering her entrée to the French equivalent of the FitzHardinges' social circle. "I am a very vain and conceited girl" who uses "too much 'I' in her writing" began the chronicle she kept on the visit, betraying her growing confidence in navigating situations that would have sunk a less assured young woman. The long hours spent reading in the library, and her knowledge of French literature and culture, primed her to handle protracted dinners that "felt like a constant sharpening of wits." While on this first extended stay with Margot and Auguste, she learned that French permitted discussions about the body's appetites forbidden in polite conversation conducted in English. People said "the most appalling things, but they never sounded anything in French," she marveled to herself after dinner one night.[31]

After proving her entertainment value on a leisurely yacht trip down the Seine, Margot and Auguste Fouquet Lemaître invited her to visit for the season three years in a row. In their company she dined and danced, picnicked at Versailles, watched plays forbidden to single Frenchwomen because of their risqué content, and strolled through the World Exposition of 1889 without a chaperone. She grew particularly fond of the Bois-de-Boulogne, the enormous park on the city's western edge; its English garden, zoo, amusement park, and tennis courts became favorite places to pass an afternoon.

Paris Exposition of 1889

French haute-bourgeoisie life fit Nell like one of the beautifully made hats she loved. In the capital of all that was chic, her distinctive dress and coloring provoked admiration rather than the "suspicious contempt" she often felt from all but the most fashionable British women her age. Paris had first become the mecca of fashion-minded aristocrats during the eighteenth century. "To be in Paris without seeing fashions is to have one's eyes closed," observed the Marquis de Caraccioli in 1772. "Fashionable people want new materials, the latest publications, modern ideas, and trendy friends . . . no one dare appear unless decked out in the new finery."[32]

Parisians reconfigured shopping after fraying sumptuary laws—that stipulated exactly who could wear what—went the way of so many aristocratic heads during the Revolution. The rise of the ready-made clothing industry in Paris promised fashion to all. The experience of buying things also changed, first in grand arcades and then in department stores like the Bon Marché, redesigned in 1872 by Gustave Eiffel, premiere architect of glass and iron. Once shopping had been a small-scale experience that involved the exchange of goods or money. Now it became as much about looking at a world of goods in spaces designed as paradises for the ladies. While window-shopping one afternoon, Nell realized how all that wanting fostered a new emphasis on the self. "Paris is truly a place to foster vanity—there are so many looking glasses in the streets."[33]

But as she accumulated proposals that had little to do with marriage, Nell learned that the odds of a pretty, penniless girl marrying up the social ladder were even worse in France. However charming, Frenchmen were even more flinty-eyed than their British counterparts about the demand for a capital contribution from a bride. The celebration of the love match—even if mostly in theory—was already commonplace in English popular culture by the late eighteenth century. A century later, what one French writer called "marriage by fascination," was still treated as an oddity.[34]

She understood the desires many men brought to women without means and wanted something more. "Mother dear for pity's sake don't talk to me any more about bills, I am a bad bargain. I am a plaything, a toy, a doll to be dressed up and then thrown aside because my bread is bran, my dowry sawdust," moans the heroine of *Dora*, a play Nell drafted in a notebook after her first season in France. "Mother why plague me to marry? They will write me verses—they will bring me flowers. . . . They will die of love—but it is a lover's love, not a husband's. . . . If the world were different! If honest men married good women without fortunes I feel I could be so tender, so devoted. If ever I meet a man who will love me for myself alone how I will love him."[35]

Disappointment produced defiance as Nell leaned into playing a sharp-tongued English miss who did not lightly suffer fools. Her embrace of Englishness—a place where she had spent very little time, after all—also resulted from her dawning realization that an unmarried Frenchwoman's freedoms were even more tightly corseted than her English counterpart's. Such strictures were treated as a necessary protection from Frenchmen eager to live up to their romantic reputations. Told that it was impossible to play an English game of hide-and-seek called Tiger because all the ladies would get kissed, Nell responded that she "was not surprised that the rules in France for 'les jeunes filles' were so strict if they had to deal with such canaille d'hommes [dogs]." Then, after conducting a private conversation with a male acquaintance "as if I had been in England," one of her handsome cousins scolded her for giving his friend the impression that she was in love. "I don't care one snap for what any conceited idiot of a Frenchman thinks," she fumed to her diary.[36]

Her lack of funds and name may have prevented a match among her cousins' set, but acting "la belle anglaise," (the beautiful Englishwoman) as her admirers called her, allowed her to enjoy the cultural attractions of Paris more freely. Visiting the World Exposition of 1889 without a chaperone, she found the "dark beauty" and "barbaric" dress of the "native" belly dancers in the "Arab Village" mesmerizing. She cajoled her cousin Sophie into taking her to "mondaine" dinner parties, explaining, "that being a 'bien élevée jeune fille Anglaise' [well-brought-up young Englishwoman] I never understood more French than I wanted to." These sophisticates made young Frenchwomen seem blindingly dull. "An impossible evening," she complained after an evening in their company, "such conversation! Fitted for idiots about the walks and the gardens etc."[37]

"With all its delights," Paris cast a spell on Nell that London never did, and one of its greatest pleasures was the chance to study Frenchmen's techniques for "making love to a woman." Nell described their variety in a diary entry on June 23, 1891, her last night before returning to London after her third season spent in France. "As no one is going to see this but myself it does not matter what I put—so out with the truth."[38]

The account began with a farewell dinner at a fashionable restaurant on the Île-de-France with Lucy and her mother—in Paris to take her home—hosted by her cousin Margot and three well-born Frenchmen. Nell returned to London with an already established taste for the fancy dining rooms of fine hotels where it first became fashionable for a mixed-sex crowd to eat out. At hotels like the Savoy, early celebrity chef Georges Auguste Escoffier fed these new multitudes by reorganizing his kitchen into specialized stations that quickly prepared the weightless soufflés and roasted meats of haute cuisine. Though Nell adored these hotels at once, the always fashionably thin young woman never took an interest in their meals. ("I loathe food" was one of the few specific remarks about a meal she left.)[39]

Lucy and Margot pleaded exhaustion after the meal, leaving Nell's "three cavaliers" to convince her reluctant mother to sail up the Seine to a carnival in the suburb of Neuilly. When rain forced the party to abandon the plan, the Comte de Coutade brought them instead to a small party held at the grand house of a duchess. "No sooner had the first bars of a valse struck then [sic] de Coutade seized me and we whirled off." Nell danced around the nearly empty salon with all three men before the rain stopped and they set off for the carnival by carriage. At the Faire de Neuilly, she rode the merry-go-round, watched a polar bear jump through hoops of fire, and delighted in the bored expression on a lion's face: "Mon Dieu, que cela m'en bêli!" (My God, this again!)[40]

The sights on which Nell lingered were the men competing for her attention. "The look about him was as if he had not wasted a moment of his 42 years," Nell wrote of Coutade. "Always en train, never bored, never tired, exquisite manners. Of a very good, old family (wisely) unmarried, witty, agreeable. Making love all the time as every true Frenchman does, but in such a neat way." He "would always say the things in the abstract, sometimes they were very forward things absolutely unsayable in another language but French but said in such a way that it was impossible to be angry—or not to listen." In contrast, Nell called her second cavalier a "modern Frenchman." More "sporting" and not so "deeply read," he had not "the least flirtatious manners either in the abstract or otherwise but like all his countrymen just as keen about a woman's points as an Englishman is about a horse." Although reputed to be "extremely naughty where married women are concerned," he was "most respectful" to her. The third man possessed a "direct power"; while dancing he looked into her eyes to "simply say, 'Je vous aime.'"[41]

Still, turmoil percolated beneath Nell's enjoyment of French high-society life. In more than five years of looking, she had rejected three marriage proposals and had now passed the age at which most women married. This meant that when Nell returned to London that fall she faced becoming one of Britain's dreaded surplus women.

"Surplus woman" was the bureaucratic term for spinster that had taken hold in Britain after a question about marital status on the census of 1851 revealed that sending so many men off to the empire had left Great Britain with half a million more women than men— and two and half million unmarried women. The statistics provoked concern about the family's decline as the moral and reproductive basis of society.[42]

The problem presented by these "unproductive" single women contributed to broader debates about women's proper role in the following decades. Fears about maintaining social stability in a rapidly urbanizing society, as well as a population large enough for imperial demands, provoked heated discussion. The dispute partially galvanized a women's rights movement that agitated for better educational and work opportunities to improve single women's chances for self-support. Others argued that surplus women could never be useful and called for their emigration to find a husband.[43]

The trouble in part emerged from how little had changed since Jane Austen had written a century before that "single women have a dreadful propensity for being poor, which is one very strong argument in favour of Matrimony." Relatively privileged middle-class girls like Nell still mostly received an idiosyncratic education not designed to produce skills for profitable work. The professions remained mostly closed; marriage and motherhood were the only properly prescribed course. By the 1880s, even the most respectable female occupations, like teaching or nursing, barely paid a living wage, since women averaged one-third of men's salaries for comparable work. A gendered imagination—that viewed women as always under men's protection in a domestic sphere—rendered women's paid employment, however necessary and commonplace, as incidental or temporary.

Such realities undercut women's ability to heed companionate marriage's rosy injunctions to follow their hearts down the aisle. For almost all, Mary Wollstonecraft's assertion in A *Vindication of the Rights of Woman* (1792) still applied: "The only way for a woman to rise in the world is by marriage."[44]

This was the reality Nell faced when she returned to London in 1891, her fantasies of a French husband dashed. There she joined Lucy and their mother in a little house on Davies Street in Mayfair, where her mother and stepfather had moved the year before in search of better doctors. But David Kennedy had died just months later, at eighty-two.

Staring down the barrel of spinsterhood, now the pressure to wed became intense.

Although still writing for her eyes alone, Nell's journal—and later her novels (often heavily laced with autobiography)—betrayed her creeping awareness of the less respectable alternatives available to a pretty, well-dressed British woman without a dowry or well-connected family. Her study of the lives of famous women who had triumphed through means other than marriage—usually courtesans and actresses—was in part an evaluation of the choice.

"I wonder if it is amusing to be an adventuress, because that is evidently what I shall become now. I read in a book all about it; it is being nice looking and having nothing to live on, and getting a pleasant time out of life—and I intend to do that!" Nell has her only red-haired, green-eyed heroine, Evangeline, announce, in *The Vicissitudes of Evangeline* (1905, published as *Red Hair* in America). Evangeline enters the marriage market knowing most matches are born of economic necessity. "If I had ten thousand a year, or even five," she muses at the start, "I would snap my fingers at all men, and say, 'No, I make my life as I choose, and shall cultivate knowledge and books, and indulge in beautiful ideas of honor and exalted sentiments and perhaps one day succumb to a noble passion.'"[45]

Armed with a heightened awareness of her exotic good looks and arresting style, Nell returned to London determined to use the "glamour of France" to finally land the right man. A tempest she triggered that winter at a ball in Devonshire did the trick. After inciting a quarrel between four friends, the tuxedo-clad men all landed in a lake. Tales of the Devonshire "lake episode" reached as far as Essex and the ears of Clayton Glyn Jr., who decided to meet the woman who had caused such a fuss. The Chisenhale-Marshes, neighbors of Clayton's, arranged an introduction at their home, Gaynes Park.[46]

Evidently, Clayton liked what he saw. Nell found the supremely confident, charming, slightly older gentleman with bright-blue eyes attractive too. Both had apparently decided the time to wed was also nigh; the haste of Clayton's proposal likely appearing at the time like a kind of ardor to his bride. Just four months after they met, the broad-shouldered Clayton Glyn stood in St. George's Church watching his bride walk down the aisle wearing a diamond tiara he had purchased on her red head.

"The living incarnation of a fairy-tale princess," thought Lucy with satisfaction as her sister entered in the gown she had made. Two years before Nell wed, Lucy had begun the excruciatingly slow process of divorcing her alcoholic husband, after James Wallace ran off with a dancer. Although recent legal reforms had made divorce possible for those outside the aristocracy, the still cumbersome, expensive, and typically reputation-destroying process meant that fewer than five hundred people divorced in Britain a year. Though both sisters skipped lightly over the subject, near the end of her life Lucy confided to an interviewer, "The six years of my marriage to Jim were the worst years I ever knew."[47]

While Nell had been husband-hunting in Paris, Lucy set her sights on the even trickier task of becoming a self-supporting single mother by designing gowns under the name Mrs. James Wallace out of a little house on Davies Street in Mayfair just around the corner

"A Gentleman's Wife," Nell dressed in her wedding outfit in 1892

from where Nell now wed. Ironically, in the end, David Kennedy had supported his stepdaughter's ambition when their mother used her small inheritance after his death to finance Lucy's divorce. Then she invested the remainder in Lucy's business, determined to help her daughter capitalize on what Nell called her sister's "genius for making clothes out of air." While keeping one eye out for the sticky fingers of her little girl, Esmé, Lucy cut out designs on the dining-room floor of the house that had been built for those who served the patricians in Mayfair's estates. Lucy never doubted she could make dresses worthy of passionate attachment. Finding the women to pay for them would be the real chore. Long an advertisement for her sister's talents, Nell's wedding party offered the perfect chance to show the assembled guests what she could do.[48]

Seven-year-old Esmé trailed behind the bride, stretching out the full court train of white brocade that flowed from Nell's shoulders. The gown's full skirt and form-fitting bodice—which showcased her eighteen-inch waist—would have been familiar features to all fashionable brides. But Lucy included unexpected elements too: a medieval band rather than orange blossoms to attach the veil and yellow edging on the typically all-white bridesmaids' dresses. The unexpected use of color and mixing of different period styles would become a hallmark of her work. Before the season ended, several guests had headed to the house on Davies Street, looking for clothes with similar charms.[49]

After the ceremony, guests made the short trip to Claridge's Hotel for a lavish reception. Then Mr. and Mrs. Glyn left for the beaches of Brighton to practice another rite created by the Victorians: the honeymoon as a special trip for the bride and groom to be together, all alone.[50]

Once a tiny, rock-strewn fishing village, Brighton had developed into "London by the sea" after doctors began prescribing saltwater and sea air as tonics for the overindulged. By the late eighteenth century, the patronage of that paragon of overindulgence, George, Prince of Wales, really set the town buzzing. His Royal Pavilion offered a sumptuous testament to the excesses of the Regency era, which so many Victorians came to define themselves against. Completed in 1823 after nearly forty years, the pavilion was built in the Indo-Saracenic style that British architects developed by combining Indo-Islamic, Indian, and Gothic architectural elements. Its intricately carved minarets, towers, and domes made of white marble glowed from atop Brighton's steepest hill like the moon. Inside, brilliantly hued Chinoiserie awaited, offering a sharp contrast to stimulate the senses. The pavilion advertised the important role the

"Orient" came to play in the erotic fantasies of so many European subjects over the nineteenth century.[51]

This "improper, Oriental-fairy-tale atmosphere" set the stage for the one true lover's act Nell ever credited to her husband. Ever more at ease with deeds than words, Clayton rented Brighton's public swimming bathhouse for their private use so as to fully "appreciate the beauty of the mermaid he married," if her autobiography is to believed. There, husband and wife frolicked naked for two days. With her milky skin and waist-long red hair, she would have appeared like a lady in one of the era's pre-Raphaelite paintings come to life.

Nell would have had very little tangible sexual experience before her wedding, the demand for chastity in a bride, particularly among the middle and elite classes, now a well-entrenched norm. Yet her age and circulation among the Parisian beau monde meant she was far from innocent in her mind. The decade-long wait, the long-practiced habit of stoking and banking her own desire, must have left her expectations impossibly high. "Love of the souls is the divine part of the business," she later wrote in one of the books she published on her philosophy of love, "but it cannot exist without love of the body. As well ask a man to live upon bread without water."[52]

The fictional honeymoons Nell created strongly hint that her sexual initiation produced few carnal pleasures in Brighton. "No one can possibly imagine the unpleasantness of a honeymoon until they have tried it. It is no wonder one is told nothing about it," one of her heroines remarks after enduring her own. "Really, girls' dreams are the silliest things in the world," she continues. "I cannot help staring at all the married people I see about—'you—poor wretches!—have gone through this,' I say to myself and then I wonder and wonder that they can smile and look gay." Another of her heroines would groan: "A second honeymoon! The first was a horrible, fearsome memory, which was over long ago, but the thought of a second . . . Oh, it was unbearable—terrible—impossible! Better, much better, to die and have done with it all."[53]

However the honeymoon went, the Glyns' homecoming was a success. Clayton's tenants met the master at the gate with a tribute that deeply touched his bride. These "grave, Sunday-dressed farmers, most of them wearing 'Newgate frill' beards and shaved upper lips, like Abraham Lincoln" freed the horses drawing their carriage from the harness. Lifting the weight of the brougham onto their shoulders, they drew the Glyns through a triumphal arch of evergreens and then down the long drive past Durrington, the Georgian manor Clayton had rented, and all the way to Sheering Hall.

The three-hundred-year-old farmhouse with the garden out back was the first home Nell could call hers. As the squire's new bride, she presided over a banquet in their honor. Servants laid out a feast under a tent for all the families around the estate to share. Heaping platters of food and a punch heavily laced with alcohol disappeared, only to be replenished again. Jokes about the couple's conjugal duty to produce an heir sent ripples of laughter through the crowd. Fireworks exploded into the dark.[54]

The fashionable lady had at last found her gentleman, concluding her own marriage plot, that storyline about a troubled courtship that had powered the rise of the English novel. Although the marriage plot had long ended with the triumph of connubial bliss, Nell's story had only just begun.

CHAPTER 3

In Sickness and in Health

The problem created by the marriage of two irreconcilable characters is a
psychological one which deserves sympathy as well as understanding.

—Consuelo Vanderbilt Spencer-Churchill, the Duchess of Marlborough[1]

In the first years of her marriage to Clayton, the most important
things took place in the silences, as Nell struggled to abide by
the rules of the circle she had worked so hard to join. "After Nell
married she was very delicate for a long time," was how her old friend
Ada Lloyd described this first, difficult phase of her marriage.[2]

The composure she had practiced over a lifetime helped, but at
moments threatened to crack open and expose the turmoil inside
over her marriage's chilly temperature. There was no place to talk
about the confusing process of adjusting to her husband's temperament and tastes, the environment of his home, or the disappointment over what happened between them in bed.

And when Nell quickly became pregnant like most brides, there
was no one to help her grapple with her fears about pregnancy and
its consort, maternal death. Like so many newly married women, her
body had suddenly become an unfamiliar battlefield over which she
struggled to regain control.

Virtues became vices as the glamorous appearance that had
attracted Clayton now complicated Nell's fit in the English countryside as she tried to assume her role as mistress of the estate. Nell had
spent the last decade learning to be an excellent guest in company
that appreciated her sharp-edged wit and elegance.

Those skills translated well among the fashionable metropolitan
elite, but they were of little help as the mistress of a humble estate

in the English countryside. Local women's lectures on her duties—about *who* could be invited to dinner parties versus garden parties, and just *where* they should sit—brimmed over "with the extraordinary ideas and prejudices that still prevailed." She learned that "brains did not count" and that those who worked for their living—whether in business, the professions, or the arts—"were ruled out" of social gatherings entirely.[3]

Many of her new neighbors appreciated the appeal of a long-lashed, doe-eyed Jersey cow more than one of Lucy's delicately stitched-together tea gowns. In Essex, prudent women at least feigned interest in farm animals, shooting parties, and the outdoors. They wore boots, without grimacing, designed to tramp about the often-muddied clay terrain. They did not wear fingernail polish—a suspicious product only recently imported from France. Nell's penchant for the varnish and preference for reading by the fire in "lovely indoor clothes" with a cat curled on her lap convinced many of the locals that she was more of a foreigner than Clayton admitted.[4]

The locals were not wrong. The routine butchering she had

Painting of Sheering Hall by Richard Harpum

observed at her grandparents' Canadian farm left her with a preference for fancy lap cats over baying dogs bent on the destruction of
small animals. Her childhood along the British Empire's edges had
also imprinted a terror of horses, a fear of the water, and an appetite
for city life that her time in Paris had only whetted. Although she
loved the splendor and quiet of wild and lonely places, she possessed
neither the interests nor the clothes that would have made it pleasurable to give them more than an appreciative glance.[5]

His wife's unsuitability for country life became apparent to
Clayton when he rented a moor near St. Fillans, Scotland, in
August for killing grouse. The elaborate meals and shooting parties
arranged around the birds' ritual slaughter ostensibly made the trip
the second, more social, stage of the Glyns' honeymoon, a practice
still common among elites in the late Victorian era. St. Fillans was
a myth-saturated town on the eastern end of Loch Earn. Evidence
of its Celtic past abounded, including a giant S-shaped boulder said
by locals to mark the spot where the druids and fairies had retreated
underground after marauders above had made things too tough. Still
advertised as one of "undiscovered Scotland's" prettiest gems, the
waters of Loch Earn feed into present-day Loch Lomond (Britain's
largest lake) and Trossachs National Park. Straddling the Highland
Boundary Fault, here the rolling Lowland landscape collides against
the majestically rugged Highland terrain. When Nell visited more
than a century ago, this was a wild and lonely place indeed, and one
that did not appear to suit the new Mrs. Glyn.[6]

Nell's surviving letters convey a vivacious woman suddenly overcome with a weary heart. She spent the first days in Scotland running up and down buttes, accompanied by near-deafening noise, to
watch the hunters (or, guns, as they were called) take aim at birds
flushed from their cover by servants called beaters. In one morning,
an ordinary shooting party of five guns—and Clayton was by all
accounts an extraordinary shot—would bring down four hundred
birds. "I could not have run another step if a bull had been after me,"
she sighed to her mother at the end of the second day.[7]

Struck with a cold, which turned into a persistent cough, a doctor pronounced her suffering from "a slight weakness of the heart."
Although the doctor declared the problem hereditary, this was

the first time Nell's heart had ever troubled her so. It would not be the last. The diagnosis led Clayton to excuse his "Dresden China Duchess" from further excursions, she reported, relishing the sympathy and attention. "The darling old angel is so good to me and so dreadfully distressed about the cough," she happily reported.[8]

Nell learned early on that illness excused her from the excursions in the countryside that she detested. She also saw that it pricked an unusual care in her husband, calling forth a solicitation and tenderness that she craved. It could easily have been otherwise in a society that preferred to wear a mask to tidy up whatever mess might lie beneath. To complain of an illness was "common," pronounced future socialite Lady Diana Cooper. "Only housemaids had pains."[9]

But Nell's health did not improve, even with her activities restricted to the dinner parties that ended each day. She now felt "too bad to be entertaining" and blamed herself for the evenings' festivities taking a dismal turn. Worried that Scotland's climate was the culprit, Clayton sent Nell home early, alone.

No record exists of Nell's feelings about her brand-new husband's decision to choose the company of redheaded birds over his redheaded, heartsick bride on their honeymoon. But she aimed an unprecedentedly direct expression of anger at a different husband days before she left for Sheering Hall. After asking her mother to send her new gowns there instead of out to the Scottish moor, she coolly observed of Lucy's recently divorced husband: "What a pity he does not kill himself."[10]

Nell returned to Essex to face what might have been her social doom until she sparked the interest of her new neighbor, Lady Daisy Greville, the Countess of Warwick, a woman she counted with hindsight to have been among her "small number of real friends." "I can remember the sensation created by the arrival of a perfectly lovely girl, with the most wonderfully beautiful red hair I had ever seen," Warwick wrote of meeting Nell at the Essex Hunt Ball of 1892. "I hope it is not unfair to say that the Country regarded such allure as indecorous. But I have always been attracted by beauty, and I became her friend."[11]

In the Countess of Warwick, Nell found a sympathetic, expert guide who demonstrated the fun to be had in the countryside. It was easy to think the fates had predestined their friendship, which became the silver lining of these early, often confusing years of her marriage. The countess claimed descent from Nell's beloved Charles II and his mistress Nell Gwynn. Warwick's example indicated how marriage could mark the beginning of a woman's story, not the end—especially if she was an upper-class wife in charge of her purse.

The sole heir to her grandfather's estate since the age of three, Warwick possessed the ineffable air of a woman raised with typically masculine rights over her known world, which included a fortune rivaling any American dollar princess. She trailed a bewildering number of titles and names like most in her class: Frances Evelyn Maynard Greville was known as Lady Brooke until she became Lady Warwick in 1893, when her husband ascended to his earldom, making her a countess. Also like many in this insular world, her intimates called her by an entirely unrelated pet name, Daisy. Generous Daisy. Lovely Daisy. Kind Daisy. Scandalous Daisy. "Daisy, Daisy / Give me your answer, do. / I'm half-crazy / all for the love of you," crooned an English songwriter that year about the woman who quickly fascinated Nell more than any other.[12]

Nell
dressed
in Lucile,
190[?]

Born in 1861, Daisy Maynard's childhood, like those of all elite girls, aimed to preserve her chastity until marriage by keeping her ignorant of the wider world. Sons were sent to boarding school as early as six years old and taught to hold their own in any situation.

Daughters, by comparison, were shadows haunting their houses. They spent their childhoods in cast-off clothes, secluded in a separate wing of a country house, and cordoned off from children who were not relations. The idea was to control daughters' every outside interaction. "It is immaterial to a gentleman as to which set in society his acquaintances move, and he can be polite to all without offending any in their several circles. With a lady it is otherwise," warned the author of *Manners and Tone of Good Society*, considered the best of the slew of etiquette books published to guide the era's many parvenus. "She, like a stately flower, does not care to descend from her parterre [formal garden], to mingle with the flowers of either field or forest; but a gentleman possesses the freedom of a butterfly, and can wander from garden to field and from field to forest *sans se deroger*" (without prejudice). Another guide reminded: A girl "cannot learn too early that her first social duty is *never to be in the way*."[13]

Frances "Daisy" Greville (née Maynard), Countess of Warwick in 1895

Hedonistic Daisy Greville dressed as Marie Antoinette in 1897

Such customs turned adult activities, conversations, and books into rumors. The hope was to send girls to their wedding nights "unbelievably ignorant," Daisy ruefully admitted. So great was the reticence to speak about sex with unmarried women, so thorough the censorship over what girls read and heard and did, that many headed down the aisle unable to name their body's parts. The practice also aimed to keep daughters unaware of how the carnal customs of their class contradicted their professed commitment to female virtue, marital fidelity, and romantic love after marriage. "Marriage—their goal, their destiny, their desire—was all in a rosy haze. Afterwards, as wives, they accepted without question the code of the day."[14]

Brides like Daisy learned the basics of reproduction fast; nearly two-thirds bore a child within the first year, more than any other class. They also quickly became familiar with what Daisy called "the code of the day," as she did after marrying Francis Greville, Lord Brooke in 1881. The even-tempered "Brookie" caught her eye during her first season; she decided at eighteen, and nearly at first glance, to wed him and no other, including Queen Victoria's youngest son. Brushing her parents' disapproval aside, she made the match at twenty, taking control of her estates earlier than would have otherwise been possible. In her first year of marriage, she miscarried and then bore a son. She was pregnant again in the third and fourth years.[15]

After giving birth to a second son who would die before his second birthday, Daisy embarked on the extramarital affairs that were one of the few sports that both sexes in the English elite (usually) played together, though on different terms. Society's politely predatory men preferred older, married women for the more elaborate affairs they staged since a gentleman (theoretically) regarded an unmarried woman of his own class untouchable. But "every married woman was fair game, the assumption being that if her husband did not look after her, that was his fault. If she happened to be in love with her husband," Nell quipped, "well that was the luck of the game." "From the beginning of our life together my husband seemed to accept the inevitability of my having a train of admirers," Daisy wrote with more than a trace of self-justification. "I could not help it. There they were. It was all a great game."[16]

The queen groused about such habits. The "higher classes—especially the aristocracy," the sovereign grumbled, "are so frivolous, pleasure-seeking, heartless, immoral and gambling that it makes one think . . . of the days before the French Revolution." This coed marital philandering likely remained even more common among the elite in France, where there had been no equivalent of Victoria's example. There, sex moralism was less pronounced, even among the middle class, and married women socialized in a mixed-sex company more than their English counterparts. An unfortunate misalliance was called a "love match" in France, but parents in both nations still defined a good marriage largely in economic terms. As a result, many among the English and French elite viewed marital devotion as "positively bourgeois. . . . Constancy was expected and admired only between illicit lovers," Nell noted with grim irony.[17]

Many in her new social circle had learned not to examine younger children too closely for resemblances to their legal fathers, since contraception was still emerging as a more reliable and widely practiced means to limit wives' pregnancies. Previous methods of fertility control—abstinence before later marriage, abstinence within marriage, withdrawal, abortion, and infanticide—failed to offer women reliable, painless options free from the fear of inflicting damage to their bodies or the repression of their sexuality. "French letters," as the English called condoms, possessed a distinctly unsavory reputation unsuitable for wives; they were crude, expensive, difficult to obtain, and associated with preventing venereal diseases, not pregnancy. Evidence suggests that the use of the withdrawal method among all classes by the 1890s helped to speed the falling birth rate that began decades earlier among the middle class. Although the withdrawal method had a high failure rate and lessened sexual pleasure, it became the preferred method to limit childbearing.[18]

Nell would humorously describe the often-heartless quality of fashionable upper-class marriages in her first novel, *The Visits of Elizabeth* (1900), which was equal parts autobiography and fantasy, like so many of her books. Details from the diaries recording her first forays into society under the less-than-fastidious care of the Fouquet Lemaîtres and FitzHardinges went directly into the book. But she did her duty in *Elizabeth*, sketching the sexual escapades typical at country house parties with so light a hand that they flew right over the heads of society's clueless girls.[19]

The author's caution was still not good enough for some. "Our elders had strange taboos" for their daughters, explained an aristocrat who came of age after Nell became society's premiere chronicler. "Almost all French books were banned. I remember pointless discussions raging over my head as to whether I should be allowed to read *The Visits of Elizabeth* by Elinor Glyn. I managed a surreptitious look at it and could see no double meanings though I was on the look-out for them." A more knowing eye would have found double meanings in its first pages, like when a married man asks Elizabeth to drop a glove outside her bedroom door on the way to bed (as a signal, and excuse, that he should pay a visit that night).[20]

In the present, real world, Lady Warwick's favorite spot to orchestrate such liaisons was her birthplace, Easton Lodge, which showcased the "curious mixture of philandering and philanthropy" that defined her adult life. Built in 1583, a devastating fire in 1847 produced its resurrection in the mock-Elizabethan style beloved by Victorians. Visitors approached by way of a two-mile drive through twelve hundred acres of parkland before entering a massive reception hall festooned with animal heads of every kind and lined by eight Siena marble columns on each side. A vaulted roof paneled in wood rose above. Impossibly tall French doors opened onto two terraces and an intricate garden. Beyond lay the park's herd of deer; two stables; a cricket ground; and Stone Hall, an Elizabethan-styled "pleasure house" nestled among a grove of ancient oaks. Here Daisy exercised her passion for horses and hunting. Here she opened a needlework school to train local girls for jobs with higher pay during an agricultural depression in 1890; this was her first step toward earning the sobriquet the "Red Duchess."[21]

Nell was not alone in considering Daisy the most "enchanting and beautiful" object to grace Easton Lodge. By the time Lady Warwick met her new neighbor, the countess had been for several years the most fashionable hostess in society's most fashionable Marlborough House set, so named for the London home, and separate social circle, that Edward, Prince of Wales established after his marriage. Queen Victoria had blamed her husband's death on the worry provoked by her eldest son's wild ways. After Albert's death in 1861, the queen had retreated from London, but judging her son "*totally totally* unfit for ever becoming King," had refused to prepare her heir for the duties of government and would forgive him only at her death in 1901.[22]

Sociable, restless, energetic "Bertie" established a virtual second court after wedding the beautiful Danish princess Alexandra in 1863. The marriage gave him access to £50,000 a year. He spent all this and more, embracing the habits of a sporting gentleman so detested by his mother and late German father. Bertie ruled from Marlborough House as the accessible face of the monarchy; the prince was known for loving music halls, pretty girls, and the pheasants he shot by the hundreds most days.

A remarkably tolerant royal host, Bertie mixed with Jews, Catholics, and dignitaries from all nations, showing a particular fondness for stage stars, the French, and beautiful American heiresses. Years later, the prince would tell Winston Churchill: "You know, you wouldn't be here if it weren't for me." Churchill's mother had managed to marry the duke of Marlborough's son because the prince welcomed colonials like the Brooklyn-born beauty Jennie Jerome, who were amusing, pretty, and rich. Prince Edward's support made possible an entire generation of half-American, half-English aristocrats. With Alexandra preoccupied by a marathon of childbearing— she gave birth six times in eight years, nearly dying during her third delivery—the prince selected a series of ladies to partner him on his ceaseless rounds.[23]

Lady Warwick took the role of Prince Edward's *maîtresse en titre* in 1889, replacing Nell's childhood idol, Lillie Langtry, in the job. Daisy became the prince's consort after she solicited his help in tamping down a brewing scandal when her lover's wife, Lady Charles Beresford, threatened to give the countess's love letters to the press. The prince hated bad publicity even more than he loved a pretty face and deftly crushed the attempt to break society's real code: "*there must be no scandal.*"[24]

Like most important codes, the broader sexual double standard meant that women and men experienced its violation differently. As Prince Edward had proven, several times, patrician men's institutionalized power ensured that exposure of their transgressions resulted in little more than humiliation. The "fear of being laughed at, of looking foolish" was the worst punishment an aristocratic man could suffer, reminded *Etiquette for Women*. (The important exception was for homosexual affairs, as the Irish playwright Oscar Wilde would shortly learn.)[25]

Public exposure of women's infidelities led to the insane asylum, divorce, or social death; the last two states being interchangeable for ladies of their class. A decade-long affair with Britain's royal social leader was an enviable way for Daisy to avoid such a fate.[26]

Luckily, Easton was only a short carriage ride from Sheering Hall. After Nell charmed the countess at the Essex Hunt Ball, the Glyn name appeared regularly in the lists of her guests printed in the local paper. Daisy's younger half-sister, Lady Angela St. Clair-Erskine, recalled what a good first impression Nell made on Daisy's fashion-minded guests when they met at a cricket match, "her very red hair glistening in the sun." Onlookers were "thrilled over her appearance," St. Clair-Erskine remembered, in a "frock that made her look as if she had stepped out of *La Vie Parisienne*" (a popular Parisian magazine that was part cultural guide, part naughty-picture paper of lightly-clad damsels in dishabille). Nell wore "another marvel" at a dinner party at Easton soon after and gave a pitch-perfect imitation of actress Sarah Bernhardt for the guests. When Angela asked who made her clothes, Nell sent the debutante to Lucy, still working under the name Mrs. James Wallace, but now out of a larger house in Mayfair. Daisy would soon follow.[27]

Lady Warwick built her legendary status on the credo "spare no effort and despise no trouble." A good hostess's "head must be a perfect encyclopedia," Daisy wrote. She "must never forget, never be ruffled, never be 'caught napping,'" particularly during country visits, when one activity melted into the next for days. There was sport to arrange, particularly for men like Clayton and Lord Brooke, who believed "a good day's fishing or shooting is second in point of pleasure to nothing on earth." There were meals that nipped at each other's heels: "Breakfast started at 9 a.m. and finished at midday. Lunch faded into tea, and dinner—supposed to be at 8 p.m.—rarely commenced until an hour later." After dinner, conversation and music lasted late into the night, since Lord and Lady Warwick disapproved of heavy gambling and drank only lightly.[28]

Daisy's fabled staff, who numbered fifty inside and nearly twice as many on the grounds, made it all possible. "It was always a problem to me when the cooks and kitchen maids went to bed," one guest complained with a petulance indicating the staff's otherwise omnipresence. "Never were there such servants as at Easton," Nell pronounced. "All the footmen were the same height, six feet tall, and they seemed to fulfil every want before you were aware of it. To see four housemaids 'doing' a bedroom in about ten minutes was quite an experience, so perfect was the drilled efficiency, while if you wanted a telegram sent to Timbuctoo [*sic*], or your train and boat connections worked out to Hades or the moon you only had to ask the magnificent [Groom of the Chambers] Mr. Hall. . . . I am sure he would have disposed of the body without fuss had any of the guests been careless enough to commit a murder on the premises."[29]

But it was Nell's description of guests' sexual shenanigans that has most interested writers later trying to peer behind society's beautiful mask. To an astonishingly uniform degree, even a relatively outspoken libertine like Lady Warwick tripped lightly over the details of her circle's erotic habits even if they could not quite follow Prince Edward's dictum *never* to put anything incriminating in print.[30]

As the "authoress, Elinor Glyn," Nell later developed a unique approach to discussing society's code, spilling the truth in her novels that kept everyone guessing who and what was real. When it came time to write her autobiography in 1937, she erased her own extramarital entanglements entirely, but society's premier novelist described this atmosphere in which a married woman might, discreetly, move from lover to lover without anyone lifting a brow. There "was no stupid hesitation or waiting upon circumstance about the would-be-lovers," she nostalgically remembered.[31]

Nell recognized another double standard at work here that had everything to do with class, even if she could not see how her own middle-class background made these seemingly heartless habits harder for her to accept. The heavenly surroundings, sumptuous clothes, and restrained manners made illicit extramarital sex feel different than if it had occurred in an alley behind a bar. "Nothing was ever allowed to appear crude or blatant and what were essentially ugly facts were made to seem beautiful, even admirable," she admitted. The "cloak of glamour that surrounded the whole matter, perhaps render[ed] temptation all the more irresistible."[32]

The delicate performance of subterfuge lent an undeniable frisson to every caress. "Above all there was *no* touching of each other even in seemingly accidental ways," she recounted, in an often-quoted remark. "It might be a lovely lady's own lover who was sitting beside her, but he would never lean over her or touch her arm to accentuate his speech, for all touching in public was taboo."[33]

The demand for absolute public decorum licensed the private expression of desire, not romantic, possessive love—which usually led to trouble, as Nell was learning fast. A religiously worn mask protected one's standing. With very few exceptions, marriage lasted unto death. Marriage preserved family fortunes and the social order on which they relied; it promoted a family's legacy and longevity. Divorce and romantic, possessive love threatened all of that and more. Becoming indifferent, even good-natured, about the "external attachments" of a spouse made a kind of sense, promising protection from confronting head-on the gales of emotion that flowed from jealousy and despair.

But before Nell could decide just how closely to follow Daisy's example, she would have to deliver her first child.

Nell did her duty, giving birth little more than a year after her wedding; the experience would turn the warring impulses inside her body white-hot. She delivered at home, like almost all women, in a house that Clayton rented on a fashionable street in London. A spare notice announced the news in Essex: "GLYN—on the 7th, at 55 Lower Belgrave Street, the wife of Clayton Glyn, Esq., of a daughter." She was hardly more forthcoming in her autobiography. "My daughter Margot (now Lady Davson) was born in June of the year following my marriage."[34]

Not much had changed since Queen Victoria wrote her eldest daughter three decades earlier: "Let me caution you, dear child, again to say as little as you can on these subjects before Alice (who has already heard much more than you ever did) for she has the greatest horror of having children, and would rather have none— just as I was as a girl and when I first married—so I am very anxious she should know as little about the inevitable miseries as possible."[35]

Such linguistic sleight-of-hand fit a time when the imaginations of even the most exacting fiction writers completely skirted childbirth's dramas. The first novelists in the eighteenth century wrote of childbirth with words that at least identified the worker and her field of labor; a woman was "brought to bed," where she gave birth. Some novelists hinted at the toil. She "was almost ready to cry out" conceded Henry Fielding of a woman large with child; she "dropp'd her burthen," wrote Daniel Defoe of a woman postpartum.[36]

A century later, the demands of modesty and good manners had erased even these timid reckonings from the page. Nineteenth-century novelists tackled diseases of the mind—sadistic cruelty, drunkenness, and madness—with aplomb. They invoked the grip of poverty with a clarity that could make the cozily situated smell the city's filthy streets. But bodily functions like pregnancy vanished from public discourse in the Anglophone world. Dickens reached perhaps unparalleled euphemistic lows when he wrote, "the ship upon the ocean made her voyage safely and brought a baby, Bella, home," the year Nell was born. George Eliot's clichés about broken flowers obscured the brutality of maternal death: "The delicate plant had been too deeply bruised and in the struggle to put forth a blossom it died."[37]

Until the discovery of antibiotics in 1937, the social history of childbirth makes such understatements read like a cover-up. Until then, nothing else rivaled the lethal threat it posed to women in the prime of their lives. Too few accounts of childbirth survive to piece together how often things went well or wrong before the rise of "man-midwifery" in the eighteenth century (previously only women attended births). But the historical record hints at the longstanding trouble; until modern times, the licensure of midwives in Britain and France lay with the Church, to ensure their ability to administer last rites. There is no doubt that maternal mortality in England and Wales during the eighteenth century was horrific. During puerperal fever epidemics, the most common cause of maternal death, lying-in hospitals periodically resorted to burying two women's bodies in one coffin. This "deep, dark continuous steam of mortality," in one Victorian demographer's words, remained unchanged in the next century, when an estimated 1 in 10 pregnant women died from childbirth complications within six weeks. The number was as high as 1 in 2 when epidemics raged. Until antibiotics, doctors and nurses were so busy tending to dying mothers that they paid almost no attention to the health of infants, which was far worse.[38]

Doctors and midwives erased these realities more thoroughly than fiction writers, recording causes for women's deaths that hid their origins in birth. Medical whitewashing only worsened as awareness improved about the contagious nature of infections like puerperal fever. The fever's germ had the habit of attaching to a doctor or midwife "and following their footsteps with the keenness of a beagle, through the streets and lanes of a crowded city," observed Dr. Oliver Wendell Holmes. "Practically every doctor who loses a confinement case receives very great blame, no matter whether he deserves it or not," complained a general practitioner to a committee studying the cover-up problem in London in 1892. "If one . . . dies on a particular street, your midwifery practice is almost ruined in that street." The camouflaging of maternal mortality led those trying to approximate its extent in Britain, Europe, and North America to inflate their findings by 10 to 25 percent.[39]

Nell likely had death on her mind during her pregnancy. The year of Margot's birth would be the second most fatal one for mothers that century in Britain. That spring a particularly virulent puerperal fever epidemic had swept through London and beyond, killing nearly 90 percent of women infected during their deliveries.[40]

If she followed the customs of her class, when she went into labor in June an obstetrician arrived during the last stages of the birth. He carried a medical case heavy with the tools of his trade: forceps and breech hook to move or remove a badly positioned baby; blunt hook, crochet, and cranioclast to crush the infant's skull to force extraction if all else failed; scissors and needles to try to repair the damage done. Though antisepsis practices had been routine in surgical procedures for a generation, the silver instruments would have been clean but unsterilized. After carefully rolling up the long shirt cuffs that were the fashion on the outside of his jacket—removing his jacket was too vulgar to consider—he likely performed a perfunctory hand-washing and got to work. Since physical examinations of female patients were "more decorous than instructive," this one likely was Nell's first. His clothes, tools, lubricant, hands, nails, nose, and throat could all have transmitted deadly bacteria into her suddenly vulnerable body. But luck went her way, and they did not.[41]

As she began pushing, the doctor would have dulled Nell's pain with anesthesia, the only new obstetric practice to take hold in a century. Introduced in 1847, tiny Queen Victoria—who used chloroform during her eighth delivery in 1853 and again in her final one in 1857—had pressed reluctant physicians to accept the drug. Mother of nine, Victoria had a terror of childbirth, an experience that she likened to an uncle as having her "body invaded by a parasite that made me physically ill and eventually split me open like the spear of a Zulu warrior." Upper-class women quickly followed the queen's example, and chloroform's use spread down the class ladder as a practice said to indicate a woman's refinement and status. "In our process of being civilized we have won . . . [an] intensified capacity to suffer," a physician explained to an international drug conference in 1892. "The savage does not feel pain as we do." Nell was lucky to have the means to safely lose consciousness. She was luckier still to survive with a healthy child. In the 1890s, 46,000 women died giving birth in England and Wales.[42]

Decades later she wrote, "my daughter was an immense joy to me," but there was almost certainly a sense of failure too. Like most everyone, Clayton had wanted a son. The British principle of primogeniture—which kept estates intact by leaving them almost exclusively to the eldest son—made the heir a virtual sun around which everything revolved. If Nell and Clayton had only girls, the estate would pass to his younger brother's boy.

Public discourse was also absolutely clear about the preference.

A survey of three hundred well-known novels published by British authors between 1800 and 1970 found just one character who ardently hopes for a daughter: an eccentric maiden aunt in Dickens's *David Copperfield* (1849–1850). "A daughter! It seemed to him unfair," bitterly thinks a new father in John Galsworthy's *A Man of Property* (1922). "To have taken that risk—to have been through this agony—and what agony—for a daughter! . . . One never got what one wanted in life." The literary record expressed the preference even after Parliament abolished primogeniture in 1925. "I didn't want to speak about her—she was a daughter, so Rex didn't much mind her being dead," explains a mother about her stillborn child in Evelyn Waugh's *Brideshead Revisited* (1945). Whatever a parent's means, only a boy could carry the family name into the future.[43]

Yet Nell later reported joy over Margot's birth, writing, "I was secretly delighted, as I knew nothing of little boys and their ways." There are good reasons to believe her. Boys were storybook creatures in her eyes; Lucy had been her childhood's only consistent companion. No flesh-and-blood brother, boy cousin, or father penetrated the carefully invented worlds of this girl who had always preferred to stay inside and read and draw and make up stories. Although her attention had turned to studying her effect on men as she came of age, Nell was too observant to think this counted for true insight into the hearts and minds of boys.[44]

Yet, there must have been a sense of deficiency, too, for failing wifehood's most serious test. She had created not an heir but merely a girl.

After surviving childbirth's rigors, Nell fell prey to typhoid: the most common and mysterious of the nineteenth century's deadly fevers, the one that had killed her father before she turned one. Flourishing best under unsanitary conditions, typhoid laid more soldiers to waste than combat until the development of a successful vaccine in 1896. It struck the intestinal tracts of poor and rich alike, causing high fevers, delirium, and a cascading series of variable symptoms that typically produced vomiting and diarrhea over several weeks. Typhoid drove waves of sanitation reform, the detective work of early epidemiologists, and a new hygienic zeal among

all classes that reflected and created "modern" ideas about what—
and who—was clean. Left emaciated and exhausted, survivors took
months to recover.[45]

A skeletal Mrs. Glyn spent the remains of 1893 at Sheering, trying to regain her strength to resume the social whirl that made life
there bearable. This extended time at home with Clayton seemed
to answer any lingering questions about whether motherhood might
cause her to embrace her role as mistress of the humble estate. She
still found only decorating and the garden of interest, happily calling
herself foolish about all other household-related tasks.

While recuperating, Nell contentedly stitched together baby
Margot's wardrobe of muslin caps, satin coats, and tiny silk dresses.
But like all women of her class, she left the round-the-clock routine
care of her infant to the nanny, Charlotte Dawson. Nanny Dawson
would stay with the Glyns for fifteen years. Such practices were
already well entrenched in an era in which most upper-class children
made only daily appearances before their parents' eyes. Clayton was
keen to keep young children at the edges of adult life. He "detested"
the sights and sounds of childhood so much that he had a nursery-
wing built onto Sheering Hall swiftly after his daughter's birth. The
homes of virtually everyone in their circle expressed variations of
the same attitude.[46]

Clayton judged his dangerously underweight wife too delicate to
undertake the rigors of a London Season in 1894. So, the invalid
sewed Margot's wardrobe, read, and wrote letters by the fire. On fine
days she sat outside in the garden pavilion Clayton had built. No
place was as perfect to Nell as the garden; friends always marveled
at her green thumb. Beyond stretched a row of willows that opened
onto a meadow bordered by a brook that marked the entrance to
Heather Wood.

The interests of husband and wife kept diverging. Agricultural
matters, fine wines, and sport occupied most of Clayton's attention
over the next year, while Nell stayed close to the garden and her
books by the fire. Clayton tramped about the woods and farm, at
times in the company of one of the bridesmaids from their wedding. Nell failed to name the bridesmaid she described as "pretty and

good-natured," the kind of woman who *enjoyed* the chance to "bathe dogs, fetch corn for colts, and go for long walks in the rain." This never-named woman made frequent visits that year, often accompanying Clayton on his outings, according to Nell.[47]

When she failed to regain her strength by autumn, Clayton took Nell, Margot, and Nanny Dawson to Costebelle, a small health resort on the Riviera that had become a favorite spot to treat English invalids suffering from lung diseases like consumption and nervous exhaustion. Set on a cliff above the town of Hyères, this was the most southern of the so-called winter stations that the British frequented on the Mediterranean's northern coast.[48]

"This place is so gorgeously beautiful that I can't describe it," Nell warned her mother before trying anyway: "Great hills covered with pines and lots more running away to the distance which is quite purple, the pines are the brightest emerald green . . . and there is a nightingale singing now." But she worried the place would be "hideously dull." At dinner she had spotted only "two men who don't look to be dying."[49]

Clayton stayed just long enough to hear the doctor's diagnosis: "a weak heart," precipitating "a collapse of the nervous system," or what doctors called neurasthenia. The doctor instructed Nell "not to walk up any hills or take any exercise," and prescribed bromide and a strict diet regimen that involved eating protein-rich foods every two hours. Then Clayton left her in the Mediterranean heat and headed back to England.[50]

After Margot's birth, Nell's blue moods and physical "delicacy"—her weight loss, heart palpitations, back pain, fatigue, and coughing fits—were among the most common of the "mob of incoherent symptoms" used to diagnosis a neurasthenic. Neurasthenia captured a constellation of health problems that had first been called *The English Malady* (1733), and had grown along with the pressures, softened conditions, and luxuries associated with "civilized" urban life.

The number of patients suffering from "shattered nerves" appeared only to worsen during the nineteenth century, with the rise of industrialization and evangelical moralists' punishing emphasis on work and self-discipline. By the time the New York neurologist George Beard finally coined the term "neurasthenia" in 1872, medical opinion generally agreed that nervous disorders had first wreaked havoc with the sensitive sensibilities of the "better ranks" before "rapidly extending to the poorer classes." Beard argued the now-pervasive "repression of the emotions" had combined with the pace of urban life—the "periodical press, steam power, the telegraph, the sciences, and the increased mental activity of women"—to drain humans' limited supply of nervous energy. The etiology reflected a pre-Freudian worldview where the suffering of body and mind had not yet been severed.[51]

By the time Nell struggled with her nervous collapse, physicians thought "clever, emotional, and excitable women" particularly susceptible to nervous depression; women composed about half of all cases in England. Doctors agreed that overwork and "wasting fevers" like typhoid could produce neurasthenia in men but believed that "the limitations of women's brains" and the "excesses of her reproductive organs" were chiefly to blame for their ailments. Medical men recognized how often depression afflicted postpartum women, but armed only with prejudices about the "second sex" rather than medical information about hormones and endocrine levels, they labeled the problem "puerperal insanity." The thrall of Darwinian science—which used women's smaller brains and reproductive function to provide new support for old ideas about their innate weakness—encouraged this view even for a patient like Nell, who had recently suffered from typhoid.[52]

More generally, the medical profession treated menarche, pregnancy, childbirth, and menopause as diseases that led to women's disorders of the nervous system and mind. The "rest cure" devised by the American doctor Silas Weir Mitchell quickly became the most popular way to treat female neurasthenics. Ideally, the cure involved a rigorous feeding schedule—forced, if necessary—no mental and physical activities, and seclusion from all but medical personnel. Massage and electrical stimulation provided nervous relaxation and prevented muscle atrophy. The cure was disastrous for women craving more, not less, stimulation. But for an exhausted, and often lonely, wife like Nell, the more relaxed version of the cure (this was the Mediterranean, not Boston, after all) helped. She left Costebelle looking like "a blooming milk maid."[53]

Yet the recovery of her good spirits failed to change Clayton's feelings for her, as she painfully learned. Shortly after returning to Sheering Hall, "an awful thing" happened on a Saturday-to-Monday visit the couple made to an Oxford friend of Clayton's. On a private tour of the garden, their host called Nell "the fairest rose in the garden" and then kissed her on the lips.

Nell claims her conscience pressed her to share the news with Clayton that evening. But it seems more likely—given her flirtatious history and the habits of their circle—that the desire to provoke jealousy to test the strength of her husband's feelings sent her into his adjoining room while they dressed for dinner. Ever droll, Clayton responded with a "delightful smile. 'No! Did he? Dear Old Bob!'" Then he turned back to the mirror to adjust the white bow tie that his groom, Billingham, had tied minutes earlier.[54]

The proposition of sharing his new wife's body with a friend amused Clayton. Her "romance was over, after only two years of marriage. It was a bitter blow." Nell's despair revealed that her desire to experience the passionate intensity she had glimpsed in Paris would not die or be satisfied by her husband's approach. For Nell was never as sophisticated as she looked, as all of her heroines desperately looking for a man to make them "feel and *feel*" later exposed. Middle-class habits of mind pressed by her mother lingered despite her best efforts. She had sworn to obey Clayton, to "serve him, love, honour, and keep him in sickness and in health; and, forsaking all others, keep only unto him" for as long as she lived. However depressed, after only two years of marriage she would not yet have been ready to break her word.[55]

We have only Nell's side of the story about her husband's decision to abandon even the pretense of resting their marriage on mutual desire and fidelity. She told it after Clayton's death and not long before her own, passing it down through her autobiography and her first and favorite grandchild, Margot's son, who took Nell's name to become the successful writer Anthony Glyn.[56]

In *Romantic Adventure* she also described her complicated rationale for deciding under what conditions she approved of breaking the marriage vows that her middle-class upbringing made it hard to forsake. Nell announced in numerous places over the years that lying—to your spouse, your children, your friends, and likely to yourself—was the most serious problem posed by infidelity. Repeatedly, she urged brides and grooms to disavow the practice of promising monogamy from the start. Men were driven to the hunt. Humans inevitably fickle. Better not to pledge at all then to risk the heartache she felt that evening when her husband contemplated her adultery with a smile.[57]

Nonetheless, she rather torturously laid out a set of conditions that would eventually explain her violation of her honor code: When a husband deliberately neglected his wife. When he courted other women. When sexual relations between husband and wife had long since ended. When the deception was open but discreet. When attempts to perform the charade of a loving partnership had ceased. Nell could not have checked off each item on her lovelorn list yet, but that could change.

As Margot grew to toddling age, the Glyns resumed the seasonal migrations of the leisure class that gave their marriage a rhythm and shape it otherwise lacked. In the spring of 1895, Clayton let a house on Sloane Street for the London season. By the beginning of August, at the season's end, the couple made what would become an annual trip to the Isle of Wight for Cowes Week, the oldest and largest regatta hosted at the "Yachting Capital of the World." A tiny port town planted beside an estuary on the Isle of Wight's northern tip, the patronage of the Prince of Wales during the 1870s had turned Cowes into a key event in the social calendar. By the time Nell attended, the regatta's eight days likely packed more fashionable folks from the United Kingdom and Europe per yard than any place on Earth.[58]

A passionate sailor, Clayton relished inspecting as many boats and races as he could. Nell's childhood on the Channel Islands' shipwreck capital left her with both a lifelong fear of the sea and a particular horror of small crafts. For Nell, only the chance to study the manners and clothes of the onlookers offset the tedium presented by the thousands of boat races crowded into the week.

The couple parted ways the morning after the regatta's concluding fireworks fizzled into the Solent, the sliver of water separating it from the mainland. Clayton headed north to Scotland for shooting and tramping. Nell went south to France with Margot and Nanny Dawson to meet her cousin Margot Fouquet Lemaître in Paris before traveling together to the Côte d'Azur. The couple reunited at Sheering Hall by Nell's October birthday, to attend the country-house parties and hunt balls that punctuated the fall and early winter. After New Year's they headed for the warmer locations popular among their set: Venice, Cannes, Rome, and Cairo were the favorite destinations to take in the winter sun until everyone headed back to England in the spring.

Ever-courteous Clayton knew how to navigate any trip in style. A seasoned traveler adept at ironing out the inevitable problems that arise on the road, Clayton had a talent for meeting old friends in new places and for making hotel managers and headwaiters smile. (His enthusiasm for every aspect of service helped.) Nell appreciated his deliberate speed. With Clayton you never rushed from thing to thing, but a certain vigor was necessary to keep up.[59]

She almost managed a grand tour that next winter of 1895, perhaps fearing that she would otherwise have to face the consumptives again with only the nanny and Margot in tow. Their itinerary called for a January departure for Rome, then north to Venice, west to Milan, and finally down to the Italian Riviera, from where they would wind their way along the Mediterranean coast to Cannes before returning home in March. Nanny Dawson took Margot to London to spend time with her grandmother and cousin Esmé. Elinor Kennedy still minded Esmé while Lucy tended to her expanding dressmaking business, opening her first proper studio on 24 Burlington Street, not far from their home in Mayfair.[60]

Nell had never been to Rome, and her description of the city still sounds apt: "Splendid old remains and the shabbiest houses all jumbled together and everyone's washing hanging out the windows . . . magnificent old Palazzos and all the streets paved with small stones and no sidewalks so it is difficult to keep from being run over." They attended receptions, dinner parties, and balls filled with the kind of guests she and her sister had long ago inspirationally dubbed "one of ours." Enchanted by her charm and beauty, an Italian prince invited the couple to several events at court.

But before they left for Venice, her body rebelled again, suggesting things were not as well as they appeared. Suddenly her heart palpitations and fatigue returned, leading Clayton to call a doctor, who "said the same again," she reported, "that I should have to be very careful for months to come about my silly heart so as not to get real heart disease." Her wings clipped, she languished on the sidelines while her husband's participation in the fun soared. An aggrieved tone crept into her letters by the time they traded Venice for Cannes. "Clayton and I have changed places," Nell fretted to her mother, "he now dances away all night and I look on. I feel for you now. It is awfully tiring when one doesn't dance."[61]

Yet the caution she took over the next weeks resulted in a recovery that left her dancing her way through the London season that spring. The chance to finally make her presentation at court was a huge boost to her spirits. Though the rite had become a much less exclusive affair by 1896, it still possessed a near "mystical significance" for the uninitiated and offered a "passport to society" that nothing else replaced. Nell "made her bow" before Princess Alexandra, wearing a presentation gown made by Lucy that trailed a typical twelve-foot-long court train. The necessary ostrich feather and tiara headdress perched on her head.[62]

"I felt very pleased with my look," Nell recalled before confessing her shock that the other participants generally lacked the grandeur and brilliance she had expected. "One could count on one's fingers the women who could stand being viewed in full regalia in the day light with impunity," she marveled. Fewer still possessed "a fine carriage," or "an air of distinction," and instead just "shuffled along." She singled out for admiration just one woman "in a shabby black dress, beautiful diamonds and rather dirty feathers in her hair, who also looked every inch a great lady." She already knew that the right air was more important than the right dress.[63]

Dressed by Lucy and exuding the charm that had landed her in this sparkling company, Nell became the belle of many balls and an enormous success. Lucy now counted not just Nell but several other notable beauties as clients, including Daisy; her half-sister Angela; the sisters' early idol, Lillie Langtry; and the great society hostess Mrs. Willie James. Nell met James performing in a charity production of the play *Diplomacy* directed by Daisy's stepfather, James St. Clair-Erskine, the Earl of Rosslyn.

"Bitten with theatrical mania," Lord Rosslyn cast "the beautiful Nellie Glyn" to play the ingénue who steals the hero's heart. According to Rosslyn, Nell stole the show when she sustained a concussion from a staged fall on the show's closing night. Lord Rosslyn recalled how Nell expertly milked her minor misstep. After she fell, he kept the curtain down for twenty minutes while she recovered, leading to "round after round of cheers for her reappearance. She was a clever darling," Rosslyn enthused. Her triumph this season turned even Clayton's head. "The past was forgotten" as her smitten husband fell in love with Nell all over again.[64]

Lucy's gowns for *Diplomacy* shocked audiences accustomed to the stiff, obviously fake costumes long prevalent on the stage. The bold colors, flamboyant eroticism, and realistic look of *Diplomacy*'s costumes led a professional theatrical director to ask Lucy if she might help him to translate visually the sexual suggestiveness of his next play, *The Liars*. Lucy jumped at the chance. Blurring the line that separated stage and street clothes, *Lucile* "did a great deal to revolutionize dress in London," recalled her client, Angela St. Clair-Erskine.[65]

Clayton and Nell sometimes crossed paths with Lucy at the swanky Savoy Hotel; the couple dined most Sunday nights here in the first restaurant in which a woman might eat without a husband and not lose face. Hotelier César Ritz and chef Auguste Escoffier got their start at the Savoy before getting sacked when large quantities of wine went missing. But the two men had already made the Savoy shorthand for a new kind of glamorous sophistication that married modern "American" comforts—like electric lights, elevators, constant hot and cold running water in private bathrooms—to Old World service. Here, looking out over the Embankment onto

Lady Lucy (née Sutherland) Duff-Gordon ("Lucile") in 1904

the Thames, Lucy's haute bohemian world pressed by aristocrats and the merely rich, whose faces were all beautifully framed by the dark mahogany paneling.[66]

The Savoy's latent sexual charge had slipped into decadence the year before, during Oscar Wilde's two trials for "gross indecency" with other men. The hotel had been the favorite trysting place for the celebrated playwright and his lovers, and several employees became witnesses for the prosecution. At the height of his fame, Wilde went to the workhouse for two years and died penniless after his release. But the notoriety seemed only to burnish further the Savoy's reputation as a place where anything and everything could happen under a cloak of unmatched elegance.[67]

Nell and Clayton divided their winter that year between Rome and the St. Remo villa of his friend Sir William Walrond, the chief Conservative whip, happily relaxing under all that Mediterranean blue. For the first time since her marriage six years earlier, she had spent a year entirely free of illness and depression.

She was pregnant when they returned to London in March. Her mother moved into Lamberts—the cottage on the estate nearest to the town of Harlow—that summer in preparation for the heir everyone hoped Nell would bear for Christmas. At thirty-four, Nell gave birth to a second child on December 18, 1898, after a much more difficult labor than her first. Bad news met her on the other side of the ordeal: the baby was another girl, a daughter she would name Juliet Evangeline, her name lending a bit of romance otherwise lacking in the event. Her body had betrayed her again.

Clayton's famous composure crumbled, along with his hope for the son who might make a legacy out of his care of the family estate. After waiting to ensure his wife would recover, Clayton did what came easiest when things got sticky. He hit the road, heading for Monte Carlo, where he could eat and drink and gamble his cares away. He spent Christmas and New Year's at the Hôtel de Paris, far from women who were not members of the demimonde. He lost a great deal of money, alongside the "dandies, roués, spendthrifts and scions of great European families" who gambled colossal fortunes away in the tiny state.[68]

"I was mercifully ignorant of this at the time or I believe I should not have had the strength to recover at all," Nell recalled in the autobiography that her infant daughter later helped her to write.[69]

She was still weeks away from getting out of bed when Clayton returned, but by May had become well enough to sit outside. By fall, she ventured out shooting one afternoon with her husband. Given how much she hated the activity, the choice seems a conciliatory gesture for her failure to produce an heir, again. But the shooting party got caught in a storm, and then days later she came down with rheumatic fever, which resulted in arthritis, the infection's most common side effect. The pain in her back and legs was so acute that she could not walk; there was talk that she might not again. The doctor blamed the soaking Nell took while out shooting. The doctor's diagnosis, however incorrect, must have given Nell satisfaction at the time. She may have failed to give her husband an heir, but she had been martyred trying to stay by his side.[70]

Still, as she lay in her bed alone, again, she knew, six years into her marriage, that something had to change.

CHAPTER 4

Marry the Life,
Not the Man

It is wiser to marry the life you like, because after a little, the man
doesn't matter.

—Elinor Glyn, *The Vicissitudes of Evangeline, or Red Hair* (1905)

Fiction alone seems to have given Woman the chance of proving that
she is, in an artistic sense, the equal if not the superior of Man, and in
this country, any history of fiction is a great measure the history of how
women writers have influenced not only contemporary life and morals,
but also the fictional literature of their day.

—Marie Belloc Lowndes, "The Woman and the Novel" (1904)

Back in her sickbed, Nell reverted to childhood habits, deciding to read her way out of her troubles. But the material she
chose was different this time. Desperate for levity, she went
looking for a more carefree version of herself in the diaries she had
kept of her first seasons out in England and France.

What she found made her laugh. She knew many considered her
witty and sharp, but the translation of those qualities on the page
surprised her. What she called her "preposterous education" left her
always intellectually insecure and eager to seek out older, learned
men for instruction. She knew bad spelling and fantastic punctu-
ation littered everything she wrote. Like many women of her class,
letter and diary writing had been a lifelong habit. But still, she had
never posed the question as to whether she could write something
anyone else would want to read. The outlook was an artifact of a

horizon so old it appeared real. Becoming a professional writer was simply not an acceptable ambition for an upper-class lady.[1]

But this blinker, once lifted, revealed a denial of her obvious talents and interests. And for all her recent illness and pain, for all the disappointments and heartache, marriage to Clayton offered a much more stable perch to share her private opinions.

At thirty-four, Nell had grown certain about the superiority of her taste. If she found her observations about fashionable society amusing, so would others. She would write a chronicle about the adventures of an innocently destructive debutante's first seasons in England and France. In a role she had often played in life, Daisy's younger half-sister, Angela St. Clair-Erskine, provided a model for what the French called her enfant terrible heroine. She would let Angela/Elizabeth tell her readers the truth about what went on behind society's closed doors with so light a touch that the innocent would not even notice the naughty things she said.

"No one imagined that I could be serious when I announced that I would write a book, but the poor invalid had to be humoured, and everybody in the house pandered to my lightest wish," Nell admitted with the air of a woman now well practiced at using her health problems to draw a kind of attention otherwise absent from her husband. Since no one at Sheering knew anything about "the business or art of writing books . . . some nice blue copy-books were procured for me from the village shop, and I began to write."[2]

This was the out-of-nowhere, I-never-dreamed-I-could-be-a-writer version of how she got her start that Nell recorded for posterity. Fantasy enlivened fact here, like many tales told by professional scribes. Most tellingly, she erased the writing that had first made her a published author in order to invent this more satisfying origin story.

Large with child the year before, and brimming with new hope in her marriage, she had written a weekly fashion column for the provincial society magazine *Scottish Life*, opining about trends and offering beauty advice. She had met the magazine's editor while rehearsing *Diplomacy* at Dysart, the Scottish estate of Daisy's stepfather, Lord Rosslyn. Her status as a fashionable beauty with a sisterly connection to the rising couturier now known professionally as "Lucile" was well known. But such a lady did not take up her pen to write professionally about her likes and dislikes. *Scottish Life's* editor must have considered it a coup to find Nell willing to write a fashion column, in the form of letters from "Suzon to Grizelda." This she did with increasing confidence until two months before Juliet's birth.

The first installment of "Les Coulisses de l'élégance" appeared on May 14, 1898, just as the season in London hit its stride. "I am sure you will be nice to me, Grizelda," opened the column, you "won't write back and tell me that from a literary point of view my letter is all wrong, my grammar horrid and my sentences not properly formed . . . I have never written a letter to be printed in my life," she wrote. The introduction emphasized the amateur status so important to her cachet as a lady who wrote for pleasure rather than cash. But then "Suzon" pivoted from playing the supplicant to assume the imperious voice that became a hallmark of the author: "I hear you are tall and lovely, but also that you stoop. No one, however beautiful, looked distinguished with round shoulders; I don't believe any ever yet stooped and conquered." Turning out a weekly column for five months taught Nell that she had "a cursed facility with words," but the letters attracted little attention.[3]

With the last installment of "Les Coulisses de l'élégance" only a few months behind her, the epistolary format was fresh in her mind as she hobbled out to the garden pavilion, still unable to walk without crutches. There she lay on a deck chair, hand resting on the blue copybook, and began to write. Lord Chesterfield's letters, long a touchstone, might also have influenced her decision to pen her first draft of the following year's surprise publishing hit as a series of letters written from a debutante named Elizabeth to her "Dearest Mamma" during her first season out in British society.

The Visits of Elizabeth began as a series of sketches strung together by their loose adherence to the marriage plot by telling a story that concludes with the heroine's happy marriage, in this case to a handsome duke. But Elizabeth's tale was not so much concerned with the search for the right man as in satirizing society's manners while offering readers an insider's tour of the elite in their natural habitat. Most of the problems Elizabeth confronts involve her misinterpretation of society's codes, like when she fails to grasp the significance of a gentleman wanting to drop a glove outside her door on the way to bed.

Nell also roundly mined the humor that arose from pricking the pretensions surrounding those residing in Britain's great "houses." "I am sure you made a mistake in what you told me, that all well-bred people behave nicely at dinner, and sit up, because they don't a bit," Elizabeth complains early on to her widowed mother, whose poor health forces her daughter to fend for herself in this often unsavory milieu.[4]

Although genteelly poor, Elizabeth's aristocratic standing—like Lady Angela, "she numbered at least two Countesses and a Duchess among her relatives"—gives her a confidence to express things directly in a way that Nell never did, at least until now. Through Elizabeth, Nell had the vicarious pleasure of cutting down to size snobby women, lecherous old men, and politely predatory husbands. *Elizabeth* reveals the nastiness below society's polish, exposing its rampant philandering in a manner that maintained literary propriety by using a code that flew over the heads of unsophisticated readers.[5]

Hoping to cheer his invalid wife with encouraging words from a literary man, Clayton took the completed manuscript to a lunch at London's Garrick Club, the first men's club that mixed gentlemen and artists together. Clayton passed his wife's words to Samuel Jeyes, an assistant editor at the Conservative newspaper the *Standard* who was a frequent contributor to the *Saturday Review*. Jeyes entertained his dinner companions later that evening by reading bits of Elizabeth's letters out loud.

Their enjoyment led him to show the manuscript to Edward Drummond, the acting editor at the leading society weekly, *The World: A Journal for Men and Women*. Founded by the journalist and novelist Edmund Yates in 1874, the *World* employed many of the techniques of the so-called new journalism that had transformed the older style of politically oriented—and heavily taxed—newspapers aimed only at elite men into mass market publications. A *World* feature called "Celebrities at Home" launched the first interviews with public figures, and its pages included an increasingly common mix (particularly in the American and French press) of investigative reporting, gossip columns, women's pages, and installments of fiction by authors like Oscar Wilde and George Bernard Shaw. Articles used a more intimate tone and lots of illustrations to attract readers at a price most working people could afford.[6]

Drummond expressed interest in publishing Elizabeth's letters serially, and so Jeyes went out to Sheering Hall to meet the author. Nell eagerly consented to the deal, and the first installment appeared anonymously on August 9, 1899. The letters "created a sensation, for frank intimacies of their kind were unknown," Daisy recalled.[7]

Elizabeth clearly knew whereof she wrote, and curiosity about the writer's identity grew. "We were electrified," recalled one of Nell's oldest friends when news of her authorship of the column spread. "She was quite modest about it and thought it was all a great joke," especially when critics charged, "that no lady of society could possibly have brain enough to write such a book and that therefore she must be some literary adventuress who had suddenly made a hit."[8]

The chance to determine the true identity of *Elizabeth*'s characters made the novel special. Aristocratic settings abounded in novels at the time, but none yet had exuded the scent that this was *true*. "Perhaps one or two specially favoured friends are able to indicate with certainty what is real and what is unreal in the book, what is imaginary or autobiographical," one critic hopefully observed. When *The Visits of Elizabeth* appeared in novel form in America the next year, a reviewer claimed, "the English have by this time pretty well satisfied themselves as to the personality of some of the characters in the book."[9]

For those in Nell's circle, reading the book carried the spiteful pleasures of schadenfreude. One turned the pages looking to see who emerged from her delicately sketched caricatures flattered or skewered. "I am not sure whether I should have been inordinately proud, or a little bit ashamed, of my photograph being used as the prototype of Elizabeth," Daisy's half-sister, Lady Angela, later coyly wondered. "But it was head turning to have had such an attractive heroine built upon what Mrs. Glyn imagined to be my characteristics."[10]

A few months after the *World* serialized Elizabeth's letters, her author was well enough to put down her crutches and appear on the stage along with four other society redheads in "The Five Senses," a tableau vivant (a century-long fad for watching live models pose silently in scenes from literature, history, or art) of the famous Titian painting. The "living picture" was presented at Her Majesty's Theatre in London as part of a benefit to aid the widows and orphans of the Boer War, the fight between Anglo and Dutch colonizers to control southern Africa's land and gold. Herbert Beerbohm Tree, the flamboyant Shakespearean actor who directed the benefit, sprinkled copper dust in the five society ladies' hair to better imitate the painter's beloved shade.[11]

Newspapers focused on the spectacle Nell presented, likely in part because of the increasingly open secret about her identity as society's leading author. "In the centre stood 'Hearing' represented by Mrs. Clayton Glyn, looking superbly handsome in a dress of bright purple velvet trimmed with sable and revealing a skirt cloth of silver studded with pearls and emeralds." Nell struck up a friendship with the evening's green-eyed, sharp-tongued organizer, Minnie Paget, the American wife of Gen. Arthur Paget, currently serving in South Africa. Paget had conquered London years earlier, becoming the model for the heroine in socialite Edith Wharton's posthumously published novel, *The Buccaneers*, about the era in which the Dollar Princesses had first reigned.[12]

Now it looked like Nell might do the same. After becoming a society wife and mother she had carved out an identity of her own as something more: society's premier "authoress." That summer an ambitious young publisher, Gerald Duckworth, approached Nell through Jeyes about expanding the sketches into a novel. A stout man with spindly legs and a small mustache, Duckworth wore a "severe smile and schoolmasterly air which disappeared" when needed. Luckily for the publishing house that bore his name, Duckworth hired Edward Garnett as a literary adviser, since many considered him the era's best reader. Duckworth's first list of 1898–1899 was brilliant by any measure, including authors Henry James, August Strindberg, John Galsworthy, and Duckworth's stepfather, Leslie Stephen. (Stephen's clubby, well-connected stepson would become notorious much later as the man who molested his half-sisters, Vanessa and Virginia Stephen Woolf as little girls.)[13]

Duckworth called on Nell at Sheering Hall to make his pitch.

Sitting in her garden pavilion, he found her face pretty and her voice warm and clear as she read the manuscript aloud to him. Very vain about her speaking voice and dramatic ability, Nell always argued that her prose was best appreciated when *heard* as read *by her*.

She agreed to write a longer version of her saucy letters for publication in the New Year and quickly expanded the manuscript by sending Elizabeth to stay with relations in France, again drawing situations and characters directly from her diaries about her first visits to the Fouquet Lemaîtres. In anticipation, Duckworth Publishers announced that November would herald the arrival of "a new Writer, Elinor Glyn."[14]

The Visits of Elizabeth became a surprise sensation on both sides of the Atlantic in 1901, making it one of the first novels marketed as a "bestseller," a new publishing-industry term in Britain and America. Writing about "The Literary News in England," J. M. Bulloch declared it "extraordinary" that a book about fashionable society's manners and morals had become "one of the successes of the season." "The person who thought of printing Elizabeth's letters describing her sojourn in various country houses, English and French, was blessed with a bright idea," concluded the *Athenaeum* in London, the era's quintessential literary magazine.[15]

Nell's obliquely indiscreet novel earned mostly good reviews for its realistic depictions, cleverness, and comic touch. Elizabeth "writes things in her innocence that have a very deep meaning, as the alert reader will soon realize," noted the *Dial*. "Her audacity, or rather that of the author, is so startling that the reader holds his breath." "There never has been a more interesting book written on the subject of the house-party," judged W. G. Robinson in *Town and Country*. "Here you have both the English and the French methods of entertaining and both very true to life."[16]

The ignoble habits of Elizabeth's noble company shocked some critics, particularly the American ones. "One is sorry to see what absolute bad manners the tea drinking English have. It seems to be their way of enjoying themselves to make other people uncomfortable," wrote a reviewer in *Overland Monthly*. The so-called

"Christian Gentleman" Glyn depicted appalled the *Literary World* in Boston: "They have as little sense of decorum, as little self-restraint as Ojibways. Marriage stands little in the way of the 'smart set' here depicted. It is hard to say which is worst, the brutal earthliness of the aristocratic British circle" or the "frothy filth of the French nobility."[17]

Like the gentlemen at Clayton's club, most critics found Elizabeth a beguiling narrator and her story worth telling, if entirely unsuitable for young ladies like the narrator to read. "English country-house life, as the occasional glimpses into it afforded by the law courts have shown, is certainly worth the study of the serious student of society," pronounced the *Book Buyer*, "but such stories as Elizabeth, an innocent young girl, tells belong to the smoking-room and the club." *Elizabeth* may have owed her start to the approval of gentlemen, but only her appeal to a much wider group explained the novel's spectacular success. The appearance that summer of an anonymously authored parody—purporting to offer her mother's side of the correspondence—announced the authoress had, indeed, arrived. "Vulgar imitation is the shadow of success," sniffed the *Saturday Review*, calling *The Letters of Her Mother to Elizabeth* "dull and coarse" compared to Glyn's "charming satire upon English and French society, written with delicate wit, and first hand knowledge of the people satirized."[18]

Elizabeth's success instantly changed the course of Nell's life, in part because Daisy had persuaded her to buck tradition and publish under her own name. Female authors had long used mostly male pseudonyms and remained out of the public eye. But Daisy argued that word would soon get out anyway; everyone in their circle knew she had written the letters. And Daisy bet that "Elinor Glyn" would sound like a nom de plume to the rest. It is hard to imagine that attention-hungry Nell needed much coaxing from the countess. She never denied loving the spotlight that fell upon her as hands grabbed the apple-green, cloth-covered book eagerly from shelves in bookstores and lending libraries all over Britain and America.[19]

The authoress quickly accumulated a number of incompatible identities. Nell was called a "pretty Londoner," a "French Canadian brought up in Paris," and an Englishwoman raised in "an exceedingly literary family." Reviewers in America broadly sketched her identity as "a lady known in English society." British readers eventually learned she was the wife of a "typical English country gentleman with a very considerable property near Harlow, Essex." All agreed the author was as attractive as her protagonist: "It is said her head has been quite turned by the success of her book, but she is so pretty that it doesn't matter which way her head is turned."[20]

Several reports noted her sisterly relationship to the rising couturier Lucile, who had "recently married Sir Cosmo Duff-Gordon." The year 1900 was a turning point in both sisters' lives as the string connecting their fortunes continued to stretch but bind. Lucy's business had grown rapidly after taking up theatre work, helped in part by her remarriage to her business partner, Sir Cosmo Duff-Gordon. An Olympic fencer and wealthy Scottish baronet, handsome Cosmo was a great supporter of his wife's enterprises and had assisted Lucile Ltd.'s expansion into an enormous Georgian townhouse on Hanover Square that same year. Lucy knew a "Lady" before her name would impress customers in her title-mad world and liked the sound herself. "All socialists and free thinkers like me in their hearts love a title if the truth were known," she admitted to her mother.[21]

The ropes of pearls, tall Russian boots, simple black smock, and Bo-Peep walking stick that Lucy wore to work announced an eccentric, commanding, thoroughly *artistic* figure who increasingly brought theatrical techniques to bear on dressing society ladies like her sister. All couturiers took their client's figure, coloring, and taste into consideration, but Lucy was the first to sell women the promise that a particular dress might make them appear like a "star"—a word that had recently slipped into English to describe an actress capable of filling a theater single-handedly. Lucile gave her gowns names that expressed the individuality of their wearers and then tailored these so-called emotion gowns and dream dresses to match their mistresses' moods. Nell helped out by naming some of the most erotically charged creations like "The Sighing Sound of Lips Unsatisfied" and "It's All in Knowing How." Lucile's peek-a-boo sensibility and preference for cascading chiffons and supple silks explained why she championed "lingerie of cobweb like finesse" that made underwear as important as outerwear.[22]

At Lucile's new Georgian townhouse, Lady Duff-Gordon also

pioneered the use of models as personalities and showcased their charms in the industry's first full-fledged fashion shows. She built a stage, installed theatrical lighting, and issued formal invitations to attend her shows. Informal tea parties in the garden blurred the line between private and public, business and pleasure.[23]

Lucy's aim was to make women's inner desires manifest on their skin and to bring their private feelings out into the air. "Dr. Freud had not yet been heard of, at least not popularly," recalled Elsie Kings, the first celebrity model whom Lucy groomed. "Here indeed was a forerunner of his theories, gamboling on the horizon of a dressmaking establishment."[24]

Some worried that Nell wanted to do something similar with her words. For however agreeable most critics found Elizabeth's company on the page, many fretted that her "outburst of lady-like eroticism" fueled a new school of romances that were "much more sensuous" than the swashbuckling ones of the past. "The cape-and-sword school of romance has had its day, for the time being at least," observed the *Bookman*, and the new fad for "sensual" and "erotic" novels like *Elizabeth* had made "the emotional point of view of the British reading public . . . very difficult to grasp."[25]

Debates over "the Woman Question" had become fiercer in the overheated atmosphere of the fin-de-siècle, leading the *Bookman* to associate Glyn with other women writers whose heroines broke some of society's cardinal rules and, in so doing, contributed to the rising clamor about the sex's proper place. "Another study of the enfant terrible, but here there is much less of narrative, and correspondingly more of art, than 'Sarah Grand' has to give us," the reviewer continued.

Frances McFall took the pen name Sarah Grand when she left her husband and adult son in the English countryside to become one of the most controversial authors in London. The same troubles drove the Anglo-Irish Grand's flight to creative independence as both Sutherland sisters: an unhappy, financially insecure childhood on the outskirts of British society; an early marriage that promised escape but delivered suffocation and sexual incompatibility; a lively, thirsty mind desperate to express all that she had held, ladylike, inside.[26]

After dozens of rejections, Grand personally arranged for the publication of what became her bestselling, most notorious novel, *The Heavenly Twins* (1893), which offered a long meditation on the dysfunction of marriages arranged around society's ideology of separate spheres that prescribed the home for woman, the world for man. The financial dependence and innocence (just a pretty word for enforced ignorance, Grand makes clear) of the novel's three heroines leads to their misery and death, including a baby born with syphilis because of the father's venereal disease (then endemic among married men). In short, *Heavenly Twins* was one long call for men to abandon the sexual double standard that licensed their sexual freedom in favor of embracing the code expected of ladies.[27]

Grand further stirred the maelstrom surrounding the Woman Question by parlaying *The Heavenly Twins*' success into a public platform from which she coined the term "New Woman." The fiery polemicist accused the "Bawling Brotherhood" of keeping women in two roles that reduced them to sexual functions: the ever-breeding "cow-woman" and the always sexually available "scum-woman." Grand's New Woman would not consent to being stamped by such stereotypes and relished taking men to task who tried. "Man deprived us of all proper education, and then jeered at us because we had no knowledge. He narrowed our outlook in life so that our view of it should be all distorted, and then declared that our mistaken impression of it proved us to be senseless creatures. He cramped our mind so that there was no room for reason in them, and then made merry at our want of logic," she wrote in 1894. "And finally . . . he set himself up as a sort of a god and required us to worship him, and, to our eternal shame be it said, we did so. The truth has always been in us, but we have cared more for man than for the truth."[28]

Grand's "New Woman" helped to bind the decade's rising feminist discontent to a troublesome symbol who roamed the world's stage by the time her novel, *Babs the Impossible* (1901) appeared alongside Glyn's *Visits of Elizabeth*. By then the New Woman had been roundly ridiculed in the British popular press as an overeducated, "mannish"-looking, humorless bore. More apocalyptically minded critics depicted her as a sexually voracious monster who threatened the destruction of Anglo-Saxon—the term that collected English-speaking, Christian, "white" people into a separate "race"—civilization. Bram Stoker's *Dracula* (1897) was the most enduring product of such fears, but many others argued the New Woman was the natural partner of the era's "decadent" male artist. "The truth is simply this," asserted Eliza Lynn Linton in *Nineteenth-Century*, "THE UNSEXED WOMAN PLEASES THE UNSEXED MAN."[29]

This association of new women writers with decadence became more fraught after Oscar Wilde's trials of 1895, which drove home the threat such figures posed to the so-called West. "The many honest people who think they hear in the Woman Movement the memento mori of a race, and the gnawing of the death-worm, are not so far wrong," warned Laura Hansson, perhaps the era's best-known New Woman critic. Born of German parents and married to a Swedish writer, the cosmopolitan Hansson made a career of critiquing the New Woman's so-called sterile intellectualism. To Hansson, the particular strength of women's rights movements in Anglo-Saxon and French cultures was a sign of their advanced "decay and corruption."[30]

Nell's vague embrace of her circle's Conservative politics, her aristocratic pretensions, and her preference for a glamorously feminine style more associated with French than British tastes, made it unthinkable that she would espouse Grand's fiery brand of Anglo feminist politics. Yet Nell would do as much as Grand to create a version of the twentieth century's New Women, who would break romantic conventions around the world.[31]

Two months after *Elizabeth*'s publication, Queen Victoria died on the Isle of Wight. The Queen's son-in-law, the duke of Argyll, likened her last hour to watching the sinking of a triple-decker ship as she briefly rallied before each successive dive deeper into the depths. The queen took her last breaths on January 22, 1901, cradled in the arms of her grandson, the German emperor, Kaiser Wilhelm II. The kaiser had arrived at Osborne House uninvited and unwelcomed by the rest of the royal family because of his country's support of the Boers, Britain's enemy in the war to control southern Africa, but was admitted to the queen's deathbed by the royal family to avoid scandal nonetheless.

The tiny "Grandmother of Europe" died as she lived, the fixed point around which her nine children and forty-two grandchildren—who married into dozens of royal houses—revolved.

Eleven days later Nell, Clayton, and Lucy sat together in the windows of London's Berkeley Hotel to watch a long military funeral procession transport the queen's body through the streets as it made its way from Buckingham Palace to the train that would carry it to the Royal Mausoleum at Windsor Castle. Enterprising young men perched in most of the trees along the route to gain a better view, looking like enormous vultures wearing caps in the grainy black-and-white footage shot by British Pathé. The new film company captured the procession that included dozens of foreign royals who had traveled to England to pay their respects.

The unprecedented pomp and grandeur of the funeral was in part the handiwork of the queen's son, King Edward VII, and augured the solidification of their new approach to monarchy. Like his government, Edward VII had recognized for decades that the United Kingdom needed the monarchy to perform grand rites that helped to bind its increasingly democratic society, and sprawling empire, together in awe. For the previous two centuries, most British monarchs had been "politically energetic but personally unpopular" within their ever-tightening field of play. The few pageants staged in the Crown's name had oscillated "between farce and fiasco." The situation had bottomed out in the decade after Nell's birth, as nearly everyone found something to dislike in the behavior of the dour, absent queen or her dissolute heir. "To speak in rude and general terms," asserted Prime Minister Gladstone "the Queen is invisible and the Prince of Wales is not respected" in 1872.[32]

In 1878, the Prince of Wales had embarked—against his mother's wishes—on a grand tour of the Indian subcontinent that aimed to revivify the spirit of Britain's remote and now largely toothless royal house. Designed to honor the native princes whose support had secured the British Raj, the indefatigable prince traveled 7,600 miles by land and 2,300 miles by sea in India alone on the trip. Over these four months he met more governors, maharajahs, and local

chiefs than any British person before. His relative freedom from religious or racial bias was on display during endless parades, dinners,
and receptions. A letter he sent to Lord Salisbury while traveling
protested the "disgraceful" use of "n——" by so many of the colonial
soldiers and staff. "Because a man has a black face and a different
religion from our own," he complained to another Lord, "there is no
reason he should be treated as a brute." The prince also satisfied his
appetites on a royal scale. H.R.H. shot twenty-eight tigers and supervised the capture of fourteen elephants to include in the menagerie
of eighty animals he shipped home. The press covered every detail of
the trip. By his return, even the satirical *Punch* earnestly proclaimed
him the "Hero of India."[33]

Not to be outdone, the queen finally agreed to participate in a
state celebration on the fiftieth anniversary of her reign in 1887 that
remade her reputation. She enjoyed the trunks of jewels deposited at
her feet, the worshipful throngs, the adoring faces. "For the first time
in the history of our land," wrote one witness, "did the Imperial idea
blaze forth into prominence, as the sons and daughters of Empire
gathered together from the ends of the earth to take their part." Ten
years later, Victoria's Diamond Jubilee showcased an even greater
confidence in the splendor and stability of its empire.[34]

The crowds now assembled for Queen Victoria's funeral witnessed the realization of the royal house's new approach. The day
was raw and damp, but the sun broke through the rain-laden clouds
and shone steadily by the time her coffin passed Clayton and the sisters. "Queen's weather to the last," intoned a man standing near Nell
and her party. The extraordinary silence of the black-clad crowds
was more unnerving than their size. For long minutes, Chopin's
funeral march was the only sound. "I have known London in all
moods, in all aspects, but never have I seen it so subdued, so grave, so
sympathetic," a newspaperman marveled. Victoria's reign had lasted
for sixty-four years. Few present could recall a day when Britain's
work had not been done in her name.[35]

The spectacle performed the magic it was meant to on Nell,
prompting the first positive words she ever wrote about Her Majesty:
"Even in the midst of my personal success and happiness it was
impossible not to be affected by the general sorrow over the pass-

ing of the Queen," she conceded of the "Puritanical" woman she
had disliked since girlhood. The silent emotion of the great crowd,
the fortitude of the elderly men making the long march from
Buckingham Palace to Paddington Station, and the Queen's "little,
little coffin" released a burst of rare feeling for England in a woman
whose national identity remained lightly rooted and confused. A
latecomer to this Anglocentric party, Nell finally experienced a sentiment inculcated in schoolchildren from a tender age: the "superiority of all things British, and the privilege of being born to the Flag."
Her rush of national chauvinism flowed from the monarch's sex.
"The reminder of the smallness, the feminine frailty of the greatest
ruler in the world, brought home to me for the first time the glorious romance of the British Empire, and the greatness of the British
race," she recalled. "A sublime spirit of chivalry must be innate in a
people whose highest response of loyalty and valour is always made
to its Queens."[36]

Nell's view amounted to orthodoxy in Britain, where both sup-
porters and opponents of women's rights argued that England's history of bowing before female sovereigns was the ultimate sign of its
progress and the justification for its "civilizing missions" abroad. In
this telling, fealty to a queen was only the most dramatic instance
of Britain's supposedly superior treatment of the female sex—
particularly in contrast to the darker, "Oriental" peoples and places
where colonial empires spread. A century's worth of paintings by
colonial powers had already made the harem the key symbol of
the Orient's alleged licentiousness and degradation of women. A
European imaginary that justified their so-called civilizing missions,
the "Orient" referred to present-day Turkey, Greece, the Balkans,
Middle East, and North Africa. (All Jewish people were also considered Oriental by much of the race science of the day.)[37]

The funeral's spectacle also provoked a more farsighted response
in Nell. "It was impossible not to sense, in that stately procession, the
passing of an epoch and a great one; a period in which England had
been supreme, and had attained to the height of her material wealth
and power," she later wrote. "Influenced by Gibbon's *Decline and Fall*
and by my French upbringing, I felt I was witnessing the funeral
procession of England's greatness and glory." Edward Gibbon's *The*

History of the Decline and Fall of the Roman Empire (1776) taught that no empire lasted. Watching that gray afternoon, she believed "the slow progress of that solemn procession marked the passing of that period of repose and security and of all those things which leisure and security imply—peace, order, confidence, contentment, rest and material well-being on the one hand; self satisfaction, blindness, prejudice, stagnation on the other."[38]

Some portion of the million English people who read a newspaper each day by the time Queen Victoria died would have shared Nell's sentiments that the established order of things was about to change. The recent British victories in the war in southern Africa could not erase the early thrashings by the Boer states' rag-tag guerilla forces. The Boer War's long slog demonstrated that the British Army was prepared only for small colonial skirmishes. The defense budget had leapt to create a ground force of 300,000 (four times larger than their enemy) that would finally defeat the Boers in 1902. But their scorched-earth tactics had already produced a stream of gruesome reports about the deaths of white Boer women and children in British concentration camps that plainly contradicted the empire's professed ideals.[39]

Less obvious, but equally significant, long-term challenges confronted the established order too. The rising industrial strength, public education systems, and militaries of the much more populous Germany and the United States had made them worrisome competitors in the race to control the future. The beginnings of massive technological disruptions loomed—cars, motion pictures, telephones, wireless services, and airplanes. Though at present just a whisper, soon their speed and light and sound would alter the feel and pace of everything. The attention swirling around the women's rights movement, and the era's many other different kinds of new women, raised the possibility that even the most intimate arrangements might change.[40]

The twentieth century would witness the fulfillment of Karl Marx's prophecy in the *Communist Manifesto* (1848): all that once appeared solid would melt into the air; those who did the melting would rule. Without its empire, without control of these new technologies, tiny Britain could not triumph over its competitors. The creation of "invented traditions" like the British Crown near the end of Queen Victoria's reign celebrated the unity of the empire's people to act as a bulwark against these tides breaking against the North Sea's shore. Mass ceremonies were necessary to maintain the national spirit under the conditions of mass society. All nations would reach for them with increasing sophistication in the years ahead. The power of the image-makers who manipulated the symbols and signs, who excelled at performances before the crowds, would only grow. And they would include women as never before.[41]

Although the newly prominent writer had suddenly joined the image-makers' ranks, at the moment Nell had other plans. Immediately after the funeral, she and Clayton traded cold, gray London for Egypt's sunny sky. She officially traveled under her married identity—as "the immaculate and well-behaved wife of an English Squire."[42]

But once in Cairo her associations with the Orient and the ancient world further freed her creative spirit, causing her to behave and to write in previously unimaginable ways.[43]

CHAPTER 5

Under Foreign Skies

What should she do with her life? This taste of change and foreign skies
had unsettled her.

—Elinor Glyn, *When the Hour Came, or His Hour* (1910)

With childbearing behind her, and her own money in the
bank for the very first time, Nell began to travel more;
this trend would only intensify in the years to come.
By 1901, a trip down the Nile and a trek out to the Giza Necropolis
had become a required stop on the Grand Tour for any well-traveled
British person, and Cairo was a favorite wintering place for the very
best kinds of people.[1]

Nell and Clayton brought suitcases of associations along with
their luggage on their many travels, especially when visiting the more
"exotic" places in the British Empire like Egypt. Over the nineteenth
century, Cairo had become widely viewed in the "West" as the past
and present capital of the Orient, a space redolent with freer modes
of erotic expression. Cairo's most famous fictional residents included
Aladdin, Ali Baba, and Scheherazade, the great storyteller of the
Arabian Nights, as Anglophone writers called the Persian folk tales
that had helped to spark their widespread fascination for Oriental
things. By the time Florence Nightingale visited in 1849, that book
shaped everything she saw. "It is the religion of the *Arabian Nights*,"
she wrote after watching men pray in a mosque, "the most dreamy,
the most fantastic, the most airy and yet sensuous religion."

Tourists like the Glyns came to the African continent's largest, most industrialized city to find a place of mystery, barbarism,
and exotic sensuality; a city of inwardly twisting narrow streets that

93

The Sphinx as Nell first saw it in 1900

opened onto colorful bazaars, where beautiful houris of the harem peeked out from behind pink veils and latticed screens.[2]

The visions that later intimidated and entertained Nell's friends in Hollywood began on this trip of 1901, when she visited Cairo for the first time. Drinking in the fresh vistas, sounds, and smells—all primed by her associations of the Orient—Nell unearthed a previously buried erotic edge. Perhaps we all dream more vividly under foreign skies.

A more conventionally Christian woman might have called her first vision a brush with the state of grace. It happened on a visit to see the Great Sphinx on the Giza Plateau, high above the western edge of that great inland sea, the Sahara Desert, about ten miles from where they were staying at the Savoy Hotel. A curving Beaux Arts building put up a few years before, the Savoy spread out over an entire city block on Opera Square in Downtown Cairo, next to the train station in the city's "European Quarter," which was modeled on Paris and home to some 100,000 Europeans. The Savoy instantly became a cultural center for colonial elites in the Middle East. Lawrence of Arabia, Henry Morton Stanley—the journalist and explorer of "Dr. Livingstone, I presume?" fame—and all manner of men indispensable to Britain's far-flung interests passed through its vast halls frescoed with Egyptian gods. On its long veranda, the British smoked their way through their "scramble" to colonize the African continent. During the First World War, the Allied military made the Savoy's 178 rooms their regional headquarters. Like the British Empire, the hotel fell to shambles after the Second World War and finally came tumbling down during the Egyptian Revolution of 2011.[3]

The Glyns had been in Egypt for two weeks by the time Nell left Clayton behind to make the trip out to Giza's Necropolis, Greek for "city of the dead." In another week they would depart for Rome. She framed the expedition in her memoir in the most romantic terms: three ladies, each with their cavalier, sallied forth by horse and camel to pay homage to the desert's stone god.[4]

The journey began after breakfast, when her party packed into a single brougham that set off west across the city before crossing the bridges that connected the island at the Nile's center to the rest of Cairo. "Les Jardin des Plantes," Khedive (viceroy) Isma'il Pasha had named the island in the river's middle for the Parisian park. Educated in France, Muhammad Ali Pasha's grandson Isma'il the Magnificent had built a palace there surrounded by a botanical garden to host dignitaries visiting for the opening of the Suez Canal in 1878. Over the nineteenth century, Muhammad Ali Pasha's dynasty had labored to secure Egypt's independence from Ottoman and European control while simultaneously taking out loans that came with concessions that furthered their encroachment. They built railroads, dug the Suez Canal and irrigation systems, expanded the military and public education systems, and made Egyptian cotton into a staple that fed mills around the world. Cairo became the African continent's most modern, cosmopolitan capital.

"My country is no longer in Africa; we are now part of Europe," Isma'il had announced at the canal's opening. One year later, the British and French convinced the Ottoman sultan in Constantinople to force Isma'il to step down.[5]

Sprawling Cairo has swallowed Giza today, but when Nell's brougham set out that first time the city's urban energy quickly drained out of the landscape after a traveler crossed the Nile and picked up El Haram Street. Pyramid Road, as the English called it, was a dusty carriage track designed to make the drive out to the pyramids easier for the visitors expected for the canal's opening. El Haram passed through open country, where emerald-green rice fields stretched out on either side of the road.

The group stopped at Mena House Hotel for lunch in view of the pyramids and to arrange for a guide to take them to see the Sphinx. A British couple had remade Mena House, once Khedive Ismail's simple hunting lodge, into a sumptuous hotel graced with an enormous outdoor pool surrounded by a stone wall low enough to allow views of the pyramids. Mena House specialized in providing "Arab" guides to take wealthy tourists to see the sights on the northern tip of this vast cemetery that stretched from ancient Egypt's capital of Memphis to its present-day one of Cairo. They planned their pilgrimage later that night, hoping to avoid "the hateful tourists" whom Nell, without irony, disdained.[6]

The desert suspended the 4,500-year-old Giza Necropolis in a sea of sand unbroken by lights, walls, guards, surrounding buildings (save Mena House), or rules. Arriving from the only road that led into the site in 1901, Nell's group would have passed the three largest of the plateau's eighty-some pyramids, including Cheops Great Pyramid. Completed in 2590 BCE, Cheops Pyramid was the last wonder still standing since Philo of Byzantium made the first such list in *On the Seven Wonders* in 225 BCE.

The Sphinx Nell saw looked like some fantastic desert plant, its neck sprouting from the sand to support a giant head whose royal headdress opened, petal like, on each side. The archaeological work that uncovered the lion's long body would come later, in the 1920s. None of the many digs before or since have answered who, when, or why the world's largest statue was built. That it is the oldest object yet uncovered in this great city of the dead is one of the few things about which experts agree.

When all but one man in her party had returned, Nell had "one of the greatest experiences of my life. No words can define the lasting effect upon my imagination, indeed upon my whole personality, of this moonlight visit to the Sphinx." She recalled:

The full moon shed an unearthly light and the luminous sand appeared pink, the shadows indigo, and the sky unbelievably blue. . . . I seemed to feel myself become a part of that Immortal Being whom these Ancient Egyptians sought to commemorate in this strange edifice of stone. I seemed to understand the mysteries of the ages, and to glimpse the true meaning of existence. The importance of the things of this world, for which I still cared so greatly, appeared to fade into insignificance.[7]

A version of this experience that added a powerful erotic dimension to the heroine's reckoning with the meaning of existence out in the desert opened her novel *When the Hour Came* (1910). A moonlight trip to the Sphinx acts as the turning point in the life of the novel's heroine, Tamara, as it did for her creator. Recently widowed, Tamara travels to Egypt, where she impulsively decides to visit the Sphinx late one night with only an "Arab" guide.

The Sphinx was smiling its eternal smile. It was two o'clock in the morning. The tourists had returned to Cairo, and only an Arab or two lingered near the boy who held Tamara's camel . . . she was alone—alone with her thoughts and the Sphinx. The strange mystical face looked straight at her from the elevation where she sat. Its sensual mocking calm penetrated her brain. The creature seemed to be laughing at all humanity—and saying—'There is no beyond—live and enjoy the things of the present—Eat, drink, and be merry, for to-morrow you die and I who sit here and know tell you there is no beyond. The things you can touch and hold to your bodies are the only ones worth grasping.'

'No, no!' said Tamara, half aloud, 'I will not—I will not believe it.'

'Fool,' said the Sphinx, 'What is your soul? And if you have one, what have you done with it? Are you any light in the world? No, you have lived upon the orders of others. Just an echo it is—that fine thing, your soul. Show it then, if you have one! Do you possess an opinion? Not a bit of it. Believe me, you have no soul. So take what you can—a body! You certainly have that, one can see it—well snatch what it can bring you, since you have not enough will to try for higher things. Grasp what you may, poor weakling. That is the wisdom sitting here for an eternity has taught me."[8]

Tamara's conversation with the Sphinx suggested Nell's struggle over feeling gradually suffocated by trapped desire. Her marriage's cool temperature, its lack of intimacy and intensity, was the tepid weather system in which she lived. She wanted passion, to pluck the day and put no trust in the future, as the ancient poet Horace wrote. *When the Hour Came* added a dramatic twist entirely absent from the author's own experience: after Tamara's conversation with the Sphinx, the novel's hero (modeled on a Russian Nell met this visit) rides up and sweeps the timid widow off her feet.

And yet, Nell also preserved an equally strong desire not to break her marriage vow over a trifling affair—as so many around her did. Before going to Egypt, she had ended a flirtation with the first man who had seriously tempted her to break her word. John Seymour Wynne-Finch was a former major in the Royal Horse Guards regiment, known for his charm and good looks even among the charming Marlborough House set in which he traveled. Finch was also a wit; when someone remarked that a wife treated her husband like furniture, he deadpanned: "Drawing room or bedroom? It does make such a difference."[9]

Though she knew it marked her as hopelessly bourgeois, Nell ended the affair before things progressed too far. She later wryly remarked that her faithfulness among their faithless set had become "almost an embarrassment" to Clayton by this point.[10]

Acutely aware of her beauty, her head turned by her recent literary success, Nell arrived in Cairo restless and wanting attention, and the men she met there made her swoon. "Godlike," and an "English gentleman of the old school," she called Lord Cromer, Evelyn Baring, Egypt's de facto ruler since 1882. A still-towering, sixty-one-year-old with a bushy silver mustache and a monocle clutched over one hooded eye, Cromer kept to the edges of gatherings, studying his cigarette. Sounding like a schoolgirl with an enormous crush, Nell described Cromer and his men as, "'Ambassadors from Britain's Crown,' lesser Caesars holding sway over the destinies of numbers of native people" who "worked selflessly, and with immense success, for the material and moral good of those whom they ruled and served."[11]

Her reaction to men like Cromer was hardly rare. The celebrated mystique of such men had made them into world figures essential to the appeal of Britain's so-called new imperialism. It is easy to see why the relentless industriousness of her imperial heroes put the men she knew back in England to shame. When you scratched the surface, many of the most successful were not typical aristocrats at all. They were men with newly made money in their bank accounts, or second sons, or the smart boys who, contrary to custom, diligently pursued their studies at England's great public schools. They had something to prove, an ambition to make their mark outside the insular lines of influence at home. Asked for the reason behind the British imperial system's success, the reply of Lord Lawrence, India's viceroy, flashed the arrogant assurance that acted like catnip to Nell: "It's not our system . . . it's our men."[12]

Because more and more, Nell's industrious, middle-class core thought the leisure class—and particularly the men—back in England really needed more to *do*. (*"You might try working . . ."* would become a refrain among her heroines in response to aristocratic men bemoaning their impoverished fate.) A gentleman like Seymour Wynne-Finch—who occupied his hours with dressing and undressing, shooting birds, and seducing other men's wives—simply failed to incite the ardor that might have turned her hankering for the touch of flesh into the deed.[13]

After a few weeks in Cairo, Clayton and Nell left her "dream country" in a boat bound for Naples and then boarded a train south to Pompeii, where the ancient ruins discovered in the eighteenth century further freed the kind of desires she was used to keeping under wraps. Every turn displayed the evidence of the Romans' worship of Priapus, God of Fertility. (Which had led historians to conclude the society's moral depravity had produced the Roman Empire's fall.) The most graphic erotic art—the frescoes of copulating couples, the life-size statue of Pan penetrating a female goat—had been locked away in the "Secret Museum" in Naples, off-limits to female visitors. But the authorities could not remove the dozens of brothels and sex clubs or the phalluses protruding from the most ordinary objects. A "sensuousness that was so extreme as to be positively sensual," suffused even Pompeian air, Nell reported. "Obsessed" with the feeling that she knew this place, she wanted only to leave it behind.[14]

Next, they continued farther south to the small seaside town of Paestum. Founded by the Greeks in 600 BCE as Poseidonia, Paestum boasts three of the best-preserved Greek temples left standing. Still off the beaten path, a lucky visitor today might see the Temple of Hera—Goddess of Women and Marriage—alone, as Nell did. After Clayton and the others left her in the inner sanctuary with the lizards, Nell experienced the vision that later led her to embrace Spiritualism and New Thought, new religious movements that believed in accessing a deeper reality through practices like meditation, reincarnation, and communicating with the dead.

Suddenly, in the temple she "saw quite plainly a number of draped figures around me. They were dancing a strange dance, and I longed to join them." She felt "almost suffocated with the intensity of weird, tigerish sensations" and "overwhelmed by extraordinary, pagan emotions" watching the dancers weave and spin around the temple, and one another, in ever tighter circles.[15]

Desire now overpowered her as it had not since watching Bernhardt perform as the Byzantine adulteress-empress Théodora. Ten years before, Bernhardt's Théodora had been "like a sudden flint touching steel to ignite the tender" of her craving for a touch she did not yet know. The overwhelming yearning she experienced left her "trembling in bed the whole night through." *Théodora's* lavish Orientalism licensed the kind of decadent heroine still forbidden on the late Victorian stage in Britain. But until this trip, almost a decade later, Nell claims to have tucked "anything sensual" away, sublimating her cravings for a carnal connection into the pleasures of fashion, conversation, and the word.[16]

(Ten years later, when the now notorious authoress finally met Bernhardt in person during the war, the two had a frank exchange and Nell learned that Seymour Wynne-Finch had been the actress's lover just before Nell had met him. Bernhardt had "loved in fact" because she "was a great actress." While Nell, "the immaculate and well-behaved wife of an English Squire," had loved "only in word." By the time she met Bernhardt, Nell understood firsthand the pains and pleasures associated with the white-hot passion she had wanted for so long. "Would I have been happier if I had taken him as fact, as [Bernhardt] has done," she wondered later, "or only more full of unrest—Who knows?"[17]

After ten minutes in Hera's temple, the vision evaporated and she left. For the rest of her life Nell insisted that the scene and sensations were as real as ordinary life. Calling such experiences "illusory settles nothing," she argued, knowing that many people did. "For what, after all, is the criterion of reality? How may I know that my clear and strong-felt sensations during such a moment are unreal, whereas those evoked by, say, the taste of a certain dish, or the smell of a rose, or the sight of a motor accident, are genuine and trustworthy?" After discussing the nature of ontology with some of the most eminent minds of her day, she would conclude that, "some external reality must exist to provide the stimulus for all these sensations."[18]

And, if that were the case, then little wonder that Nell believed that outside forces beckoned her now to join in the dance of life and embrace the pleasures of the flesh. The historical record of her life all but disappears until her return to Egypt the following winter. It was as if the buzzing, unreal quality of her life—as society's beauty became society's most celebrated chronicler—obliterated the traces. But on her next visit to Cairo in January 1902, she had the chance to make her dreams into something she could touch.

◇ ◇ ◇

This time the entire household went. Margot and Juliet, ages nine and four, Nanny Dawson, and Nell's mother, Elinor Kennedy, all packed their trunks for a three-month stay.[19]

On this trip, Nell behaved at times like a woman possessed. "What had Egypt done for her?" wonders her heroine Tamara in *When the Hour Came:*

> Lifted just one pretty white eyelid, perhaps. Stirred something which only once or twice in her life she had been

Nell and Margot ride camels in Giza in 1902

dimly conscious of. Everything had been a kind of shock to her. A shock of an agreeable description. And once driving at night in the orange groves of Ghezireh, after some open-air fete, the scent and intoxicating atmosphere had made her blood tingle.[20]

Nell's blood more than tingled at Khedive Abbas's ball the night she met the Russian nobleman who became the model for Tamara's perfect lover. The "most physically attractive creature I ever met," she called the grand duke Boris Vladimirovich of Russia near the end of a life spent consorting with some of the world's most attractive, powerful men. First cousin to Russia's last emperor, Tsar Nicholas II, Boris was a tall, broad-shouldered, charismatic extrovert who hated to be alone. Favored and spoiled by his mother, the grand duchess Maria Pavlovna, he became a "world class womanizer, absolutely unscrupulous" and "the terror of jealous husbands." "Of all the Romanovs, Boris was the one more likely to be shot by a husband than by an assassin," an acquaintance recalled.[21]

On a world tour designed to separate him from a mistress, Boris paused in Cairo where he acted "just as I described" in her novel *When the Hour Came*, Glyn coyly noted in her autobiography. Holding her tight, he gracefully whirled her around the floor and into a quiet corner, where he pressed a kiss on her neck that "burned into her flesh. In all her smooth, conventionally ordered life she had never experienced such a strong emotion," Tamara thinks after the dashing Russian lets her go. In real life, the encounter with Boris left Nell longing for more similarly passionate connections and wanting to visit the Russian Court. Luckily, Boris's mother was the Romanov Court's most prominent hostess and would later give Nell an entrée that made it possible to set *When the Hour Came* there. (Never write about places unseen was already one of Glyn's top rules.)[22]

Such sexually charged experiences cracked Nell's well-practiced self-control, sending her creative energy into unfamiliarly explicit erotic territory. She posed in a tableau vivant as Lorelei, the Siren whose song slipped into German folktales during the Romantic period. For long minutes she stood onstage covered only in a body stocking, yards of green chiffon, and her red hair, swinging loose to her waist. A symbol of women's sexual availability and power since antiquity, the modestly covered heads of so many women in the surrounding streets offered potent testimony to the belief in the magic a woman's hair was said to work. The bright red color of Nell's would have emphasized her image as a dangerous seductress.[23]

But after the performance, she fell prey to pains in her side so agonizing that only morphine gave her relief. For weeks she lay in bed as the throbbing came and went. Prince Hussein, the eldest son of Khedive Abbas, invited the terribly thin and pale Nell to recuperate on the Jardin des Plantes. Though just a few acres in size, the intricately landscaped island in the Nile appeared much larger. Legend had it that each night gardeners removed every faded bloom.

In the "enchanted air" of this garden "straight out of the Arabian Nights," Nell felt well enough at once to write her second novel, *The*

Reflections of Ambrosine (1901). What if she had bowed beneath the pressure that Lucy's first husband put on her to marry the brash millionaire? The answer to that question inspired a novel whose central dilemma is whether or not its high-minded, miserably married heroine will break the seventh commandment—no adultery—with a character modeled on Seymour Wynne-Finch, the enticing man Nell had just rejected.[24]

So conspicuous was Finch's resemblance to Ambrosine's love object, Antony Thornhirst, that friends took to introducing Finch by the name of his fictional twin after the book's publication. "A beautiful mover" on the dance floor, with mocking "cat's eyes" of green, Thornhirst speaks with an "alluring" voice and has a wit "as light as thistle down." Nell took other characters from her life, resurrecting Grandmother Saunders's spirit in Ambrosine's impoverished French grandmamma, who raises the heroine to the ancien régime's rigid code.[25]

But Ambrosine's more genuinely aristocratic (and therefore less morally rigid) grandmother teaches her that "one may do as one pleases as long as one behaves like a lady." And yet Ambrosine waits two hundred and fifty pages even to kiss Sir Antony's lips (and long after her husband has taken up with another woman). It was as if Nell wanted to inflict her own sexual frustration and confusion on her readers. "I longed, passionately longed, for him to take me in his arms and let me lie there forever—fused in some bliss I did not yet know," Ambrosine thinks after Antony begs her to spend the night early on. "I have been a child and asleep—now I am a woman and awake," she continues, "but dearest, there is something beyond all this for you and me—there is the seventh commandment—I cannot share myself between two men."[26]

Tortured Ambrosine conveys the confusion of a woman made miserable by the moral code of the company she keeps even while believing wholeheartedly in their superiority. The author's growing dismay over her circle's dedication to self-interested pleasure also snakes through the novel. "I wish he would go into Parliament," a dowager says of charming Sir Antony. "He would not give himself the trouble," someone else replies. "That is just it. The ablest people are so lazy." Ambrosine's boorish middle-class husband is the novel's only hardworking man. "We have always eaten and drunk too rich food and wine in our class, and have not had enough to do, so we can't help being as we are," explains one lady.[27]

Ambrosine sold decently when published later that year, solidifying Nell's reputation as England's "leading novelist of modern manners." But its serious, sad, unhappily married heroine disappointed readers looking for another witty, single Elizabeth. Some also worried that the author endorsed an immoral view. "The suggestion that refined vice is preferred by persons of taste to honest vulgarity requires more than a novel to establish it," one critic demurred, refusing to accept the author's premise: that aristocratic settings and glamorous clothes made so-called immoral behavior less troublesome than if performed by poorly dressed people in a saloon.[28]

Nell's pains had disappeared while she composed the novel that vented so many of her sexual and emotional frustrations in the sweet-smelling Jardin des Plantes. She left Cairo in early April alone, the nearly finished manuscript tucked into one of her dozens of trunks. Nanny Dawson and Mrs. Kennedy shepherded the girls back to Sheering alongside Clayton, who planned to check on the progress of spring before meeting Nell at the Grand Hotel in Rome.

She reveled in the attention she received in Rome on her own. "Lady Rodd arranged a dinner for me to meet some 'very clever people who will interest me.' What it is to be an authoress!!" she wrote her mother. She sat for a portrait bust by the sculptor Waldo Story. Born in Rome, educated at Eton and Oxford, Waldo Story traveled in a circle swimming with American and British creative luminaries. Story wore pantaloons with enormous checks and a "carefully studied squint and air of nonchalance." He parroted the American idea of an Englishman even as his American roots defined him: his grandfather was Joseph Story, the nineteenth century's most influential Supreme Court justice; his father, W. W. Story, was a sculptor, writer, art critic, and pivot in Rome's expatriate community who had passed down his art studio to his son.

By the time Nell sat in Story's vast, sunny studio, his signature already adorned dozens of marble likenesses of British elites and the voluptuous statuary ornamenting their estates, like the *Fountain of Love* at Viscount Astor's Cliveden. Story alternately praised Nell's beauty and criticized her vanity, drawing her into the group that gathered at his apartment in the Palazzo Barberini, the Baroque palace built for the new pope in 1623.[29]

Surrounded by frescoes and sculptures of naked emotional intensity, Nell grew bolder than ever before, behaving in this exclusively creative company with an abandon that she later erased from the official record of her life. She wore men's clothes about town and went target shooting where she "killed a champagne bottle at a hundred yards! & *rode* a horse. Clayton won't believe it," she wrote to Story's wife, Maude.[30]

When Clayton finally joined her in Rome, they began motoring to nearby towns, bumping through the hilly countryside in the Panhard of the American ambassador. Motoring in one of Europe's first automobiles, Nell finally found a sport she liked.

But then the mysterious pains in her side reappeared with an intensity that flattened her high spirits. A pattern emerged, as illness and anxiety followed when Nell could not speak or act out her desires, a feeling that her husband's company often instigated or intensified.

Clayton arranged for his wife to see Dr. Axel Munthe, a Swedish physician whose training in Paris made him a kind of early psychiatrist. "One of those modern doctors who are more occupied with healing the soul than the body," was how the Roman press described the man whose small practice near the Spanish Steps catered mostly to wealthy Anglo-American ladies. Like many of his patients, Nell felt seen, heard, and spoken to honestly by this man who believed in forcefully sharing his opinions and then letting their subconscious do most of the work.

"He wore a soft, close cut beard, and very peculiar spectacles," Nell recalled, not realizing the forty-five-year-old was going blind. "The lenses were so immensely thick that it was impossible to see the colour or expression of his eyes, and thus he produced in me that rather uncanny sensation of being watched by someone unseen."[31]

Some found the quality unsettling, calling Munthe a "mesmerist," or worse. He confessed a "certain ability to lead people. . . . I do believe that it depends on a definite talent for judging people, but this is not enough," he wrote. "Sometimes it seems to me almost to

be 'demonic.'" (During World War I, with anesthesia in short supply, Munthe became revered for easing the pain of dying men by
repeating words of hope and comfort while laying his hands on their
heads.)[32]

Nell's pains never got her classified as a hysteric, but many neu-
rologists called neurasthenia the little hysteria, grouping it inside the
nervous disorders they believed originated in women's sexual and
reproductive dysfunction. By the late nineteenth century, doctors
considered such nervous disorders a virtual plague among women of
all classes. Many historians now tie the explosion of the diagnoses
to the rise of the study of sexuality per se and to how the sexuality
of respectable white women grew steadily more shameful, suspect,
disordered, unintelligible: more "hysterical," in a word.[33]

Ancient attitudes about women's voracious sexual appetites
still pooled around "Oriental" or darker-skinned, often colonized,
women. They showed up in the obsessive interest that European
artists and playwrights paid to history's "dark ladies," (or femmes
fatales), like Théodora, Salome, Medea, Lady Macbeth, and the
Sirens. It spilled over onto the personas and attitudes of actresses
like Bernhardt, who played them. Most successful female performers
used such conventions to their advantage.[34]

But except for a radical few, most white people came to believe
that unbridgeable differences separated the sexuality of "dark"
women from white ladies. Even metaphorically, a great actress like
Bernhardt—whose Jewishness classified her as Oriental in the race
science of the day—could not hope to play both kinds of parts. One
was either a Siren or a Lady among the fin-de-siècle theatre crowd,
who found the idea of female metamorphosis too monstrous for
entertainment. "A genuine fear of a woman actually *acting*," circulated around the stage because of a concern about "the actress being
corrupted by the moral impurity of the character, or, most significantly, of becoming someone else, of finding within herself other
selves to become."[35]

Before he came to specialize in helping society ladies heal their
pains, Munthe had made debunking hysteria his pet project. His
internationally bestselling autobiography, *The Story of San Michele*
(1929), concocted a dramatic story about an adventure as a medical

student under Jean-Martin Charcot, the neurologist made famous by his work on hysteria and hypnosis. Munthe fancifully claimed to have liberated Charcot's best-known hysteric, Geneviève, from Salpêtrière, the giant Parisian hospital where her hypnosis-induced fits had transfixed hundreds of onlookers in its amphitheater.[36]

Nell used Munthe's supposed advice to craft a turning point in her autobiography, *Romantic Adventure*. Here she said the good doctor's description of her "in his case-book was 'The Syren'" and that this sexy lady's suffocation had made her sick. But she had only played that role once on her honeymoon, she protested. (If her diaries are to be believed, she remained the "immaculate wife of an English Squire." That was of course the point.

Attributing the naming of her sexual frustration to Munthe followed the kind of playing with mirrors she liked by having other characters express views that Nell herself could still not say aloud.

Why take responsibility for saying the hardest things? Why risk speaking aloud all that she had been praised since girlhood for keeping tucked inside? So much easier to put your words into other mouths. So much easier to leave everyone guessing just what was sincerely felt and what had merely been observed. Better for her reputation and for posterity, better for everyone to let Munthe say it.

Traveling alone, the couple left Rome for Lucerne in May of 1902 where Nell's first sight of the Swiss Alps in springtime made her dream of playing the Siren again with an intensity that changed the outcome of both Nell and Clayton's lives. After her husband laughed at her "spring fancies," Nell felt "much aggrieved at his want of sympathy" and "flew to [her] journal for comfort," writing "detailed descriptions of love-scenes with an imaginary lover in this idyllic setting."

Irritation over their sexual and temperamental mismatch led to a rare argument between the couple when Nell asked to buy a magnificent Siberian tiger skin displayed in a fur shop's window in a Lucerne hotel one rainy day. Typically generous Clayton refused. "It was bad enough to have to travel with a woman who had thirty-seven new dresses" and "a train of antique admirers," she said he explained. Traveling with a giant dead feline crossed the line, particularly when she was "too like the creatures anyway."

Armed with a large royalty check from *Elizabeth*'s sales, Nell returned and bought the tiger's skin herself. Clayton later found her in their hotel suite stretched out on the hide in front of a fire, caressing the tiger's fur. "He laughed so heartily at me that I was snubbed and never reclined on tigers again," she claimed (oddly, given the existence of several widely circulated publicity photos that later showed her doing just that).

Later, Nell would give the incident a happier ending in the most infamous scene in her notorious sex novel, *Three Weeks*, in which a glamorous older woman seduces her beautiful young lover by masturbating on the back of a great dead cat. Nell would pour all the sex she fantasized about in the Alps into the novel, earning her "title among prudes and Puritans as a dreadfully 'immoral woman'" and forever coupling her name "with the picture of a woman lying on a tiger skin" ("undulating" was the word she actually used in the novel). The cruel irony for Nell was that her "imagination was roused to the worship of Love not by possession of its joys, but by a longing for them."[37]

Once again, the established pattern held true: after Clayton's rejection at the hotel, the pain in her side returned and only intensified once they rejoined the girls at Sheering Hall. Physical pain had become the means to express her thwarted desires.

Dr. Munthe had advised trying "the cure" at the Bohemian Mountain Spa, Carlsbad, if her pains resumed. So, Nell took Munthe's advice and left Sheering for Carlsbad. "The pains come every day but not as violent as they were," she wrote to Waldo Story not long after arriving in the town perched in the Bohemian hills above the narrow valley carved by the Ohre and Tepia Rivers (in the present-day Czech Republic). Carlsbad rose like a layered cake into the hills to accommodate the health seekers who arrived in droves. By the 1890s, 50,000 patients came each year to soak in the hot mineral springs, drink the waters, and walk along the miles of paths laid out through dense woods of oak, pine, fir, and beech trees.[38]

Nell appeared "a very strikingly fashionable and delicate-looking little woman" when she arrived in July, according to an acquaintance there. Always on the border of painfully thin, she had lost more weight and thought she looked like she felt: "old and just terribly run down." "I was put on chicken and champagne with a little brandy in the morning to stop the wasting," she reported to Maude Story, describing a diet sure to leave one more relaxed. "I feel so lonely and far away from all my dear ones. The babies' photographs make me cry." But she still thought it "wise to be alone without them for really getting well, as their anxious faces get on my nerves."[39]

Part health resort, part writer's retreat, Nell found intellectual, literary-minded company there like Story's salon in Rome. The judge Sir Francis Jeune and his wife, Mary, became companions. The Jeunes introduced her to Sir Gilbert Parker, the recently knighted Ontario-born novelist, and his American wife, Amy. In between the talks and the walks and the seven glasses of metallic-tasting mineral water she reluctantly drank each day, her spirits revived and she quickly finished *The Reflections of Ambrosine*. She showed the manuscript to Parker, who praised the novel. Suspecting it might encounter trouble because of her more matter-of-fact descriptions of society ladies' pursuit of their extramarital pleasures, Parker urged her "not to mind criticism or accusations of immorality and to 'go straight on.'" By the end of summer, Nell reported a complete turnaround. "I have had enough," she wrote, referring to the mineral water she detested, "but I think it has cured me as I have no more pains now."[40]

Gilbert Parker's advice shrewdly recognized that critics would not like *Ambrosine* as much as *Elizabeth*. As the novelist predicted, some faulted Nell's more direct engagement with "all the clandestine wickedness that underlies the whole fabric of English society." It is a "vulgar story of vulgar people, vulgarly told," another sniffed.[41]

Nell regularly returned to Carlsbad over the next few years for pleasure, not pain. As Munthe suspected and Cairo first illustrated, the pleasures of writing and of travel banished or kept her pains at bay. Travel to places outside of Britain—especially if the setting encouraged a freer sensuality and emotional register—offered escape from the boredom and anxiety that too often accompanied her family life in the English countryside. And the writing that inevitably flowed in these settings soothed her bruised heart by permitting her to vent her feelings while earning the attention she craved.

While Clayton sailed and hunted with the guns, she spent the following August and September at Carlsbad talking and walking and playing "tigre" (hide-and-seek) in the woods with the kind of imperial statesman she now liked best, Lord Alfred Milner, who became a close confidant and lifelong friend (and some say temporary lover). Knighted for his success in "modernizing" Egypt, Milner had become high commissioner in South Africa and governor of Cape Colony, where he had waged war against the Boers, making "Milnerism" a term of abuse for many by the time they met.[42]

Nearing fifty, Milner was tall and lean, with almost as much hair in his handlebar mustache as on his head. Depicted as married to his work, friends considered him warm, generous, and skilled at attracting beautiful, spirited women when he had the time. The year before he had begun a secret affair with the fiery empire supporter (and married) Violet, Lady Edward Cecil. Even after Violet finally

"His Excellency Sir Alfred Milner and Staff in Cape Town," 1900

married Milner in 1921, she remained jealous of Nell, forbidding her daughter from reading Nell's books.[43]

Some sources say that Milner and Nell began an affair on this trip that ran hot and cold for decades. Nell's diary suggests the affair with Milner was never consummated (likely helping to explain why they could remain lifelong friends), but their cerebral flirting in the woods rings out of her next little book. Penned in Milner's company (who possessed the spirit of Socrates, she came to believe sincerely), *The Damsel and the Sage* (1903) is a short metaphysical dialogue between the two characters about the meaning of life and love. "Oh, hush, Sage!" the Damsel observes near its end, frustrated with all his reasons for prizing serious pursuits with other men over love. "Come, shave off your beard, and put on a velvet doublet, and return with me to the Court. See, life is short, and I am fair."[44]

On this visit Nell also grew much closer to one of London's most important socialites, Minnie Stevens Paget. The connection proved valuable in both Paget's native America and in Britain. It helped that Minnie Paget appeared like one of Nell's favorite characters, Becky Sharp, come to life. The first American heiress to marry into English society, Minnie was imagined as a buccaneer by Edith Wharton when she sailed from Boston to London in the 1870s. Paget became a matchmaker for those who followed in her wake, assessing them with "her hard green eyes" before introducing them to the royal circle she knew so well. Nell admired how this plainspoken, commercial-minded, energetic American now in her forties had steered her own course through life.[45]

"I think you would find me very much changed for the better. I am not nearly so vain in the way that used to irritate you so, do you remember?" Nell wrote to Waldo Story after returning from Carlsbad. "I believe happiness has altered the bad things. I have had a year of intense happiness." Nell would publish two novels back to back that displayed her steady drift toward full-blown love stories and her sense of humor's return, as she reverted to the lighthearted, "French" philosophical tone she had used in *Elizabeth*.[46]

Dedicated "to the women with red hair," *The Vicissitudes of Evangeline* (1905)—published in America as *Red Hair*—helped to solidify a new image of redheaded women as possessing unusual sex-ual power. In the novel, everyone tells the "penniless adventuress" that no one will marry her because of her "wicked" looks. "You beau-tiful siren," hisses the older brother of the man Evangeline loves. "You are coaxing me. How you know how to use your charms and powers; and what *man* could resist your tempting face!" Generally well received, the novel was noted by one reviewer as having the "peculiar charm of an engaging feminine personality, which almost disarms criticism even in the act of provoking it." While another predicted: "Doubtless all fashionable restaurants will now swarm with heads prodigal of red."[47]

About the time *Evangeline* appeared, Nell had developed a seri-ous interest in another man who stimulated her Siren side. Dashing, lively, and ten years her junior, Alastair Innes-Ker, also of the Royal

Glyn family posed under an "Arab" tent at home in the garden in Essex, England

Horse Guards, was the second son of the duke of Roxburghe. At one house party they appeared together in a tableau, Alastair playing the devoted Boswell to Nell's Mary Queen of Scots, another infamously beguiling redhead.

After performing with Alastair, Nell wrote *Beyond the Rocks: A Love-Story* (1906), her first third-person narrative about a heroine's search for true love after her family auctions her off to "a fat, short, prosperous, middle-class Englishman who had accumulated a large fortune in Australia, accidently." She named the novel's heroine Theodora, after the "dark lady" played by Sarah Bernhardt who had inspired her own sexual awakening in Paris long ago. But it was a *New York Times* description of Evangeline that captured the warring impulses in the author's heart. Evangeline may have been named for Nell's favorite "dark lady," but her heroine was still "as beautiful as the dawn, as innocent as a baby, as pure as the stars," as the *Times* wrote.[48]

The dilemma driving *Beyond the Rocks*—will or won't Theodora succumb to Hector, a charming rake modeled on Innes-Ker— dramatized Nell's own struggle, again. With his "deep and arresting" voice and "way of looking straight into the eyes of the person he was talking to," Theodora sees that Hector "belonged to the tribe who . . . could never be husbands." But she loves him just the same.[49]

"What can her husband be about?" wonders Hector after they meet. "What an intoxicatingly agreeable task to wake her up!" he thinks after an evening out in Paris in Theodora's company. "He lived in a world where the awakening of young wives, or old wives, or any woman who could please man, was the natural course of the day. It never even struck him as a cruel thing to do," the novel's narrator observes.[50]

Nell's first official "love story," *Beyond the Rocks* earned almost universally bad reviews, but also sold better than any of her books since *Elizabeth*. This commercial success suggested greater rewards if she could further free the creative and erotic impulses first loosened under foreign skies. From the novel's rise in the eighteenth century, the literary genre had promised its always heavily female readership information about sex and the wider world. And now, after Nell's experiences in the Orient and the ancient world, after unburdening

her heart in Rome, after consorting with a creative cast of characters, she had become more of an independent personage in her own
right than before. And the more Nell embraced playing the role
of the peripatetic, romantic authoress, "Elinor Glyn," the more life
led her to imagine the kind of increasingly explicit erotic escapades
about which so many wanted to read.[51]

Harnessing the power of glamour: Nell dressed in the manner of her Tiger Queen from *Three Weeks* for her first American book tour

Act II

GLAMOUR

CHAPTER 6

Writing *Three Weeks*[1]

She ran over those most delightful substitutes for bodily dissipation, novels.

—Mary Wollstonecraft, *Mary* (1788)

For the whole fifteen years of her marriage Nell had waited. Ever the proud mistress of restraint, she kept her longing for a lover under control. She wrote and she traveled and she flirted and she danced. She visited doctors and took their cures, all in hopes of keeping her "feverish unrest" and the "terrible attacks of pains" in check.[2]

When the Glyns returned to Sheering in the fall of 1906, the normally slack wire of tension between them stood taut after a rare argument erupted over Nell's latest flirtation, Alastair Innes-Ker. The argument followed a summer in which Alastair had acted like a member of their family, traveling with the Glyns to Paris, where they left fourteen-year-old Margot at a finishing school for the year. Alastair charmed Lucy and made an excursion to see Versailles alone with Nell. Then the group went on to a house party hosted by the Lyon family at Glamis Castle in Scotland, where Clayton uncharacteristically announced that he'd had enough of the young man's company.

Essex was awash in Indian Summer, bringing the nicest weather of the year. Clayton happily busied himself with preparations for another season of shooting as the petals on the last roses curled inward. Beyond her beloved garden the long row of willows that led down to the meadow and the stream had turned yellow-green. Further still Heather Wood flamed with oranges and reds, as if foreshadowing the ear-shattering scenes to come. Nell had learned the first rule of the wood from Clayton upon arriving at Sheering Hall as a new bride: "women must not walk there, they will disturb the pheasants—only the feet of keepers must tread these sacred paths" was the lesson she recorded in her diary. Though she had always "longed for some place [she] could be alone," Nell had given up years before trying "to penetrate among the trees even in winter." But she had never ceased to wonder what lay inside this mysterious forest so close and yet "ever défendu—a forbidden corner—an unexplored land."[3]

A story she had spun for her friends before the fire at Glamis Castle one rainy day would not stop making circles in her mind. The recent brutal murders of King Alexander I of Serbia and his queen consort, Draga, partially inspired the tale she told. Alexander I had braved the wrath of public opinion and his mother to marry Draga, a well-educated widow who was twelve years older than him. Serbians had called Draga a wicked seductress before making her the first queen killed by her people since Nell's adored Marie Antoinette. Unable to shake the tragedy and romance of Draga's tale she decided to write a novel about a doomed affair between an older, sophisticated married Slavic lady and the innocent young man she ennobles with her love.

She set off down the garden path to the pavilion and wrote *Three Weeks* "to melt the frozen ache" that was her heart. Here, to the sound of the gunshots she despised, she wrote *Three Weeks* in just twice that time. She "wrote breathlessly for hours and hours on end, hardly conscious at times of the words which were pouring into [her] brain." Writing *Three Weeks* provided a typically indirect means to retaliate against Clayton. Having complied with his instruction to send Alastair on his way, she now wrote a love story in which she described in precise detail drawing a beautiful young man who greatly resembled him into her arms. *Love is tangible. It means to be close—close—to be clasped—to be touching—to be One!*[*] Nell's heroine needlessly explains to her besotted lover.[4]

---

[*]   All italics in this section are quotations from Elinor Glyn's *Three Weeks* (New York: Duffield & Company, 1907). Here I try to capture the almost hallucinatory quality and enormous significance EG imparted to writing and publishing this novel by working her words into my own through the use of italics rather than quotation marks.

In giving sole focus to a romantic plot line whose language and sexual content skirted just inside the periphery of what it was possible to print, she transgressed her entire culture's code. Few women (let alone society ladies) who were not stars like Sarah Bernhardt managed to avoid the personal disaster that association with even fictive sexual scandal spelled. Her sex novel's publication irrevocably changed the course of her life.

Like all turning points, this difficult moment would create opportunities too. The notorious novel would make her far better known than ever before, as the book's focus on a miserably married woman's pursuit of happiness outside the conjugal bed found an appreciative audience of readers around the world. The novel's insistence that sexual compatibility was a key component of a successful courtship pressed the marriage plot in an eroticized direction (the lovers in *Three Weeks* marry in spirit, if not in law), laying down the template for the genre that got called romance novels (but not Romances) by the 1920s.[5]

Three Weeks' popularity and the talk it spawned most everywhere opened up a path for Nell to become a celebrity author, a status that few women writers had ever achieved (at least while alive). That role would encourage Nell to create an authorial persona that complemented her heroines, as most celebrity male authors had, from Charles Dickens to Mark Twain.

Writing *Three Weeks* also made one thing about its author quite clear: after all the long, lonely years of her marriage, she knew exactly what she wanted in bed.

Now this is an episode in a young man's life, and has no real beginning or ending. And you who are old and have forgotten the passions of youth may condemn it, began the novel whose author turned forty-two as she began to write. What followed was an extended celebration of the redemptive powers of sexual pleasure when performed in the key of glamour.[6]

The novel's simple plot focuses on a three-week adulterous affair initiated by an older, *intensely soignée* Slavic queen traveling incognito in Switzerland. The mysterious heroine, called only

Lady, spies a callow English aristocrat named Paul and selects him to become her lover. The novel traces, from Paul's perspective, the heroine's seduction and education, carnal and otherwise, of her *great, big beautiful baby.*

Glyn's rich descriptions of his often-fervid state of mind and the gorgeous settings in which they make love and travel occupy much of the book until, nearing the end, Paul awakens alone in their Venice hotel room to find a note explaining Lady has left forever to protect his life. After nearly dying of *brain fever,* Paul slowly recovers to learn his lover's husband was an insane Slavic king. Forced to return, Lady gave birth to a son who looks just like Paul. Soon afterward the mad king murders his now unnecessary spouse. The queen's loyal servants quickly kill the king in revenge. Paul draws comfort from knowing their child will grow up to be king and ends the novel alone, but transformed by her love.[7]

Millions of *Three Weeks* readers went to this racy book looking only for the sex scenes. Nell admitted as much in an introduction she wrote for the American edition, published months after the British one: *And to all who read, I say—at least be just! And do not skip.* For despite the rapid tempo imposed by the affair's short duration, the Lady's first lesson to her lover emphasizes the importance of taking things slow:

> *This was maddening—unbearable. . . .*
>
> *And suddenly she crept close and leant down over the ivy. 'Paul,' she whispered. 'I have come, you see, to wish you good-night!'*
>
> *Paul stood up to his full height. He put out his arms to draw her to him, but she eluded him and darted aside.*
>
> *He gave a great sigh of pain.*
>
> *Slowly she came back and bent over and over of her own accord—so low that at last she was level with his face. And slowly her red lips melted into his young lips in a long, strange kiss.*
>
> *Then before Paul could grasp her, or murmur one pleading word, she was gone. And again he found himself alone, intoxicated with emotion under the night sky studded with stars.*[8]

Tall and straight and strong with *curly hair of gold and blue eyes*, the twenty-two-year-old Paul resembled Alastair. Into her hero Nell poured all her misgivings about the poor romantic results produced by the limited upbringing of so many aristocratic British men. *Paul had left Oxford with a record for all that should turn a beautiful Englishman into a perfect athlete. Books had not worried him much! The fit of a hunting coat, the pace of a horse, were things of more importance, but he scraped through. . . . Life was full of certainties for him. He was certain he liked hunting better than anything else in the world for instance.* Sent abroad by his parents to forget an unsuitable interest in a parson's daughter, this *Sleeping Beauty* desperately needs someone to stimulate his curiosity about finer things than the slaughter of small animals.[9]

Paul first encounters the mysterious woman with the black hair, white skin, and ruby-red lips who will do just that in the dining room of a *sedate Swiss hotel. . . . Do you know Switzerland?—you who read. Do you know it at the beginning of May? A feast of blue lakes and snow-peaks . . . and the exhilaration of the air. If you do, I need not tell you about it. Only in any case now, you must see it through the eyes of Paul. That is if you intend to read another page of this bad book.* All the love affair's settings—Lucerne, the Alps, Venice, Cairo, and the Giza Necropolis—tracked the itinerary of Nell's trip with Clayton three years earlier, when he had mocked her romantic yearnings and refused to buy her the Siberian tiger skin.[10]

For many critics, one of the most notorious aspects of her "bad book" was her reversal of the typical sex roles. Here the older, worldly, "dark lady" heroine uses her near magical powers to seduce the golden-headed hero and give him a crash course in the senses. Freed from the blinders that had blinkered his tastes, Paul could *notice just the beauty of things—and forget to gauge their sporting possibilities.* This appreciation of aesthetics is a necessary prelude to his sexual awakening. The Lady *is certainly not pretty, certainly not,* he observes early on. *Well shaped—yes—and graceful but pretty—a thousand times No!* Under her spell, Paul throws himself into *an adventure which savoured of the Arabian Nights.*[11]

Comparing Nell's book at the start to that great compendium of Arabic and Indian folktales known in English as the *Arabian*

Nights would have whet readers' appetite for an erotic explicitness that skirted the boundary of what could be said in print without provoking a lawsuit.

Two decades before, Sir Richard Burton—the acclaimed "Orientalist" who wrote the best-known translation of the *Nights*—had managed this feat. Near the end of a lifetime spent as both an agent and apostate of empire, Burton turned to undermining the social purity movement's grip over British literary culture by translating into English a set of "classic Oriental texts," including the 1700-year-old Hindu text on erotic love, *Kama Sutra* (1883), and *The Book of the Thousand Nights and a Night* (1885). Both sold well despite the outcry. "Now that I know the tastes of England, we need never be without money," he wrote his editor and wife, Isabel.[12]

Burton's depiction of the female characters in these texts really set the censors roaring. "Readers have remarked," he noted, "with much astonishment that they find the female characters more remarkable for decision, action and manliness than the male." Adding insult to injury, he argued that the sexual technique of the Orient's men surpassed those of the Occident. "Moslems and Easterners in general study . . . the art and mystery of satisfying the physical woman," he explained in the *Nights* lengthy footnotes and appendices. "While English men have the finest women in Europe and least know how to satisfy them."[13]

Burton's words might have come from Nell's lips, but it would take her much longer to put such opinions into print. Over decades, she crept toward candor about the role sexual frustration played in sending her down the garden path at Sheering Hall. "Why I Wrote Three Weeks" appeared in 1920, after the so-called repeal of reticence in Anglo-American literary culture that followed the First World War. There she admitted only a longstanding curiosity about why England had produced no "cases of supreme passionate loves which have made history," wondering, "if it was because Englishmen were naturally cold, or because Englishwomen were not capable of inspiring these great passions?"

Sounding like Burton, Nell blamed the problem on so-called Anglo-Saxon culture's tendency to sweep sex and psychological introspection under the rug. This had necessitated making Lady "a Slav":

"That race possesses the passion and the intensity and the capacity of psychological deduction more than any other." Nell wrote her heroine was, "a complete woman in whom the mental and the spiritual and the physical were equally balanced. . . . The reason she has been condemned is because in England and America we have tried always to eliminate the red out of the spectrum. Passion and anything to do with the physical must always be ignored and 'taboo.'"[14]

In her autobiography, *Romantic Adventure*—published three decades after *Three Weeks*, two decades after Clayton's death, and one decade after Freud's ideas about the dangers of sexual repression gained broad purchase in Anglophone culture—Nell finally admitted the role that sexual frustration played in creating her sex fantasy. The novel was the result of "the limitations and deprivations of my married life. My imagination was roused not by possession and its joys, but by a longing for them," she wrote. "My romantic temperament craved for a lover." She called the book "everything to me" and an "outpouring of my whole nature, romantic, proud, and passionate, but forever repressed in real life by the barriers of custom and tradition, and held fast behind the iron mask of self-respect and self-control" that had been "locked round my throat by Grandmamma in Canada long years before." That deeply ingrained training made writing *Three Weeks* "a fierce rebellion," a rare moment when she let loose "the syren within."[15]

The seduction of *Three Weeks* unfolds with the speed of a set of skillful fingers unfastening a row of tiny buttons along the spine of a woman's evening gown. This deliberate pace leads Paul to notice his Lady's painstaking attention to every detail; this is the first step in his sensual education in becoming a suitable lover. As always, Nell luxuriates in the settings, but it was her sensuous descriptions of what happened inside several hotel suites that left the deepest impression on readers' minds.

Much like the *Arabian Nights* storyteller, Scheherazade, Lady teaches her *Sleeping Beauty* that the imagination is the most powerful aphrodisiac. Paul must learn to use his before she will orchestrate their *wedding night*. When Paul enters the Lady's bedchamber for the first time, he finds a hotel room redecorated to appear like a place for the *favorite in the harem.* Here he found:

> . . . *a room as unlike a hotel as he could imagine. It may have had the usual brocade walls and gilt chairs of the 'best suite,' but its aspect was so transformed by her subtle taste and presence it seemed to him unique. . . . The lights were low and shaded, and a great couch filled one side of the room beyond the fireplace. Such a couch! covered with a tiger-skin and piled with pillows, all shades of rich purple velvet and silk, embroidered with silver and gold. . . . The Lady had reached the couch, and sank into it. She was in black still, but gauzy, clinging black, which seemed to give some gleam of purple underneath. . . . 'Come,' she said. 'You may sit here beside me and tell me what you think.'[16]*

Quickly grasping the importance of the tiger to his queen, Paul sends her another one the next day. (It's easy to speculate that Clayton must have wished many times that he had just bought his wife that damn tiger skin while shopping that day.)

When Paul returns to her suite a second time he encounters a vision suggesting his sexual satisfaction is at hand: *There in front of the fire, stretched at full length, was his tiger—and on him—also at full length—reclined the lady, garbed in some strange clinging garment of heavy purple crepe, a scarlet rose between her lips. Paul bounded forward, but she raised one hand to stop him. 'No! You must not come near me, Paul. Not yet. See, you must sit there and we will talk.'[17]*

The Lady proceeds with a game of erotic show-and-tell that became the novel's most infamous scene and linked Nell's name to tigers for the rest of her life.

> *She gave a movement like a snake, of joy to feel its fur under her, while she stretched out her hands and caressed the creature where the hair turned white and black at the side, and was deep and soft.*
>
> *'I have got your skin—for the joy of my skin!' And she quivered again with the movement of the snake. . . .*
>
> *'I'm so glad you like him,' he said in a choked voice. . . .*

'And oh! Good God! If you knew how you are making me feel—lying there wasting your caresses upon it!'. . .

'I'm not wasting them. . . . He was my lover in another life—perhaps—who knows?'

'But I,' said Paul, who was now quite mad, 'want to be your lover in this [life]!' Then he gasped at his own boldness. With a lightening movement she lay on her face, raised her elbows on the tiger's head, and supported her chin in her hands. Perfectly straight out her body was, the twisted purple drapery outlining her perfect shape. . . .

'Paul—what do you know of lovers—or love?' she said. 'My baby Paul!'

'I know enough to know I know nothing yet which is worth knowing,' he said confusedly. 'But—but—don't you understand, I want you to teach me—'

'You are so sweet, Paul, when you plead like that. I am taking in every bit of you. In your way as perfect as this tiger. But we must talk—oh! Such a great deal—first.'[18]

The Tiger Queen's flirtatiousness surpasses even Nell's, as she kisses, caresses, and weaves a web of stories around her lover, creating scenarios that she controls with a sure hand. *You are maddening me!* Paul cries midway through, still waiting for their *wedding night.*

'Do you think I am a statue or a table, or a chair—or inanimate like that tiger there? I am not, I tell you,' and he seized her in his arms, raining kisses upon her . . . which, whatever they lacked in subtlety, made up for in their passion and strength. 'Some day some man will kill you, I suppose, but I shall be your lover—first!'[19]

Since role-playing is an essential element in the Lady's erotic repertoire, Paul's display of force signals he is ready for the next step in his sensual education. At long last she orchestrates their wedding night on a bed of rose petals in a secluded hotel high in the Alps. Tellingly, Nell treats the consummation with a blasé air; this means quite a lot to Paul, but not so much to the Tiger Queen. A quick study, Paul realizes that he must become versatile and bold as their sex scenes swing between unfamiliar erotic restraints and freedoms.

Given her love of the Russian empress Catherine the Great and her familiarity with decadent writers and the Parisian demimonde, Nell's Tiger Queen likely drew inspiration from an infamous text, *Venus in Furs* (1870). Leopold von Sacher-Masoch's heavily autobiographical novel tells of a man whose dream of speaking to "Venus in Furs" leads him to become enslaved to a dominatrix. Masoch's lust for a different kind of erotic existence was inspired by the titular Titan painting and the commanding Russian empress Nell put at the very top of the "List of the World's Twenty Greatest Women" she later made. Russia's most powerful monarch of the eighteenth century, Catherine was well known for having her way with beautiful, learned younger men. Nell's heroine conducts her affair much as Catherine the Great might have, directing Paul in ever-more-elaborate scenarios in which they trade positions of dominance and submission, acting by turns mistress, master, queen, king, mother, child, and *worshipping slave.*[20]

Love should be voluptuously passionate, the Tiger Queen insists:

> *She bent over and kissed him, and smoothed his cheek with her velvet cheek, she moved so that his curly lashes might touch her bare neck, and at last she slipped from under him. . . . Then a madness of tender caressing seized her. She purred as a tiger might have done, while she undulated like a snake. She touched him with her finger-tips, she kissed his throat, his wrists, the palms of his hands, his eyelids, his hair. . . . And often, between her purrings, she murmured love-words in some fierce language of her own, brushing his ears and his eyes with her lips all the while.*

But in what can only be read as a rebuke to society, above all, love refused to share:

> *A woman will stand almost anything from a passionate lover. . . . He may beat her and pain her soft flesh, but if the motive is raging love and interest in her on his part it only makes her love him the more. The reason why women become unfaith-*

ful is because the man grows casual, and having awakened a taste for passionate joys, he no longer gratifies them—so she yawns and turns elsewhere.[21]

The Lady's last lesson was one engrained in her creator since she crouched under the table at Government House in Jersey, waiting to see Lillie Langtry all those years ago: a woman of temperament and independence must learn how to triumph over scandal. *In all ages it is unfortunately not the simple good women who have ruled the hearts of men,* she reminds Paul before her mad, drunken king of a husband forces her to return home. *If this is so, that would prove that all the very clever women of history were immoral,* he replies with bewilderment.

The Lady laughs. *Immoral! It is so quaint a word, my Paul! Each one sees it how they will. . . . If one remains the faithful beast of burden to one man, one is counted in the world a moral woman.*[22]

By the standards of modern erotica, *Three Weeks* contains very little sex. How quaint, how easily shocked they were, it is possible for us to think, reading the novel today.

But even allowing for the much more restrictive obscenity publishing standards at work in the English-speaking world in 1907, the novel painted a startlingly innovative, sensuous picture of the way people could have sex. All the slow caresses, the smooth talk, the long, strange kisses, the flamboyant undulations on the tiger, and on each other, all the role-playing involving the imposition of restraint and force are precisely the point of the erotic education that the Lady offers her eager pupil.

More than any other modern novel made widely available in English before, *Three Weeks* made explicit the strength of women's sexual desire, the different quality of its character, and the failure of so much of contemporary culture to register or understand both. The novel's content offered a virtual substitution for what so many lacked: a woman who could take charge of the situation and make sure everyone had a good time, in and out of bed.

Reading the sex scenes in *Three Weeks* more than a hundred years later means taking into account what Glyn could not write in her day. (At least, not with the hope of broad circulation and without the fear of imprisonment.) It also means acknowledging what is still hard to say in our day: sexual compatibility between women and men did not come easily after two centuries of sexual miseducation in the West. Such a fact undoubtedly accounted for the novel's refrains: *we must talk, take your time.*

Nell began writing books midway through the long arc of modern sexual miseducation about female desire that emerged, paradoxically, with the rise of sexual freedom during the eighteenth century. In this period, parts of the so-called West began the transition to systems of work, thought, and political forms that enshrined distinctive principles of individual equality, privacy, freedom, and sexual difference. Popularized perhaps most effectively by the upstart genre of the novel, the new common sense of sex judged men as rapacious and inconstant sexual beings and women as passive and, increasingly, passionless or hysterical ones. By 1886, many cited the opinion of the German sexologist Dr. Richard von Krafft-Ebing to summarize the dominant medical view of the sexuality of respectable Anglo-American women. "Woman, when physically and mentally normal and properly educated, has but little sensual desire," Krafft-Ebing opined. "If it were otherwise, marriage and family life would be empty words."[23]

The publication of *Three Weeks* coincided with another shift in ideas about the nature of female desire, as men like Sigmund Freud and Havelock Ellis began to resurrect the sexuality of respectable women from its social death. But when Nell wrote, such incendiary attitudes circulated only among the cognoscenti of highly educated scientists. And virtually all of the men in the new fields of sexology and psychology continued to view female desire as passive and properly satisfied by penetration alone. Freud first popularized the new theory of the vaginal orgasm, which influenced both medical and lay attitudes until the 1970s. The emergence of this new orthodoxy created the expectation that "normal" women preferred sexual techniques that contradicted both classical and current observations about the importance of clitoral stimulation to the female orgasm.[24]

To recover women's sexual desire, Nell's novel drew upon the ancients' attitudes toward female sexuality that had recognized the clitoris as "the seat of a woman's pleasure" and the medieval underpinnings of the "Romance" that had opposed passionate, sensual love with the stabilizing institution of marriage. (Think of how the passionate love between Queen Guinevere and Sir Lancelot in *Le Morte d'Arthur* destroys her marriage and therefore the kingdom Camelot.) As in medieval Romance, the tragic outcome of *Three Weeks* justified (in Nell's mind at least) the utterly exuberant nature of the love scenes by proving how the depth of the lovers' feelings were a force that could not be denied (much like Guinevere and Lancelot's). For some, lovers who risked all for passion proved the noble quality of their act. The cornucopia of sexual practices alluded to in the novel also fit better with the approach to lovemaking used in medieval Romances and ancient texts.[25]

Readers must have enjoyed Nell's method. Upon publication, *Three Weeks* bounded to the top of bestselling book lists in both Britain and America, where it stayed for months. Equally impressive, Nell's so-called sex novel, as critics quickly categorized it, continued to attract readers steadily over the next two decades, even as it spawned a host of imitators. This enormous popularity also suggests that its appeal crossed gender lines. Although romance novels by the 1920s had become increasingly viewed as for ladies only, at the beginning of the twentieth century this was not the case. The many fan letters and thank-you letters Nell received from servicemen during World War I attested to how much they liked her Lady too.[26]

Three Weeks became a cultural touchstone for at least two generations of readers eager to imagine a new kind sexual openness between women and men. But the world that *Three Weeks* celebrated—where a woman orchestrates the satisfaction of her own desires with incomparable style—was yet to come for its author or the vast majority of her readers. That fall of 1906, not hope but anger and desire drove Nell's white-hot composition in the garden while the beaters flushed the pheasants from the trees and Clayton shot them dead.

Funneling her frustrations into her most dramatic imaginative escape yet, Nell created an "exotic" heroine who swept aside society's rules to seize what she wanted with both hands. Only in hindsight would she realize that her Lady changed everything. For in writing *Three Weeks*, the conservative-minded author unwittingly became a radical.[27]

CHAPTER 7

Trash

'Tis NOVEL most beguils the female heart.
Miss reads—she melts—she sighs—
Love steals upon her—
And then—Alas, poor girl!—good night, poor
Honour!

—George Colman, *Polly Honeycombe* (1760)

It is capable of doing incalculable harm to all classes and conditions of
women and men. Its principles carried out would mean social chaos, and
the love—God save the mark!—it describes is animality, sugared up by
literary skill and given a false twist at the end, which does not fool me
for one.

—*St. Paul Bellman* review of *Three Weeks* (1907)[1]

Daisy advised Nell not to publish *Three Weeks*. She warned that its adulterous heroine, lengthy scenes of steamy eroticism, and violation of society's cardinal code—*No talk*—might result in the ostracization of her friend. Nell hesitated. Set for publication in April of 1907, that month Duckworth announced the "postponement of Elinor Glyn's latest novel, 'THREE WEEKS,'" until "the autumn."[2]

Duckworth & Company stoked anticipation during the delay. All that spring the canny publisher took out advertisements in London's leading literary magazine, *The Athenaeum*, updating readers on the progress of the novel's release. Then suddenly an announcement appeared: "TUESDAY, JUNE 11, is the Publication Day of the New Novel by Elinor Glyn, entitled *THREE WEEKS*—An exceptional vogue for this book is anticipated, necessitating the printing of a very large Edition."[3]

In the intervening months, changes shook the Glyn family's foundation when Clayton put Sheering Hall up for sale and moved everyone in with Elinor Kennedy at Lamberts, the modest cottage close by. Clayton's decision to sell the estate's last property of significance was the clearest sign yet of their deepening financial woes. The troubles had left no trace in Nell's archive until this point (besides the decision never to live in the family home, Durrington, and then to sell it after Juliet's birth).

Nell's letters to her husband in this period allude to financial arrangements she had agreed to over the years that a more business-minded woman might have recognized as signs of impending fiscal doom. But they also indicate that the two had never directly discussed their money problems until this juncture. (This habit of silence about difficult subjects seems to have held over *Three Weeks* too.)[4]

The decline of Clayton's fortunes followed that of the landed gentry more broadly, which had accelerated into a free fall by this time. Even with the greatest frugality, rising taxes on land and falling agricultural prices had made it nearly impossible to sustain a society lifestyle without other sources of income. No one would call Nell and Clayton anything but spendthrifts. Clayton's aristocratic disdain for sordid money matters encouraged his taste for gambling with the same lavish abandon with which they traveled. Like many in his situation, he had been quietly addressing his mounting debts by auctioning off his patrimony one piece at a time while his family looked the other way. However good a face they put on squeezing into Lamberts, the fiction that the "Glyn Estate" supported their extravagant habits had ended.[5]

The move was a reunion of sorts too. Juliet and Margot, now nine and fourteen, already spent so much time at Gran's house (as everyone called Nell's mother, Elinor Kennedy, by this point) that Lamberts had been enlarged years before to accommodate them. Nell was glad to join them there, she wrote Waldo Story. Sheering Hall had never been a happy place for her. But this creature-comfort-loving woman must have felt a sense of vertigo falling down the social ladder and finding herself under the same roof as her mother, again.

They made do, building an annex for Nell that she grandly called her "Trianon," after Marie Antoinette's private residence at Versailles. These would be the first rooms she could call her own. The private annex was also proof of the still seemingly unremarked-upon fact that everyone's fortunes increasingly depended on leaving Nell in peace to do her work—now more than ever. "I would like you to see the new hermitage very much," she wrote Waldo Story when it was done. "Just a sitting room, a bedroom, a bath room, a room for my clothes, and a room for my maid," she explained. "It is joined to the house by a veranda and no one is to come in unless I ask them—not even Clayton. And over the door is to be written, 'Leave care behind all ye who enter here.' It is to be a place of peace and quiet and grey walls and soft colours and plenty of green."⁶

Gran, who genuinely enjoyed supervising the girls, was at the center of this still-unacknowledged project. The trust and warmth that had failed to take root in Nell's childhood had slowly been replaced by mutual dependence and appreciation after Nell became a mother. Moving in together would test this fragile accord as increasingly Gran grabbed the chance to perform a reprisal of her role as the placating, pampering good wife for Clayton's benefit. Gran supervised the rich dinners that had made Clayton fat and kept his wineglass and brandy snifter full, just as he liked them. She played the endless card games that bored Nell silly. She always took his side, at least until the end.

The pressures of this new domestic situation may have been what swept away Nell's doubts about sending *Three Weeks* into the world, though she never admitted as much. To the public, she continued to claim that only desire, not financial necessity, ever prompted her to put pen to paper.

Although he could not have anticipated the enormous attention the novel stirred, Gerald Duckworth knew full well that its open challenge to the genteel literary code that still reigned in Anglo-American publishing made it a very different kind of book. Duckworth and Nell were quite close by this point. Whenever she finished a new novel, she would deliver it to his office at 3 Henrietta Street, Covent Garden, and then read it aloud to him. Her books, she argued, lost their proper effect when read in silence. Extremely proud of her voice, she read slowly with long dramatic pauses. Duckworth would meekly put aside all other work to listen, while Margot often waited patiently in the hansom outside. It was the mark of a gentlewoman to be able to read aloud beautifully, the author believed. All her heroines had the skill, or acquired it.[7]

For her part, Nell admitted this novel was different on the book's opening page, admonishing readers that: they *must see through the eyes of Paul. That is if you intend to read another page of this bad book.* After publication, advertisements emphasized the novel's suitability only for adult readers in the prime of life: "A study of a strange woman. An episode in a young man's life. A novel for those who are neither young nor old," one tantalized.[8]

Daisy had been right. Nell quickly learned how little had changed in the two and a half millennia since the so-called father of history, Thucydides, wrote, "The greatest achievement for a woman is to be as seldom as possible spoken of."

Critics greeted the novel's appearance with "hot, blushing denunciation," remarked one of the few (anonymous) defenses published that June. "It is the old, old story. Mrs. Glyn has chosen to write of a passionate and a beautiful love episode between persons who have not previously been married. That is her offence, and for it, of course she must suffer the abuse of those most trustworthy of Mrs. Grundy's spokesmen—the daily reviewers," the *Bystander* wrote. "Dare to show in any other than an odious light the conduct of such a couple, and damnation is yours." Most of society shivered and turned its back on the redheaded authoress.[9]

Branded as immoral, inane, or both, *Three Weeks* quickly became one of the most excoriated works of popular fiction published in English before the Great War. The "sudden passion of two strangers for each other and their abandonment to it takes more literary genius in the telling than Elinor Glyn possesses," sniffed the *Academy*. A "Man of Letters" in the London *Bookman* decried it as the worst sex novel yet in "The Fleshly School of Fiction: A Protest against the Degradation of the Modern Novel." Such books "belonged to a tribe now increasing at a rate without example, of shameless and shameful fiction," the anonymous gentleman railed. "Yesterday, Paris almost alone spread the plague. To-day it rages in London."[10]

Daisy, as well her friends from Carlsbad Spa, Minnie Paget and Alfred Milner, stood by Nell. But most did not. Society had long ostracized—or "cut" as her circle said—women for far less. People cut women for the appearance of breaking society's rules whether they were guilty or not. Cutting avoided angry words in favor of making someone vanish into thin air. Invitations dried up, streets were crossed to avoid chance meetings, and eye contact was avoided when all else failed. A chilly civility became the best Nell could hope for from most in her once large social circle. From now on, the best sorts of people in Britain might concede to having met the authoress, but few would admit to knowing her.[11]

King Edward VII, that great despoiler of married women (who had moved on from Daisy to a fresher married mistress), forbade mentioning the novel's name in his presence. Eton's headmaster, Edward Lyttleton, banned the novel, setting a precedent followed by the other "ancient" boarding schools. Eventually the circulating libraries, many booksellers in the United Kingdom and the country of Canada, as well as the city of Boston censored the novel as obscene. A federal judge in the United States ruled that it could not be sent through the mail.[12]

Nell did not accept these judgments easily. "I want to ask your advice about what I consider a great injustice," she wrote to Ralph Blumenfeld, the editor of the *Daily Express*, the upstart rival of Lord Northcliffe's populist tour-de-force, the *Daily Mail*. A journalist and successful businessman from Wisconsin, Blumenfeld had moved to England permanently in 1892 and helped to import the new journalism that aimed to attract the ever-expanding audience of literate people in the English-speaking world. His reputation was made when the *Express* became the first newspaper in Britain to put news on the front page rather than advertisements.[13]

"Smiths bookstall have refused to sell my book on the ground of its impropriety," Nell fumed. The decision had enormous commercial consequences. Begun in the 1860s to offer properly vetted books along Britain's expanding railway lines, WH Smith and Sons had become Britain's largest book retailer, with over six hundred bookstalls. Along with the critical establishment, Smith's bookstalls and the circulating libraries enforced the genteel code that governed the literary marketplace. "They sell Maurice Hewlett's *Open Country*," she protested, "where the heroine lives with a man as his mistress for eight years and then goes and lives with another man for life—no marriage. Why are these people and most of the critics so vile to me? Do we live in [a] free country or not?"[14]

In her autobiography she called the outcry "a curious commentary on the stupendous hypocrisy of the Edwardian age." The scorn heaped upon her for writing a fictional example of customs practiced by so many real society women rankled until she died. "It was secretly considered quite normal in society circles for a married woman to have a succession of illicit love affairs, during the intervals of which, if not simultaneously, intimate relations with her husband were resumed," she reminded her readers. Yet these same people "condemned as highly immoral" a fictional depiction of "an exotic foreign character in the throes of a single passionate romance, for which she pays willingly with her life."

Society's fake outrage must have been particularly galling since Nell was one of the few married women in her company who had remained chaste in body, if not in spirit. What Nell did not admit was that for society to have done otherwise would have been to tacitly confess the uncertain parentage of too many peers.[15]

Nell's protest was equal parts telling and untrue. It seems likely— given the vogue for Orientalist images of the sexually licentious East—that she hoped using an "exotic, foreign" heroine to brazenly break her marriage vow would protect her from condemnation, or at least blunt its edge. But whatever her race, the Lady's glorification of a woman's right to pursue her heart's desire outside the bounds of matrimony proved too much of a blow to the era's genteel literary code to go unpunished.

Society, and seemingly most everyone else, read on amidst the rumpus. Although "bishops and headmasters inveighed against it," Cecil Beaton devoured *Three Weeks* under the bedcovers at Harrow. Beaton credited it with "breaking down much of the remaining Victorian hypocrisy." The novel created "a furore," recalled Nancy Cunard, the ocean-liner heiress and future poet, avant-garde muse, and radical activist. "There cannot have been many well-appointed houses without the novel, aptly bound in purple." Its "beautiful, perfidious, dashing" heroine was "exactly what I wanted to know about." She "blazed awhile across the repression of my childhood," Cunard exhaled with stars still in her eyes.[16]

Three Weeks was a global sensation. The Russian free-love anarchist Emma Goldman called it "magnificent—a masterpiece . . . a declaration of independence," in an interview in the *St. Louis Post-Dispatch*. Two grand duchesses in Russia admired the novel so much that they invited its author to visit the Romanov Court the year after its publication. The Duchess of Edinburgh admitted to Nell how much she had enjoyed reading the novel in bed.[17]

Such confessions by elite and radical readers suggest the wishful thinking exercised by the Dublin reviewer who blamed "naughty little school girls and erotic housemaids" for the novel's popularity. The English society biographer Anita Leslie's opinion about the basis of the book's popularity was closer to the mark: "It did not merely appeal to the romantic aspirations of kitchenmaids, but to the kitchenmaid in the heart of every great Lady in Europe"—and, as Nell would soon learn, to the hearts of some of their great gentlemen as well.[18]

The attempt to hold silly young women, likely from the working class, responsible for the phenomenal success of *Three Weeks* betrays the popular novel's long association with satisfying the tastes of juvenile, often lightly educated readers for stories of sentiment, romance (and later sex), for—in a word—trash. Since its emergence in the eighteenth century, the modern English novel had suffered under the weight of its reputation for providing women readers with such fare. Men reputedly read philosophy, history, biography, travel (and pornography). Women read religious tracts, poetry, and novels: good, moralistic ones that taught them the importance of sentiment and honor when well chaperoned; bad "amatory" ones preoccupied with sex and romance when left to their own devices.[19]

Ladies also often wrote these popular novels that literary critics walled off from "serious" (increasingly defined as realistic) fiction as the nineteenth century wore on. As the American novelist Nathaniel Hawthorne complained to his publisher from England in

1855: "America is now wholly given over to a damned mob of scribbling women and I should have no chance of success while the public taste is occupied with their trash." All five American authors to qualify as "bestsellers" in the 1850s (determined as a sale to 1 percent of the population, which in that decade meant 225,000 books or more) were women writing unabashedly heartfelt, sentimental tales. Only much later would Hawthorne and Herman Melville join this club.[20]

The situation in Britain was slightly less troublesome. Charles Dickens and David Makepeace Thackeray appealed to a huge public on both sides of the Atlantic. But as the fiction-reading marketplace grew enormously after the 1890s, many of the most popular living novelists in Britain were women too. The very term "bestseller" likely first circulated alongside the astounding popularity of the English writer Marie Corelli (a pseudonym for Mary MacKay) who specialized in exotic settings, mystical forces, and suspense. "Bestsellers" were not only commercially successful but also the most talked about books around town. Although these women writers were widely read, most critics loathed their rejection of realism and use of female protagonists whose crooked moral compasses, by the light of their times, often made them resemble villainesses as much as heroines.[21]

The development during the nineteenth century of a genteel literary code throughout the English-speaking world aimed to keep the novel's moral threat in check by consigning books that violated its demands—particularly for virtuous heroines—to the critical rubbish bin or the courts. Since no government censorship of fiction existed in either Britain or America, the code was the handiwork of easily shocked readers and easily cowed writers, publishers, libraries, and booksellers like WH Smith & Sons, who refused to sell *Three Weeks*. This meant that social-purity reformers like the National Vigilance Association (NVA) in London had to bring a case against "obscene" books that found an audience. The NVA, and Anthony Comstock's Society for the Suppression of Vice in New York, did their work in the name of protecting women and the working class from the poisonous influences of bad books.[22]

In 1889, the NVA got the English publisher Henry Vizetelly sent to jail for translating and publishing novels by realists like Émile Zola in France. By the late nineteenth century, France's different obscenity laws had made French the lingua franca for stories about sexual desire. Vizetelly was not a martyr to art, however, but a commercial innovator who had brought from Paris the idea of selling cheaper, one-volume editions of novels directly to the public (rather than the three volume, "Triple-decker novels" loaned out by subscription libraries). Vizetelly publicized these novels' franker sexual subject matter by advertising that their "Realistic," "French" content was "without abridgement." Much of the Anglo-American establishment considered these French novels cause and consequence of the nation's more decadent, unstable political culture. "Look at what such literature had done for France," warned a Member of Parliament. "Its poison was destroying the whole national life."[23]

By the time Nell married Clayton in 1892, what could be written about sex in English was at once more tightly corseted than ever and starting to come undone. Of the late Victorian English authors, bestsellers like Marie Corelli had pressed the hardest against the genteel code with the fewest repercussions. Corelli's enormous commercial popularity short-circuited the normal methods of containment. Though Nell considered Corelli's descriptions of upper-class settings a joke, *Three Weeks* built on her sensational romances as well as the work of New Women writers like Sarah Grand, who exposed the vice lurking in the most seemingly moral of marriages.[24]

But Nell's adulterous, sexually sophisticated "dark lady" was also unique, leading many to throw the novel into a scandalous new bucket of fiction called the sex novel. A term coined by journalists that became fashionable after 1905, the sex novel fell into a different category of erotica than so-called pornographic literature because it emphasized sexual psychology as much as stimulation and focused more on interior sensations than particular acts.[25]

Both sexes composed sex novels. (H. G. Wells, Hubert Wales, and Somerset Maugham wrote other well-known examples.) But critics still blamed women writers for this new epidemic of immorality on the page. "The record of fiction of the last twenty years is full of cases where women have written books that no man would have dared signed—books that were naked and unashamed," wrote the influential critic Percival Pollard in a scathing, and widely reprinted, review of *Three Weeks*.[26]

To be fair, the carnal focus of *Three Weeks* stood out even in the fleshy company of other sex novels. Henry De Vere Stacpoole's *The Blue Lagoon* (1908)—the other Edwardian sex novel fixated on its characters' erotic awakening—features one sex scene, just half a page long. (It also has a birth scene the mother manages to sleep through—undoubtedly how the event appeared to many fathers of the day: I woke up and there was a baby!) By contrast, *Three Weeks* reads like a series of long, richly imagined lovemaking scenarios strung together by a simple plot.[27]

The press also roundly blamed the trashy tastes of women readers for the popularity of sex novels. "Readers—chiefly women—who make the fortune of English fiction" spelled the end of the "tenderhearted tradition of Scott, Dickens, and Thackeray," the London *Bookman* warned. Such assumptions about the readership for sex novels made some sense, given that women continued to read much more fiction than men. "At every age girls read more than boys," a guide for children's literature announced. "Millions of young girls and thousands of young men are *novelized* into absolute idiocy. Novel readers are like opium smokers," worried another.[28]

This awareness could be used for mercenary ends. "I am often assured that feminine rather than masculine tastes decide the number of a novel's sales, and that a reviewer should bear this in mind if he wishes accurately to forecast its vogue." This forced the astute author to ask, "What is the feminine taste in the novel?" The answer was plain: "A story which has the relations of the sexes as its pivot," he answered. "The wise man will, therefore [secure] for the lending shelves of his library the following volumes, which have the merit of dealing with the theme of sex thoroughly, vividly, and sympathetically:"

> "Three Weeks." By Elinor Glyn
> "Life's Shop Window." By Victoria Cross
> "The Yoke." By Hubert Wales
> "Emancipation." By James Blyth[29]

Three Weeks' phenomenal commercial success was a watershed for the publishing industry. Its commercial triumph changed mass cultural conventions for how to write about sex and represent female desire. (Roses between the lips, rugs by the fire, and sexy lingerie would all become clichés signaling women's erotic intent deep into the twentieth century.) Decades before the 1960 obscenity trials of D. H. Lawrence's *Lady Chatterley's Lover* (1928) made the novel an international cause célèbre, Nell's *Three Weeks* began the project of grappling more frankly with the force of female sexual desire.[30]

While the controversy over her immoral novel and reputation rippled through the press and society, Nell spent the summer at the London Ritz plotting a visit to America to "boom" the novel and working on turning *Three Weeks* into a play. A successful theatrical run could bring in far more money than a book. And the Glyns were suddenly desperate for money.

Nell had finally learned the full extent of the family's dire financial situation from their accountant, Walters, while living at the Ritz. After the meeting, Nell wrote to Clayton, "I have always done what you wished up to now—whether it has been good for any of us is another matter. But it is my idea always to do what you wish, so I willingly do this too." She had approved the use of her marriage settlement to finish paying off their creditors. "Can you tell me the exact sum that the children will have at our deaths?" she asked. "This is the only point which distresses me. Two girls could not live on 260 pounds except in the greatest poverty. Everything of any value now is sold."[31]

She met Walters again just days before her departure for New York City. "He seemed to think the outlook quite hopeless," she reported. Nell left her husband's inability to step into the breach unsaid, making the point by emphasizing her sole responsibility for salvaging the family's fortunes instead. "I felt suddenly like a hunted animal with the whole weight on my shoulders," she confessed. From here forward, the Glyns would depend entirely on what Nell earned. Later she would admit that when presented with the choice to sell her body or her words, she leaned harder on her pen.[32]

Margot, Juliet, and "Gran" (Elinor Kennedy) 191[?]

Nell erased this financial reckoning from her autobiography, claiming only to have learned the full extent of their financial woes after she returned home from her American trip. To have admitted that financial considerations, even in part, drove her actions would have required abandoning her still dearly held posture that money was never a motivator, that she wrote only when the spirit moved her. And given the immoral reputation of her book, such an admission would have exposed her to charges of peddling smut for mercenary ends. But with creditors pressing, and so many of the right doors in England slammed shut, she had no choice but to seek her fortune in the New World. "I will work," she assured Clayton, "and try and bring things round somehow."[33]

Her letters to her husband also betrayed how financial anxieties justified a public reinvention that gave her access to a wider world and a less restrained emotional register. Rather than prompting her to retire in shame, the notoriety surrounding her novel presented prospects that a bold heart might seize. "Now when I have had time to think something in me is rising and stronger than ever," she told

Clayton. Tasked by their accountant "to make money and settle it in a trust that could not be touched," Nell could cast the freeing of personal ambition as wifely duty. "I said I believed in my star and was going to America for no other purpose than to make money." And as every British writer learned after Charles Dickens's spectacularly successful tour a half century before, there was so much more cash there for the taking than anyplace else. By 1897, the author of *Who's Who in London* could justifiably assert, "a great author visiting America is received with more attention than a Prince or Chief Justice."[34]

While Nell sailed aboard the *Cedric* of the White Star Line to salvage the family's prospects, Clayton and her mother would take the girls to Asia, a lavish trip presumably funded by the royalties rolling in from *Three Weeks*. Like Nell's choice to spend the summer at the Ritz, the family's extended travel revealed the difficulty of getting the couple to change their spending habits. Gran and the girls spent the week before her departure in London to see her off. They saw Lucy's latest theatrical collaboration, *The Merry Widow*, "so we could laugh and be gay and keep Margot from fretting, her eyes are full of tears so often when she looks at me and Juliet says she cries sometimes at the thought of parting" for months.[35]

Nell used admiring men to buffet the tempest swirling around her that summer—and made sure Clayton knew about it. She held a small farewell dinner her last night in London, dressed in "a most remarkable robe of vivid green velvet which contrasted well with her Titian hair," according to one of the reporters who now trailed the notorious authoress's every move. Gran, Margot, Juliet, Lucy, Alastair Inness-Ker, and Sir Alexander Condie Stephen attended. An author and diplomat, Stephen had helped her plan the trip. "Dear old Sir Condie" was "doing all kinds of things for me re: America," she wrote Clayton weeks before she left. "One of the most chivalrous generous friends" she ever made, Stephen did not try "to make love like all the rest," but was simply "kind and friendly and appreciating my brains," she goaded Clayton.[36]

This October voyage to America was a grand adventure and the chance to prove her mettle to the world. She felt "independent and gay" and freer then since she had "gone to Paris as a girl." Weather permitting, these luxury liners could turn the Atlantic crossing into one long party for those traveling first class.

By chance or design, the Duchess of Manchester and her mother—two society ladies who had not "cut" Nell after her scandalous novel's publication—traveled on the same ship. Formerly Consuelo Yznaga of Louisiana, the duchess was one of the first American heiresses to gain the social capital in Britain denied her in New York. (Edith Wharton's *The Buccaneers* included a sympathetic character based on Yznaga, her friend since childhood.)

During the eight-day crossing, the Duchess of Manchester schooled Nell on how to handle her awaiting countrymen and women and the nation's press. For there would be reporters, she warned, since "the stormwind of a vast and sudden notoriety" swept the authoress across the Atlantic, as Mark Twain observed.[37]

The duchess explained that the sensationalistic and emotion-laden style used by most American journalists meant a preference for vivid stories about dramatic individuals. American reporters rewarded charismatic personalities. They would craft a compelling persona of Nell and situate it in a stirring tale, whether she liked it or not. Best to accept this and try to make nice with the press in order to shape the narrative herself. American elites also loved a title and equated British accents and French associations with superior breeding and culture. Though her aristocratic connections had frayed, she should milk them and her European upbringing for everything she could, the duchess recommended.[38]

Nell embraced playing the "role of 'Elinor Glyn the famous authoress'" wholeheartedly on this trip. She arrived in New York's harbor in a downpour so heavy that she could not see the Statue of Liberty through the mist. Still, the reporters "swarmed round" her on the dock, asking "crisp, direct questions; no feeble fecklessness" or "beating about the bush" here. She did her best to answer in the rain, but then announced she would hold a press conference the next day in her suite at the Plaza Hotel.[39]

"I am not at all like the English," she clarified in her first interview that emphasized her connection to Continental mores. "I have French blood, you know, and Irish. I don't look English, do I? You have never seen an Englishwoman who looked like me?" Glyn asked. He hadn't, the *New York Times'* reporter conceded. She poked fun at a recent *Times* review that called the novel "Prurient and worse yet—Dull." Just imagine calling it dull.[40]

This was not a book tour in the conventional sense; it was instead a chance to visit her many friends from New York, people who included a *Who's Who* survey of the American elite. She would begin with a visit to Mrs. Frederick Vanderbilt's country house at Hyde Park, then return to New York City to see about turning her novel into a Broadway play. But above all, she claimed to be "in search of material for my next novel" which would feature "a typical American gentleman as a hero. I admire American men," she said, adroitly buttering up the gaggle of mostly American men arrayed around her. "Their courtesy to women wins me. In that respect, I must admit their superiority to Englishmen. I like American girls too—for their independence. Then, too, Americans have such an acute sense of humor. You don't have to explain things to an American more than once, as you do men of other nationalities. I am anxious to find out why that is so."[41]

The savvy authoress had in fact timed her arrival to the publication of *Three Weeks* by Duffield in the United States, an edition that included an "Introduction to My American Readers," written because of "the misunderstanding and misrepresentation it received from nearly the entire press and a section of the public in England." Glyn reproved, "The minds of some human beings are moles, grubbing in the earth for worms. To such 'Three Weeks' will be but a sensual record of passion," she conceded. "But those who do look up . . . will realize that to such a nature as 'the Lady's,' passion would never have run riot until it was sated. Kind reader, *to me*," she explained, the Lady "appears a noble woman, because she was absolutely faithful to the man she had selected as her mate, through the one motive which makes a union moral in ethics—Love."[42]

The critical response to *Three Weeks* in America was more crushing than in Britain, where reviewers specialized in the art of sniffing dismissal. American critics vented their fury at full throttle instead. *Current Literature* called the novel "equivalent to one long orgy, broken only by reading in Latin from 'The Golden Ass of Apuleius'" (the sexually explicit Roman novel). "Elinor Glyn Outdoes Herself in the Line of Audacious Fiction," shrieked a *Chicago Tribune* headline. "Her Latest Book, 'Three Weeks' Appears to Be About Twenty-one Days Too Much." "Most folks," reported the *Brooklyn Eagle*, "will think it is not a book that should be placed anywhere save in the fire." "It is a nasty book and that seems to be the reason it has become so popular," the *Philadelphia Inquirer* announced. "Mrs. Glyn is obviously a woman of knowledge and experience," a Boston reviewer sneered. "She deals with a forbidden theme in a way that would be forbidden if it were possible to forbid anything in modern English fiction." All agreed the novel made her the leading representative of women's writers' attempts to bend Anglo-Saxon culture toward looser Continental mores, accusing her of spreading "Gallic," "French," or simply "Continental" attitudes into Anglo-American culture.[43]

A few accepted that her association with the French romantic tradition justified her exploration of the conflict that arose between a powerful *sensibilité* and society's rules. According to French philosophes like Rousseau, *sensibilité* distinguished humans from other animals by allowing them to translate physical sensations into moral relations. The Rousseau novel that some credit with inventing romantic love, *Julie, ou la nouvelle Héloïse* (1762), told of an illicit passion inspired by a woman's *sensibilité*. "The story is one of the Rousseau class," judged a Louisville critic of *Three Weeks*, "depicting intense passion, relieved, somewhat, from grossness by intellectual passages and a love of beauty in nature. It is well-written, tragic; it has no moral aim." The literary magazine *Town Topics* also argued the Lady's love expressed a higher ideal. The editor disliked most women writers' treatment of passion, but declared, "Now, suddenly, there is redemption for the sex by an Englishwoman—for Elinor Glyn is that, as far as I know—who paints what some might call an illicit passion with so much poetry, so deep an appeal as surely to lure the applause, if not the tears, of the sternest moralist of us all."[44]

More staid newspapers like the *New York Times* struggled to even name the subject of *Three Weeks*. "The attention of French writers . . . has been focused upon phases and problems which writers in English have habitually avoided," reminded the *Times*. "It is not the province of fiction to discuss such problems as obsess the imaginations of Mrs. Elinor Glyn . . . let us keep our senses and refuse to allow the erotic to shatter the rounded integrity of true art." Concern about the influence of such newly prominent female authors ricocheted across the country, decrying how the "scarlet-crested Elinor Glyn wave that had deluged our once peaceful literary land" threatened a tradition committed to gentility for a century.[45]

In the face of such attacks, Nell conducted a charm offensive of epic proportions, flattering the press any chance she got. She paid tribute to American journalists' "good sense, courtesy, and directness of inquiry" and took pains to separate them from the voices of the literary establishment. "'CRITICS IDIOTS,'—Mrs. Glyn; But the Author of 'Three Weeks' Finds American Reporters Charming," a *Times* headline announced. 'I know that the critics have condemned the book severely. But it does not disturb me in the least. With 50,000 copies sold last month and the books still selling, I think I can stand a little criticism, don't you?'[46]

Becoming the "authoress Elinor Glyn" took work. "I never go 'off guard' for a moment. It would not be safe," she wrote her mother. Everywhere reporters lavished attention on her unusual looks and elegant dress. "If you can imagine an orchid with red hair you will gain some idea of the picture Elinor Glyn presented to the Pen and Brush Club," observed the *Washington Post*, "as she lifted her five feet six inches on . . . an improvised stand and faced an assembly, fairly purple—her favorite color—with excitement. 'Exotic,' one onlooker gasped."

"Love," she told her audience, "is a trinity—body, soul, and a desire to reproduce love's image." "A long shivery pause" followed her words, according to the *St. Louis Post-Dispatch*, before she defended her lovers. "They were obliged to suffer and pay the penalty," she continued "as people always pay for breaking the laws of man. God is above such action; he does not make man pay." Her rejection of the seventh commandment—thou shalt not commit adultery—only sent more shock waves through the press.[47]

◇ ◇ ◇

Nell's glamorous appearance was crucial to her ability to convey such daring expressions about sexual morality. "A distinctively modern visual property," glamour, as Glyn practiced and promoted it, nonetheless traded on a number of traditions and attributes—power, wealth, leisure for self-cultivation, mobility, beauty, style, theatricality—once confined mostly to aristocratic circles. Part of glamour's power lay in its ability to make the theatre of courtly life into something fit for the industrial age's wider audience.

Glamorous women like Nell and her Lady displayed an open yet licit form of eroticism that was deployed but contained, carefully controlled rather than wantonly discharged. Distance was key— whether exercised through the formality imposed by patrician codes of restraint, the privacy of reading, or the reproduction of an image. Distance enhanced the promise of erotic possibility without ceding self-control, allowing a woman to enjoy her sensuality without sacrificing her self-respect. On this trip, Nell brought glamour to the market, using it to further her desire for more independence, sexual frankness, and economic power.[48]

Like many celebrities who flourish in the public's eye, Nell's persona drew power from its possession of seemingly mutually exclusive parts. The trick allowed her to circulate ideas that she claimed personally to abjure. The press followed her lead, promoting her as part continental authoress, part proper English wife and mother of the "Most Beautiful Girls in All of England." The quintessential English lady part offset the blasphemous ideas espoused by the Continental authoress. Large photographs of Nell posed between Margot and Juliet accompanied articles that described her time reading, writing, and supervising her daughters' education at their country house in Essex.

The conservative English lady pose made plausible her protestation that she had not "meant to advocate free love. . . . I have a husband, an English squire, whom I love with all my heart and two daughters to whom I am devoted." She continued, "I painted the picture of an unconventional woman but her views are not my views." She had "no desire to rebel against society. It is as useless as running your head against a feather bed or a rock fence. One smothers; the other breaks." Though she called wives' position unjust, she observed that "the woman who offends conventional laws now pays the penalty of death. A hundred years from now it may be different."[49]

To the dear Aunt –
from
Elinor Glyn
June 1908

The other half of Nell's celebrity image: the "immaculate wife of a country squire"

Anxious to see *Three Weeks* on the stage, Nell eagerly attended a dinner in November that the Broadway producers Charles and Daniel Frohman threw in honor of Mark Twain and the authoress. Twain, the pen name of Samuel Clemens, was the first American writer to perfect the cult of the author by matching his fiction to his image in a way that audiences adored. Now Nell stood poised to do the same. "They made speeches and [Twain's] speech was splendid. They treat me like a Queen and I have nothing but adulation and the highest praise of *Three Weeks*," she wrote home.[50]

Nell enjoyed Twain's company—"a most quaint, amusing man," she privately called him. The feeling was mutual. At dinner, they agreed to meet later to discuss her novel. In his autobiography, he called their frank talk "the damnedest conversation [he] ever had with a woman," suggesting how little men and women discussed such subjects at all. Twain later described her novel's plot this way: the lovers "recognize that their passion is a sacred thing and that its commands must be obeyed. They get to obeying them at once and they keep on obeying them and obeying them, to the reader's intense delight and disapproval, and the process of obeying them is described, several times, almost exhaustively, but not quite."

Although Clemens privately confided his admiration for her book, Mark Twain refused to publicly defend the novel, as Nell implored him to do. Clemens had "a large cargo" of opinions that were not for print. The author's plainspoken, homespun image did not include supporting Nell's insistence that sexual passion was a key component of life.[51]

In November, Nell reported to her mother that "Lucy wants to come for December and I think it would be splendid for her if she would ever have enough control of herself to be careful all the time of what she said and did." Lady Duff-Gordon had just spent the happiest summer of her life, as the sisters' fates continued to follow one another on parallel tracks.[52]

In the midst of the most brilliant society season that London could remember in years, *The Merry Widow*'s opening had supercharged Lucy's professional reputation. The English designer of note had become a couturier sought after by wealthy women the world over after transforming *The Merry Widow*'s new face—a "shy and diffident" young chorus girl named Lily Elsie—into a star. Producer George Edwards had asked Lucy to design Elsie's dresses for the operetta and to help the actress acquire a personality befitting her status as a leading lady. Treating Elsie like one of her models, Lucy redid her hair and then taught her to dress, walk, and talk like a sophisticated woman of the world. When Elsie triumphed, she effusively praised Lucile's role in her success. Elsie's "Merry Widow Hat" had also made an enormous splash. Black, wide-brimmed—measuring a full eighteen inches across—covered with filmy chiffon, and festooned with piles of feathers, the hat would become *the* fashionable object for ladies for three years running. Ever a plunderer of the past, Lucy's inspiration was the Duchess of Devonshire's famed "Gainsborough" hat from the eighteenth century.[53]

When Lucy arrived in New York City for the holidays, she introduced Nell to several friends in the city's haute bohemian Sapphic set, including the first celebrity interior designer, Elsie de Wolfe, and her longtime partner Elisabeth Marbury, the pioneering theatrical and literary agent and heiress. Marbury agreed to help Nell secure a deal to produce *Three Weeks* and passed the script to Alla Nazimova, the great classical actress and "Russian siren" who had made her name playing controversial heroines like Henrik Ibsen's Hedda Gabler. For a few weeks it appeared Marbury had arranged the perfect match. The press reported, "Nazimova will make a feature of the tiger skin scene" from "the vulgarest, but the most talked of novel of the hour." But by Christmas, Nazimova had rejected the proposition for reasons that remain unclear.[54]

Lucy joined in the commotion her sister caused as the two women did the town "without their husbands," as newspapers slyly noted. They took a "Slumming Trip" to Chinatown, a fashionable practice among the wealthy interested in looking at how the so-called other half lived. "I was most insistent that we see everything," Lucy told reporters. "Of course the opium smokers were shown to us. Poor wretches, they looked so ill." Ever outspoken, Lucy raved about American cocktails to the press, promising to try each one of the "delicious concoctions" to decide which recipes to bring back to London. Altogether the sisters demonstrated that the behavior of some "fashionable ladies" from England could surpass even the "sangfroid and independence" of the "American Girl" who obsessed the imagination of so many writers.[55]

The sisters were "blooming," Nell told her mother, and enjoying the company of Sam Newhouse, an admirer she had met in London who had made a fortune in copper and silver mines out west. Although Newhouse longed to show her western America, she would not make it off the eastern seaboard on this trip. "I prom-ised you I would win the game if ever I had my head completely and I am doing it. You will feel when you see me you have a rock to depend upon the future," she wrote. "My millionaire friend Sam Newhouse" told her "every man in New York has a copy and nothing else (besides business of course eternal *business*) is spoken of in the clubs. If I had not such a sense of humor I should become insupport-able from the ravings and flattery I receive."[56]

Perhaps under the influence of her outspoken elder sister, Nell made a rare misstep with the press while Lucy was in town when the "Pilgrim Mothers" invited her to speak at their annual dinner. "After Perusing 'Three Weeks'" just hours before the author arrived, the "PURITANICAL PURITANS" refused to let its authoress occupy the speaker's table at the Waldorf Astoria, placing Nell at "an incon-spicuous place in the receiving line" instead. "Why did you write it?" one woman reportedly asked when seated for dinner. "Because I enjoyed writing it," the author retorted. "Well, if that's the kind of thing English women write, I'm proud I'm an American," her table-mate rejoined.[57]

Nell spoke to the press from the Plaza Hotel the next day about the widely publicized "snub." Her alleged comments set off a back-and-forth with club members that became front-page news from coast to coast for weeks. "Never in all my young life have I seen such an aggregation of dowds, frumps, and tabbycats," women who were, "breastless, slab-hipped, pancake-footed frights," Nell was quoted as seething. Headlines snapped back: "ONLY 'FRUMPS' ARE ENGLISH, SAY THE MOTHERS TO MRS. GLYN" and "REPLY TO MRS. GLYN: 'COARSE,' THE PILGRIM MOTHERS SAY OF AUTHORESS." "MRS. GLYN DEMANDS APOLOGY FROM 'FRUMPS' AND 'DOWDS.'" On and on the feud went until by the New Year, she had become, "ELINOR GLYN, THE NOVELIST WHO HAS UPSET NEW YORK."[58]

Nell's bad-mannered attack on her Puritan hosts, as much as her "bad book," likely drew the forces of "Comstockery" into the fray. The term—coined by the *New York Times* and popularized by George Bernard Shaw in 1905—referred to Anthony Comstock's work to protect the public from material with the remotest whiff of sex (including birth control, which Comstock opposed even more rabidly than woman suffrage). A Puritan raised in Connecticut, Comstock created the New York City Society for the Suppression of Vice and successfully lobbied to pass the "Comstock Law," which outlawed sending "obscene, lewd, or lascivious matters" through the mail.

A portly, balding man with a mutton-chop mustache, this "weeder in the garden of the Lord" destroyed fifteen tons of books during his career. No doubt incensed over the insult to his forebears, Comstock took up his "cudgel" against *Three Weeks*, asking the U.S. district attorney to investigate if the novel violated the federal prohibition he had fought to pass. The New England Watch and Ward Society also moved to suppress the novel. "Sex Novel Banned; Mrs. Glyn's Book Boycotted in Boston," announced the *Times*. "The book is still procurable in New York and I understand that booksellers there are busy filling hundreds of orders from this city." Days later, newspapers reported Comstock had his way, "'Three Weeks,' Called Obscene, Will Be Barred from Mails."[59]

By the time Nell returned to London in February, wearing "purple, her famous warm hair, and a smile," the attacks by the critics and Comstock had helped to make *Three Weeks* what publishers call a runaway sale, demonstrating what became a truism over the twentieth century: sex sells, even—if not especially—with bad publicity. The trip had rewarded her courage, set the outline for her professional persona, and hinted at the enormous size of the literary market for sexy love stories about glamorous women and their men.

"I am sorry to go," she told reporters before she sailed. She assured them she would return soon and that she had never called the "Mothers" tabbycats and frumps. "They are sparrows, not cats," the proudly feline author corrected. "The reporters caught my spirit, but they didn't catch my words." In any case, "the outrageous way the Mothers treated me has not dimmed my admiration for Americans as a whole."[60]

Nell's persona as an authoress who mixed British savoir-faire and Continental eroticism into one glamorous package captured the imagination of the American press. This reception foreshadowed what would be a long and lucrative relationship between Nell and the United States. "The one thing that counts in America is self-advertisement of the most blatant sort," explained Lucy, who would open a salon in New York the next year. "Publicity which we would set down as incredibly bad taste is taken as a matter of course there, and one has to realize from the start that the louder you blow your own horn the more likely is it to be heard above the noise of your neighbour's. I advise those whose lungs are not strong enough for a contest of this sort to keep out of it altogether."[61]

Ever the more outwardly restrained sister, Nell's temperament allowed for greater calculation with her public relations campaign. Before she left, she gave a long interview to an influential society writer at the *Washington Post.* The resulting profile defended her as "having the spark of genius," remarking, "quiet natures often possess the greatest reserve of mind and soul." Nell admitted that *Three Weeks* was not the Pilgrim Mothers' kind of book. "She is writing for a new audience," the paper agreed. "It is not that her works are intended for an audience alleged to be intellectually superior to that catered to by the old school of novelists. It is that she appeals to an advanced sensibility."[62]

The authoress had become a glamorously modern woman whose notoriety—as much as her words—had helped to make the topic of women's erotic desires *the* subject on everyone's lips.

Nell returned to chilly, wet London in February, where influenza promptly forced her into bed. For two weeks she cocooned in her suite at the Ritz, alone. Her mother, the girls, and Clayton were in Japan. She missed them as she lay in bed utterly exhausted by the triumphant tour.

But there was always so much work to be done, so many reporters to woo. When she recovered her strength, she hosted several journalists in her suite to ensure they understood the international sensation she had become. Stage managers everywhere were "anxious to produce her much discussed novel." Equally exciting, plans were "afoot for an operatic version of 'Three Weeks' by Puccini." She would pop over to Paris to see about that. But she had left her heart across the Atlantic and planned to return in a matter of weeks to arrange for the theatrical production of *Three Weeks* and to gather material for a new novel about Elizabeth's adventures traveling in

America without her husband. "The Americans delight me," she told the reporters, remarking, "In America all are equal and reporters have a right to be free and easy."[63]

In a show of her increasingly savvy publicity skills, she had timed her second American trip to the announcement of *Elizabeth Visits America*'s publication that fall. She was "very tired," she confided to her mother, but needed to return to research a novel that would exploit her momentum. ("Never write about an unvisited place" remained one of her firmest writerly rules.) To Clayton she presented a cheerier face. "Have no worries or trouble about money," she reassured him. When the family met in San Francisco for their long-planned rendezvous, she would "be there with all that is wanted, waiting for you on the pier! You never thought much of me in the past I know and perhaps I was a poor thing, but now I have proved I have brains and am of some use, so I hope you will love me a little dear pet. I am full of beans and courage and successful ideas."[64]

Much like Elizabeth would in her next novel, Nell made a solo voyage to New York on the *Mauretania* this time, the latest, greatest ship of the Cunard Line that broke the Atlantic speed record on that voyage. Having traveled no further inland than Washington, D.C., on her previous visit, this trip she immediately set out to see the far western spaces about which Europeans had long fantasized. She had already judged much of the East Coast elite—not just the awful Pilgrim Mothers—ridiculous in their social pretensions.

"I am tired of this sham civilization and fearful riches—only bourgeois underneath and bad taste. I want the wild," she wrote her mother shortly after her arrival. "My mind has expanded so you won't know me and I hope you will like me better. Anyway I am growing rich and that is something."[65]

She spent this trip constantly on the move, leaving New York immediately by train to make the thousand-mile trip to Detroit by way of Niagara Falls. "Here for a Day, Not Three Weeks, Elinor Glyn Authoress of Erotic Romances in Detroit" announced a local paper. "ELINOR GLYN, A WOMAN OF RAVISHING BEAUTY ELUCIDATES ULTRA FINE POINTS OF LOVE AFFAIR IN HER RENOWNED EROTIC STORY, 'THREE WEEKS,'" another headline proclaimed. Calling her "the most talked of woman in America, because of that erotic outpouring of a feverish amour," the reporter surfaced the expectations surrounding her persona. "That she has red hair, combined with the fact that she has written a novel that people have carried about carefully wrapped from view" had led people to call her the reincarnation of Becky Sharp. Three decades after Thackeray's wickedly fun antiheroine captured her own imagination, the press draped the character's fashionable mantle around Nell's shoulders, for better and for worse.[66]

The comparison to Becky Sharp reflected the naughty reputation Nell had earned, one she sometimes fanned and other times struggled to contain. Her red hair and white skin looked "exotic," she conceded in an article she wrote for William Randolph Hearst's massive newspaper chain entitled "Why I Am Misunderstood." But underneath she was just a fashionable society lady and mother who happened to write novels when the spirit moved her. After a lonely, bookish upbringing, she had married only to learn that life in the English countryside "bored me to death." She was a city person. "To see clever friends and go to interesting dinner parties, to meet the diplomats, high politicians, and really intellectual charming people is agreeable and I think that is my milieu."[67]

The beautiful authoress explained she was not a wicked woman, but a student of psychology, and defended her heroine's actions in the context of the novel's "very modern situation." Her Lady's loveless marriage left her "free to love where she might choose. Mind, I say free ethically—not conventionally. I am a great student of logic and psychology and philosophy and I know I'm right," she pronounced with the finality only possible with an upper-class English accent. "Do tell people I am not so awful. I love Americans and I want Americans to love me."[68]

After quickly touring Detroit, the "Authoress of Passion" took the train to Chicago for a two-day stop to attend a banquet held in her honor, then headed on to Santa Barbara. "Elinor Glyn Lauds Divorce," reporters at the banquet proclaimed. "People are so happy in Chicago," she reputedly told them, "because divorce is so easy, I suppose. It seems to me it might brighten our social life in England if divorces were more easily obtained." She boldly spoke about "methods of lovemaking, old and new, the divorce question, highballs" and the trend of women smoking cigarettes. "We could all of us be good and true if the person we love went on being demonstrative. It is the cold matter-of-fact devotion that kills love and makes one want to look elsewhere to find it again." Her "stunning" clothes attracted attention everywhere she went. "Gray with gray veil that swept the floor like a bridal gossamer," one described, before adding how it was "the masculine verdict that Mrs. Glyn knows how to dress."[69]

On her way to San Francisco, Nell learned that her family had returned directly to England rather than meet her on the Pacific Coast as they had planned. The longed-for respect from Clayton was not yet forthcoming.

Two years before her visit, a massive earthquake had ignited a blaze that had turned 80 percent of San Francisco into ash. By the time the rains came, four days after the fires began, San Francisco, San Jose, and Santa Rosa had almost vanished in the smoke and a quarter of a million people were left homeless. "Surrender was complete," said writer and resident Jack London, one of the few American writers Nell admired. When she visited, a massive rebuilding effort was under way that would leave San Francisco a much more elegant place than before.[70]

Awestruck by the city's destruction, she spent two nights at the Fairmont Hotel, where she met Mr. and Mrs. William Graham. Prominent society members in Santa Barbara, the Grahams would take Nell south to the palatial Italianate villa they had recently built on twenty-three oceanside acres. She barely managed to avoid another public snubbing at the hands of local socialites when they attended a ball that night. "Quaint as it seems now," she recalled, "whether you were 'for' or 'against' *Three Weeks* was quite an important matter in the United States, in the spring of 1908."[71]

Propositions of all kinds piled up. Doggerel by Walter S. Trumbull in *Lippincott's Monthly Magazine* captured the provocation the authoress posed to the disapproving and approving alike as she made her way to Southern California:

SERVED HER RIGHT
A certain young girl in East Lyn
Tried writing like Elinor Glyn;

After taking one look
Mommer burnt up the book
And Popper he spanked her like syn.[72]

Fellow Spiritualists, Nell had met Eleanor Graham in Paris and
the couple now exposed her to "the ideas of 'New Thought' propa-
gandists," which would deepen her faith in the powers of her own
mind during the years to come. Closely related to Spiritualism,
Theosophy, and Christian Science, New Thought emphasized the
cultivation of positive thoughts through meditation to manifest
"Inspiration, Power, Health, and Prosperity." While visiting their
estate in Santa Barbara, the Grahams gave Nell several books on
the subject and introduced her to a local medium in Los Angeles.
Although still a small town, Los Angeles was already one of the
most important centers of New Thought in the world. As a well-off
and relatively well-educated white woman, Nell fit the typical profile
of New Thought's early leaders and converts.[73]

Already quietly convinced she was psychic, Nell found what
she called New Thought's "Hindu thinking"—its belief in reincarnation and the ability to communicate with the spirit world—
congenial to her developing suspicions about how the universe
worked. No doubt New Thought helped to control her anxiety
about all the sudden changes and pressures swirling around her,
helping to channel Nell's worries about her family's uncertain
future into useful activity. She began meditating for an hour each
day, a new lifelong practice, and diligently practiced visualizing the
success and riches that had become the chief incentives in her life.
New Thought taught her that all her success was not just earned,
but likely predestined.[74]

There was always so much to be done, so many people to charm.
However much she relished the attention and opportunities, she
required time alone to maintain her equilibrium. And with the publication of *Elizabeth Visits America* looming, she badly needed to find
more time to write. Arrangements had finally been made for the
actor and producer James Hackett to stage *Three Weeks* in St. Louis.
But worries about state censorship and local opposition lingered in

Missouri. A scathing editorial, "Mrs. Glyn's Land of Promise," called
Hackett's planned production "distinctly discreditable to American
taste rather than to American morals."[75]

Sam Newhouse had joined Nell in Santa Barbara to take her
to one of his silver mines, along with his niece, a few of her female
friends, and Count Léon de Laborde of Paris. Although called only
"the Utah millionaire" in the press, Newhouse was the child of
Jewish immigrants, raised in New York City, who had made his fortune in copper and silver mining in Colorado, Nevada, and Utah.
A man of lavish tastes, he had become smitten with the authoress
the year before while spending time at his London mansion. On this
trip, Newhouse (separated from his own wife) propositioned Nell,
having decided that any husband who allowed his beautiful wife "to
travel around alone could be squared." She genuinely appreciated his
hospitality and company, but Newhouse—a "shortish, square man of
immensely strong physique" and "about as plebeian looking as it was
possible" for a fabulously rich man to appear—sparked no reciprocal
attraction in Nell. All her years on the marriage market had taught
her no amount of financial stress or uncertainty about the future
could force her to pretend unfelt desire.[76]

But now she had at last secured a way forward that did not
require catching any man's eye—at least, not one whose attention
she needed to rely upon for long. As the group passed through Reno
on the way to visit two of the area's booming silver mines, she found
that increasingly the men she saw caught hers. "Going west, the
figures of the men seemed to be less thickset and more loose-limbed
and athletic, and in the mining camp they reached perfection," she
recalled with still perceptible relish.

They went first to Rawhide, where gold and silver had been discovered a year earlier, and then on to Stingaree Gulch. Nell gambled
at one of the thirty-six saloons that had sprung up on the mining
camp's "gay white way" in just one year. Six hundred women who
worked in the instant town's saloons poured onto the street after
learning the author of *Three Weeks* was visiting. The women reportedly followed Nell wherever she went, including to a banquet in
her honor held under a tent that lasted far into the night. "I have
travelled from Budapest to Bombay, from Boston to Bakersfield, and

there are few experiences I have not had or people I have not met, but I would not give last night's experience for them all," she told reporters.[77]

The next day, Nevada's governor, John Sparks, escorted their party down into a silver mine. Nell called the men working there "the most perfect gentlemen I have ever met as a class and quite the most beautiful creatures," in a letter to her family. "I shall make you thrill when I tell you of our adventures and how nearly your mum was shot. The last camp was as wild as any Bret Harte story." She repeated the praise to the press before she left, calling "the Western miner the highest type of American. Yes, she actually compares the workers of Goldfield and Rawhide to the cream of the British nobility," an incredulous reporter wrote.[78]

On her way back to New York to return to London on June 14, she gave an interview to a gaggle of reporters in Salt Lake City that illustrated how much she had embraced playing the authoress of an exceptionally naughty sex novel. "Elinor Glyn: 'Marriage Vow Is an Insult to God,'" shouted the headline. "With rare exceptions present day marriages become platonic relationships," she explained, and thus "an insult to God." Since love was "beyond the control of human beings so utterly" she warned that the promise of eternal love often resulted in "hypocrisy."[79]

There was no turning back now, no cutting her personality down to a size that fit in the elaborate cage that had contained it for so long. As she sped across the country on her way back home, it is easy to imagine her reckoning with how a year of expressing so many of the opinions that she had long held inside had changed not just how everyone saw her, but her outlook on life.

She crowed to her mother about having become a self-made woman. "For the usual quid pro quo of men," she wrote in a welcome-home letter to Gran, "I could now have had a million settled upon me and 100,000 on each of the children but I have refused every suggestion and the whole of my fortune has been made out of my brain and in perfect self respect."[80]

CHAPTER 8

The Word Became Flesh

What is this thing called love?

—Elinor Glyn, Heather Wood Diary

Nell returned to England to find her family in turmoil. Clayton had "wantonly gone to the Jews again," she wrote to her mother, and then wagered the money away at Monte Carlo, again. A gambler with no more collateral to mortgage could not go to a bank. A black-market loan from a moneylender—at 100 percent interest or more—was his only chance to secure a pound. She was "heartbroken coming back after my hard fight" to find out about his betrayal in her absence. All was "black but God will pull us through somehow."[1]

Nell's assumption that Clayton's moneylenders were Jewish reflected Britain's rising anti-Semitism as much as the ethnicity of the men to whom her husband turned. The association of Jewish men with the job dated to the medieval period, when the Catholic Church first required them to take up the "dirty" work of lending money with interest. Centuries later, the rising anti-Semitism that followed increased Jewish immigration to Britain produced the 1905 Aliens Act, which restricted their migration for the first time, as well as a highly publicized series of investigations into the "Jewish" practice of making usurious loans. These dramatic press stories about Jewish loan sharks had revivified and cemented the association of predatory lending so firmly onto Anglo-Jewry in the public mind that one Jewish activist recommended barring men who did the work from synagogues.[2]

Clayton's health had collapsed under the weight of these enor-

mous financial pressures and the accumulated decades spent drinking fine brandy and smoking expensive cigars. Working with the
family accountant, Walters, Nell prevented a public spectacle by
borrowing funds from Lucy; business at Lucile was going so well that
plans were afoot to open branches in Paris and New York.

From here forward the family relied solely on Nell's pen and personal connections for support. "One long nightmare of reoccurring
financial crises," she called the years between *Three Weeks* and her
move to Los Angeles after World War I. A never-ending flow of
fresh debts required many "hastily written novels, the advance payments on which were already mortgaged to some pressing creditor,
or urgently required to pay the household bills or school fees for the
children."[3]

Returning in the midst of Clayton's steep decline, Nell took more
control over the future of her daughters, now sixteen and ten. She
had seen to it that her "babies" spoke "French perfectly." But beautiful Margot needed more polish to make her coming-out to society
a success. With her heart-shaped face, cameo-like features, and large
blue eyes, so like Clayton's, Margot had always been the prettier of
the girls—not as arresting as her mother, but just as lovely in her
own way. After she returned from her year in Paris, Margot would
attend another finishing school in Dresden, with her governess,
Dixie, in tow. Juliet's always evidently sharp mind required a good
boarding school that would provide the more systematic approach
that Nell's education had entirely lacked. Juliet would begin at
Eastbourne in the fall of the next year. That was the plan, one that
handily removed Nell's daughters from the spectacle of their father's
rapid deterioration and left her free to travel and write. How she
would pay for it all was the question.[4]

Supporting the family in the manner to which they were
all accustomed meant long hours alone writing in her Trianon.
Although attached to Lamberts by its covered walkway, the suite
isolated her from some of the drama unfolding inside the house. She
was happy to leave Clayton's care to her mother. Their interests and
habits had always been more aligned. The two now appeared like
the devoted couple that she and Clayton had never been. Still, her
husband's deterioration unnerved her. She would "creep to the win-

dow" as she worked at night. "There is always a light in that other window no matter how late—even to the dawn. What is happening there?—are ghosts talking to one who suffers—If one knew—if one could help—Alas! the weary mockery of it all—to jest & to laugh—to keep the ball rolling—that is the duty."[5]

The publication of *Three Weeks* had made Nell notorious, as Daisy predicted, but also famous. The two usually went hand in hand for a woman in the public eye, she had learned. On her return to London, whether or not *Three Weeks* was obscene became the talk of the town as the courts, publishers, book buyers, librarians, and schools bandied the question about. Boston had prohibited the novel's sale just days before Nell sailed home from New York. Showing unusual nerve, her American publisher Duffield had directed a representative to sell a copy of the novel to a Boston police officer in order to arrange a test case. A superior court found him guilty under the state's obscenity law and issued a fine. Duffield appealed the decision to the Massachusetts Supreme Court, arguing that words like "obscene" were impossibly vague.

The judge thought otherwise. Obscene, lewd, and lascivious were ordinary words, he retorted, "and may be assumed to be understood in their common meaning by an ordinary jury." In any case, he believed that the authoress had "disclosed so much of the details of the way to the adulterous bed" that she provoked "not the spiritual but the animal." The New England Watch and Ward Society (responsible for the initial ban in Boston) blamed Nell's "devotion to *Three Weeks*' advertising" for provoking "a veritable deluge from England of fashionable novels of the free love school." By the time she settled back into Lamberts to write, the American Library Association had called for the suppression of all novels with a similarly "immoral tendency." The six largest circulating libraries in Britain followed suit. Then word came that opposition in St. Louis had caused James Hackett to back out of producing *Three Weeks*.[6]

All the troubles in America over translating her novel to the stage had led Nell to sign with the literary agent Curtis Brown, who provided essential connections to agents who might work on her behalf in the United States. An American journalist working in London, Brown had helped to launch a new profession when he founded his eponymous agency in 1899. "The agent's business is world authors, or those who might become world authors if given a fair opportunity," he explained in *Contracts*. No longer would her first publisher, Gerald Duckworth, take his long customary commission. Instead, Curtis Brown would earn 10 percent for negotiating his infamous client's increasingly far-flung deals in magazines, newspapers, and the variety of editions of her books published in multiple languages.[7]

Undaunted by the outcry, Nell made a remarkable decision before turning to write *Elizabeth Visits America*. She would direct a "dramatization" of *Three Weeks* in London that summer. A single matinee would prove her critics wrong and make possible a theatrical adaptation of the novel, she believed. Everyone knew a successful play promised the kind of financial rewards that were almost impossible to earn in print. So, she would undertake a private staging of her romantic tale to prove its morality and secure a producer. She knew that many had damned the book only by reputation. She would invite all of society—who would not miss the spectacle no matter their views of its author—and shut the critics out. She would show them that her Lady's passion was ethically pure, if technically unlawful. She would change their minds.[8]

Nell continued to insist that only a Russian could capture her heroine's so-called civilized savagery and only an Englishman Paul's strapping innocence. "I want no American with padded coat sleeves to play Paul," she told a reporter. "He must be English. I have no objection to American players," she added, but her hero and heroine demanded "an Englishman and a Russian woman for the proper interpretation of the parts."[9]

She made a quick trip to Paris to interview actresses in its large Russian émigré community. She failed to find the right leading lady, but a meeting with the Grand Duchess Cyril of Russia, called Ducky by her friends, resulted in an invitation to visit the Romanov Court the following winter. Ducky and her mother-in-law, Marie Pavlovna, the Grand Duchess Vladimir, had both read and loved *Three Weeks*. Nell had a feeling for the Russian character, they reported. Why not come and study the country firsthand so that she might set a novel there? "Everyone always writes books about peasants," complained the grand duchess. "Come and write one about how the real people live."[10]

In Paris, Nell also paid a flirtatious visit to the eminent French sculptor Auguste Rodin that captured the attention of the press. The two talked art as she toured the Hôtel Biron, the eighteenth-century château in the heart of the city that Rodin had converted into a workshop and residence. "ELINOR GLYN HAS A LONG SECOND TOE; SHE GIVES THE SCULPTOR RODIN A PEEP THROUGH SILK OPEN-WORK STOCKING," newspapers teased as she kept her name in the news, but failed to find the right actress to play her Lady.[11]

Convinced that no British actress could play her Tiger Queen, she returned to London and boldly cast herself to star opposite the twenty-seven-year-old English actor Charles Bryant. "Paul is beautiful," she wrote to her mother after reassuring her that a check for expenses was on its way. "6'3 tall and a shape like a footman and quite a gentleman," she continued. "We shall look lovely at all events." The choice revealed the eye for spotting talent that would later serve her so well in Hollywood. Bryant had spent the last several years performing on stages across America and would soon return to New York, where he would catch actress Alla Nazimova's eye. His next big role was as the "husband" of the Russian actress widely known inside artistic circles for preferring women's romantic company in her private life.[12]

Two days before the performance, the press announced the dramatic casting choice: "MRS. GLYN HER OWN HEROINE," shrieked headlines across the ocean. "London Learns That Author of 'Three Weeks' Will Play Tiger Skin Lady." They also learned she would pay for the performance herself at a cost of $3,750; a sum on which a middle-class family of four could live comfortably for two years. Nell never hesitated to lavish her resources on her art as long as she had the cash. Pure class, movie producer Samuel Goldwyn later called the trait.[13]

Nell professed shock for the rest of her life that the public insisted on confusing the author with her heroine. But this was more theatre, more "typically aristocratic" pretense that commercial considerations were beyond her care. She had stepped in and out of playing the Oriental siren on her American book tour to catch the public's fancy. Now she disappeared into the role of the Lady entirely in the adaptation of her novel that she quickly wrote herself. With only a few weeks to rehearse the show before the fateful performance, she spent all day rehearsing and evenings in bed resting and memorizing her part. "All is chaos," she wrote to her mother from the Ritz, "but they assure me it will be right in the end."[14]

Nell certainly created an alluring portrait onstage. A surviving photograph captures her at the story's climactic moment, stretched out on the Siberian tiger skin in a racy Lucile creation; a sleeveless V-neck tunic of gossamer chiffon, embellished only with a metal string of beads that runs down her shoulders and under her breasts. She gazes fiercely at the camera from under an enormous pile of plaited hair wound into a fantastic shape atop her head while leaning against the head of the world's largest cat, her arm curled around his neck. By any estimation she earned the doggerel (reputedly

Nell playing her Tiger Queen from *Three Weeks* on a London stage in 1908

written by the Irish playwright George Bernard Shaw) that chased
her across the century:

> Would you like to sin
> With Elinor Glyn
> On a tiger skin,
> Or would you prefer
> To err with her
> On some other fur?[15]

There would be only one chance to get this right; one matinee
on a hot July afternoon at the prestigious Adelphi Theatre on the
Strand, the street along the Thames dotted with most of the West
End's theaters. Sir Walter Scott's novels had resounded from the
Adelphi's stage for years before Charles Dickens suffered through
his theatrical debut there. Newspapers reported that "the most fashionable audience" seen that summer blocked the theater's entrance
with their luxurious automobiles and carriages drawn by "high step-
ping horses." Ladies and gentlemen packed into the Adelphi's fifteen
hundred seats, which rose like a triple-decker cake around the stage.
Footmen in black coats and knee breeches handed round purple pro-
grams before the curtain and refreshments during the intermission
between the second and third acts. As Nell predicted, though most
of society no longer claimed to know the authoress, they turned out
to watch her attempt at redemption for her bad book.[16]

 Enterprising journalists wormed their way into the event despite
Nell's strict instructions that this was an invitation-only affair.
"Everybody one's seen every day for years is here," the Duchess of
Rutland was heard to say after surveying the audience from her seat
in the stalls. The Duchess "had not brought 'her girls,'" a reporter
slyly noted in a story that ran in American newspapers from coast
to coast. The "British peerage had representatives galore, young and
old, male and female," remarked another reporter, before listing the
notables present who included key American figures who had failed
to cut Nell—like Minnie Paget, Mrs. Waldorf Astor, and Mrs. John
Jacob Astor. Diplomats from all over Europe packed in alongside
denizens of the American and British stage.[17]

Most remarkably, Edwardian society's supreme hostess, Alice Keppel, shared a box with Mrs. Willie Page. Keppel had replaced Daisy as the *boudoir belle* of the Prince of Wales and had become very rich in the process once he became king. A shrewd and buxom Scot, Keppel made an art of perfecting the cardinal rule—discretion at all costs—that Nell stood charged with violating. It's impossible to know what King Edward's beloved mistress thought of the show that sultry afternoon, but we know her lover forbade any mention of "that vulgar novel" in his presence until he died in 1910.[18]

The king's stunning act of hypocrisy betrayed a series of paradoxes at the heart of his short reign. An instinctive Conservative like his mother, Edward's now-similarly corpulent person represented his embodiment of all that was English. Yet his cosmopolitan side adored Paris and considered the company of Liberal politicians and prime ministers more fun than those who held political views closer to his own.

Edward helped to reinvent the modern monarchy as a series of solemn, "ancient" rites even as he indulged a well-publicized taste for music halls and the company of high-spirited, pretty women and entertaining, rich men—whatever their provenance. (Some historians suggest that the prevalence of successful new-moneyed Jewish men in his circle may have contributed to rising anti-Semitism in these years.) His preferences validated the growing appetite for women who followed their sexual passions where they led, even as he publicly scorned any woman like Nell who openly admitted as much. King Edward VII was thus both recognizably loose and "modern" in ways that brought him closer to his subjects while insisting on a role that reinforced the notion of unbridgeable, "natural" divides throughout the British Empire.[19]

Nell may have looked the part of her Lady, but by design the dramatization that she wrote conveyed none of her novel's erotic abandon. Much of the audience departed in disappointment after the second act when the opportunities for "passionate lovemaking" had passed. The critical consensus declared that Anthony Comstock would have approved the show in New York.

Yet, incredibly, the Office of the Lord Chamberlain, George Redford, forbade a public performance. Since admission had been free, Nell had lost a great deal of money on the gamble that the production would result in a commercial theatrical run.[20]

As the king's hypocrisy suggested, the mere idea of the seductive heroine in *Three Weeks* was too hot for the guardians of Anglo-Saxon propriety to endorse. The novel's celebration of a woman's adulterous pursuits was bad enough. But its animating assumption—that Anglo-Saxon lovers desperately needed an Oriental education of the senses—was simply too audacious to stage, however restrained her adaptation. Edward Lyttleton, the headmaster of Eton, Britain's toniest training ground for boys, conceded as much to Nell. A first-class cricket player and son of a baronet, Lyttleton might have played Paul as a younger man. He admitted that reading the novel had changed his mind about its morality. But he still refused to lift the school's ban, for fear of the trouble that the parents of his students might rain down on his head.[21]

There is no doubt that Lord George Curzon, Marquess of Kedleston, liked what he saw that sweaty afternoon. An imperial statesman who had recently resigned as India's viceroy, Curzon was far more of an "Oriental expert" than the leading lady on the stage.

At forty-nine Curzon commanded the attention of all eyes just by walking into a room. Tall and good-looking, he was an impeccable dresser with large hazel eyes and skin like a milkmaid. As if to hint at the passionate nature behind his enameled façade, he accentuated his surprisingly full lips with a clean-shaven face—an unusual choice in these mustachioed days. Curzon watched the performance with Nell's friend Lady Minnie Paget, the American buccaneer turned inveterate matchmaker. It's easy to imagine Paget whispering a thing or two about her friend's less visible charms in his ear as they sat together in a box.

Nell learned that George succumbed to temptation with the seriousness of purpose that he brought to all his tasks. The next day he sent Nell the skin of a tiger he had killed in India, along with a note applauding her courage and an invitation to tea. The two had met at parties over the years, but this would be their first of many unchaperoned tête-à-têtes.[22]

◇ ◇ ◇

Nell fell deeply in love for the first time, with a brave and arrogant aristocrat whose life had recently blown apart. Born in 1859 at the vast and neglected Kedleston Hall, George was the second of ten children and heir to lands in Derbyshire held by his family for more than seven hundred years. He dismissed this fact with typical economy. They were "a feeble lot," since "no family could have remained in possession of the same estate since the twelfth century, had they manifest the very slightest energy or courage." Almost an anachronism in his own life, as many said, Curzon grew into the model of an eighteenth-century gentleman in a Palladian pile built as homage to the glories of the Roman past.[23]

He exuded the combination of noblesse oblige and supreme confidence that Nell found irresistible. In private he could be as sweetly sentimental as he was unbending and caustic in public. This dual nature may have been the legacy of a childhood spent under the care of distant parents (his mother died at thirty-seven, not long after her eleventh birth) and a sadistic governess. The daughter of a prison warden, Ellen Paraman was a talented teacher. She was also a "brutal and vindictive tyrant who persecuted and beat us in the most cruel way," Curzon later said. She "established over us a system of terrorism so complete that not one of us ever mustered up the courage to walk upstairs and tell our father or mother."[24]

Determined to add distinction to an ancient line, Curzon pursued political work and women with nearly equal passion for the rest of his life. A horseback-riding accident as a child left him trapped inside a metal corset and often in crippling pain. The injury created another tender spot underneath his hard shell that pulled on the hearts of the women who knew him best. Brilliant and compulsively driven, he won all the top prizes as a student, first at Eton and then at Balliol, Oxford's most intellectually lively college that was already regarded as a "kindergarten" for imperial statesmen and diplomats. While at college, Curzon earned his own lifelong defining doggerel:

My name is George Nathaniel Curzon
I am a most superior person,
My cheek is pink,

My hair is sleek,
I dine at Blenheim once a week.[25]

After Oxford, he became a bold and compulsive traveler for almost a decade, trading studying and philandering for navigating remote parts of Russia, Central Asia, and the Far East. This was the beginning of a process that had made him one of Britain's leading so-called Oriental experts; recently elected to the House of Lords, he would eventually become its leader and foreign secretary.

His oratorical abilities and administrative talents led many to predict a future as prime minister. "He has a great deal of intelligence it is true," admitted one opponent, "but he has more temperament. Self-confident, ambitious, masterful, hard—he is determined to be the master of men and he will be."[26]

"Naturally attracted by Americans," as Nell came to realize to her chagrin, George married the beautiful Brooklyn heiress Mary Leiter in 1895. True to the stereotype of the headstrong American girl, Mary had been the one to court him, tracking him in her patient way for five years. After Queen Victoria made him her last viceroy of

Nell's greatest love: George Nathaniel Curzon, Marquess of Kedleston

George Curzon dressed as the viceroy of India in 1903

India, George and Mary left for Calcutta with their two baby girls. Curzon was not quite forty, the youngest man ever to occupy the office. Supportive Mary presided next to George as he ruled over British India at its apogee. "I hardly think I could bear" the loneliness and isolation of the office, he confided to a friend, "if it were not for Mary by my side."[27]

Believing possession of the subcontinent the key to Britain's continued status as a world power, Curzon set about reforming the corrupt bureaucracy of the British Raj. He also used the world's largest military to partition Bengal, setting the province's Muslim and Hindu population against each other; the decision earned him damnation from many. Then he lost an argument with Gen. Herbert Kitchener over whether there would be continued civilian, or newly enhanced military, control over the Indian Army. Kitchener had been the strategist behind the scorched-earth tactics that had won the Boer War. Curzon resigned and returned in humiliation to England in 1905. The next year Mary died trying to give him a longed-for son.[28]

To blot his grief he filled his days. He became the chancellor of Oxford and an active member of the Royal Geographic Society and the National Association Opposing Woman Suffrage. He gave lectures whenever asked and poured his energy—and his dead wife's fortune—into restoring and writing the histories of a series of crumbling historic British estates. Even unemployed, Curzon always worked.

Except when he played. "His leisure is always more spent with women than with men, they are more his natural companions," Nell wrote in the "pen portrait" she drew of her lover deep into their affair. She had already indirectly written about Curzon's nature through one of the characters in her novel *Halcyone* (1912). Next she filled a notebook with her elegant script on the subject of George. Curzon's most skilled biographer would praise her unpublished essay, "Portrait of a Great Man," for its insight.[29]

The title of "Portrait of a Great Man" bore no hint of irony. Her at times cringe-inducing reverence threaded through all of its eighty pages. "Some people are indeed born master and some slaves—this Great Man is a real master—a born ruler," she concluded near the end. "If the machine of democracy does not crush him," and "if given the chance," she avowed that he would be "the noblest ruler since Augustus Caesar elevated Rome."[30]

Yet her hero worship did not blind her novelist's observant eye. The manuscript took pains, perhaps even found its purpose, in describing the faults that might prevent this destiny. His "egregious self confidence" led him to assume "his own personal scope of sight is the only one," she cautioned. He failed to take the feelings of others into account and ignored the effects his words. "No one," she wrote, "has a greater art of crushing with a polished sentence." He was a poor judge of character who forgot "that games of chess are sometimes lost through not considering the possible movements of the pawns." Such habits might act as "a great barrier to his ultimate career" and result in tragedy, she warned.[31]

But it was a revelation to spend time with a man who shared her preferences and tastes. George hunted on occasion, but "is not a sportsman if that is taken to mean an ingrained desire to go out and kill something," she noted with satisfaction after years of watching Clayton do just that. Interior decorating and garden design, fine art and fashion, Greek and Oriental philosophy and history, travel and sparkling talk were some of the many interests the lovers shared.

Since her most important relationships were the ones she filtered through her mind, it made sense that she fell hardest for a man who "dazzled" her with his "marvellous brain," "delightful outbursts of humour and fun," and "brilliant wit." Unlike "most strong characters," who wanted only to hear themselves talk, Curzon could be an excellent listener when he chose. "His two greatest pleasures are first *work* [underlined twice] and then really brilliant and intelligent conversation." The same was true of her. Each fell under the spell of the other's quick wit. When deep into their affair, George once asked Nell why her daughters were *so* much more intelligent than his own, she replied, "Well the mother does make a difference!"[32]

Always with one eye trained on history, Curzon carefully culled his many love affairs from his personal archive, but scraps survived elsewhere. George possessed a "rare gift: il sait aimer" (he knew how to love), sighed the American-born novelist Pearl Craigie, who'd had an affair with Curzon before his engagement to Mary. "Alone among the libertines," he was "always kind to women—young or middle aged or old" and "spoke well of his mistresses" after ending affairs. Nell went even further in praising his capacity to charm. George "could fascinate man, woman, or child, and turn the most venomous middle-class antagonist . . . into a strong partisan." When he tried.[33]

But she also knew that Curzon, an aristocrat's aristocrat, served only "God, King, and Country." This outlook did not shift even after the Liberals' landslide victory against the Conservative Party in 1906 set in motion changes that loosened the Tories' long grip on the kingdom's social and economic levers. The most dramatic reversal of political power in Britain to date, the election of 1906 brought an administration of professional politicians to power. Some of them even hailed from humble backgrounds, like the new Welsh president of the Board of Trade (and future prime minister), David Lloyd George. Though it was not clear yet how far things would go, over the next few years Britain began building a welfare state complete with old-age pensions and minimum wages. The "People's Budget" of 1909 operated from the revolutionary assumption that redistributing wealth—particularly through new land taxes aimed directly at patricians—was good for everyone.

The only pressure that made high-handed George bend was "the chatter of his group of women friends," as far as Nell could tell. Part of a like-minded circle of aristocrats called "the Souls," the chattering women had been Curzon's closest companions since his Oxford days. The madly prolific English writer H. G. Wells called visiting with the Souls "like going to a flower show and seeing what space and care can do with the favoured strains of some familiar species." Members took pride in their learning and acute aesthetic sensibility while practicing the same sexual freedom as the Marlborough House set. Arthur Balfour (who resigned as prime minister just before the Conservatives' disastrous defeat) officially led the Souls, but the group actually spun around several magnetic women, preeminently the four Tennant sisters, Charlotte, Laura, Lucy, and Margot. Curzon was their prize peacock, and they shared him badly, Nell learned.

Even the well-educated, beautiful, and immensely rich Mary Leiter had wilted under their scrutiny. "I must say no more critical set exists in the world than the friends," Mary wrote home after her marriage. "My path is strewn with roses, and the only thorns are the unforgiving women."[34]

A beautiful, mature authoress, trailing sensationalism and scandal, could never hope to gain the unforgiving women's approval, even if she was more moral and accomplished than all the Souls' leading ladies. Morality was not the issue, though, Nell knew. George was "perfectly indifferent to moral worth" in a woman. "So long as they are ladies outwardly and amuse him," he cared nothing about a woman's "general virtue" or "sexual morality." Even "virtues of goodness and truth and broadmindedness and mental integrity" were not necessary in women, because he did not consider the female sex "equal souls" who demanded "that scrupulous sense of honor with which he would deal with a man."[35]

The heated opposition to Britain's burgeoning movement for woman suffrage—led by empire-builders like Curzon and Nell's old friend from Carlsbad, Alfred Milner—indicated how many Conservatives shared George's view, including Nell. "Are the majority of women who come into the busy life of a great man," she wondered, "creatures calculated to elevate his opinion of the sex? Viewed without rosy spectacles, are women as a whole worthy of chivalry and respect? Or only of toleration, physical worship, kindness and protection?"[36]

Curzon valued women like Mary, who furthered his ambition. He appreciated those "regarded as worldly successes" and "envied for their social positions." He enjoyed their beauty and indulged a particular penchant for redheads when he could, believing the coloring suggested a passionate temperature that burned as hot as his. But far and away what mattered most to him were other men. (Tellingly, wife Mary is the sole woman to make the index of a recent history about his time as viceroy.) Women "were of no real importance in his scheme of things," Nell reasoned, because his "leisure is so rare" that it did "not amount to anything great in his life."[37]

Knowing all this seems to have made him more, not less, attractive to Nell.

George overwhelmed her senses, appealed to her mind, and flattered her snobbish side. In the company of this hardworking, handsome Lord, she could no longer exert the kind of control she had exercised over her flirtations in the past. He was "so physically attractive that he arouses passion even in the many friendships which he holds casually," she ruefully admitted. A "sensation of sex" always crept in because of the "intensely magnetic tremendously powerful male fascination" he possessed.[38]

Nell checked all the boxes on her list of when she thought it permissible to break her marriage vows. Then she seems to have dived headlong into her first full-blown romance by the end of 1908. At age forty-four, it is easy to imagine that she believed there was no time to waste.

Luckily for her, George seems to have applied his brilliant mind in bed. "A most passionate physical lover" she called him—"superbly virile, vital and voluptuous." He delivered in private the kind of intense focus she had wanted for so long, enjoying women "in the spirit in which other men like fine horses or good wine," savoring each beautiful line and nuance of taste. "He rules entirely—and when a woman belongs to him, he seems to prefer to give her even the raiment which touches her skin, and in every tangible way shows absolute possession, while *in words* avoiding all suggestion of ownership, all ties, and all obligations upon either side. It is extremely curious."[39]

Indeed. The Siren had met her match.

Desire could make you unrecognizable to yourself, twist everything loose that had once seemed fixed. Nell had become well practiced at imagining how sexual attraction could contort a person. No longer just society's "leading novelist of modern manners," critics now considered her métier and trade as calling forth "the sharp gradients of ecstasy or despair" stirred by "giving full play to uncontrolled passions."[40]

But Nell had never personally experienced such intense emotions until beginning her carnal education with George. Edwardian Britain's most notorious sex novelist quickly learned how little she could control the effects of passion on herself. She knew "love, not worship" was "the medium of happiness." Yet she banished every other male admirer from her life "to be freer to lavish worship on

[her] idol." "I would let him put his feet on my hair—give my white body for his cushion & my soul for his plaything," she confided to the diary she filled with all the things she could not say to George; the one unlike any other private writing she left behind.[41]

She of "the tiger tribe" set herself inside "a cage with iron bars" to subdue her instincts. She—who was "not sweet and good but desired & denying"—would try to wear a "mask of calm" over the passion that raged inside. She would "be meek, be patient, be a side interest," she chanted to the diary. She would conduct their relationship in a secret box apart from the world.[42]

She would learn to wait. "Of all the weapons of a Lover silence is the cruellest," Nell complained to her diary while waiting, once again, to hear from George. "Poor women!—let none deceive themselves—what a man most desires to do that he will find time for—even if he snatch it from sleep."[43]

She found the practice hard. "A wild rebellion is in me," she confessed at least a year into the affair. "There is a magnet here in England & I am a needle & between the two there are all sorts of paltry obstacles & some great ones & I feel I could scream to the night—tear me a path—sweep them aside let me be free to follow my heart. I think I will go to the zoo and watch the tigers in their cages. I know so well what they feel."[44]

Since playing her Lady in London and then catapulting straight into an affair with George, Nell had spent most of her time not with her lover but trying to write her family's way onto solid ground. Her letters to Clayton from this period are at least as poignant as the journal into which she poured all her angst over George. The confidence in her star that she brought back from America dimmed under the strain of the "racing chasing life" she led. The pains in her side returned. She constantly sought some recognition from her husband and mother for her efforts that did not come.[45]

She agreed to a loan on a new life insurance policy that the accountant Walters took out and then pleaded with Clayton "not to incur anymore debts," counseling "any extras we can only have when the money is actually in hand from my work." They must learn to economize—she suggested they try to live on £1,500 a year at Lamberts—in order to invest the fee she would receive after finishing her next book. The alternative meant "a cruel spur hanging over" her to work constantly "whether I feel in the spirit not."[46]

She reluctantly borrowed money from Lucy (again) to take Margot to Monte Carlo so her daughter could better recover from the scarlet fever she had caught at finishing school in Dresden. There Nell set about finishing *Elizabeth Visits America*, now a year past the originally promised publication date. "I am forcing myself to write hours every day to get it done," but she feared it was "not amusing in the least." With the £500 advance that she received from Duckworth for the book, she paid back Lucy, settled the family's debts, and then went briefly to America to try to "boom it" so that the novel might "sell in the thousands like *Three Weeks*."[47]

Elizabeth Visits America fizzled. Americans failed to appreciate all of Nell's criticisms of them; British critics found Elizabeth's latest visits surprisingly dull. So the authoress headed to Saint Petersburg in December of 1909 to spend the winter at the Russian Court collecting more material for the novel that would become *When the Hour Came* in Britain, or *His Hour* (in America and on film, the latter title to be used going forward for simplicity).

Her knack for making a splash was on full display visiting Grand Duchess Marie Pavlovna the Elder at Vladimir Palace, where the Romanov Court seemed blithefully unconcerned with Tsar Nicholas's incapacity to manage the unrest spreading through his empire. Nell's letters to her mother and the girls focused on her social success. "I am having a gorgeous time," never in bed "before 2 am," and "am supposed to be a wit!" she reported. The woman Nell referred to as "my G.D." was the great-great-great-granddaughter of Empress Catherine the Great. The recent widow of Tsar Nicholas's uncle, the GD had long acted as the Romanovs' chief hostess because of Tsarina Alexandra's discomfort with the role and her ambitions for her sons. Known for her interest in literature and the arts, the GD's spectacular collection of jewels would support her children in exile after the Revolution. An admirer of *Three Weeks*, the GD asked Nell to read it to her aloud in her private chambers.[48]

Nell celebrated even the most outrageously despotic qualities of the Russian royals. "I went out to a party in the most splendid palace you could imagine a private person living in," she exclaimed. The cold was "unbelievable," "sometimes the coachmen become insensible on the boxes waiting," but "you can keep them out all night. This is my kind of country—a real autocracy," she wrote, exhibiting the deepening of her Conservative political views that occurred during her imperial sojourns and relationship with George. "An enchanting people—as simple as one great family and absolutely human and no airs—deeply read and properly educated" and "full of heart sentiment—ugly, polished, and attractive . . . so kind and homey and splendid at the same time." "Everyone is curious to know why I know the Grand Duchess so well. It makes me laugh. I am being feted and . . . like everything. I am not only trying to as in America," she admitted. "I shall write something wonderful," she concluded in the cheery tone she typically used with the women in the family.[49]

To her husband she told a different tale. "The drain of writing all day and going out all night is tremendous," she complained in March. "My brain is numb. I must put [the manuscript] aside and look at it with fresh eyes" later. "You must admit I have a certain amount of backbone, haven't you?" No letters from Clayton to Nell survive, but it seems no praise for her fortitude ever came. "I feel absolutely deserted," she fretted in a letter in April, "not a word from anyone since I came." Although she believed the hero of her novel "a sweet young man," she was "not pleased" with *His Hour*, she admitted from Moscow. "It is stiff," but "I must work. I have 200 pages done but in writing it has to be 360 so you see I must go on."[50]

Nell dazzled the Russian Court by night and wrote furiously by day, all the while missing George. Their immediate families, and George's closest friends in the Souls, were the few exceptions to the rule that they conduct their relationship in secret. Curzon had met Clayton and Nell's mother at Lamberts several times before Nell left to visit the Romanov Court. References to "her friend" and "Lord C" peppered her letters from Russia to her mother. As became heart-sickeningly clear, Clayton seemed to embrace tacitly his wife's affair for the financial assistance it might bring.

Luckily, Nell was wrong about *His Hour*. The novel cemented her reputation as an author who "knows everyone, sees everything, goes everywhere and is, as becomes the sister for the inimitable Lucile of Hanover Square, a connoisseur in gowns as well emotions." "'His Hour' is a sexual novel. It is magnificently sexual," announced the novelist and influential critic Arnold Bennett, in a review about this difficult romance between the English widow Tamara and the Russian prince Gritzko. Gritzko wanted Tamara, "with the extreme of amorous passion," Bennett concluded after extensive quoting from the book. To overcome her doubts about his suitability, Gritzko led Tamara "to believe that he had raped her. She, being an English widow, moving in the most refined circles, naturally regarded the outrage as an imperious reason for accepting his hand." Bennett praised the circulation libraries' decision to let *His Hour* sit on their shelves (though he suspected the reason was Glyn's lengthy dedication to her "G.D."). Above all, he hoped that the choice signaled a loosening of the stays strangling the subject of sex on the page.[51]

Whether critics praised or damned the book (and many considered it further evidence of Nell's "sad deterioration" into "the morbid preoccupation with sensuality in the modern school"), they found the hero and Russian setting too compelling to ignore. Several likened Gritzko to Byron, the Romantic poet and beautiful Lord famously called "mad, bad and dangerous to know" by one of his many lovers. Griztko's wild exhibition of aristocratic privilege was the polar opposite of the hypercontrolled George.

But the novel seemed to capture Nell's own discomfort at finding herself in love with a man she could not trust. "Mrs. Glyn is a realist," wrote Sidney Dark in the *Daily Express*. "She realizes . . . that the real things are not always the 'nice' things. . . . As one reads, one thinks all the time of Versailles before the Revolution, with its elegant, immoral aristocrats dancing while their doom was being prepared. I have always been skeptical about the possibility of a Russian revolution. But Mrs. Glyn has almost persuaded one it is inevitable."[52]

The *Academy* detested the novel, but conceded Glyn expertly exploited the commercial logic that had taken the publishing world by storm. "Tempting exotic fare" like *His Hour* held an "irresistible appeal" for so many different kinds of readers looking for a guidebook about how the modern heart worked, the journal groaned. "To fathers who delight in sacrificing their leisure hours to eliminating those books which they consider unsuitable for their daughters' perusal; to wives anxious to solve the riddle of why their husbands have fallen so short of their youthful romantic ideals; to daughters who long to lift the veil which hides the great mystery of their dreams and desires; and to younger sons, who, about to enter the field of amorous adventures for the first time, desire to carry with them an air of experience and long acquaintance with the charms and weaknesses of the opposite sex."[53]

As Gritzko stirred readers' pulses, Nell received more bad news from the beleaguered Walters: Clayton should leave the country, he advised. Otherwise, Walters feared he might face arrest because of another batch of his debts incurred for secretly purchased alcohol and gambling forays that Nell could not, or would not, pay. The remaining record makes it impossible to say which, for certain, but suggests that Nell thought settling these debts would force the sacrifice of comforts she deemed essential for the girls and herself. Juliet stayed in boarding school at Eastbourne, but the rest of the family headed across the Channel, where Nell deposited her mother, Margot, and Clayton—now bloated nearly beyond recognition by drink and failing health—in Saint-Raphaël, a medieval fishing village that had become a popular seaside resort for tourists like so many towns along the Côte d'Azur. Then she turned around and headed back to London in hopes of seeing George.

They met at a favorite trysting spot upstairs at the Cavendish Hotel (still known today as the Elinor Glyn Room). The hotel was well known in rarefied circles for such intimate tête-à-têtes since many respectable women still preferred this ambience for a private meeting with a man to the more public space of supper clubs.[54]

At the end of the night George told Nell they must end things as "Lovers & be only tender friends." She had provoked jealous barbs from the female Souls, who thought him too distracted by her charms. His servants chattered about them, he explained; he knew his valet read every letter that she sent. Worst of all, their affair had disturbed his peace of mind and diverted him from his important work.[55]

So Nell took the emerald earrings George offered as a parting gift and left the hotel by way of its secret exit through the stable yard. She walked "out into the darkness full of troubles all alone," wondering how "two people the very night of causing each other to flame with passionate desire" could "suddenly be friends."[56]

Nell left England and headed back to France. "The atmosphere of Paris suits me, here, & in Russia, there are no quaintly jealous women. They understand & appreciate what they are good enough to call my 'esprit,'" she wrote from the city that offered the best location to try to patch her broken ego back together. She sat in the familiar hotel room "like a person risen from the dead," troubled by how little she had learned from her past lives about love.[57]

Then she went to the Louvre and wandered among the ancient Greek deities until she found Aphrodite, the goddess of love, beauty, and desire. Two thousand years before on the tiny, sun-bleached island of Milos "her divine face, her column of a throat, her perfectly set head" had looked out across the Aegean Sea that gave her birth. Now tourists thronged about her feet in a cool marble hall, gazing up at the breasts that pointed toward the heavens beyond the vaulted ceiling. "What can life mean for us modern people—was she, this Venus, ever storm tossed by love & tortured even as I? No," Nell decided, "she could not have been."[58]

"The part that hurt most of all," was that "there was no thought of me—no tender regret that you must cause me pain—No wonder as to whether it would be good or bad for me—Simply no single thought but that—*it must be*, because it was best *for you*." Byron's Don Juan was right, she decided: Man's love is of man's life a part; it is a woman's whole existence. "And the greater the man the greater the selfishness in him," she argued. "I cannot conceive of any possible combination of circumstances which could cause me to be indifferent to the effect of any action of mine upon you—or cause me to calculate what was best for *my* life & *my* work, & *my* ambition to do my duty, regardless of any thought for you—But I love you not *because* of your noble mind, your greatness—Nor *in spite* of your selfishness—but just because I do—& you are you."[59]

After regaining her equilibrium a bit, Nell joined her family in Saint-Raphaël. Determined to prove her intelligence to George, she returned to writing *Halcyone*, a novel that had preoccupied her on and off for the last three years. It would be one of her worst. The impossibly pure and penniless heroine, Halcyone, incessantly quotes

Greek philosophy and communes with tree spirits while her arrogant, thoughtless lover, John Derringham (modeled on George, of
course), equivocates over whether to marry irritating Halcyone or an
insufferable rich American who cares only for his title.

Nell made a friend in Saint-Raphaël, the metaphysician
F. H. Bradley, who explained *Halcyone*'s particularly learned tone.
The greatest English philosopher of his generation, Bradley had
trained as a classicist before becoming the most original and influential of the British idealists. The mind more fundamentally ordered
the universe than matter, he argued. Reality was spiritual, and feelings captured reality better than thought. Nell's reading in New
Thought philosophy, a branch of idealism that emphasized its practical application, prepared her for their talks. Bradley gave Nell a
system in which to place the spiritual beliefs that she had been wres-
tling with for years.[60]

Never married and twenty years older than Nell, Bradley became
another of her "antiques," as Clayton had long ago nicknamed the
series of influential older men whose devotion Nell collected the way
George amassed country houses. Bradley was the model for Arnold
Carlyon, the Oxford don who tutors young Halcyone after deciding
she is that rare thing: a woman who possesses a soul. Carlyon was far
and away the novel's most interesting character. The two exchanged
books. Bradley read *His Hour* while Nell pored over his masterwork,
Appearance and Reality (1896).[61]

She wished George could see her here, walking though the
purple-and-green wooded hills beside a sea that turned ultrama-
rine at the horizon, discussing love, reincarnation—they were both
believers—and philosophy with one of the era's greatest intellects.
"Would it make any difference in my value for you?" she wondered.
Would it change his mind?

Then a letter arrived that made her heart race and her hands turn
cold. George wrote that he had hosted some friends for a Saturday
to Monday at Hackwood House but felt only exhausted when they
left. The pains in his back were so bad that he could not sleep at all.
Hackwood whispered constantly to him of joyous times spent there
with her. He did not write "I miss you," or "I made a mistake," but he
said it all the same.

When Christmas came a few days later she had a vision of George while she sat beside Margot in a small French church while an old English parson "discoursed upon the graves of loved ones far away." She saw George in the private chapel at Hackwood House, dressed in a gray overcoat. His head drooped and his face bore no trace of his usual arrogance. And she knew that she would write to say that she wanted only to see him again.[62]

Nell returned to London with Margot a few weeks later to learn from Lucy that Clayton had another "bill out to the Jews" that her sister had paid. "Lucy has been most kind but she has a way of doing kindness[es] that doesn't always make one feel happy about them. However until I can work to pay it all back there is no use thinking about it. She has been most kind," Nell wrote to their mother.[63]

By the time a friend or relation or her pen cleared one debt, her husband confessed to another obligation taken out in secret. This time Curzon made the £1,200 loan that saved them, after extracting a written oath from Clayton that he would never resort to such desperate measures again. It is easy to speculate that any tender feelings that might have lingered in Nell toward Clayton would have ended with the loan. Since everyone knew Clayton could never repay George, it likely felt like her husband had extracted a price from her lover for keeping quiet about their affair.

Desperate to repay her sister and lover, Nell appealed for work to her friend Ralph Blumenfeld, the editor of the *Daily Express*. Blumenfeld promised £1,000 if she delivered a new novel to begin serialization in eighteen days. *The Reason Why* (1911) was the result; Nell always called the novel her worst. "When I have finished this lurid tale for the *Express* I have to have a week's rest and begin on *Halcyone* again—I have four chapters but that has to be finished by 11 June." Although padded and formulaic, *The Reason Why*'s heroine, Zara—another exotic, bitter beauty married off to ensure her family's financial security—was more engaging than the pretentious Halcyone. When *The Reason Why* became a bestseller Nell learned that how much pain she took with her words mattered little to the bottom line.[64]

That spring she and Margot spent several weeks motoring through Italy while Juliet remained in boarding school. Her mother stayed with Clayton, abetting his accumulation of debt. "He wrote me a letter proving himself an injured creature and plainly proving a 'wife with a motor car and smart clothes' must be at fault and that everyone would say so. The hideous injustice of it leaves me wordless," she wrote in a rare show of anger. "If you read his letter you would think it was an injured angel with an extravagant wife who took all and left him without enough to buy his enlarged boots for his illness with. I have grown into a stone."[65]

In 1912 she leased "a tiny house on Green Street" in London and tried to bring Margot out to society as best she could, presenting her at Court that year. She hoped that having her own house would provide the kind of privacy that would attract her distant lover. But George barely visited the house on Green Street. Obsessed with making his way back into the political thicket, he was busy fighting a losing battle to prevent the Liberal Party from abolishing the House of Lords' absolute veto power on new legislation.[66]

But the couple continued their tucked-away lunches and dinners. They spent the occasional long weekend together, usually in the company of their girls (who acted as chaperones, likely for the benefit of his servants). One weekend at Hackwood House, Curzon humored Nell's interest in Spiritualism, inviting a well-known Russian medium, an older "peasant woman," whom Margot remembered "smelt very strong" of drink. The girls became close. Curzon's daughters—Irene, Cynthia, and Alexandra—treated Nell like the surrogate mother, or close aunt, they did not have. The following year, she traded the small house for a suite at the Ritz, whose anonymous staff made it the most discreet address in London.[67]

However hard to pin down, her lover asked the brilliant Hungarian-Jewish portrait artist, Philip de László, to paint his lady-love in 1913. De László had moved from Vienna to London in 1907 after promising his wife, Lucy Guinness of the banking family, to raise their children as Anglicans. Conveniently, painter John Singer Sargent's retirement that same year left an opening for someone to capture the era's most formidable figures on canvas. De László took the job. "Has any one painter ever before painted so many interesting and historical personages?" wondered his great patron, Lord Selborne.[68]

Nell asked de László to pose her on a tiger skin that matched her hair. "If you knew the strange effect tiger skins have on me! The touch of the tiger awakens some far-off savagery—some former life when I was unhampered and could kill—or love—when I desired, without having to consider civilization. Now I am in a cage and live off bread and milk, and wear sapphires," she explained.

Although de László evaded her request, the finished portrait possessed an unusual intensity that the painter called "diabolic." Nell appears as part regal author, part visionary exotic—just "the persona, the mask" she wanted the world to see, as one critic noted. Age fifty, she sits on a thronelike chair in front of a velvet drape the color of dried blood, wearing a peacock-blue brocade cape and matching gown, clasping a book in her right hand. The dark surroundings emphasize her pale neck and copper-colored hair, wound around her head like a crown. A sapphire-and-diamond *tikka*—jewelry often worn by Hindu and Buddhist Indian brides—sits at her third eye. A gift from Curzon, the *tikka* symbolized the ideal fusion of male and female in the tantric system.

This tacit acknowledgment of her relationship with India's former viceroy likely also accounted for why the unusually vivid portrait became "A VERY MUCH DISCUSSED PAINTING," reproduced in several society magazines and displayed in the fourth annual exhibition of the National Portrait Society in London. "Elinor Glyn is an enigma, and so is the picture," observed one critic. Curzon called it "a masterpiece of modern times" and a "superlative likeness."[69]

Nell had finally experienced the kind of passion about which she had dreamed and written for so long. She would not trade the experience for anything but had learned firsthand what many of her heroines had always suspected: even a true passion could be as transitory as the English sun. Passion had done very little to change the material circumstances of her life for the better. That had been left to her and her alone.

She felt so much world-wearier now, as her family's ever-hazardous financial situation left her always furiously writing to pay the bills. *Halcyone* appeared in 1912, followed by three more books in 1913:

The Contrast and Other Stories, The Point of View, and *The Sequence.*
She learned to worship "the new God of Money," as she ruefully
recalled. "Society, in the old meaning of the word, still existed," she
wrote of these years immediately before the Great War. "But it was
no longer the fairy ring within which danced a circle of families
entitled to enjoy its privileges on account of birth and tradition"
alone.[70]

Yet the accident of birth still defined expectations about how to
behave when disaster struck, as Lucy and her husband, Sir Cosmo
Duff-Gordon, learned while traveling aboard the *Titanic* on its
maiden voyage. The old order's utter purchase on the levers of society may have been slipping, but everyone would soon see how much
force they still carried after the tragedy exposed how unprepared the
British elite were to handle the enormous challenges that lay ahead.

CHAPTER 9

Surviving the Worst

A great liner stealing through the vast loneliness of the Atlantic, the sky jeweled with myriads of stars overhead, and a thin little wind blowing cold and ever colder straight from the frozen ice fields, tapping its warning of approaching danger on the cosily shuttered portholes of the cabins, causing the look-out man to strain his eyes anxiously into the gloom. Inside this floating palace warmth, lights and music, the flutter of cards, the gay lilt of a German *valse*—the unheeding sounds of a small world bent on pleasure. Then disaster, swift and overwhelming, turning all into darkness and chaos, the laughing voices changed into shuddering wails of despair—a story of horror unparalleled in the annals of the sea.

—Lucy Duff-Gordon, *Discretions and Indiscretions* (1932)

It isn't likely I shall ever forget the screams of these people as they perished in water said to be 28 degrees. At this point I was being brought up as a typical British kid. You were not allowed to cry. So as a cool kid I lay down in the bottom of the lifeboat and went to sleep.

—Recollection of an eight-year-old *Titanic* survivor

—Was this story about Sir Cosmo Duff-Gordon the only story that was set on foot about the people on board the ship?
—That is all, Sir, the cowardice and the money. It was the only story that was in the papers.

—British wreck commissioner's inquiry into the *Titanic* disaster, July 1912

While Nell fretted about her lover and how to pay the bills, Lucy and her husband, Sir Cosmo Duff-Gordon, survived an ordeal—the sinking of the RMS *Titanic*—that foreshadowed the appalling scope of things to come when the Great War began two years later.

The *Titanic* disaster exposed the hollow core at the center of Britannia's claim "to rule the waves." Incompetence, poor training, and hubris set the stage for this catastrophe and the next. Yet many newspapers charged that the Duff-Gordons illustrated the worst problems the calamity exposed. Their public vilification—as the cowardly baronet and his too-ambitious, showy wife—displayed how much expectations for their sort remained the same since Victorian times in spite of the all the modernizing forces that drove the luxurious steamship across the North Atlantic.

Long before she stepped aboard the *Titanic*, Lucy had earned a reputation as the "naturally brave one" in the family, according to her instinctively cautious little sister. A "terrible tomboy," who "had absolutely no fear of anything of earth, I could climb trees that very few of the boys could climb," Lucy boasted in her memoir. "My love for dolls was my only feminine trait at that time, and I was secretly sensitive about it, as it gave the boys, whom I envied with all my heart, a chance to tease me."[1]

A shipwreck the family endured returning to Jersey in 1875 tested Lucy's mettle early on. When they encountered "a dreadful winter gale," their small vessel struck "the famous Casquets rocks," where it hung "battered on every side by the huge waves," Nell recalled. "To be wrecked on the Casquets is to be cut to ribbons," wrote novelist Victor Hugo, who lived for decades near the long sandstone ridge that arched above the Channel. "Rockets were sent up but as there was no wireless signalling in those days, we had no reason to be sure that our plight was known," Nell continued. "My mother held us silently by the hand, too well drilled by Grandmamma to show the slightest fear, although several of the other passengers were screaming." Lucy "was not a bit afraid, and I believe she even thought it all a great adventure," her sister admiringly observed. "But I was filled with a kind of superstitious terror," she admitted. "In my pagan imagination, storms and disasters signified the anger of the gods, and I did not believe we should be saved."[2]

Lady Lucy Duff-Gordon, known professionally as Lady Duff or simply Lucile, was the most famous woman aboard the *Titanic* when the world's largest moving object set sail on April 11, 1912. Lucile had become the most quoted, photographed, and perhaps criticized couturier of the day, and still the lone woman in the field. There was little competition for distinction among the women on board the luxury liner's first and final voyage. In total, two-thirds of the paying travelers, and all but 23 of the ship's 685 crew, were men. Even the wealthiest woman in this largely male world—Madeline Astor, the nineteen-year-old second bride of the richest passenger, John Jacob Astor IV—was known as so-and-so's wife.

Lucy had not traveled on one of Britain's ever more opulent, oceangoing steamers since opening her salon in New York the previous year. But now urgent business called her to New York from Paris, where she was opening the third branch of Lucile Ltd. in the heart of enemy territory.

Lucy was not a woman prone to premonitions. That was Nell's territory. But she had experienced an immediate and lingering resistance to sailing on the *Titanic*'s maiden voyage. Sir Cosmo decided to accompany his nervous wife on the last-minute trip in the gallant manner befitting "the finest dueller in England." (He had silvermedaled at the Athens Olympics of 1906.) No lover of the sea, this was his first Atlantic crossing. Once on board, "nothing could persuade me to completely undress at night," Lucy later claimed. "The fact remains that though I have crossed the Atlantic many times both before and since I have never had [this feeling] on any other occasion. Something warned me, some deep instinct, that all was not well."[3]

Lucy boarded Lifeboat 1 one hour and thirty minutes after an iceberg sliced open the so-called unsinkable *Titanic* like a can opener. It was 1:10 in the morning, and the boat was already listing to the port side and down at the bow. In another hour the great ship would split in two and head toward the bottom of the sea. There were 2,200 people aboard and lifeboat seats for 1,170 passengers, at most. The *Carpathia* would pick up barely 700 survivors after dawn.

Lucy had "absolutely refused to be separated" from her husband until this point, as she wrote to her family after finally arriving safe on land. She and her twenty-nine-year-old private secretary Laura Francatelli, whom Lucy called Franks, had each grabbed one of Cosmo's arms when the crew pressured them to join the women and children being herded off the ship. Then Cosmo saw a "small row boat" with seven seamen aboard preparing to depart and "asked if we

Rendering of the *Titanic*'s lifeboats being picked up by the *Carpathia*, 1912

might all get in." "Please do," the officer replied, likely because "there were no women and children about anywhere," as Lucy explained to her family. Two more American men got in before the crew started lowering the tiny craft down the seven stories that separated the boat deck from the water.[4]

Lifeboat 1 was among the first half-dozen boats launched after the ship hit the iceberg while traveling at top speed just before midnight. Smaller than the proper lifeboats, it was one of two emergency woodcutters kept ready to rescue someone fallen overboard. Many passengers huddled on the decks were reluctant to trade the enormous ship for a small boat that would be lowered slowly, unsteadily down into the night.

From above, the few boats already floating on the glassy water would have looked like teacups bobbing in the vast, dark sea. Like all the boats launched from the starboard first-class deck, Lifeboat 1 held less than 50 percent of its capacity (12 of 40 seats). But this particular craft was also unusually full of men (10 of 12 passengers).

On the way down there was "an anxious moment" when "one of the ropes stuck." Already packed with four sets of oars, the small craft went terribly askew. A lifeboat drill had been canceled the day before; now the crew struggled to control the boats descending from the crooked ship. The most experienced sailor at the task filled no boat to capacity until the very last ones, for fear they would split in two. We "were nearly falling out of the boat into the water," Lucy recalled, "and then someone cut something from above," the boat evened out and finished its descent. As the men rowed away from the ship, Lucy felt seasick and promptly vomited down her moleskin coat. Then a cry from Cosmo drew her attention back to the water:

"My God! She is going now!"

   I turned and saw the few remaining lights of the *Titanic* shining with steady brilliance, but only for a moment, and then they were gone. A dull explosion shook the air. From the doomed vessel there arose an indescribable clamour; I think that it was only at that moment that many of those poor souls on board realized their fate. A louder explosion followed and the stern of the great ship shot upwards out of the water. For a few seconds she stayed motionless while the agonised cries from her decks grew in intensity; then, with one awful downward rush she plunged to her grave through fathoms of water, and the air was rent with those awful shrieks. Then silence, which I felt I could not bear; I felt my very reason tottering. I lapsed into unconsciousness, from which I was aroused by a dreadful paroxysm of sea-sickness, which persisted at intervals through the rest of the night. Between bouts of my horrible sickness I could see the dark shadows of icebergs surrounding us.

That description was as close as Lucy ever came to admitting that she lost her cool when the great ship went down.[5]

   The day after arriving in New York, she wrote a letter home. "You know how I have always said I longed for adventures and sensations. Well I have had it this time and no mistake," she wrote her family. "The only part that was *personally* awful was my seasickness when we were afloat on the ocean. . . . Such a sight of course I hope I shall never see again and the horror *horror* of the poor drowning creatures' cries. . . . It was a weird sensation—us all alone in a little boat out on the Atlantic in the black darkness and no one near watching for a light—but I was never for a moment afraid and knew we would be rescued." Now Lucy was "very tired," she conceded, and had closeted herself inside the hotel suite to focus on the work that had called her to New York.[6]

Nell's vision had been vindicated. She had insisted to their mother that Lucy would turn up even when the Duff-Gordons—traveling under a different name to avoid publicity—were not at first listed among the saved.[7]

And then another kind of storm washed over Lucy and Cosmo. Before leaving the *Carpathia* Lucy had asked the crew to sign her lifebelt as a keepsake to carry home. Someone snapped a photograph of the group grimly standing together on the deck. "LADY DUFF GORDON GOT SOUVENIR NAMES ON HER LIFE BELT," headlines sneered. Shortly before the *Carpathia* had reached land, Cosmo had pressed the £5 checks he had promised to the crewmembers on Lifeboat 1 while they were all waiting for rescue that night. They would need to replace the sailors' kits they had lost to the sea to get new work, Cosmo explained.[8]

"TALE OF 'THE MONEY BOAT,'" newspaper accounts shrieked as a story about Sir Cosmo bribing his way to safety surfaced the class tensions swirling around the lists of names of those who had drowned and those who were saved. Contrary to public expectations, many poor children had died, while most wealthy men disembarked in New York physically unscathed.

Some of the Duff-Gordons' trouble originated with an interview Lucy had given to Clem Edwards, a reporter she knew through her work as a fashion columnist for America's most successful newspaper magnate, William Randolph Hearst. Edwards had appeared at a dinner at the Ritz that Lucy's friends had planned after retrieving the couple and Franks from the dock. The fanciful tale Clem Edwards spun—under Lucy's signature—focused on her unseemly happiness over their survival.[9]

Not all publicity was good publicity, and no value carried quite the same cruel report as courage and its consort, cowardice, Lucy and Cosmo learned as reporters found a hook to hang the tragedy around their posh necks. "RESCUE STOPPED BY DUFF-GORDONS" and "SIR COSMO OPPOSED SEA RESCUE," learned newspaper readers across the globe. The Duff-Gordons became the only civilians called before

THE ATLANTA GEORGIAN AND NEWS: MONDAY

SIR COSMO DIDN'T THINK OF LIVES OF DROWNING

Possibility of Saving Titanic's Victims Never Occurred to Duff Gordon, He Admits.

LONDON, May 20.—Prominent society people, including members of the nobility, turned out again in full force today for the government's inquiry into the Titanic disaster. The attraction was the presence of Sir Cosmo and Lady Duff-Gordon at the hearing, and the introduction of further evidence relating to their behavior at the time of the disaster.

Among the members of the nobility present were Prince Albert of Schleswig Holstein and Prince Leopold of Battenberg.

Sir Cosmo was recalled and questioned keenly by Sir Rufus Isaacs, the attorney general.

"I don't know what officer told me to get into the lifeboat," said Sir Cosmo in answer to a question. "From what I have learned since I believe that it was Fifth Officer Lowe. I did not know Lowe and I have been told that he approached my wife and asked: 'Are you ready to leave, Lady Duff-Gordon?' but I did not hear this."

Sir Cosmo was questioned closely as to when he had offered each member of the crew manning the lifeboat a five-pound (£25) note. The witness was a little vague on this subject. Referring to his escape from the ship, he said:

Saw No Others Near Empty Lifeboat.

"I simply saw an empty lifeboat, and as I had two ladies with me I asked the officer in charge whether I could accompany them. There were no other passengers near, so far as I could see."

Sir Cosmo said he did not hear any order given on board the ship that women and children should be saved first.

While the witness was testifying dispute arose between counsel as to the nature of the questions, and Attorney Henry Duke, counsel for the Duff-Gordons, served notice that he intended to call Duff-Gordon to the stand to refute reports which had been circulated about her.

Witness pleaded faulty memory when asked whether he could hear the cries of passengers in the water pleading to be saved.

"It never occurred to me that we could save anybody," began the witness. When one of the lawyers angrily broke in with "you considered when you had saved yourself that all others might perish? Do you think that question fair?" asked Lord Mersey. "This witness's position is bad enough now."

"I intend to press that question," answered the lawyer, at which there was a burst of applause from the crowded galleries.

Denies Trying To Bribe Sailors To Row.

Mr. Harbinson, a lawyer representing families of some of the third steerage passengers, wanted to know if anyone in the lifeboat had given orders or made suggestions what to do. The witness replied that one man gave orders all night. Then Harbinson wanted to know if Sir Cosmo's offer of £35 to each member of the crew had any effect.

"Why don't you put your questions plainly?" demanded Lord Mersey. "Here is what you want to say," and then turning to the witness, Lord Mersey demanded: "Did you promise the seamen rowing your lifeboat five pounds apiece to row away from drowning people?"

Sir Cosmo's face blanched, but before he could reply Harbinson was on his feet.

"That is precisely what I wanted to say," he cried.

"Then, why didn't you say it?" queried the presiding judge while applause again rippled over the galleries.

Sir Cosmo denied that he had bribed the boatmen and he also denied testimony that he had made arrangements with Ismay to have a lifeboat put at his personal service.

Lady Duff-Gordon followed her husband on the witness stand. She declared that it was not a question of choice with her about getting into a lifeboat. She said a seaman picked her up and pitched her bodily into the boat.

LOCAL GARMENT WORKERS TO SPEND DAY AT FALLS

Factories in Atlanta employing members of the United Garment Workers of

---

Big M. E. Conference Is Working Overtime To Elect 7 Bishops

MINNEAPOLIS, MINN., May 20.—With only eight days left in which to wind up its business, the general conference of the Methodist Episcopal church today began what was expected to be the busiest week of the session. Seven bishops must be elected before adjournment, May 28. The secretaries of the benevolent boards must be selected, the editors of the official church papers named, the agents of the book concern chosen and three-fourths of the work of the conference transacted. Of the 75 reports of committees so far received in the conference only sixteen have been acted upon. Some of the questions still to come up will call for lively debate, and if the conference fails to dispose of all the business before adjournment today it is believed the length of the sessions will be increased.

The sixth ballot for bishop, ended Saturday night, is to be counted this morning. It is expected that the result will be announced at noon. There was much speculation among the delegates as to the possible effect the stand of the candidates for the bishopric on the amusement question might have on their election.

Nine of the twelve candidates voted to eliminate the dancing clause of the Discipline. The majority of delegates voted for its retention.

INDIAN DOCTOR HAD NO LICENSE

An Osage Indian, giving his name as Dr. G. L. Gray, of Oklahoma City, Okla., who recently came to Atlanta and opened offices in room 21, Inman building, is behind the bars at police station in default of $500 bond and must answer to Recorder Broyles for posing as a physician and practicing here without a license. Detectives Coker and Hamby say Gray has admitted to them that he is not a doctor, although at first he protested that his business was perfectly legitimate.

Gray advertised himself as an Osage Indian specialist, and is said to have done an extensive business. Detectives confiscated a lot of medicines in his office, and, among other things, found a bottle of green fluid, which, they say, is nothing more nor less than knockout drops.

The arrest of the "doctor" followed complaint by Fayne Almond, a farmer living near Oakland City, who was one of his patients. Almond says he came to Atlanta with $100 and that he had only $12 when the Indian specialist finished with him. Almond was stopping at the Randolph House, and when he moved from there he drove to the Gate City hotel. Gray is said to have led the patient to believe he would be taken to his mother's home.

Judge Broyles today fixed Gray's bond at $500, and set the preliminary hearing for Saturday morning.

DEMOCRACY'S MEET AT HA[...]

Debutante Daughters of Democrats Take Leading Part in Notable Gathering.

WASHINGTON, May 21.—The wives and daughters of Democratic leaders assembled at a harmony breakfast today in honor of the memory of Dolly Madison. The guest of honor was Mrs. Mary Cutts Craig, a granddaughter of Mrs. Madison's young sister, Anna Payne.

The decoration scheme and the menu served in every possible way to revive the "Dolly Madison" atmosphere. The breakfast, the women of the national Democracy declared, signified the "unification of the Democratic party."

The guests at the party included descendants of presidents and vice presidents. Prominent women present were Mrs. Woodrow Wilson, Mrs. Oscar Underwood, Mrs. Champ Clark, Mrs. William Randolph Hearst, Mrs. Judson Harmon, Mrs. Henry D. Clayton, Mrs. Norman E. Mack, Mrs. Grover Cleveland and others.

Prominent among the debutante daughters of Democratic leaders were Mrs. Lucy Hoke Smith, of Atlanta, and Miss Genevieve Clark, daughter of Champ Clark.

$100 Worth of Good Time Gone
GINGERCAKE HICKS DID IT

Clarence Herman Hicks is only ten years old and black as a burnt gingercake, and his whole attire wouldn't weigh eighteen ounces or bring eight cents at an auction, but he cost Atlanta business men $100 worth of time, delayed traffic in Peachtree street twenty minutes and nearly ruined the day's business for a restaurant. And he did it all by falling off a trolley car.

them are loafers, but there are bankers, brokers, lawyers and merchants in the bunch. Average them up as being worth 50 cents an hour. There's $81 worth of good time gone.

The trolley conductor and motorman lost five minutes each getting a record of the accident, and the passengers were delayed. Twenty-eight automobiles stopped and the chauffeurs climbed out to find what the excitement

---

BIG [...]

The Ch[...] announced [...] vested in [...] The prob[...] vested in [...] done in [...] will be car[...] thing at [...] nection an[...] be asked [...] Not onl[...] fine cattle [...] various a[...] South are [...] Only po[...] erected on [...] grass leade[...] will be ad[...] structed u[...] positions [...] from all o[...] The pla[...] in the So[...] which the [...] Indi[...] To estab[...] convention

---

Duff-Gordons branded cowards in the *Titanic* aftermath

the British Board of Shipping's inquiry held in London into the causes of the disaster. During the inquiry, two sailors from Lifeboat 1 testified that Lady Duff-Gordon had protested a suggestion to row back to help those freezing to death in the arctic waters. Lucy worried that their boat might be swamped, the two men claimed.

From the witness box, Lucy denied such a conversation ever took place, though she admitted her acute seasickness made it hard to remember much but the sound of the oars. The other seven sailors aboard reported that no one mentioned returning to help.[10]

The man in charge of the boat, George Symons, also denied that Lucy had ordered them to abandon the drowning. A twenty-four-year-old lookout, Symons said that "using [his] own discretion," he had decided it was too risky to head back toward the cries. The Board of Trade lawyer, Mr. Scanlan, pressed Symons to admit this decision impugned the honor of all aboard.

—Did you attribute to cowardice the fact that your passengers did not all ask you to go back?

—No, Sir. I never had a thought in my head of cowardice.

—Looking back on this whole incident, and considering that you had a boat practically empty, with only five passengers, and accommodation for fifteen or twenty more, was it not cowardice that prevented the passengers and the crew from going back?

—No, I cannot see that.

—Can you give any other account? Can you account for it in any other way except by the exercise of what you are pleased to call your discretion?

—That is right, Sir. That is the only thing I can see.

—You admit it was cowardly?

—No, I do not admit it was cowardly.

—Is not a seaman, when the passengers in his boat are in danger, expected to run risks in order to save life?

—Quite so.

—The Commissioner: This is mere argument, Mr. Scanlan.

—Mr. Scanlan: I shall not press it further, My Lord.

—The Commissioner: Have a little mercy on the man.[11]

Class mattered a great deal to who survived the accident. Then, as now, chiefly for the access it provided. Then, as now, children felt the yawning differences calibrated to its effects most acutely. Two-thirds of the children traveling third class perished in the icy water, while all the others on board survived. Men of Sir Cosmo's class survived at more than the rate of men traveling second and third class combined. But the shipping industry's appalling safety standards explained the locked gates between the decks that separated the classes, the canceled lifeboat drill, and the fact that there were too few lifeboats to fill.[12]

In the end, only one boat returned to help the drowning. "Did you return to the wreckage immediately after the 'Titanic' had disappeared?" Senator Smith asked Harold Lowe, the Welsh first officer who sailed his boat back toward the cries. "I did not," Lowe replied at the American inquiry. "Had you any reason for not doing so?" continued the senator. "I had." "Would you mind telling me what it was?" "Because it would have been suicide to go back there until the people had thinned out," Lowe answered with characteristic directness, "a drowning man clings at anything." Picking his way through the floating bodies, Lowe found just four men still alive. After being fished out of the water, one of them promptly died of shock.[13]

It is impossible to know the full story of what occurred in Lifeboat 1 that night, but a few things are clear. Lucy was profoundly shocked by the circumstances in which she found herself. Her reason tottered. Then she likely did what many trauma victims who succeed in moving on used to do; she scrubbed her memory of the event as clean as she could. "Since being safe on land, I am afraid I am a coward, my nerves had gone, but I do not show it, as I am constantly battling with it," wrote Lucy's secretary Franks to a coworker days after the disaster. "Poor Madame gets worse, every day since we have been here, but she was so brave, & calm all through it. I have never imagined anybody so wonderful, but now unfortunately the reaction, so you see, we have not seen anything of New York, hardly been out of the bedrooms & Sitting room of the Hotel."[14]

To be "THE WOMAN WHO ROWED AWAY FROM THE DROWNING" was to reveal the "monster" who lived inside, according to the author of one of the many books published on the disaster's centennial,

repeating the accusation first hurled a century before. Like those
of the past, this present-day account seemed to delight in cutting
this "fashionable, exotic, and more than a little bit showy" woman—"whose ambition knew no bounds"—down to size.[15]

The more things change, the more remains the same. Or as Lucy
put it on the first page of the autobiography that she published the
year before her death: "I do not think that, on the whole, it is good
for a woman to have temperament. It is much better for her to be
[a] vegetable, and certainly much safer, but I have never had that
choice."[16]

Cowardice was, however, to be expected from a woman. "WOMEN
OF THE TITANIC: WHY THE DROWNING WERE NOT RESCUED," intoned
Lord Northcliffe's *Daily Mail*, Britain's bestselling newspaper that
"ruled England," according to the *New Yorker*. "Officers failed to go
to the rescue of the drowning people 'because of the ladies,'" the
paper explained in the widely spread "chivalry made them do it"
defense of the men who lived.[17]

But profits continued to pour in at Lucile after the disaster and
her career burned white hot. The shadow the tragedy cast on Lucy's
life was visible in the beginning of her marriage's end and in her
decision to embrace America and avoid London whenever possible.
She had had enough of noblesse oblige to last the rest of her life,
Lucy wrote to her family before beginning a self-imposed exile that
lasted more than a decade, almost entirely without Sir Cosmo by
her side.[18]

Not so for the husband who remained in Britain until he died. A
tall and handsome first-class sportsman, with a dignified bearing and
loads of charm, stepped onto the most splendid, oceangoing vessel
ever built in April 1912. The boat and the man both appeared to be
irrefutable evidence of the British Empire's glory, of how Britannia
had come to rule the waves and the world.

By May, Cosmo Duff-Gordon would be damned for living. At
the inquiry in London, his behavior would be condemned in comparison to men like John Jacob Astor IV, who had gone down with
the ship. (Though only after inquiring if the "delicate condition" of
his young second bride—Madeline was pregnant—might not war-
rant a seat by her side?) Though decisively cleared of bribery charges,

Cosmo was held accountable for tending to his sick wife rather than rousing his fellows to go to the rescue with their lightly filled craft. "According to the way that we have been treated by England on our return we didn't seem to have done the right thing in being saved at all!!! Isn't it disgraceful," Lucy fumed to Nell and her mother.[19]

"Did you, Sir Cosmo Duff-Gordon, on the night of that tremendous tragedy behave as a gentleman or as a coward?" Scanlan demanded at the inquiry that resulted in changes to the shipping industry's safety practices. The answer was clear.[20]

At the inquiry, Cosmo Duff-Gordon stood revealed for who he was: an unusually solicitous husband with little facility for explaining himself, a man whose noblesse oblige led him to believe too little was enough. Cosmo had survived the worst and lost what mattered most. "Now a man can be accused of all sorts of things and get away with them without losing the respect of other men, but call him a coward," Lucy wrote, "and his own kind will turn on him and make him feel it for the rest of his life. At least that is what happened in my husband's case."[21]

This broad commitment to what made a man a gentleman held when the Great War started two years later and younger versions of Sir Cosmo began leading their men out of the trenches, into No-Man's-Land, and to their deaths. Determined to prove their valor as the warrior class, Britain's elite would die proportionally far more than any other social class during the four years of war.[22]

Increasingly heartsick over her gentlemen's conduct, Nell, along with Margot and Juliet, had spent the year before men everywhere started marching to their deaths living in a small apartment on the outskirts of Paris near Nell's beloved Versailles. The official reason for the move was to further Juliet's studies and to introduce Margot, after "coming out" in London the previous year, to the French society her mother knew so well.

But like Lucy, Nell had also wanted to escape England's cold shoulder. Parisians relished a woman skilled at turning heads, and she thought this move just might be for good. "I adore France. France is where my home is. For me France always means exquisite joy. The other places one loves, and one is a patriot for England. But France! France for me means light and joy," she explained in newsprint after the war came.[23]

Paris had also removed Nell and her girls from witnessing Clayton's continued decline. In the Parisian suburbs they could live "peacefully and cheaply" and Nell could "write and have my wits kept up," she explained to her mother before taking the girls across the Channel. "I cannot support anyone if I cannot work and these troubles destroy my power of working."[24]

The dynamic established from the time of her first American tour through the months she spent at the Romanov Court had continued: Clayton spent more than he had and then borrowed at usurious rates; then Nell scrambled to pay off the worst and to keep them in a semblance of the style to which they were all accustomed. The hardest part for Nell was the blame Clayton directed her way for being too extravagant as she bitterly remarked to her mother before nearly begging Elinor Kennedy to take her side as her husband's health bottomed out.[25]

So Nell was in Paris with her girls when war began after seven Serbian nationalist suicide bombers, packets of cyanide in their pockets, set out to assassinate Archduke Franz Ferdinand and his wife, Sophie, during a visit to review military forces stationed in Sarajevo. The largest city in the Balkan territories of Bosnia and Herzegovina—recently annexed by the Austro-Hungarian Empire from the Ottomans—was not a safe place to be for the deeply unpopular heir of the region's latest ruling power. But this summer visit coincided with the fourteenth anniversary since the archduke had defied the emperor's wishes to wed the insufficiently royal Sophie. Determined to celebrate their anniversary openly for the first time, Ferdinand had agreed to the trip since a troop review was the one loophole that permitted a public appearance with his wife.

As they drove from the train station a tossed bomb hit the car behind them. The archduke checked on the injured parties and then proceeded on his way. Sophie calmed her husband when he lost his temper giving a speech before the town hall, and then together they visited the wounded members of their cavalcade at the hospital. She

Nell in 1914, wearing Curzon's jewel-encrusted *tikka* on her forehead

sat next to him as they returned to the train station after the archduke cut the visit short.

"Sophie, Sophie, don't die, stay alive for our children!" he pleaded
after one of the assassins fired a revolver twice from point-blank
range into their automobile. Sophie was likely already dead; minutes later, so was Franz Ferdinand. Within a day, newspapers readers
around the world could recite the archduke's dying words. "It was if
a storm were sweeping through the monarchy," an Austrian newspaper declared, "as if History had inscribed the hideous axiom of a new
epoch with a blood-red pen."[26]

Thirty-seven days later, a war began that ended the Ottoman,
Russian, and Austro-Hungarian Empires and an estimated 20 million military and civilian lives. At minimum, 21 million more people
carried away permanent scars.

The simple cause for the eruption of the greatest catastrophe
yet unleashed by man upon mankind was clear: the assassination
of the archduke on June 28, 1914, led Austro-Hungary to declare
war on Serbia, triggering a set of mutual alliances and secret treaties
that quickly pitted it, Germany, and the Ottoman Empire against
Russia, France, the United Kingdom and all its dominions, including Canada, Australia, and India, the latter of which alone sent
1,250,000 soldiers to the fight.[27]

Deeper explanations for the conflict have set historians arguing ever since, producing debates of remarkable complexity. Most
agree that imperial rivalries to control Africa's and Asia's raw goods
acted as the slower-burning fuse that detonated that August. Quests
for colonies and alliances had generated both a military arms race,
led by a recently unified Germany, and a fetid nationalism that
ensured vanity and national honor would play a starring role in
explaining why so many went to their deaths. Widespread acceptance of a crude kind of social Darwinism—that argued only the
"fittest" races would prevail in the death struggle that was life—had
lent these imperial pursuits the patina of scientific "natural law."
Now they convinced many that the very terms of civilization were
at stake. All this plus a large measure of incompetence made an
Armageddon that was unthinkable to most people just months earlier appear suddenly like fate.[28]

The Great War, as it was called until the outbreak of World War II, would be memorialized for many grisly firsts. Two produced most of the others: it was fought around the globe, another fruit of empire, and with an approach called "total war." Total war obliterated many of the distinctions that had formerly separated military men from civilians. Those who remained behind the lines were now a part of the "home front"—a term first used in 1914—and expected to devote all their energies to winning. Ever more detached and distant ways of killing—machine guns, grenades, submarines, artillery tanks, long-range missiles, Zeppelin balloons, planes, and poison gas—eased the production of indiscriminate carnage of civilian and military populations alike. (The British lost 60,000 men in the first day of the Somme, still a record for the most men killed in a single battle.) Governments on both sides commandeered industry in service of the war effort, rationed almost everything, and began the wholesale conscription of single (and then married) young(ish) men. The assumption of more "male" tasks by the "ladies" and thoroughgoing propaganda campaigns that called any dissent traitorous were also characteristic features.

Germany's brutal invasion and capture of neutral Belgium on August 4 (to get to Paris quickly to try to prevent a two-front war with Russia and France) had early on distilled total war's determination to punish the enemy's entire society. Soon after, the British began a naval blockade to starve the German people into submission using similar logic. Total war quickly demonstrated that almost everyone, under the right conditions, was a war criminal in the making.

Looking back, Nell remarked on "how oddly ignorant we all were of the possibilities of the political situation" during the July before everything changed. Though the "sense of coming calamity was in the air . . . no one appeared to associate it with war." As the days ticked by toward the beginning of France's destruction, the trial of Madame Henriette Caillaux—a former prime minister's wife who had murdered the *Figaro*'s editor for publishing her love letters to another man—dominated French news. Public debate in England remained fixed on the subject of Irish Home Rule even as negotiations between the men at the top heated to a boil. Nell, Margot, and Juliet went to Versailles to watch the fireworks on Bastille Day. The next day *Gil-Blas* reported that the "famous English writer" had staged a reading of her books to a gathering of nobles and prominent society personalities, including Lucy.[29]

Lady Duff-Gordon was in town visiting the Parisian branch of her couture house, which had proved an instant success with visiting Americans, celebrities, and the demimonde. The increasingly introverted Cosmo had largely retreated to his Scottish estate after the *Titanic* disaster. Lucy continued to court the spotlight, turning Lucile into an internationally recognized brand name cultivated through advertising endorsements and regular (ghostwritten) columns on "Lady Duff-Gordon's Latest Styles," for *Good Housekeeping*, *Harper's Bazaar*, and Hearst's newspapers. Booming business at Lucile's couture salons kept her traveling to oversee the artists who now drew many of the designs for the lingerie and dresses inspired by her free-flowing, femininely sexy style.

Living as extravagantly as her celebrity clients, Lady Duff-Gordon was a familiar face throughout Europe and North America as the "Greatest Creator of Fashions in the World" who now kept a string of young, dandyish "assistants" in tow. That year, trouble over Lucy's "boys" caused the Duff-Gordons to separate, personally if not professionally, for the rest of their lives. Lucy stayed in America for the duration of the war, where she opened another branch of Lucile in Chicago that Cosmo and the other directors resisted. The directors wanted her to focus on taking the brand Lucile from the "classes to the masses" through a deal with Sears, Roebuck & Company, which she duly attempted too.[30]

That weekend, the last before the war, they all went to a party at a château outside of Paris. Guests included the Austrian ambassador who caused a mild stir by abruptly departing for Paris. Austro-Hungary declared war on Serbia the next day. Nell had seen Paris first at the dawn of its Belle Epoque. Now she and her girls left just days before the obliteration of that "beautiful age" began. They were lucky to have booked passage across the Channel months earlier in order to attend the regatta at Cowes. As Europe mobilized for war overnight, hotels and businesses closed, the banking system froze, and armies commandeered transportation systems. Weeks later, some 200,000 Americans were stranded all across Europe.[31]

They returned to an England still almost entirely unaware of the real news and to a social class preoccupied by whether to postpone Cowes Week. Less prepared than the other Great Powers, the British would have the most work to do expanding and transforming their military when the United Kingdom declared war on Germany on August 4 for its violation of Belgium's neutrality. Four days later, Parliament hastily passed the Defense of the Realm Act (DORA) without debate, ensuring that anyone caught spying or spreading rumors could be tried in military court. DORA also put all communication systems under the control of the War Office, which imposed draconian censorship measures on the press, making it a crime to "spread reports likely to cause disaffection or alarm among any of His Majesty's forces or among the civilian population."

Although Britain arguably boasted the most powerful organized women's movement (along with the United States), suffragists quickly suspended their campaign for the vote. Parliament set aside the question of Irish Home Rule. "Spy fever" gripped the country, turning its many recent immigrants from Central and Eastern Europe into "enemy aliens."[32]

Nell and her daughters threw themselves into supporting the war when most upper-class women still thought needlework for the cause to be sufficient. Determined to preserve the peace of mind that came with distance from her mother and husband, Nell moved into the London Ritz while the girls settled back in with Elinor Kennedy at her London apartment.

Only fifteen, Juliet lied about her age to join Margot at the Voluntary Aid Department (VAD) doing clerical work. Organized under the Red Cross, the VAD organized tens of thousands of mostly middle- and upper-class British women who donned uniforms to support the war effort by performing tasks that freed men for fighting. Once the endless procession of stretchers started returning, Juliet became an assistant surgical nurse at the London War Hospital.[33]

Nell joined the executive committee of the Women's Emergency Corps, a group of "England's best known women writers," who raised funds to support middle-class women—"actresses, artists, musicians, authors, typists, and short hand writers"—who had lost their jobs. She also worked the midnight shift three nights a week as a bus-girl at a canteen in Grosvenor Gardens that served hot meals to soldiers passing through Victoria Station on their way to the fight. "I was never a good waitress, always stupid and muddling," she admitted, "but I could sweep and clean nicely, and finally became one of the most expert of the washing-up staff."[34]

However poor her waitressing skills, she made an impression on the men she served. "Dear Madam," began a letter that an officer she met there later wrote to her on behalf of the 700 men in his division of the British Expeditionary Forces now stationed at the Western Front. "At the request of the rest of the 'boys' I am asking if you could send us a copy or two of some of your works, for we have all read your book 'Three Weeks' and are admirers of your works," he explained, adding that after having "been out here over a year reading material is hard to get."[35]

During the day, she began the novel that became *The Career of Katherine Bush* (1916). Katherine was Nell's first heroine of lower-middle-class origins, a radical departure for someone who had only written tales about people with pedigrees like the thoroughbred horses they loved. The novel's more democratic tone, and Katherine's preoccupation with making a living as a secretary while educating herself for finer things, matched her times.

In September, a slim set of nonfiction essays entitled *Three Things* appeared that betrayed her growing confidence in speaking directly to her polyglot audience about contemporary social problems. "The Old Order Changeth," the first essay boldly declared, and this would require new approaches to marriage and motherhood if individuals were to achieve "the three essentials to strive after in life. Truth— Common Sense and Happiness." Published in America by William Randolph Hearst's International Library, the book marked Nell's first deal with the publisher who helped to facilitate her emergence as a transatlantic expert on modern romance rather than a scandalous novelist of dubious morals.

Written mostly while living in cynical, sophisticated Paris, *Three Things* emphasized how much had changed for the "modern woman."

Most should expect to get an education and to work; motherhood would be just one element in the lives of many. Man "must learn to treat the modern woman as a comrade," she declared, "a creature to respect and consult, who he cannot rule just because he is a man and she is a woman." Divorce should be made as easy for the so-called masses as it had become (legally at least) for the classes—so long as it was not merely to legitimize an affair.[36]

But however much the circumstances of many women's lives had begun to change, *Three Things* warned readers that men's natures remained the same. Women who forgot that men were still "polyg-amous animals" would only suffer, exposing Nell's hard-won accep-tance that George could no more change his fickle, self-interested ways than a dog could become a cat. She knew that the racy prestige her persona sold—part high society, part exotic sex novelist—had made her "strong enemies among his friends," as she wrote to Margot. The Souls had long whispered to him that marriage to her—were it to become possible—would spoil any chance to escape from the political wilderness in which he had languished for too long.

Now the war had presented the opportunity for Curzon to lead again, as he joined Prime Minister Herbert Asquith's coalition cab-inet and began pressing the indecisive PM to introduce compulsory military service. This gave George even more reason to hold Nell at arm's length. So Nell had recommitted herself to the New Thought teachings she had learned in America, which helped her to "behave with serene dignity" because she trusted "higher forces" would work things out, she reassured her daughter. A favorite medium had coun-seled that her karma was "this strange withholding by fate of hon-ors from those [you] love most." The prophecy did not suggest much improvement in her personal life, but hour-long meditations each day kept her focused on positive thoughts and deeds. Only two things mattered to her now, as she wrote the girls: securing their happiness and spreading messages to help the world survive these times.[37]

"The pleasant prospect you hold out for my sex comes at just the time when everyone is too busy to avail himself of the numer-ous opportunities about," the press baron, Alfred Harmsworth, Lord Northcliffe, joked to Nell in a note confirming *Three Things* would receive a prominent review in his newspapers.[38]

Northcliffe—who published more than a third of the news-print read each day in Britain—had been among a small clutch of Conservatives who had been drumming for years that war with Germany would come. Northcliffe's papers had helped to brand the invasion of neutral Belgium as the "rape of Belgium." He helped to instantly turn "Englishness" into everything "Germanness" was not. By the time *Three Things* was published, just one month into the war, a single issue of Lord Northcliffe's *Daily Mail* called Germany's Kaiser Wilhelm a lunatic, barbarian, madman, monster, modern Judas, and criminal monarch. As Queen Victoria's grandson, the kaiser shared the Hanover family name until the Great War led his cousin, King George V, to adopt the more Anglo-sounding "Windsor." "He has utterly ruined his country and himself," King George wrote. "I look upon him as the greatest criminal ever known for having plunged the world into this ghastly war."[39]

With their circulation soaring to unprecedented levels, news-papers would never be quite so influential again. But attacks on Central Powers leaders and descriptions of the brutality of their armies were about the only war-related topics the British and French censors allowed. All the Allies initially refused to accredit reporters with their armies, instead issuing War Office bulletins about their progress that were as brief as they were vague. The call to patriotism and to aid "little" Belgium helped to reorient a public unprepared for war.

Lord Northcliffe was not impressed by the War Office's efforts to use newspapers to aid recruitment for the kingdom's still volunteer-only forces. "The chief hindrance to recruiting," Northcliffe complained to Prime Minister Asquith, "is where as the German public are supplied with the work of photographers, artists, cinematograph operators, and war correspondents, our people have nothing but the casualty lists and mutilated scraps with which it is impossible to arouse interest or follow the war intelligently."[40]

So when a French propaganda organization asked Nell to return in the summer of 1915 to write articles for the American press, she jumped at the chance to trade the relative security of London for Paris. Six months into the war, some Allied leaders had begun to recognize (as the Germans had from the start) that the press needed to be managed—not simply suppressed—like any other critical resource. Everyone knew the Americans did not want to join the fight. Nell re-crossed the Channel in June determined to help convince them otherwise.

Nell moved into the Ritz rather than living alone in her apartment in the suburbs. Paris was gloomy and quiet. There was no frolicking in the ballroom or along the surrounding streets, which were even darker than London's at night. The capital of all that was unimportant, as the French president Georges Clemenceau once called Paris, had ceased to celebrate life's pleasures.

Yet however different the city appeared, the miracle was that Paris still spoke French. One month into the war, the German Army had been close enough to see the Eiffel Tower. The French government gave up the capital and fled to Bordeaux, but the man left in charge, Gen. Joseph Gallieni, would not abandon the City of Light. Then luck (a map found on a German officer) and technology (the first reconnaissance air flight) told him exactly where to take the fight. Gallieni called up racing cars, private automobiles, buses, and 600 cranky cabbies to convoy 6,000 soldiers—previously ensnarled by the railway system—to a spot where they halted the Germans' heretofore-inexorable advance.

Fought over just three days in September 1914, the First Battle of the Marne was likely the most significant one staged in Europe. Paris's survival forced Germany into a two-front war—against the Russians to the east and the rest of the Allies to the west. Afterward, both sides dug into ever more elaborate networks of fortified trenches separated by No-Man's-Land—the strip of graveyard through which one side periodically tried to advance. Barbwire slowed attempts to cross the space to a deadly crawl, while machine and heavy-artillery gunners mowed the men down.[41]

The Western Front—a roughly 450-mile defensive line that cut across the northeastern corner of France—was where the war in Europe was lost and won. Deliberately staged as a battle of attrition, the generals got what they wanted: over three years the front never moved more than a few miles in either direction. The land for miles around it was left "just a mass of deep shell craters, filled with water" a place where "tanks, all shot to pieces" littered burned-over fields.[42]

Reporting on this type of war was almost impossible without official access to the fighting zone, as many frustrated journalists had learned. In the war's opening months, correspondents who made their way to the Western Front in defiance of Allied military orders routinely faced arrest. "Almost unbelievably stupid, unsatisfactory, and inefficient," fumed one of the many neutral American journalists who ignored them. The situation meant that much of the news about the war's progress in Britain came from stories first published in the still neutral United States, where censorship rules did not apply.[43]

Nell's invitation reflected the Allies' creeping awareness of the necessity of keeping pace with their enemy in the management of news. Within weeks of the war's start, the Central Powers had launched a charm offensive with the press, accrediting more than one hundred reporters with its army to publicize its remarkable weaponry and to combat the image taking root in neutral countries of them as "barbarian Huns." Now, one year into the war, Nell's invitation reflected the Allies' determination to beat the Germans in the battle for hearts and minds. Rather than simply sanction reporters like the Germans had done, the Allies would offer war tours to important "molders of neutral opinion," including editors, statesmen, university presidents, and popular novelists like Nell.[44]

While waiting to get the necessary paperwork for her first tour of the Western Front, Nell visited wounded British troops during the day and worked on *Katherine Bush* at night as the French Army's attempts to retake the industrialized north produced only horrific casualties.

But her foray into the life of a war correspondent was delayed when a wire from Margot the first week of November called her suddenly back to England. Clayton was dead. Having been assured by his doctors that his condition was stable, the girls were "horrified" by the news. He "passed away quite peacefully and without any pain," Margot soothed Clayton's sister, Nellie.[45]

The marriage that had provided Nell's first stable perch was over. "The tragedy of these last years is too sad to talk about is it not?

Poor, poor dear Clayton, I know it was the disease and not his kind and generous soul," Nell wrote his sister after the funeral. "I have never really felt any resentment against him although it has often been very cruel, the things that happened. . . . Life is a strange tragedy altogether and we have to go through with it as best we may." The thing for her now was to "work very, very hard for the next few years and build up a future for the girls," she concluded to her sister-in-law. To Clayton's cousin John, she claimed relief that Clayton "never knew of the fresh grief and worry" he had caused the family because "of the fresh debt she now had to pay." John had been trying to remember Clayton "in the old days," he responded. "He had a great personality and was such a fine, good looking young man, but always so dreadfully extravagant beginning from his Oxford days."[46]

The news of her husband's death was still a shock although her life had moved on utterly without him years ago. Clayton's death could not but stir old memories of how much this charming, handsome, generous, and (seemingly) well-situated man's proposal had meant to her when she was just twenty-seven.

That a man like Clayton would pick her only for her beauty and charisma had made it seem like anything was possible, seeding a confidence that she could will her dreams into something she might hold in her hands. His romantic rejections had almost immediately crushed her hope that her husband would ever deliver the passion and understanding she craved. But Nell had long ago recognized that her marriage was the basis for everything else and offered her reputation a protective screen that nothing could replace. She had already grown expert at seizing the rights and privileges that came with being the family's sole breadwinner, conducting her financial, professional, and romantic affairs as she thought best. Now with Clayton's death another vestige of tradition's hold on her receded into the past.

Further evidence of tradition's grip on England arrived on her return when Judge Younger, in London's Royal Court of Justice, denied her claim to copyright infringement because a burlesque film of *Three Weeks* was made without her consent. Calling Glyn's "free love" novel "grossly immoral, both in its essence, in its treatment, and in its tendency," Younger declared it unworthy of protection. He particularly emphasized the need to protect women from further infection by Nell's bad ideas. Her novel was "a mischievous glittering record of adulterous sensuality masquerading as superior virtue" calculated to teach young women "that she may choose without danger the easy life of sin."[47]

The allegedly wicked widow traded time between the London Ritz and one of George's country houses that winter, visiting wounded soldiers and finishing *The Career of Katherine Bush*. The novel's first installment was due to appear in magazines in both the United States and Britain before its publication later that year. Nell's visits to the hospital made the writing hard.

"I can't work this morning. I am so full of yesterday," she confided to Margot. "Oh such cases since the last week, enough to break the heart. I talked to 400 of them . . . their courage is superhuman, two of them were dying and I assure you I had all I could to keep from crying," she confessed. "All the officers left alive of the 10th are here and I am going to take them roses tomorrow. I have not seen officers yet but the soldiers love a nurse. . . . I chuffed and joked and made them laugh. . . . I have developed the art of speaking to them. . . . But each time I come away I have that strange feeling of the nearness of eternity and of how little this life matters."[48]

When she finally finished *Katherine* a dispute over its morality erupted with Ray Long, the editor of William Randolph Hearst's *Cosmopolitan*, a middlebrow magazine that reached over a million mostly women readers. Ray Long worried Americans would fail to sympathize with a heroine who emerged unscathed and unrepentant after taking a lover. Indeed, Nell's novel endorsed her heroine's choice: "To be twenty-two and in love for the first time in life, with an extremely delectable specimen of manhood—to be free as air—answerable to no one—untouched by backward or forward thoughts, unworried by tormenting speculations as to whether the affair was right or wrong—wise or unwise. This made the cup worth drinking, and Katherine Bush knew it," she wrote.

Nell agreed to add some regret to her heroine's decision to have sex with a man she had no intention of marrying, but she refused to change the story's basic arc. In *Katherine*, the affair is a necessary step in her middle-class heroine's education and proves no obstacle to finding romantic bliss (with a duke, of course).[49]

Each serialized installment of *Katherine* in *Cosmopolitan* began with an "Editor's Note" that prepared readers for the moral ambiguity to follow. "Elinor Glyn belongs to the school of fiction-writers who devote their powers to an unsparing and critical consideration of life. She does not invent romances," Long warned. A heroine "too daring for hypocrisy," Katherine "estimates the probable cost of power, and calmly prepares to pay it. You cannot approve of her early code, but the intolerable circumstances of the dull, mean environment of her girlhood help to explain, without excusing, a character of such astounding determination and competence. Here's another Becky Sharp—a new 'Vanity Fair,' in which British society is exposed with a Thackerayean scalpel!" At fifty, Nell had finally published her homage to the heroine who had inspired her most as a girl.[50]

Her novel's ambitious, morally complicated heroine fit wartime Britain's tastes better. *Nash's and Pall Mall Magazine* promoted it simply as a "brilliant novel" that "stimulates deep and sober thought" and reviews were her best since *Elizabeth*. "By several degrees the best piece of character-drawing" Mrs. Glyn has achieved, the *Daily Telegraph* declared, before calling the heroine "a distinctly real creature, the product of social ambition bred in a vulgar surrounding and of calculating cleverness that wins its way in the end." "Let no one who has an old-fashioned preference for the stock moral read 'The Career of Katherine Bush,'" cautioned the *Illustrated News of London*. "It is far too revolutionary, too subversive of social discipline to be *virginibus puerisque*" [acceptable for maidens and youth], but "Katherine's enterprising career makes a very lively volume." "What distinguishes Miss Bush is the masculine character of her method," the *Times Literary Supplement* observed. "It is courage and deliberation, the simple triumph of character, which transforms the shorthand typist living in Brixton, the daughter of an auctioneer and the grand-daughter of a butcher, into a duchess acclaimed as worthy of the hand of the most eminent of the dukes."[51]

By the time *Katherine* appeared, women had been included in the National Registration Bill, marking their official absorption into the war effort as the British government began conscription of men for the first time. Feminist leader Emmeline Pankhurst deserved much of the credit, having organized a mass demonstration—with the support of the minister of munitions, David Lloyd George—demanding women's "right to serve." Women's participation in the labor force in Britain had soared, rising 23.7 percent (more than any other nation) as working-class women left domestic service for factory work in droves, and middle- and upper-class women volunteered for positions in the government, often as nurses through the VAD, or to head charities supporting soldiers and refugees.[52]

All that past year, in between the writing and the visiting soldiers and the traveling, Nell had spent whatever time he offered with George. She had few illusions left about her lover. In *Halcyone*, vanity always drives the course of the Curzon-inspired character of John Derringham. "Fool to sit there and eat your heart out. Why live like a nun away from the world?" she had fumed to her diary while writing the novel. "He does not value you the more for it. He enjoys his life and his friends, his life full of interesting things," she lectured herself. But as with so many cravings of the heart, intellectual awareness failed to alter her feelings or change her behavior.[53]

Having never considered divorce, the circumscribed terms of Nell's relationship with George had at least remained fixed in her mind, whatever her fantasies. The future possibilities raised by her husband's bad health had flitted into her conversations with Margot and Juliet before Clayton died. Her daughters were curious about the relationship, having become almost like cousins with George's daughters, Irene, Cynthia, and Alexandra, during their many visits together at Hackwood, Crag Hall, or another of Curzon's country houses. Nell taught Alexandra, called Baba, how to paint. Her bond with Cynthia, or Cimmie, grew especially strong. Born with a wayward spine, all her short life Cimmie turned to Nell for the maternal advice she found nowhere else.[54]

None of these women appears to have known about the other beautiful, married redhead George had met just weeks after Nell had returned to London from Paris. "My heart is just calling to you all day," Grace Duggan wrote to George by August. "Believe me my darling great big man, I think I must have been waiting for you always as I can't describe how complete I feel. . . . Teach me to please you in every way, not only in passion." At thirty-six, Duggan was nearly fifteen years younger than Nell and married to a wealthy, infirm Argentinian oilman who had come to London as a cultural attaché. The post allowed his American wife ample opportunity to chase her favorite pastimes, horse racing and love affairs. In a strange coincidence, Grace's husband died just two weeks before Clayton, leaving Duggan a wealthy widow of childbearing age.[55]

Could sharp-eyed Nell really have failed to notice any change in George all that year while he juggled visits between his two redheads? News of the war, always the war, filled everyone's minds as the Allies suffered defeat after defeat, and the lists of the dead grew impossibly long. George was busier than ever. Still a member of PM Asquith's coalition cabinet, Curzon had become the new president of the Air Board and had begun conspiring to push the prime minister out of power. Asquith had proved too indecisive to wage war effectively, George and most everyone agreed.[56]

The war, always the war, might have explained why George failed to visit Nell much even in Somerset, where she had taken up residence to oversee the redecoration of his latest acquisition, Montacute House, at the end of the summer of 1916. The request seemed an honor, given her history-minded lover's obsessive interest in such tasks. Montacute's steeple-like chimneys, balustrades bedecked by armored figures, and paneled baronial hall—all almost untouched since Elizabeth I's day—made it the most perfect Tudor stately house still standing.

All autumn Nell pored over new interior schemes. Irene's bedroom became a symphony in pink, while parrots flew along Baba's walls. Purple and orange velvet draped Curzon's chamber, where three of his Indian tiger skins prowled across the purple carpet on the floor. During breaks from reinventing this beautiful pile, Nell wrote her "Portrait of a Great Man." Into early winter this woman who preferred curling by the fire with her pen and a book clambered about in Montacute's drafty rooms, cut off from the world (George would have no telephone disturb the original quiet), coaxing the house back to life.

Here, standing on a stepladder one late afternoon just before Christmas, a servant brought Nell tea and the *Times*. She climbed down from inspecting the drapery's fastening and picked up the newspaper, looking for reports about how George was faring under the recently installed new prime minister, David Lloyd George. Nell had once detested Lloyd George, but like most everyone else had grown to admire the great Liberal reformer for his success at supplying the munitions needed so desperately at the front. When Lloyd-George superseded Asquith on December 7, 1916, he brought both Curzon and Nell's old flame, Alfred Milner, into his supreme War Cabinet of Five.

But instead of news about George's return to the center of power she read that the Marquess Curzon of Kedleston had become engaged to marry Grace Duggan. Ever a man defined by opposing sides, the classic English snob had again demonstrated his weakness for redheaded, nouveau-riche, American wives.

Nell left Montacute and went back to London, where she burned the many letters George had sent over their eight years together. Curzon would do the same. His attempt to erase Nell from the record of his life included scratching out her signature in the visiting books his housekeepers kept. Still, Grace Duggan Curzon remained hotly jealous of Nell for all the years of their marriage.[57]

Only Lucy's reactions to the end of the love affair remain. "How is Aunt Nellie? We are in our ignorance infuriated at the matrimonial news in the papers here," she wrote to her daughter Esmé from America, where she was cementing her position as the era's leading British couturier. By 1916, "Lady Duff-Gordon's Latest Styles" and Lucile were everywhere one looked: splashed across the newspapers and magazines in the fashion columns she regularly (ghost)wrote; onstage at the Ziegfeld Follies revue; in the special catalogues that Sears, Roebuck & Co. mailed across the country; and on the bodies of celebrities like dancer Irene Castle and movie star Mary Pickford.

"What did she do the country house for!!! We boil when we think of the ungrateful sneaking cad," Lucy fumed to her daughter. She went further to their mother. "What faith can one have in 'noblesse oblige' anymore? Not that I've ever thought anything of them—I think the English aristocrats unless you are really one of them, are in their set, or you are an American millionaire, are a vile set of cruel snobs."[58]

Although the sisters' attitudes toward the aristocratic code had been miles apart since childhood, the wave of events exposing society's hypocrisies over the last decade had likely brought their views closer together. Nell had been ostracized by most of her former friends for writing about the kind of affair their set had long condoned. She had witnessed the pillorying of her brother-in-law for taking the chance to save his own life, like so many other men of his class had done. She had tried to ease the suffering of soldiers led to their slaughter by younger Curzons in the name of honor in a war that statesmen everywhere had promised would be quick. And now she had been dishonorably dumped by her nobleman for another American millionaire.

If the supposed noblesse oblige of Curzon's kind had ever protected those around them, she knew, unequivocally, that times had changed.

With no man to tie her up in knots for the first time in decades, her daughters leading independent lives, and the world around her crumbling, Nell had reached a turning point. Who knew what was next?

CHAPTER 10

World Split in Two

Even when you win a War, you cannot forget that you have lost your generation.

—Alan Lascelles

"In 1917, I died." The reporter looked into her serious, sea-foam-green eyes. "In 1917," Nell repeated:

> I died. I sat before my glass and I saw an old woman who said: You are physically broken, you are spiritually dead, you are morally bankrupt. And the reflection in the mirror only bowed its head and agreed. Then, suddenly, something happened. I looked in the mirror again, and it was as though a challenge was flung back at me from its depths. I said to myself, I am not going to be an old woman, either in body or in soul. I am not going to give in. And I didn't.[1]

Nell was fifty-two when George broke her heart for the last time. She knew by then that when disappointment threatened to crush, the best medicine was to direct her pain into labor and let her adventurous side lead her back into the light.

She lobbied George Riddell, another of England's press barons, to return to France to finish what she had tried to do before. She would go this time with papers in hand to travel behind the lines to write about the Western Front's horrors. She would add her famous voice to the chorus imploring the Americans to finally join the fight.

The Americans declared war the week before she moved back into the Paris Ritz. Germany's pursuit of unrestricted submarine warfare had inflamed American public opinion. Then, as American merchant ships started heading to the bottom of the sea, the British decoded a German telegram to the Mexican president asking him to join the Central Powers, attack the United States, and take back their stolen lands. President Woodrow Wilson had had enough: "Neutrality is no longer *feasible* or desirable where the peace of the world is involved," he declared when asking Congress to declare war in April 1917. "The world must be made safe for democracy. We have no selfish ends to serve."[2]

The Germans had counted on ending things before the United States could send enough men to tip the scales. Narrowly reelected the year before on the platform "He Kept Us Out of War," the American president was in no rush. Wilson's determination to enlist a million men to fight under American command before joining the fray seemed to play into the enemy's hand. Wilson wanted to put enough firepower behind the country's loans to claim a bigger say in the peace. American troops would not deploy in force in France until a year later, in April 1918.[3]

It was not clear if the Allies could survive the wait. By the time Nell returned to Paris, the French were well on their way to suffering the greatest percentage of casualties of any belligerent nation involved in the conflict. A nation of 40 million was fighting Germany's 75 million almost entirely on French soil, the Supreme Allied Commander General Ferdinand Foch kept repeating. (After the war, even the tiniest French town would hold a monument etched with an impossibly long list of their Great War dead.)

The nearly yearlong German offensive at Verdun during 1916 had tried "to bleed France white" by attacking a point necessary to France's defense, indefinitely, until Germany's greater numbers ground out the win. When Verdun ended, 700,000 men were dead, but France had not fallen and the Western Front remained unchanged. The Battle of the Somme—staged by the British in part to divert Germans from Verdun—claimed over a million more lives.[4]

Then war midwifed revolution in Russia during the winter of 1916–1917 and the end of the three-hundred-year imperial dynasty of the Romanovs Nell knew so well. With the economy in chaos and millions of unarmed peasants already sacrificed to the

Eastern Front—where their soldiers had been deserting in droves—
the Union of Soviet Socialist Republics started peace negotiations
with Germany. In March 1917, the USSR signed a treaty with
Germany, forfeiting 30 percent of their territory to quit the fight.
The Central Powers now turned their full fury toward France.

When Nell moved back into the Ritz in April, Verdun was a
symbol of French grit and self-sacrifice, but their army was near collapse. That month mutiny struck among infantrymen, spreading to
nearly half of those stationed at the Western Front. A mixture of
executions for the ringleaders and better conditions for the rest controlled the problem there. But antiwar fever spread throughout the
home front, reaching factories and the school system. French leaders
would keep the world as ignorant as possible about the severity of
the situation for decades.[5]

Living amidst so much death and destruction for so long likely
explained the desperately gay façade many upper class Parisians
presented, according to Nell and many other observers. Paris now
slipped a step in her heart for the first time. "What has happened
to the gallant French nation that I used to adore?" she wondered
to her diary at the time. "So much of the aristocracy here in Paris
seems to be just *fine de race*," or decadent, as the English said. "Vice
is Rampant in Paris," she reported. "Lesbians dine together openly,
in groups of six sometimes, at Laure's . . . Men are the same."[6]

Nell found the superficial concerns that so many French women
of her class fixated upon particularly disillusioning. Before the war,
the women's movement in Britain had been far stronger. During wartime, the two nations' approaches to women's proper roles evolved
differently. Women in both countries would join the war effort by
doing everything short of serving as combatants.

But only British women received public acknowledgment of
their service when the new PM David Lloyd George established
the Women's Army Auxiliary Corps and the Women's Royal Naval
Service at the behest of leaders of the suffrage movement. The organi-
zations paid competitive wages and celebrated women who freed men
to fight at the front by acting as clerks, cooks, and drivers behind the
lines. Even though most continued to perform stereotypically female
jobs, propaganda images showcased them doing "men's work" near

the combat zones, or on the home front in munitions factories. Such images helped to decouple citizenship from manhood, as individuals who risked their lives to serve the nation became worthy citizens regardless of their sex, while male pacifists, "shirkers," and conscientious objectors had their rights challenged in the press and the courts.[7]

Although French working-class women had worked in factories more than their British counterparts before 1914, their labor participation in all classes grew much more slowly during wartime, and the meanings attributed to their labor remained narrowly defined as civilian. Images of women in France—where pronatalism had been a growing force for decades—emphasized motherhood as women's primary role, presenting it as their national duty and most important source of fulfillment.[8]

The different faces that French and British women wore during wartime taught Nell that she was more English than she had previously recognized. Nell knew very well how important exquisite standards were to French identity, but the elite Parisian women who still openly obsessed about looking their best disturbed her. Nell had privately fretted over a Reboux hat that had arrived damaged before she left on her first trip to the Western Front. But she found the public expression of such trivial concerns offensive while "Big Bertha" shot cannons over the city's medieval walls each night.[9]

The war years shifted Nell's political orientation and brought new sympathy for the experiences of working people too. After cleaning up at a canteen or caring for men while they died, many British women from the upper classes—long the class least interested in suffrage—could not imagine holding themselves so aloof from the world of politics again.

She openly repudiated views she had held just years before. "I used to be an anti-suffragist and the most arrogant of conservatives," she confessed in "MRS. GLYN SAYS WAR MEANS END OF SNOBS," an interview she gave before returning to Paris. "Now I am a suffragist and a democrat. This war means the death of cult and snobbery, except the snobbery of brains," she continued in an article syndicated across America. "I think it may be justly said that all but a very tiny percentage of Englishwomen in every class have shown that woman is capable of as glorious a courage, as steady a devotion, and as patriotic a sense of duty to the state as man."[10]

The next month she finally got her chance to see the Western Front firsthand. After making out her will, she made the first of several tours of areas recently liberated from the Germans (who would recapture their rubble months later) with an American Red Cross officer. The VAD even sent Margot and Juliet to accompany their famous mother on one trip. A snapshot shows them all perched on a small hill of bricks in uniform, serious faces looking out from under their caps.

No army attached women journalists to their troops, and they remained a tiny minority of firsthand reporters. But several intrepid female writers received tours of the Western Front once the Allies recognized their importance to maintaining home-front morale. After becoming prime minister, David Lloyd George's first meeting was with the newspaper magnates George Riddell, owner of Britain's biggest circulation-getter, the *News of the World*, and Harry Levy-

Nell visits the Western Front with Margot and Juliet 191[?]

Lawson and Lord Burnham, of the *Daily Telegraph*. Lloyd George knew that success depended on enlisting American support and keeping the home fires burning. Like most, he subscribed to the belief that women writers could best reach women readers through the so-called woman's angle. "The real story of the war is never at the front, it is in the hospitals and the homes," declared the *Saturday Evening Post*'s editor, George Horace Lorimer. Lorimer sent mystery novelist Mary Roberts Rinehart, who became the first journalist to visit the front-line trenches.[11]

Many of the women given wartime tours were popular novelists (May Sinclair and Edith Wharton were others) who traded on their literary skill and familiarity with the public to draw in readers, establish the truthfulness of their reports, and make the terrors they witnessed palpable. "Men, alas! have had to grow so familiar with the sight of the horrors of war that perhaps they can no longer feel in the measure what a woman would who sees the desolation for the first time," explained the letter that introduced the articles in her series that ran in American newspapers from San Francisco to Boston and from Atlanta to Detroit. "I want to tell you of Prince Eitel Fritz's pleasure house, and of the sinister burning of St. Quentin—and of the terrible fate of the poor girls from the villages," she continued. "The Germans have soaked God's earth with blood and trampled underfoot the sacred things. . . . For indeed, as in the ancient myths, 'The fierce dragon has passed, and with its scorching breath, laid waste to the land.' "[12]

She used all her descriptive powers to help American readers visualize this villainous enemy. "I am still so stunned by the sights that I have seen and the things that I have heard that I hardly know how to begin to write about them," began her account, "Glimpses of a German-Made Hell." Nell relentlessly focused on the emotional impact of what she saw. "Bailly was a place of the dead, and the whole country round also," she wrote. "There were no signs of cultivation—for the entire civil population has been rendered homeless and the rich fields remained untilled. . . . The sensation was that one was in a dream—that it could not be true that the passion of men should so destroy all created things . . . often on this journey I have with difficulty kept back my tears."

"In the Track of the Barbarous Hun," variations of which ran in dozens of newspapers, railed against the German Army's atrocities: children torn from their mothers' arms so that they could be put to work; married women and teenage girls left "*enceintes* (pregnant) from the assaults of German officers"; medieval churches bombed and desecrated with naked drawings of Frenchwomen kept hostage in German "pleasure houses." Long after it "became the fashion to pretend such things were invented for the purposes of propaganda," she defended the accuracy of such reports.[13]

She tried to re-create the conditions under which soldiers lived and died. "Author Visits the Trenches Where Men Lived in Straw Like Rats," took readers along on her tour. "After a perilous advance over newly mended roads, we came to the part where the struggle was most desperate of all—'No Man's Land.' . . . The scene is one vast waste, looking much like the alkaline desert one crosses on the way to San Francisco." Although terribly claustrophobic in the best of times, she climbed down into the labyrinthine network of tunnels "in most places still deep in sordid red slush, many too low to permit any man to stand upright. Probably you have seen what a trench looks like on the cinematograph?" she asked. "No picture gives you the feeling of the real things, for there is the color, the stench, and the knowledge that one is standing upon the spot where human beings have sacrificed their lives."[14]

The scenes she witnessed behind the lines prompted Nell to aid the suffering around her more directly. Although she had long considered clubwomen irritating busybodies (an impression that her dust-up with the Puritan Mothers in America had only confirmed), she became vice president of the society of the Secours Franco-Américain Pour la France Dévastée, a charity designed to help resettle French and Belgian refugees. The experience taught her the utility of (New) England busybody-types. "Our President was Mrs. Prince, of Boston. We had a great many grand French names on our Committee, but those who did the real work were either English or American," she wryly noted. A letter to William Randolph Hearst described the "scenes of pitiful terrible misery" she had seen before imploring him to use "his infinite power" to publish a set of articles appealing for funds to support the work of Secours Franco-Américain

in his newspapers that reached one-third of Americans. "Each village as it becomes re-inhabited and self-supportive would be an
object more likely to rouse the sympathetic response of Americans
who love their own homes," Nell reasoned.[15]

Hearst agreed, and the appeals on behalf of French refugees
began that summer. "Try to imagine it, kindly people who are reading this in your sheltered house. All the neat little houses crushed
to powder and where they once stood are now deeply dug trenches,"
she urged. "Oh! you who are reading, will you not give what you
can—thanking God all the time that though America sends her
brave sons to fight for the cause of freedom, no American homes can
be desolated, nor American women outraged. . . . All we can do is to
try our utmost to bring back some hope—some life—some comfort
to this stricken country."[16]

She enlisted her sister's help raising funds, since Lucy was sitting
out the war in still-prosperous America. After needling "Lady Duff-
Gordon, the arbiter of elegance and the autocrat of fashion," as the
New York Times called her, about not doing her part, Lucy agreed to
stage a charity event for New York society called "Fluerette's Dream
at Péronne" to benefit Secours Franco-Américain.

A story Nell had shared with her sister about a young model
she had met living with her family in a cellar in Péronne (a town
inside the war-torn Somme region), inspired the "musical fantasy."
As German bombs explode overhead, Fleurette dreams of her life
in Paris before the war. Scenes with her finely dressed friends at
parties and on shopping trips—where they try on the latest Lucile
creations—fill the stage until she awakens to confront the horrors of
her present. Staged at the Little Theater in the fall of 1917—before
Americans started arriving in force in France—the lavish fashion
spectacle was such a success that a vaudeville booker asked Lucy to
helm a twenty-five-week tour across the United States.[17]

Lucy had declined such invitations before but claims to have
accepted this one in order to donate most of her $2,500-a-week
salary to various war charities. The truth was more complicated.
Although not yet apparent to most Americans, Lady Duff-Gordon's
fashion empire was coming apart at the seams. The Paris and
London branches of Lucile Ltd. had both closed, the Sears, Roebuck

catalogue had failed to attract mass-market interest, and a lawsuit decided in the New York Court of Appeals that year had assigned the sole use of her professional name to her former agent, Otis Wood. Dramatic changes in fashions—hastened by wartime restrictions and needs—favored a more streamlined chic in the style of the rising couturier Coco Chanel. Chanel's severe, simple styles, like her little black dress, would make the trendiest prewar fashion houses look old-fashioned to the rising generation of younger tastemakers.[18]

This made the war years a watershed for both sisters, but for entirely different reasons. Looking back from a distance, the arc of their lives pivoted in different directions for the first time. In these years, Lucy's fortunes took a nosedive from which she never recovered. During the same time, Nell's stature and spirit—free and independent and no longer looking for a man for the first time—rose higher with each passing month. "I was, I am almost embarrassed to admit, extremely happy in spite of the terrible casualty lists which still appeared every two or three days," she admitted of her years in wartime Paris. But she believed many women who had the opportunity to do war work similarly "seemed to find peace and satisfaction."[19]

Because of her popularity in the United States, the French government also enlisted her help welcoming American servicemen, who in April had finally begun pouring into France at a rate of 10,000 a day. "The men landing from the ships are most magnificent," Nell wrote with relish to her mother after a tour of the American bases. Her "greatest wish" was that her speeches would help them to "realize we really are brothers, and that all our interests are the same."[20]

Nell's speeches to servicemen reflected the pull to publicize a "special relationship" between the so-called great English-speaking democracies. "Now boys, when you know the English better you will see that they are just capital good fellows, exactly like yourselves," she said in one she delivered dozens of times. The nations were "after all blood relations," the only two that "both play games" and "both have got 'cussedness'! . . . The French have gallantry and courage and many other fine virtues but we—Anglo-Saxons—have pre-eminently cussedness—we stick it." In another she warned, "the French and the British are suffering a holocaust of our bravest and best," exhorting: "You are going to avenge them, Boys, and bring new life to tired France, and the strong arm of a comrade to England."[21]

She gave loads of interviews to American journalists (that invariably reminded readers she was the "famous author of *Three Weeks*"), praising American soldiers for saving the Allies' morale. "Bestial Hun Brutality Contrasted with Wonderful Spirit of America," declared one; "America Has Revived the Spirit of France," shouted another syndicated as far away as Shanghai.[22]

All that last year of the war, Nell woke most mornings to see what had survived the artillery bombardments that barraged the city overnight. So familiar became the air-raid sirens that she sometimes remained in her bed at the Ritz.

"The terrible danger in which the Allies stood at that time was well understood by all of us," she recalled thinking during a particularly long air raid that had sent her down to the hotel's center hall to sit jumbled together with the other resident-guests in the dark.

> And as we sat there steadfastly refusing to feel the least alarm when the 'zoom-zoom' of the attacking aeroplanes was heard overhead, our mental attitude towards the raids was an odd reflection of our real feelings about the War. No doubt remained now as to whether the attack would come; we could hear the explosions as the first bombs fell on the outskirts of the city, and the sudden cutting off of the engine as a Gotha swooped to drop another one nearer to the hotel. The only doubt remaining was as to the whereabouts of the next explosion and what our fate would be after the fall of the impending blow. And so with the future of the War.[23]

Nell's fears about having become an old woman without purpose had evaporated in the war's light, which dispelled so many of her past passions, personal vanities, and concerns. Her identity and roles as a woman—as a daughter, society beauty, wife, mother, scandalous sex novelist, and mistress—had defined every aspect of her life.

Learning to live with the existential uncertainty of each day made it possible to set aside the focus on her personal ego in ways that had previously been impossible. She had found a bigger role entirely. She felt "no longer a woman but something else," as she explained to CC, an old friend in the British Admiralty.

"I am inclined to doubt this," he replied. "The Ethiopian cannot change his skin nor the leopard his spots." CC wondered if she were not suffering from the same confusion caused by the interruption of so many of the governing features of sex roles during the war. "The girls have lost their heads, what the result will be to the population of England I do not know," he groaned, before philosophically conceding, "Fighting and love making have I fancy gone hand in hand ever since there has been any of either which is just so long as the world has been populated by human beings."[24]

British newspapers had been voicing CC's alarm for years, as images of emboldened women embracing male "vices" and behavior along with their jobs proliferated in wartime. Cartoons, fiction, and newspapers all agreed that a visible transformation in women's manners, dress, and speech had occurred. Women's "looser morals"— their swearing, smoking, and wearing of shorter skirts (and even pants!)—provoked reams of commentary.

What varied in the reports was the interpretation given to these palpable deviations from past norms. Some commentators assumed the changes were temporary wartime aberrations; others believed they were simply the most dramatic sign yet of an ongoing rot. The publication of *Married Love* (1918) by the academic Marie Stokes— which discussed in heretofore unheard-of scientific detail the mechanics of birth control and techniques to cultivate female sexual pleasure to achieve "great sex"—gave a scientific imprimatur to the subject that Nell had long advanced in her novels. A good marriage demanded recognition and attention to women's sexual pleasure.[25]

But even if the home front appeared beset by still poorly understood social forces, by late summer the Americans had decisively changed the math at the Western Front. On August 8, Germany's "Black Day," Americans helped the Allies to smash through the lines and advance by kilometers, not yards. The assault wiped out sixteen German divisions in just a few days.

In September, Germany's top military strategist, Gen. Erich Ludendorff, demanded the kaiser sue for peace at any cost.[26]

That month Nell wrote a remarkable essay, "When Our Men Come Home," about what the war's end might mean for her sex. Published in Hearst's *Cosmopolitan* magazine, the article marked a new relationship with the media mogul. Her literary agent, Alfred Brandt of Hughes, Massie & Co., had arranged a three-year contract with Hearst's International Magazine Company that offered her considerably more money than she had been paid for such work before. The contract reflected her new stature as a public figure—as a person of "brilliant intellect," as the essay's introduction noted—particularly in America, where most of her reporting had appeared. American movie companies had also begun adapting her novels into movies with success. Although she had no involvement in the process, her name had been used heavily in promoting adaptations of *Three Weeks* (1917), *The Reason Why* (1918), and *The Career of Katherine Bush* (1919). Hearst likely saw signing her up as a sure bet.

No one doubted that the advancement of women's equality with men seemed at a crossroads after the war. During and immediately after it, many women secured the right to vote for the first time in most of the nations involved in the conflict. By 1920, France would stand alone as the only so-called Western democracy in which a majority of women had not been formally incorporated as citizens in important new ways, although in the U.S. South huge numbers of African American women (and men) were still disenfranchised by Jim Crow. But important questions remained as to whether the 1920s would see more fundamental changes in women's ability to exercise influence and power in public like the men.

"When Our Men Come Home" argued that further changes were afoot to equalize women's status. "Realize it at once, my sisters! For us, as a sex, a new era has been born. We have, at last, in some measure been given freedom. The bondage imposed upon Woman by Man's superior strength is broken, possibly forever." During the war, women from all classes in England and America had discarded "ways which Man has half contemptuously characterized as 'feminine'" and "every pre-War restriction as to the intermingling of the sexes" had been swept away. "Now for the first time in centuries, many recognized that 'morality' was not the same thing as 'sex-fidelity' to one partner."[27]

This abandonment of many of the conventions and moral strictures governing the performance of proper femininity had promoted changes in Anglo-American women's economic opportunities, social freedoms, and moral development, Glyn believed. Still, she warned that "although woman's chance has come," they must not "ever forget, that we are given our new freedom because we seem to have made good in this awful moment." She warned that "Man still possesses brute force, which can club us back into bondage if we irritate him too greatly by overarrogance in our demands."

Women had to tread carefully, in other words, and to use all their charm to prove themselves "worthy of the new liberty," lest they lose their gains so recently won.

Paris, 1919.

In the Hall of Mirrors, at the Palace of Versailles, Nell tottered, wilting after the hours spent standing on a bench, waiting for the peacemakers to come and sign their hands.

It was June 28, and a gorgeous summer day after a cold spring had passed while the great men talked and talked. Nell had joined their conversations from her corner table at the Ritz. Her rare entrée to the men's inner circle had been smoothed by her new stature as a commentator on world events as well as her old friendship with Alfred Milner, brought by Lloyd George, and her new one with George Riddell, the press baron who was as close to a Boswellian-confidant-scribe as the prime minister would get. (Lloyd George would make Riddell the first divorced peer in 1920.)[28]

Luckily, the PM had left his foreign secretary, George Curzon, in London. Though Curzon knew more about the Ottoman Empire than almost anyone present, the Welsh Baptist prime minister was an outsider among Curzon's fancy folk and had learned to tolerate his patrician foreign secretary as a necessary evil only when the war was on. Having viewed George as a rival for Nell's affections long ago, the newly married and semi-retired Alfred Milner likely relished sharing the details with Nell about Curzon's unhappy marriage, which had given him no male heir in the end.[29]

All that long, cold spring Nell was in her element with these men, at times listening, at others holding forth on the social subjects that would take center stage as the conflagrations of war receded. "A remarkable woman with great insight into character—a sort of female philosopher," Riddell called her in his diary about the peace conference. "In some ways she is what you would expect, in others quite the reverse," observed the man who had turned an ailing newspaper, *News of the World*, into Britain's biggest one by stoking people's interest in celebrities, gossip, and scandal.[30]

The noted Irish portrait painter William Orpen—there to paint the official portrait of the treaty signing in the Hall of Mirrors— took credit for bringing Glyn and Riddell together. That spring, Nell, Riddell, and Orpen shared many memorable dinners in the backyard garden of Laurent restaurant. In her "pleasant, modulated voice, under the trees and twinkling stars," Nell would hold forth on "many things about life" until long after dinner, Orpen fondly recalled. "Why men did not keep their wives; the correct way to make love; the stupid ordinary methods of the male; what the female expected; what she ought to expect; and what she mostly got."[31]

For her part, Nell thought Riddell brought the witty, irreverent spirit of the French philosopher Voltaire to the peace conference. She also became quite fond of the Welsh prime minister, whose legendary charm with the opposite sex only encouraged the further leftward listing of her views. "Although his English is perfect," she observed to her diary, "he struck me as such a purely Celtic type that I felt that I was talking to some foreigner who spoke English well rather than to the British Prime Minister."[32]

Riddell asked Lloyd George to include Nell as a reporter among the sixty guests allotted to each of the Allies' Great Powers—France, Great Britain, the United States, Italy, and Japan. "A very awkward number," complained Woodrow Wilson. "If it were restricted to say ten it would be easy to make a selection, but if one has to select sixty there are certain to be many heart-burnings." Dignitaries, generals, admirals, high-ranking officials, and journalists jockeyed to be among the guests. Rumor had it that outrageous sums changed hands for seats.[33]

As one of Lloyd George's sixty, and officially in her capacity as a special correspondent for Riddell's *News of the World*, Nell packed into the long glittering rectangle of the Hall of Mirrors with the other lucky ones and waited. She was one of only a handful of women in the room. Remarkably, Lucy was there too, having returned to Paris recently and finessed an invitation from the French embassy on account of her exceptional efforts to raise funds for France. Nell never mentioned her sister's presence there that day, likely irritated she managed to witness the end of a world altering event that she had spent watching from the sidelines in America.[34]

It was the fifth anniversary of the shots in Sarajevo; now the Austro-Hungarian, Russian, and Ottoman Empires were no more.

"A hushed hum of voices, the grave faces of the statesmen and delegates silent at their table," Nell wrote. And "then waiting, waiting, waiting, waiting, with increasing tension of nerves, and at last, from the end by the Queen's apartments, five depressed looking men emerge, frock-coated, spectacled, unprepossessing. These are the Germans. Look at them well." Excluded from the negotiations, an Allied guard ushered "five plebeian German men" into the room only at the last moment.[35]

Newsreels captured their late arrival in the first major treaty signing staged as much for the camera's eye as for those present. "How can you concentrate on the solemnity of a scene when you have men with cameras in every direction, whose sole object is to get as near as they can to the central figures?" one observer huffily wondered. Nell agreed. "The whole scene looked commonplace and undignified. A sorry end to a magnificent tragedy," she wrote in an article in *The Ladies' Field*.[36]

A document of failed hopes, the Versailles Treaty left "no one satisfied," as President Wilson admitted to his wife on the trip home. The signing ceremony—between "the Allied and Associated Governments and the German State"—marked the German Republic's reluctant debut. "Not the proud kingdom of Prussia, or the Empire of other days, but just a new-born republic, which tomorrow might be gone," Nell wrote.[37]

The Signing of Peace in the Hall of Mirrors by William Orpen (1919)

The Versailles Treaty redrew boundaries and borders across the world; the mirrors in Orpen's painting of the event prophetically suggested their shaky quality. In tiny Europe alone, the treaty created Finland, Austria, Czechoslovakia, Yugoslavia, Poland, Hungary, Latvia, Lithuania, and Estonia. The comparative care taken by the peacemakers in drawing new European lines was apparent nowhere else. The winners, the so-called advanced nations, used a mandate system to distribute amongst themselves territories seized from the German and Ottoman Empires in the Pacific, Africa, and the Middle East. But riding the anti-imperialist sentiment sweeping the world, Wilson had forced the other winners to let a new League to Enforce Peace oversee these occupied lands. To the league fell the impossible task of making the winners hold their spoils "in a sacred trust of civilization" until their occupiers deemed them capable of "the strenuous conditions of the modern world."

The relationship laid bare the era's white-supremacist logic: civilized societies—defined as the descendants of Northern Europeans—had to assume what the great imperialist-mythmaker Rudyard Kipling had called the "white man's burden" and teach all the brown-skinned peoples to fit into their schemes—with threat of force hovering just behind their lofty words.

Woodrow Wilson was the most powerful champion of this new internationalist order. But after his long absence in Paris, he returned to the United States to find another league—the League for the Preservation of American Independence—mobilizing against him by touting the founding fathers' warnings against permanent, entangling alliances with the Old World. As Wilson's health collapsed because of a series of (secretly) worsening strokes, he brooked no compromise. "We have got to accept or reject it," he declared in his last public statement. By the year's end, Wilson had won the Nobel Prize for Peace and lost his League.[38]

Ironically, perhaps the only thing clear that day to many of the witnesses who had angled to be in the Hall of Mirrors was that no one wanted to be there in the end. Nell found the ceremony not just poorly staged and organized, but awash with the anticlimactic, unsettling air that so often suffuses any too dearly won victory.

"As I stood there upon the tottery bench," she wrote in her report, "feeling that I must take care to be able to keep my balance, a sadness fell upon me. I did not want to see any more. It seemed as if the peace of the world must be as insecure as my own footing upon the bench had been. There was no glory, no triumph, no enthusiasm—there was not even any emotion. And over and over again in my head rang the Latin words *Sic transit gloria mundi*." Oh how quickly the glory of the world passes away.[39]

That winter Nell retreated to Egypt to see how the Giza Necropolis had fared. The sight of the Sphinx had its typical salutatory effect. All the troubles of her fifty-five years did not amount to one handful of the surrounding sand. Widowed twice at the war's start—once in fact, and once at heart—she had emerged at its end confident in her ability to make a meaningful life entirely on her own. Ironically, the high priestess of passion had found she liked living a life where her interest in affairs of the heart was more advisory than personal.

In Cairo, a society season "as brilliant as any prewar year" was under way among the large number of English people who had returned to the capital, including her now-married old friend Alfred Milner. Nell and her magnificent clothes created as big a stir as ever. For a dinner at Sultan Fuad I's palace, she wore a gown of silver cloth, a wreath of vivid green leaves in her red hair, and emerald-and-diamond earrings so long they tickled her shoulders. "I have just read one of her books with a smile," a member of the court confessed. Now, having seen the author in the flesh, he could "imagine how easy it must have been for her to write it."[40]

Outside the palace walls things had changed enormously since she had first danced the night away underneath Lord Cromer's monocled gaze. Alfred Milner's letters had warned her about the problems "the recalcitrant 'Nationalists'" had been giving him. After the treaty signing, Milner had returned to Cairo to tamp down the rising cries of nationalism that had erupted when Egypt's First Revolution had unfolded over 1919. Mass demonstrations turned to uprisings, demanding an end to the British Protectorate system. Continued fighting in the streets would lead Milner to recommend to Foreign Secretary Curzon that a treaty-alliance replace it. After another year of fighting, the British finally recognized Egyptian independence in 1922.[41]

From Cairo, Nell accepted an invitation from the queen of Spain—Queen Victoria's granddaughter, Princess Victoria—to visit and write about the court of Alfonso XIII. Over the next three months she wrote a series of articles—later expanded into *Letters from Spain* (1924)—for Hearst's *Cosmopolitan* that advertised its colorful folkways (bull fights, of course) and preservation of the aristocratic habits and privileges that had vanished in so many other places.[42]

All the interviews and articles, all the war tours behind the lines and the speeches at the military bases, all the conversations with world leaders in Paris, had taught her that she could speak directly to almost anyone and that they would not just listen but would also take her ideas seriously. As she watched many women slide into depression as their opportunities to be useful shriveled up, Nell knew that her dearly won independence and peace of mind demanded that she continue this work.[43]

By the time Nell's letters from Spain began appearing in Cosmopolitan, her many readers likely thought a press agent had timed their release to advertise her international cachet and standing to her new colleagues in the American movie business. For in Spain another, even more remarkable, invitation had been forwarded to her: Mr. Jesse Lasky, vice president of production at Famous Players-Lasky Studio, wanted to bring Europe's most eminent authors to Los Angeles to write for the motion picture business. Would the famous authoress consent to become one of them? Would she visit America to see the work of making movies and then try her hand at writing a story for the screen?

In her autobiography, Nell acted as if she accepted Jesse Lasky's invitation at once, almost on faith. In fact, she returned to London, where her agent, Albert Brandt, negotiated with Famous Players' representative, June Mayo. Her contract with the world's largest motion picture company outdid the one she had signed with Hearst International months before by quite a lot. Famous Players would pay her $3,000 to travel to New York and on to Los Angeles in a Pullman drawing-room car—the fanciest possible way to make the cross-country trip—accompanied by her personal maid and dressmaker, Ann Morgan. The contract also promised $10,000 (equivalent to $147,000 in today's dollars) for an original story synopsis, or adaptation of an existing novel, accepted by the company.[44]

But the portrayal in her autobiography of the decision to accept Famous-Players' offer instantaneously likely captures her intention to seize this new opportunity at all costs. She had seen only a few pictures to date, including an adaptation of Three Weeks, which she detested. But by 1920 no one could miss the crowds lining up outside movie theaters. Although she knew nothing about writing for the screen, she was confident in her appeal to a large, polyglot audience on both sides of the Atlantic. And she "felt certain that a great new art was being born, which would profoundly influence the whole world." At last, "here was a unique opportunity to spread the ideals and the atmosphere of romance and glamour into the humblest home."[45]

So Nell returned to Paris to pack up her most essential belongings. Then she boarded the *Mauretania* and chased adventure back to the New World again.

Nell, as "Madame Glyn," ready to go to Hollywood

Act III

POWER

CHAPTER 11

At the Hollywood Hotel

> The mysteries inherent in the new art created a feeling of isolation
> on the part of its performers. They spoke a silent language, a different
> language . . . but they felt a camaraderie with all the other members
> of their clan. This bond gave them the assurance they could create
> their own laws, devise their own moralistic codes, establish their own
> habits and behavior. This isolation made them feel temporary, reckless.
> No doubt that subconsciously they feared the magical bubble would
> soon burst and they would run scurrying back to their Brooklyns, their
> carnival shows and their villages to continue an existence more closely
> allied to life as it was—rather than as it was imagined.
>
> —King Vidor[1]

Jesse Lasky met Nell on the gangway when the *Mauretania* docked
in New York, eager to whisk his so-called eminent author to
her hotel and then a press reception. The vice president of production at Famous Players-Lasky Studio, later Paramount Pictures,
had just made the five-day train trip from the West Coast, where he
supervised making 102 feature films a year.

A native San Franciscan and former vaudeville musician and
promoter, Lasky was the genial counterpart to the company's steely
Hungarian president, Adolph Zukor, who carried himself with
a princely air befitting the president of the world's most powerful
motion-picture company. (Despite everyone in the business being on
a "first name basis five minutes after they met, no one ever calls this
man anything but 'Mr. Zukor,'" observed director Cecil B. DeMille
of his boss.) After meeting "the green-eyed novelist" with "the flaming red hair," Lasky hastily arranged for a photo shoot. Someone as

adept "at drawing attention to herself as Salvador Dalí" needed pictures to illustrate the copy, he concluded.[2]

On their way to meet the press, Nell grabbed a leopard-skin rug that she imperiously bestowed upon Lasky with "a queenly flourish" when a promenade struck her as better than folding anonymously into a car. "A nightmare," was how Famous Players' bespectacled vice president recalled his stroll with the "fleshy leopard pelt" on one arm and the eye-catching writer on the other. A man with a "smile that seemed to come and go as it was needed," Lasky likely pasted one on his face in that moment, knowing their little parade illustrated what made this elegant and eccentric British lady such a find. Here was an author whose whims were promotional stardust. In an industry built on just such magic, no one doubted the value of Nell's talent for playing the role of the slightly scandalous, and impossibly worldly, celebrity authoress who could keep reporters and fans alike wanting more.[3]

Nell asked the reporters waiting at the Ritz to call her "Madame" Glyn (haphazardly spelled with and without the "e" over her years in Los Angeles). She knew "the Americans love a title so" and was as eager as ever to draw the cloak of romantic and artistic license associated with France over the role that she played in public. Madame Glyn explained that since the Great War had changed all social relations, the modern lovers she wrote about would need to change too. "I must find a new type of hero, because all the old types are dead, I mean, killed in the war," she gravely declared.[4]

The difference between the world she had left and the one she now met at the Ritz in New York could not have been starker. She had seen firsthand how the war had devastated victors and vanquished alike. By the time she left war-ravaged and debt-soaked Europe in the fall of 1920, unemployment was rife, inflation had soared, and austerity measures had been taken that would help to ignite the greatest global depression yet seen. Conditions had produced wave after wave of refugees. But in America Nell could see at once that "the War had not caused much excitement even at its height, and now, appeared as a remote event of little general interest." Americans were proud of their part winning in the war ("a predominant part it was believed," she mocked), "but it touched her very little."[5]

Yet, from the moment she landed in New York, Nell seemed eager only to turn her back on the profoundly uncertain arrangements she had left behind her. She had arrived to write a "picture play" to illustrate the romantic logic of postwar conditions, she announced at the Ritz. Her hero would be "an American business or professional man over 40 years of age," a man "of energy, ambition, and daring." He would possess, above all, a quality called "It." "Something in you which gives the impression that you are not at all cold, but could be awfully loving if you wanted to, and would really enjoy dozens of kisses from the right person—that makes 'It.'"[6]

Fresh off the boat, Nell had coined a polite way to discuss the impolite subject on everyone's minds in an era in which most still did not have an acceptable way to talk about pregnancy or childbirth, let alone sex. "It" must have sounded like beautiful music to Jesse Lasky, a former trumpet player, who knew full well what Nell could only have suspected: the American movie industry had a sex problem that threatened to destroy everything that Lasky and many others had labored so intensively to build.

In addition to her expertise managing the sexual scandal associated with the modern woman, there were other reasons that Nell had inadvertently picked the perfect moment to break into the American movie business. Even before the war, motion pictures had been an extraordinary example of America's corporate dynamism. In 1910, the film industry had been a WASP-controlled (via inventor Thomas Edison's Patent Trust), geographically dispersed business churning out all different kinds of short films just ten or fifteen minutes long. Nickelodeons—the first indoor spaces devoted to movies—were typically crude converted storefronts. Movie actors were anonymous, uncredited performers flickering before an audience mostly composed of working-class men who popped in anytime, day or night.[7]

All of this had changed by the time Nell arrived in New York after a group of mostly Jewish immigrants like Adolph Zukor began to wrest control of the film business away from Edison's first trust. A Hungarian orphan who stood five-foot-four, Zukor had made his first fortune in the fur business in Chicago and then funneled the profits into nickelodeons and penny arcades. Determined to "kill the slum tradition" in the movies, Zukor started Famous Players Film Company to focus on making longer "story pictures" that showcased famous actors from the stage. Zukor aimed to attract more white women as fans, whose patronage had long spelled greater respectability and profits at the theatre.[8]

But Zukor had quickly recognized that the public's attention had fastened *not* onto stage stars of the past like Nell's old favorite, Sarah Bernhardt, but on ingénues of the screen like Mary Pickford. So Zukor hired Pickford, "America's Sweetheart," whose popularity powered his company's rise. Then he joined forces with Lasky to create the largest film-production company yet seen. A star system, long a feature of the stage, rapidly turned recently unknown, cash-short actors into fabulously wealthy personalities known far and wide. Feature-length narrative silent films, always accompanied by music, ran in gorgeous new theaters often retrofitted from the stage. Such tactics paid huge dividends as the numbers who flocked to the movies soared, making motion pictures the most popular form of entertainment ever seen.[9]

By 1920, the American movie business had become the nation's fourth largest industry—behind steel, automobiles, and railroads—and was about to begin another decade of astonishing growth, aided by a political realignment that fall. Disillusionment over "Wilson's War," and the promise of a "Return to Normalcy" had put big-business-minded Republicans in control of Washington in the first presidential election after the passage of women's suffrage. "The country needs less government in business, more business in government," declared Warren Harding, whom Zukor and most of the industry's other titans had supported. Now, as European powers struggled to rebuild and rearm, America's big men removed the few restraints shackling corporate growth and set about conquering the globe through trade.[10]

The biggest cloud on the moviemakers' horizon was a looming culture war over the industry's influence on the sexual morality of youth, as Nell would quickly learn. Even before the war, prescient journalists had bewailed the tolling of "Sex O'Clock in America," as scientists, activists, and politicians argued about contraception, prostitution, masturbation, and the manners and morals of the

young. After it, the topic had become one of the most contested subjects of the day. If Europeans blamed the war for behavioral changes
most visible among its "bright young things," Americans more often
turned their fire on the so-called un-American influence of urban
popular culture. Dance halls, jazz clubs, and the movies all showcased the talent and customs of those from the so-called margins
of society, like the "new negroes" leaving the rural South, the "new
women" flocking to work in cities, and the "new immigrants"—the
southern and eastern European Catholics and Jews who had poured
into the country in the decades before the war.[11]

By the time Madame Glyn arrived, many parents blamed the
movies' "Hebrew" producers, déclassé stars, and "Sex Pictures" for
spreading habits like dating, "treating," and premarital petting to
their once-respectable daughters. And "with the Prohibition question out of the way, pictures will furnish the most fertile field for sal-
aried reformers," warned one of the few Midwestern producers in Los
Angeles. "The post war revolution of manners and morals" had left
the industry "caught in the middle between youth and their elders,"
Zukor agreed.[12]

Moral reformers reversed the direction of influence. "Sex is the
one potently dominant idea in the minds of the men who are gambling in the public taste," warned the former head of Pennsylvania's
film censorship board, Ellis Oberholtzer in *The Morals of the Movie*
(1922). Oberholtzer and his allies in the women's clubs had begun
calling for federal oversight of the medium that the Supreme Court
had stripped of free-speech protections and ruled "a business pure
and simple" in *Mutual Film Corp. v. Industrial Commission of Ohio*
(1915). In *Mutual*'s wake, five states and too many cities and towns
to count had created censorship boards that pre-screened and cut
every foot of celluloid. Similar legislation now pended in thirty-six
states, threatening to "reduce all motion pictures to 'entertainment
for children,'" the *Exhibitors Herald* wailed.[13]

Yet the kinds of sexually provocative stories and personalities
that seemed designed to inflame the moral reformers kept showing
up on screens. "Did I have any love stories to sell?" writer Frances
Marion said a studio boss at Selznick Pictures asked her when she
returned to Los Angeles after trying to report on the war in France.

Director Lois Weber had given Marion her start a decade earlier, teaching her how to write "scenarios" (the early term for screenplays). Already one of the industry's highest-paid writers (and the future winner of two Academy Awards), Marion had written most of Mary Pickford's biggest hits before the war. Now she dashed off *The Flapper*: "a love story to feature the modern girl who, irked by convention, had joined the erring youth revolt and kicked over the traces."[14]

Although the flapper first emerged in working-class women's freer habits before the war, it was the movies that turned her silhouette into the reigning symbol of women's sexual liberation in the 1920s. Pictured as a slip of a girl with bobbed hair, the flapper smoked, danced to jazz, and generally pursued a good time like one of the boys. Her fashions advertised the physical mobility so many young women flaunted, as hemlines went up, ornamentation went down, and the accentuation of breasts and hips disappeared to create a streamlined shape that made men's and women's bodies appear equal in scale for the first time in nearly two centuries.

"Reckless and unconventional, because of their quest in search of self-expression," was how Zelda Fitzgerald described the figure she embodied in literary-minded circles after her husband's debut novel, *This Side of Paradise* (1920), "cast a spell across the nation." "None of the Victorian mothers—and most of the mothers were Victorians— had any idea of how casually their daughters were accustomed to be kissed," wrote Fitzgerald in his account of college students, a subset of the 1920s flaming youth. "I've kissed dozens of men," confesses one of his heroines. "I suppose I'll kiss dozens more."[15]

Weeks after the publication of *This Side of Paradise*, Selznick Pictures released *The Flapper*, starring the Ziegfeld Follies star Olive Thomas, playing a rich, headstrong young woman who heads to the city for fun. The wife of Mary Pickford's only brother, Jack, Olive Thomas fit the part. Although the couple looked like "innocent looking children," Marion called them "two of the gayest, wildest brats" around town. Months after *The Flapper* opened, Thomas's drug-related death in Paris gave moral reformers the perfect ammunition. "OLIVE THOMAS' DEATH INQUIRY BARES ORGIES," screamed the *San Francisco Chronicle*. "It may be time, at long last," a Boston paper opined, "for the government to investigate the goings-on in Movie Land and perchance take over the running of the various businesses from its libertine leaders."[16]

Given her long-standing fondness for libertines, Nell was well prepared to assume the part of Madame Glyn, the world-famous authoress whose age and war-tested savoir faire lent her an imposing edge that she would wield to keep the bohemian young friends she would make in line. The extremely thin Nell had also filled out a bit in her fifties, the additional pounds adding more gravitas to her already formidable personality. This more regal Madame Glyn who boarded the train to Los Angeles was just the woman to teach the movie industry's workers how to behave in a manner that would help to smooth the acceptance of their unconventional behavior, onscreen and off.

The real problem, as she had yet to learn, was that in reality no one of influence in the movie business was interested in listening to what the British writer had to say.

After the five-day cross-country trip in a super-luxurious Pullman car, the Super Chief roared into L.A.'s Moorish-domed train station, and Jesse Lasky escorted Nell out to the Hollywood Hotel.

Located at the corner of Hollywood Boulevard and Vine, the Hollywood Hotel had been the area's community center since 1903, when seven hundred teetotaling Midwesterners had arrived in the area in search of better weather and real estate deals. Two years later, the elderly chocolate heiress Almira Hershey bought the rambling stucco-and-frame building with long verandas and employed Myron Hunt and Elmer Grey to remodel it in their signature Mission-Moorish-Victorian style. American flags flew from cupolas covered in Spanish tile. New wings featured a chapel and music room. Imported palm trees screened the balconies, verandas, and the garden that went into the courtyard out back. Potted ferns dangled from the ceiling of the wood-paneled dining room where Hershey hosted weekly dances at which only nonalcoholic beverages were allowed.[17]

The same year this odd edifice reopened, the flickers—as

many still called the movies' immigrant-heavy, bohemian crowd—discovered Los Angeles, and boy did things change fast. Southern California possessed many of the resources the business needed most: sunshine, varied scenery, lots of cheap land, and civic boosters with a historic knack for ballyhoo. A City of Dreams, its boosters crowed, projecting hopes for an easier life under the Pacific sun onto the still sleepy pueblo of Los Angeles. In flight from a brutal Chicago winter, the Selig Movie Company responded to this "Come to Southern California" campaign and finished *The Count of Monte Cristo* (1905) on Laguna Beach. It was the first movie ever shot in California.[18]

After Jesse Lasky and his brother-in-law Samuel Goldwyn (born Gelbfisz in Warsaw) opened Lasky Feature Play Company in New York, they sent their friend, actor Cecil B. DeMille, west to direct the company's first film. DeMille set up shop in a barn he rented a short walk from the Hollywood Hotel and shot *The Squaw Man* (1913), likely the first feature film ever made in Hollywood. Several other production studios opened in the area. By 1915, Universal Film Manufacturing Company charged 25 cents, box lunch included, to tour its enormous new production lot in North Hollywood. Famous Players' Studio had spread out over several blocks to include offices, labs, wardrobe buildings, warehouses, and a large stage with a retractable glass roof. The "back ranch" held facades for exterior shots: a medieval European village, a Lower Eastside sidewalk, a dusty Old West Main Street. By 1917, the flicker's invasion of Hollywood was so complete that whenever anything unexpected happened the locals looked around for a camera. (That year Hollywood's city council banned shooting in the streets, to no avail.)[19]

Nell was just one of 100,000 new residents who made their way to Los Angeles each year from 1920 to 1924. The film industry—along with the tourism and real estate development it promoted—powered L.A.'s explosive growth; the year she arrived Los Angeles shot past San Francisco to become the West Coast's largest metropolis. Construction was everywhere. The orange and lemon groves that had once surrounded the town were disappearing and the graceful pepper trees along Hollywood Boulevard "had been chopped down so that the tourists could have a better view" of store facades built like "windmills, huge wieners, bulldogs, jails and brown derbies."[20]

Now California's leading industry, the flickers paid some 35,000 Los Angelenos $1.25 million a week—not including the "extras" paid to wait on call. Landlords who had warned "no Jews, actors, or dogs allowed" had "removed those obnoxious signs and doubled their rents," Frances Marion bitterly recalled. There was simply too much money to be made. The best place to stay within walking distance of several studios, the Hollywood Hotel had suddenly "bounced into prominence like a bewildered country maiden bequeathed a fortune," quipped Charlie Chaplin, one of its many later-famous residents.[21]

Nell had left behind a hungry world, still nursing its open wounds, and arrived in this blue-sky-land on the edge of the Pacific Rim that time seemed to have forgot. It must have felt dizzying, and disorienting, for this mature British lady, used to conversing with statesmen on matters of war, peace, and the wayward heart, to have arrived suddenly at this ramshackle hotel in a still largely pastoral setting where the sun blazed an astonishing 320 days a year.

Southern California appeared Edenic to Nell in contrast to the world she had left. It was simply made of "paradise and flowers," she marveled in an early letter to her mother. And after a lifetime spent assessing the slightest nuance and variation in visual detail, she could not help but notice that her surroundings also included the most beautiful crowd of young people she had ever seen—even if most were frightfully dressed. Everyone she met appeared not just healthy and whole but exuded a "fresh, well-nourished look" and was shockingly young.[22]

This was not her vanity speaking. Nell, more accurately, should have called herself Grande Dame Glyn. At fifty-six, she was at least a decade older than most of the men with whom she would work and often two or more than the women. Nell's only exact contemporary in her new working environment would be media tycoon and native Californian William Randolph Hearst, now in Los Angeles constantly after opening Cosmopolitan Pictures to promote his twenty-three-year-old mistress, actress Marion Davies. This would be the first period since her coming of age when Nell's beauty would have little part in influencing the judgments about her that others would make. Nor would her hard-earned stature as a cosmopolitan celebrity author who had long lived at the center of world events matter much on this faraway coast if she could not translate her cachet into a currency that counted *now*. Her imagination, sharp humor, charisma, and matchless style would be put to the test here as never before to determine if she could conjure the power she would need to succeed.

For she knew that it was her future that was in doubt. The pressure of providing for her daughters was past; both Margot and Juliet were on course to marry well-established, and significantly older, men in the months ahead. Juliet planned to wed her former boss at the Ministry of Transport, the Liberal Welsh politician Sir Rhys Rhys-Williams, whose war service had earned him a baronetcy. Margot, on the rebound from an affair (that ended because of her mother's racy reputation, family lore claims), had quickly agreed to tie the knot two months later with Sir Edward Davson, "a notable figure in the West Indies" trade. Long her mother's favored companion, lovely Margot would retreat to the edges of the family scene and into the trials of her mostly unhappy marriage.[23]

Showing a ferocious focus on the task at hand, Nell would skip both of her daughters' weddings back in London. She still had "nothing fixed to live on," as she fretted to her mother in a letter explaining her decision to move so far away. And she knew better than to hope some man would change that fact. "It is imperative for me to work to secure something while I have the chance," she asserted, so that she could "retire on just comfort—not even riches" and finally "settle down."[24]

At the Hollywood Hotel, Nell met an international crowd of literary types loitering about the veranda looking "as if they had come to the wrong address." Unconstrained by voices, silent movies "spoke a silent language, a different language" capable of seamlessly absorbing the tongues of all nationalities into one aesthetic whole. And with financial opportunities booming in America like no place else, the motion-picture business began attracting creative talent on the make from all over the world.[25]

Nell quickly learned that she and her fellow eminent authors were the result of a competition between Lasky and Samuel Goldwyn to see who could bag the most literary names for the screen. Barely

Hollywood's "Eminent Authors," Joseph Henabery, Glyn, and Somerset Maugham

literate in English, but with high aspirations to make only the very best movies, Goldwyn began a "game of authors" to make his new company stand out in the ferociously competitive business. George Bernard Shaw and H. G. Wells had rejected Goldwyn's offer to write for the screen, but he convinced several popular American writers like Rupert Hughes (uncle to Howard) and Mary Roberts Rinehart (of "the butler did it" fame) to try their luck.[26]

Not to be outdone by his former partner, Jesse Lasky focused on writers who conveyed a "foreign angle," from an upper-class, British milieu that exuded the sophisticated atmosphere the studio sought, including Somerset Maugham, Sir Gilbert Parker, and Madame Glyn. Lasky recalled the "international sensation" provoked by Glyn's "titillating English novel" back before he had ever worked in motion pictures. Now he wagered that an author who had rode her scandalous bestseller to fame more than a decade earlier might be just the person to "fashion a slinky story" for actress Gloria Swanson's first starring vehicle.[27]

In reality, Nell quickly learned that this game of authors was little more than what the Americans called a publicity stunt. "No one wanted our advice or assistance, nor did they intend to take it. All they required was the use of our names to act as shields against the critics." Her old friends Sir Gilbert Parker and his American wife, Amy, staying at the hotel, had explained as much. The Parkers lasted into spring and were a comfort as she got her bearings. But the WASPish Somerset Maugham and the Belgian poet and playwright Maurice Maeterlinck vanished not long after Nell arrived. "I look back on my connection with the cinema world with horror mitigated only by the fifteen thousand dollars I received," Maugham fumed to another eminent author after departing for France. The more gregarious Maeterlinck, who spoke no English, lasted long enough to submit two rejected scripts; one allegedly featured a hero who was a bee.[28]

Nell had confronted worse obstacles. Recognizing she knew nothing about the work at hand, she asked Jesse Lasky if she might watch her upcoming leading lady's work on her current film, *The Affairs of Anatol* (1921), directed by Cecil B. DeMille. Days later, she was playing bridge on-set with Lady Amy Parker in DeMille's latest "marriage and divorce" picture.

A former actor, DeMille created the prototype of the director general as a man who marshaled his troops in the service of epic display. From a theatrical family with New England roots, "CB" had taken instantly to Southern California. Now forty and nearly bald, he wore whatever hair he had left closely cropped. Leather puttees wound up to his knees (snakebite protection, he said), encasing the jodhpurs into which he tucked a crisp white button shirt. CB strode about on-set in this pseudo-colonial martial garb with a megaphone in one hand and a riding crop in the other, trailed by a prop person with a collapsible chair. The lifelong conservative racked up hit after hit using a formula that blended sex, moralizing about sin, and spectacle.[29]

Although Nell liked CB at once, she could barely stomach *Anatol*'s vision of romantic intrigue set among the American elite. The dramedy about marital infidelity lacked passion, just for starters. Wallace Reed was not a convincing romantic lead. Though Nell thought Reed looked ravishing in a tuxedo, the studio's biggest male star exuded a sporting, big-brotherly air devoid of the necessary naughty charm. (He was also badly addicted to narcotics and alcohol, as Gloria Swanson learned on the shoot.) She thought *Anatol's* sets tackily overblown—stuffed with chintzy bric-a-brac, they hardly conveyed the glamorously sleek, modern look needed. The women's costumes were overdone and ostentatious. Although Gloria Swanson aimed for sophistication, Nell thought the barely twenty-one-year-old woman looked more like a chorus girl. But then, almost everyone she had met so far looked common, as she complained to her mother, and by her aristocratic standards they were.[30]

After her week on DeMille's set, Nell saw that she would have her work cut out for her. So, she set about transforming the two adjoining rooms she had charmed out of Almira Hershey at the Hotel into a makeshift suite that communicated the exotic, cosmopolitan glamour that was her trademark. The dozens of trunks that had traveled with her from Paris along with her dressmaker, Ann Morgan, and Blinky, the personal secretary she hired, would also be essential to this task. The trunks spilled out scarlet drapes for the windows and bedspreads of gray velvet and piles of purple silk pillows to turn a single bed into a cozy divan. Carefully selected books—on the British aristocracy, Renaissance art, ancient history, and philosophy—lined shelves installed along the walls. De László's portrait of Nell that Curzon had commissioned hung next to a photograph of Margot and Juliet dressed in their eighteenth-century costumes for that long-ago Cairo ball. Another portrait featured her sister Lucy, still very well known in Hollywood even though her American shops had closed and Lucile Ltd. was no more. Two Siberian tiger skins—the first her purchase, the second George's calling card—escaped their trunks to make a couple on an Oriental rug. An exquisite set of tarot cards, a smiling Buddha, and a crystal ball acquired on the recent trip to Egypt landed on a center table.[31]

When Gloria Swanson arrived for tea later that week, she thought the room appeared like "a Persian tent" and Madame Glyn like "something from another world." Nell's now artificially red hair was "wrapped around her head like an elaborate turban" and Swanson recognized at once that her "teeth were too even and white to be real." (She had painfully acquired a set of dentures in Paris earlier that year.) Nell also sported the first false eyelashes the actress had ever seen. "Although old enough to be my grandmother, she got away with it," Gloria saw at once.

Nell "talked a blue streak," pacing around her crowded rooms in the small steps required because she refused to wear glasses though now terribly nearsighted. "People in America are very direct. I rather like that. I am very direct myself. It saves an enormous amount of time. And at my age, time is very precious to me. You children don't realize yet what has happened, I know. But you will," Gloria recalled her explaining. "Motion pictures are going to change everything. They're the most important thing that's come along since the printing press."[32]

Nell's easy projection of supreme confidence would have been a surprisingly familiar variation on a type the young actress would have known well. Although Swanson called the world of 1916 not just "a man's world, but a business controlled entirely by men," she had learned that sometimes things worked differently in the picture business after trading work at Essanay Studios in Chicago for work at Mack Sennett's Keystone Studio in Los Angeles. She had enjoyed the improvisational Sennett system of making pictures, but not playing "a dumb little cutie." Gloria had no intention of spending her time forever "having her skirts lifted and dodging flying bricks." An encounter with Clara Kimball Young—a dramatic actress who had opened her own production company—suggested a different path. "In what other business," Swanson wondered after a dinner at Kimball Young's, "could this delightful elegant creature be completely independent, turning out her own pictures" and "dealing with men as her equals"?[33]

The movie colony was no utopia for the female sex, but Nell had unexpectedly landed in the ideal environment to exercise her ambition to become a new kind of star author. At the time of her arrival, motion pictures were the least sex-segregated of America's major industries. Standards were admittedly bleak and racial stratification was rife, limiting opportunities almost exclusively to white women. Whispers about the casting couch circulated, and men far outnumbered women in the most powerful roles. But in the movies' fluid industrial landscape, workers moved in and out of different roles, and powerful actresses routinely formed their own companies. Others took leading parts behind the camera as writers, directors, and editors. Lois Weber was Metro's director general as much as CB was for Famous Players. They also filled the ranks of the publicists, culture reporters, and all manner of more traditional support positions. It would take a century for Hollywood to again employ, in the entire industry, the number of women directing movies at Universal Studios alone the year that Madame Glyn arrived.[34]

A spotlight had landed on the movie colony's new home, and women journalists working in a press corps that soon rivaled only Washington's for size, seemed to revel in drawing attention to the unusual conditions under which many women worked and played. Journalist Louella Parsons (whose later radio broadcasts from the hotel's ballroom during the Depression were the basis for Busby Berkeley's musical comedy *Hollywood Hotel* in 1937) became the era's most influential movie columnist by celebrating these women as pioneers in the west's latest gold-rush industry. "When Horace Greeley penned those immortal words, 'Go West, Young Man,' he failed to reckon with the feminine contingent. That of course was before the days of feminism," Parsons excused. "In the good old days when Horace philosophized over the possibilities in the golden west he thought the only interest the fair sex could have in this faraway country was to go as a helpmate to man." But "in the present day, if milady goes west, she goeth to make her own fortune."[35]

Gloria Swanson had been working in the movies long enough to know that making her fortune required getting people—reporters like Parsons, studio bosses like Lasky and, through them, the public—to take your charisma seriously. By the end of their first tea, Swanson believed she had found just the person to help her fashion the right image to match the sophisticated kind of modern women she wanted to play.

Gloria had already leapt from comedic foil to dramatic lead in films like *Don't Change Your Husband* (1919), one of the "marriage and divorce" pictures written by Jeanie MacPherson and directed by DeMille. ("One of the best-known scenario writers in the business," Parsons called MacPherson, who had been an actress and director before becoming CB's primary collaborator.) Lasky had asked

MacPherson and DeMille to tap the buzz surrounding the nation's skyrocketing divorce rates, revealing feminine fashions, and flaming youth. "What the public demands to-day is modern stuff with plenty of clothes, rich sets, and action . . . full of modern problems and conditions."[36]

Now Gloria faced the ultimate challenge for an actor: an above-the-title role in *The Great Moment* that would test if she could open a picture. But Swanson knew she lacked not only *just* the right image onscreen but also, and perhaps more critically, the right celebrity persona. Swanson had read *Three Weeks* years before, recalling it as an opening salvo in the struggle to end the sexual double standard by celebrating a woman who "*enjoyed* her amorous conquest," believing "that love-making is an art like any other." Already headed to a second divorce trial—where her husband charged her with multiple counts of adultery—Swanson needed just the kind of help Madame Glyn had to offer.[37]

At their tea, Nell recognized that Gloria was smart and brave, however common. She would make an excellent pupil. "Egyptian!" Nell pronounced in the voice Samuel Goldwyn described as sounding "like the lonely wind blowing through the pine trees." "Extraordinary, quite extraordinary. You're such a tiny, dainty little thing. But of course if your proportions are perfect they can make you any size they want, can't they?" (It is still true that many actors are often much shorter than people expect.) "But . . . my . . . dear," Nell drawled, carefully spacing her words for effect, according to the awestruck young woman. "Your proportions are Egyptian; anyone can see that when you turn your head. *You have lived there in another time.*"[38]

Here was a new element in the character Nell played for her public after coming to Hollywood. Whether consciously or not is hard to say, but once arrived in Los Angeles, Nell began to announce her esoteric views and psychic gifts for the first time, far and wide. "I believe that in some previous incarnation each of our souls dwelt in the body of an animal," she avowed over an illustration of "Elinor— the Tiger," in one of her first *Photoplay* interviews. The image of Madame Glyn she crafted now positioned her as an Oracle-like figure capable of seeing into the heart of any matter by drawing on her entrenched spiritual belief in reincarnation, the law of karma, and her own mental powers to make her visualizations materialize.[39]

The popularity of New Thought in southern California likely encouraged Nell's new openness about her religious practices. California possessed more New Thought centers and healers than anyplace else, and Nell quickly befriended a female medium in Los Angeles who remained an unnamed but important presence in much of her writing during this period. Most of the religion's leaders and converts were well-educated and relatively well-off white women like Nell, who embraced mental healing through meditations focused on manifesting a better life. The medical establishment and intelligentsia heaped scorn upon in it: "probably the most preposterous lunacy ever invented by man" (or rather, woman), H. L. Mencken called New Thought. But this may only have intensified some women's interest in a philosophy that promised their own minds, rather than the opinions of men, held the key to their health, happiness, and success. And like most everyone in the 1920s, Nell's meditations trained her mind on producing wealth.[40]

Like her commitment to New Thought, playing a part in public had also become a familiar strategy to soothe anxiety. The balance between tradition and innovation, between the elegant lady and the sexy siren that she had first assiduously cultivated on her *Three Weeks* book tour in America was still apparent. But Nell's cultivation of the role of Madame Glyn also conveyed her hard-won confidence in her powers to flourish even amidst heartbreak and war. She would channel this confidence in the power of her visions to create the grander, queenlier persona of Madame Glyn—part glamorous grande dame, part cosmopolitan oracle. Her success playing the role of Madame Glyn bolstered her authority working in a new medium where her previous fame and reputation only partially translated.

"There are no accidents my dear," Nell assured Gloria, her narrow, sea-foam-green eyes staring deeply into Swanson's big blue ones. "We simply live out what was meant to be."[41]

What was meant to be was that Gloria seized the chance to become the first protégée whom Madame Glyn mentored to stratospheric heights. Before their first tea ended, Nell had convinced Swanson to hitch her star to Madame Glyn. Swanson would follow her redheaded friend's well-modulated orders about how to dance, dress, talk, and walk whenever possible. With the help of her dressmaker, Ann Morgan, Nell would reshape how Gloria appeared to her fans. Swanson's fussy dresses would give way to a kind of slinky simplicity that Nell herself now favored. Her fluffy hair became a dark satin cap that emphasized her small well-shaped head, long neck, and enormous eyes. Nell and Morgan would make Swanson the industry's first glamour queen, setting the stage for her to become the first Hollywood actress who would marry into the aristocracy when she wed Henry de La Falaise, Marquis de La Coudraye in 1925.[42]

"Rubbish, my dear, absolute rubbish," Nell called Lasky's warning that Gloria's new motherhood would destroy her sex appeal. "You are the new kind of woman altogether—daring, provocative, sensuous," she imperiously explained. "I am sure religiously-minded people will be *reassured* to learn your love life takes a normal course. If motion picture producers knew what sex appeal was they would have no need of me, now, would they?"[43]

After settling into the new suite that fed the right vibrations she needed for her creative work, Nell turned to convincing the producers that she was more than just the usual literary figure with no appetite for what making movies required. She took "a lot of pains" with her first original story for the screen, writing the required 4,000 words about a temperamental, aristocratic Englishwoman's sexual awakening by a hero brimming with "It."

Nell's decades-old fascination with western American men shaped *The Great Moment*'s dream lover, Bayard Deval. After her heroine, Nadine, meets Bayard on a trip to visit her father's silver mine in Nevada, she breaks "the bonds of English conventionality" and dumps her sleepy fiancé. A builder of the modern world, Bayard is an engineer who is also desert-tough enough to satisfy Nadine's buried gypsy-side. When a rattlesnake bites the wayward heroine, Bayard expertly sucks the poison from her breast with a finesse that leads her to want to settle down. Nell called her story, "an exciting tale, of *The Taming of the Shrew* variety."[44]

Lasky accepted the scenario, making Nell the first of the eminent authors to succeed at telling a tale fit for the screen on her first attempt. Then he passed it on to the scenario department to add more suspense and the comedic touches that Nell came to dislike. Next one of the studio's many continuity writers would turn the story into a shooting script that detailed the technical requirements and staging for each change of scene.

While she waited, Madame Glyn set about modeling elegance, charm, and good manners to her young coworkers at the Hollywood Hotel. "Of all the people I ever waited on Mrs. Glyn was the nicest and kindest and most considerate. I never knew her to be cross—not even at breakfast," declared one of the waitresses where she ate each morning. She rekindled her love of dancing at Almira Hershey's weekly soirees and launched a Sunday teatime literary salon. When her hungover colleagues showed up, they were mystified that actual tea was the only beverage. Nell "was not content with merely putting elegance into her plots," recalled one regular attendee, writer Anita Loos. The expert wisecracking, brunette pixie (who wrote *Gentleman Prefer Blondes* in 1925) recalled that Nell "was hell-bent on bringing refinement to the film colony."[45]

When Charlie Chaplin appeared one Sunday afternoon, Nell declared him "an old, old soul" who had been a princess in a previous life. Nell could be "a little overwhelming at first," Chaplin admitted, but the British transplants from opposite ends of the class ladder quickly grew very fond of each other. Charlie learned that she could not only make but take a joke. ("You're not as funny looking as I expected," Nell observed after first meeting the Little Tramp. "Neither are you," he retorted, to her delight.)

They both recognized that each knew how to inhabit a role that captivated the attention of the world. Charlie and Nell would become frequent partners at charades and in other escapades on land and sea over the 1920s. Like Charlie, her "narratives and comments usually kept a whole roomful of people laughing." Charlie embraced the hedonistic pleasures of early Hollywood's raucous bohemian scene, while Madame Glyn's humor at times derived from her seriousness about setting and enforcing better manners in this unruly milieu.[46]

"What a wonderful country this is! A divine climate, and a happy-go-lucky way of living," she wrote her agent, Hughes Massie, days before Christmas. An American who had long lived in London, Massie had pioneered the profession of literary agency when he began selling the works of Americans abroad. The charming go-getter had personally taken over Nell's affairs from the "dislikable but effective" Albert Brandt before she left for the United States. But after only three months, Nell saw that Massie's large literary firm, based in London and New York, was quite distant from this new show business in which the old rules did not seem to apply.[47]

"I have been waiting until my first scenario should be finished to let you know how things are going. It is complete now, and delivered and accepted, and will be begun after Xmas, and then another arrangement must be made with the company," she reported happily. Then she turned to the real subject. "It is perfectly impossible, even with the cable" to manage negotiations, "with you so far away and all the principals *here*," she wrote. "I shall do it myself after having expert advice on the spot," she continued, indicating her rapidly growing comfort operating in the movie colony alone. "You know me well enough to know that your commission will be exactly the same on all the Lasky transactions," she reassured him, "but I must arrange the details myself here at the fountain head."[48]

Rather than return home for Juliet's marriage to Sir Rhys Rhys-Williams in February, Madame Glyn stayed in Los Angeles over the holidays to launch a highly publicized search to find the right actor to play her hero in *The Great Moment*. Family lore claims she might have failed to make the trip because she considered the Welshman far too old for her brilliant girl. At fifty-seven, Rhys was thirty-three years older than his bride and just one year younger than Nell. In her novels, young women's marriages to much older men always end disastrously (Juliet's to Rhys would not, but Margot's to the seventeen-years-older Edward Davson would.)[49]

But prioritizing work was by now a firmly entrenched habit for this breadwinner mother. The only surviving comment from the time suggests her ferocious commitment to mastering the task at hand. "I believe there is a fortune in the moving picture industry," she explained to Massie. "But there is a terrible amount to learn in the technique, and I doubt if I shall be able to return to England before the summer."[50]

Although still a neophyte at filmmaking, Madame Glyn quickly demonstrated her mastery over the arts of using her celebrity persona to capture the attention that helped to fuel the American silent film industry's spectacular growth in the 1920s. "Tiger Skins and Temperament," her first interview in *Photoplay*, found Nell posed on her signature rug in her suite, Egyptian incense wafting. Here she airily announced American men could simply not make love, a claim sure to earn lots of publicity for the Tiger Queen, as the fan magazines often predictably called her.

Madame Glyn's command of Orientalism dazzled reporter Delight Evans, who nonsensically described her both as a "very, very well connected," "old citizen of the world" and as "an absolutely fantastic 'houri'" (one of the young virgins said to await devout Muslim men in Paradise). Screen tests proved no actor could treat his sweetheart differently from his aunts or sisters, she complained. Unless she found an actor with "It," she could not teach romance-starved American girls "a desire to be loved as European women are loved."[51]

Madame Glyn leaned heavily into the French provenance she had earned when explaining why the sexual repressions and hypocrisies of Anglo-American culture prevented most actors from expressing "It." "In Filmdom's Boudoir," continued the point. Published under her elegantly scrawled signature, here she called "It" that "strange magnetism that attracts both sexes," the quality exuded by "tigers and cats—both animals being fascinating and mysterious, and quite unbiddable." Actors should remain single in order to gain "It," she argued, rather than take advantage of America's more liberal divorce laws. How many "foolish, ordinary" wives and "boring, exacting" husbands, she wondered, had suffocated their partner's creative growth? Aligning herself with the French romantic tradition and its production of the first bohemia to house the modern artist, she reminded readers that in her beloved Paris, everyone knew that "marriage is good, and art is good—but they do not appear to assimilate to perfection."[52]

The announcement that Milton Sills—who had zero "It"—would star opposite Gloria revealed that Nell had no influence choosing the hero. But she knew that outcome hardly mattered. Perception mattered more than reality in the shorthand of celebrity culture.

"Before a foot of film had been shot—she knew that she had the public hanging on every word," her first protégée boasted.[53]

When *The Great Moment* went into production, Madame Glyn astonished everyone by treating her role like a serious job. The story was out of her hands; Lasky had made that clear. She also had no influence over Swanson's costumes. But she shuddered about sets like a stately mad hatter determined to make the scenes of British society life look realistic, ordering the grips (the industry's moving men) to rearrange and replace offensive objects. "She ain't a bit like the other authoreens we've had around here," one complained, "They'll go off and leave you alone."[54]

"Humiliating," she called the situation to her mother. "Every person connected with the production studios," she later huffed, "was absolutely convinced that he or she knew much better how to depict the manners and customs of whatever society or country they were attempting to show on the screen than any denizen of that country or society." Since Hollywood had suddenly become *the* international film capital and fashion trendsetter, its movies during the 1920s increasingly strove to reflect the highest levels of society. But the vast majority of the polyglot film folk came from modest backgrounds; if they had traveled at all, they had likely done so in steerage.[55]

Nell's constant interference on the set over what she later conceded were at times trivial details left director Sam Wood fuming. A former real estate developer, Wood had apprenticed as CB's second director for years, developing a solid, workmanlike approach to his task. Wood did his best to ignore the omnipresent British lady. But "appalling rows" erupted after he argued they should move the snakebite from Swanson's breast to her wrist to avoid trouble with the moral reformers. Nell won a rare victory when Lasky agreed the bite should stay low enough to preserve the scene's steamy charge.[56]

Still, the work appealed to Nell. She had always liked a challenge, and after burying conflict for so long she found this open airing of disagreements at times exhilarating. Working with people who seemed to thrive on argument, and with whom she had no real ties, permitted her to live out loud as never before. And there were internal intricacies to this medium, she began to see; a need to take what those around her called the screen angle into account.

Milton Sills, Gloria Swanson, Nell, and the tiger skin on the set of *The Great Moment* (1921)

"The great problem with the usual author, is that he approaches the camera with some fixed literary ideal and he cannot compromise with the motion picture viewpoint," Samuel Goldwyn bitterly observed when explaining why his "game of authors" failed so spectacularly. The "medium demands first of all tangible drama, the elementary interaction between person and person and person and circumstance," Goldwyn wrote. The usual author could also not endure a collaborative storytelling process in which the image ruled.

"Words fail to describe the scene that follows" became perhaps an apocryphal line in one eminent author's screenplay that still made a point. Even with the best actor, internal psychological motivation only got you so far in front of a camera.[57]

But Nell had never been the usual author. To spot the wrong note almost instantly in any look or setting was the virtual birth-right of Lucile's little sister. And in her stepfather's library long ago she'd come to believe in the magical glamour of appearances that were accompanied by just the right words and touch. Now with her intuitive third eye honed to razor-sharp precision, she felt ready to spread her romantic visions to the world.

She also knew that Lasky would, whatever her actual influence, promote *The Great Moment* under the name of "the world famed author of *Three Weeks*." Even before shooting began, advertisements announced the movie would be "written especially by Elinor Glyn and supervised by her." As spring gave way to summer, ads contin-ued to hammer home the point. "This picture has some names to conjure with," the *Exhibitors Herald* reminded theater owners shortly before it opened. "First there is the author, Elinor Glyn, famous as the writer of 'Three Weeks' and other novels; second there is Gloria Swanson, who is elevated to stardom."[58]

"Sex and the Photoplay," a full-page editorial that appeared in *Motion Picture Magazine* under Nell's byline, aimed to stifle the crit-ics' prospective yowls. "What after all is this Sex Bogy?" she asked. "You might just as sensibly attack the practice of eating bread, as to attack every subject which has to do with Sex. . . . It is the life force of the world," and "while humans are of a certain age it is the mainspring of all action." Taking aim at the censors, she advocated a democratic solution in this increasingly democratic age, arguing, "this matter should be left in the hands of Public Opinion."[59]

Like the vast majority of silent movies, *The Great Moment* is lost, making it impossible to see. But the box office vindicated her approach. "The public doesn't seem to be able to get enough of Elinor Glyn's first story for the screen," reported the *Exhibitors Herald* months after the film opened in August. "It's a picture that will cause talk," one theater owner warned. Several others remarked that female patrons particularly liked the movie's several daring situ-

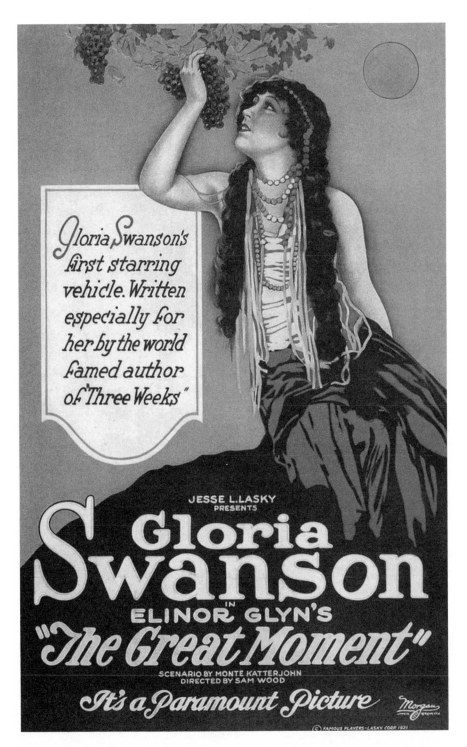

Poster from Nell's first movie, *The Great Moment*

ations. "The snakebite incident sent a thrill through the audience. It is one of the big moments of the picture," another gushed.[60]

"*The Great Moment* is having a wild success! At last they see what I can do," Nell gloated in a letter home. After having so many of her opinions ignored on the set, the film's box-office returns had earned her "devoted friends and admirers." She had proved her genuine value in this new medium in just a matter of months, even if the critical response was almost as bad as the box office was good.

"Nothing more sensational has been seen on the screen, even in the most horrible moments of the serials," advised Edwin Schiller in the *Los Angeles Times*, connecting Glyn's racy heroine to the hair-raising exploits of serial queens like Pearl White. "Boob bait, with a great deal of sex strewn around everywhere," Robert Sherwood fumed in *LIFE*. According to Sherwood, the film proved that Madame Glyn was simply "of the box office, by the box office, and for the box office," rather than a civilizing force. Still, like any business, the financial bottom line was what mattered most to producers, most of the time.[61]

What was still in doubt was whether Madame Glyn could subdue the tempest whipping up over Hollywood's sex pictures and the outrageous, often gender-bending, behavior of the men and women inside the bohemian movie colony.[62]

CHAPTER 12

Babylon or Bohemia?

Women can—and do—exactly what they like here for they work, play,
love and draw their paychecks on exactly the same basis as men.

—Mary Winship, "Oh Hollywood! A Ramble in Bohemia" (1921)[1]

—Are you married?
—No, I live in Hollywood.

Nell had landed in her element almost at once inside the movie colony. After *The Great Moment*'s success, she "seemed to take over Hollywood. She went everywhere and passed her fearsome verdicts on everything. 'This is glamorous,' she would say, 'This is hideous,'" reported Gloria Swanson, who often made the social rounds with her that year. "Her British dignity was devastating, as she baby-stepped through this or that dining room or garden party, people moved aside for her as if she was a sorceress on fire." Her height helped, as she admitted to her mother. The film folk had "tiny bodies—none over 5'4 high and mostly about 5 foot. I am *tall!*"

The first *Vanity Fair* cartoon to offer a peek at Hollywood and its industry-defining personalities placed Madame Glyn towering above a row of tiny stars, including Charlie Chaplin, Douglas Fairbanks, Mary Pickford, Alla Nazimova, and Gloria Swanson. Nell stands center stage, mysteriously swathed in a mantilla, staring at the viewer as if to ask: *So? What do you think?*[2]

Madame Glyn's status as a writer was notable even in an industry in which women pioneered the craft of screenwriting, headed the first scenario departments, and wrote 50 percent of copyrighted scripts from 1911 until the end of the silent era in 1929. Although surrounded by women made rich by writing—June Mathis, Anita Loos, Frances Marion, Ouida Bergère, Josephine Lovett, and Jeanie MacPherson, to name a few—Nell had managed indisputably to become motion picture's star author, male or female, in a matter of months.[3]

Much of her role's magic lay in a sleight-of-hand that substituted the glamour of her upper-class white European identity for conventional moral respectability in ways that confused the substance of the two to her advantage—and to Hollywood's. In the United States, her evident wealth and white skin counted for so much more than in Europe. In the unusually mobile, multilingual, and multi-hued society of the United States, law and custom pitilessly fixed people with darker skin at the bottom of society's scale no matter their other characteristics.

This meant that Madame Glyn's lily-white skin, upper-class British accent, elite associations, and box-office success gave her singular leeway to promote a more titillating approach to romance without inflaming the moral reformers too much. The inherent conservativism of the aristocratic context that surrounded the author and her stories and lovers also helped, elegantly cloaking their celebration of sexual passion often centered on the heroine's pleasure. In a manner her old friend Daisy, the Countess of Warwick, would have recognized at once, Nell skirted the censors by using the power of glamour—chic clothes, superb settings, gorgeous faces, and carefully orchestrated caresses—to transmute more explicit and often illicit depictions of heterosexual passion into the most exquisite love.

Offscreen, Nell's cultivation of the role of the film industry's cosmopolitan grandmother, wise to the ways of the world, would give her enormous influence over her young coworkers so recently thrust before more eyes than any public figures before them. Her queenly censure of disorderly conduct, if not high spirits, cowed many into tamping down their wilder ways in her company.

Even before Madame Glyn arrived, before the term "Hollywood" slipped into wide usage, astute observers had begun comparing the movie colony to a bohemia, that quintessentially modern metropolitan neighborhood of creative expression and romantic self-reinvention first publicized in Henri Murger's *Scènes de la vie de bohème* (1851). Although the Latin Quarter remained the standard for bohemia, in the succeeding decades many communities of penniless, free-spirited, ambitious artists and other wayward souls came to embrace the term as capturing their challenge to bourgeois standards. In the twentieth century, bohemian spaces made more room for women to act as artists and lovers as well as muses and mistresses. L.A.'s bohemia would intensify this association with the female sex's move toward greater equality and freedom of expression. Although racial stratification was endemic, white women even in the industry's emerging "pink-collar" workforce earned a living wage and enjoyed full political rights. And the top salaries in the film industry included many women, displaying how this bohemia featured women artists as never before.[4]

After the war, the national press began to regularly describe the movie colony as a bohemian third space, a "city within city," some place on the "edge of town," where "clannish" and "outlandish" customs set the trends desired and criticized by others in equal measure. "The colony's outlandish ideas," warned Anita Loos in *Breaking Into the Movies* (1921), were the same ones "always associated with artists—a bohemian spirit which is the same whether in Hollywood or the Latin Quarter of Paris." Valeria Belletti, a secretary at Goldwyn who dreamed of becoming a writer, was equally emphatic. "You have no idea how glad I am I left New York," she wrote home. "There is no place so full of romances as California, especially Hollywood," before admitting it "at times reeked too much of the flesh." But at least "the bohemian colony in Los Angeles" had "real artists and not fake ones like you find in the Village."[5]

Although Nell could have gotten away with just about anything inside the movie colony's bohemian party scene that spring of 1921, dancing with handsome young men was the principal risqué activity in which she indulged. Nell avoided the smaller, racier dives to exercise her old pleasure whirling around on polished floors with men in tuxedos in the swankier places springing up along Wilshire and Sunset Boulevards. The most elegant new venue became her preferred spot: the Ambassador Hotel's intimate Patent Leather Room, where it "was always impossible to get in without a reservation unless you were Elinor Glyn," Swanson learned. If Nell's party met a crowd waiting near the maître d', she "simply looked shocked and imperious until, as if by magic, a front table materialized." To the wailing rhythms of the hottest jazz west of Kansas City, Nell quickly learned all the latest dances like the Charleston, Black Bottom, and Cake Walk in front of a row of cameras.[6]

Nell's regular partner that year was a handsome Oklahoman actor, Dana Todd (who danced *marvelously*, Swanson sighed). Todd was the first in a long line of little-discussed, much-younger men who squired Madame Glyn about town during her Hollywood years. What happened after hours between Nell and her often-decades-younger admirers is impossible to say based on the remaining historical record. Certainly, there would be few doubts about the after-hours activities of a similarly well preserved and well-situated single man. Nell's impeccable pose of stately grandeur, as well as attitudes about middle-aged women's lack of sexual appetites, likely prevented the gossip columnists from discussing the subject.

While in Los Angeles, Nell repeatedly told her mother that she was happy to be free of romantic entanglements. But over the years, the traces left by Nell's bevy of admirers appeared in the private cor-

The Cocoanut Grove at the Ambassador Hotel

respondence of younger British women like Juliet and the socialite and actress Lady Diana Manners Cooper. Both were aghast at the devoted attention younger men paid to Nell.[7]

Still, as Nell well knew by now, the American public's response to her was more tolerant, and not just because of her upper-class accent and European associations. Here, the governing logic of consumer capitalism meant a greater acceptance of the idea that what was permissible was what the public bought. If you could get away with it—and Nell did, as Swanson and so many others instantly recognized—more power to the individual, even if that individual was a nakedly ambitious woman.

For Madame Glyn's stature as Hollywood's glamorous grande dame was priceless to moviemakers whose workers often embraced a freewheeling bohemianism that made an easy target for moralists to attack. Calls for 100 percent Americanism that first arose during the war would crest in 1924 with Congress's passage of the Johnson–Reed Act, which virtually halted the entrance of new immigrants. The censors had grown bolder and restive about the dangers posed by the film industry's un-American producers, love stories, and stars. That year Henry Ford launched a campaign to publicize the danger of a "Movie Trust" controlled by "five or six degenerate Hebrews." The Federal Trade Commission had also begun investigating Famous Players-Lasky for monopolistic practices even as the recently revivified Ku Klux Klan became the decade's largest social movement by fomenting fear about the danger immigrants posed to "native-born," Protestant, white Americans (or WASPs, as they would soon be called).[8]

Although danger stalked the new immigrant-led film industry from all sides, it continued to court trouble by releasing more sex films, some of which were foreign imports, to boot, like the Berlin-made *Madame Du Barry*—a lavish court spectacle about the infamous mistress of King Louis XV who sleeps her way to the top of French society. The German film industry had been the only European one to flourish during the war. After 1914, film production among the Allies ground to a halt, since the production of celluloid and ammunition required the same chemicals. The opposite was true in Germany. Before the war, the German film industry had lagged far behind France and Italy and imported most of its films, but after Allied-made, anti-German propaganda films flooded the country, the government took control of the industry and consolidated all production and distribution at UFA—a gigantic, state-subsidized studio in Berlin. Charged with improving the quality and quantity of German movies, UFA succeeded.

Still, the German market was tiny; at the signing of the Treaty of Versailles, 90 percent of all films screened in Europe, Africa, and Asia were American-made; the figure for Latin America was closer to 100 percent. And only the United States possessed the enormous advantage of having a domestic market large enough to recoup the expense of making, distributing, and promoting the ever-more-lavish feature films that became moviegoers' preferred fare.[9]

Once the Weimar Republic came to power in 1919, it transferred the company into private hands, making UFA the leader in the All-Europe cinema movement that aimed to compete with Hollywood. UFA produced artistically and technically excellent films like *Madame Du Barry* that held an international appeal, which Hollywood producers had renamed *Passion* for its American release. The film was a critical and commercial hit, but the outcry over its immorality had left a state censorship board in New York, the industry's largest market. In what became a familiar pattern, *Passion*'s star actress and director—Pola Negri and Ernst Lubitsch—ended up in Hollywood rather than transforming the European cinema world.[10]

But no movie burned hotter in this year of pyrotechnical displays than *The Four Horsemen of the Apocalypse* (1921), which became Nell's favorite film of the decade. The *Four Horsemen* turned an unknown Italian actor, Rudolph Valentino, into the screen's first male sex symbol, starring as a dissolute Argentine heir and ladies' man extraordinaire. The wild intensity of Valentino's popularity illustrated the truth of what Madame Glyn had been saying since she had arrived: fans wanted a man with "It"—that 100 percent American lovers seemed unable or unwilling to supply.[11]

June Mathis, head of Metro's scenario department, had insisted Valentino play the hero in her adaptation of Victor Ibanez's best-selling novel about the Great War's catastrophic costs. Mathis knew the well-born Italian tango dancer possessed the necessary seductive power and grace to break out of playing gangsters (or "heavies") to play Julio, a tango-dancing, Argentine rich boy ultimately redeemed by the war. A critical and box-office smash, the *Four Horseman* dropped "the continental hero, the polished foreigner, the modern Don Juan" into Hollywood's "unsuspecting midst." Valentino's image as the Latin lover perfectly fit Madame Glyn's ideas. "Women, whether they are feminists, suffragettes, or so-called new women, like to have a masterful man make them do things," Valentino reportedly declared. Mathis and her protégé decamped to Famous Players when Metro failed to reward the actor. "More sheer animal magnetism than any actor before or since," Lasky always said.[12]

Nell had instantly identified Valentino as one of the very few actors in Hollywood with loads of "It" and had lobbied for him to play her hero in *The Great Moment*. Instead, Lasky rushed his new property into production on *The Sheik* (1919), a bestselling romance that had Madame Glyn's fingerprints on every page. Set in the North African desert, E. M. Hull's "bodice ripper" charts the sexual awakening of Lady Diana Mayo at the hands of a beautiful and brutal Arab sheik in a manner that closely resembled Glyn's *His Hour*. (Hull's choices as an author bore no resemblance to Glyn's; after the novel's success, she hid behind her initials in the English countryside.) Independent and superior, Diana rejects several passionless Anglo suitors. "Marriage is captivity," she tells one, "the end of independence." Valentino's sheik spies this "white gazelle" and arranges for her kidnap. In his tent, "the close union with his warm strong body robbed her of all strength," leading her to submit to her "hatefully handsome" captor.[13]

"We all saw ourselves in the role of Diana Mayo," pined a future Glyn protégée, romantic novelist Barbara Cartland, after reading *The Sheik*. "We all longed to be abducted into the desert and to be forced by sheer violence into obedience by an all-conquering male." A Chicago student agreed: "The more I saw the picture the more I fell in love with the handsome hero," she admitted. "I resented him for his abrupt and brutal manners but still I used to care for him." "Oh, what a Lucky Girl to have enough money to make a trip like that—a trip across the wild desert with only Arab guides in her company," exclaimed another. "Seems like an ordinary picture," one theater owner reported, "but as a lady patron remarked, 'How that man can love.'"[14]

Nell got the man she and everyone else wanted for her next film: Rudolph Valentino would star opposite Gloria Swanson in her adaptation of *Beyond the Rocks*, directed again by Sam Wood. The film would begin shooting in November, allowing Nell to take a needed vacation to Europe that fall. She received the same flat fee and guarantee that her name would appear lavishly in the film's publicity and on the screen. She also promised Lasky a third story within six months of the film's completion.[15]

In the months before she left, Madame Glyn cemented her place within the movie colony by claiming a coveted spot within its least bohemian crowd: the circle of Mary Pickford and her second husband, Douglas Fairbanks. Before their marriage, the pair had joined Chaplin and D. W. Griffith to create United Artists as a pipeline to distribute movies owned by the people who dreamed them up. "This is necessary to protect the great motion picture public from threatening combinations and trusts that would force upon them mediocre productions and machine-made entertainment," UA's first statement declared in 1919. "The lunatics have taken over the asylum," joked the president of Metro Pictures, Richard Rowland. "Actually," replied the distributor Arthur Mayer, "the founders of United Artists displayed the same brand of lunacy as Rockefeller, Morgan, or DuPont."[16]

The most business-minded of the partners, Mary Pickford had tottered on the brink of scandal the year after UA's creation, when word broke of her separation from her first husband, Owen Moore. But the public forgave all when she quickly married the swashbuckling heartthrob Fairbanks. The riotous reactions prompted by the couple's 1920 European honeymoon made the crushing scale of modern celebrity clear. "A royal reception," a New Zealand newspaper called the estimated 100,000 people who met their train in London. Like "a lynch mob—except that it was smiling," Fairbanks said of the crowd that mobbed the tiny couple at a charity event a few days later. Some 200,000 people waited for the couple in Paris; by Moscow, 350,000 met their train.[17]

On their return, the couple moved into Pickfair—their estate set on eighteen acres in Beverly Hills and designed in the mock-Tudor style of the English country houses Nell knew so well. Here the couple established themselves as models of wedded bliss (a rarity among film folk) and propriety, making Madame Glyn an ideal ornament for their table. The hyper class-conscious Fairbanks never let anyone with the right accent who possessed even a pseudo title like Nell's to make it through Los Angeles without an invitation to dine. ("Hello, Doug," Chaplin said to his friend one morning. "How's the duke?" "What duke?" Fairbanks asked. "Oh, any duke," he scoffed.)[18]

Pickfair was a dry environment, which Nell appreciated. This stance was in stark contrast to most film folk, and the rich more generally (including President Harding), who openly drank their way through their well-stocked wine cellars, since Prohibition outlawed only the sale, transportation, and manufacture of intoxicating spirits. Fairbanks, an early health nut, forbade alcohol, while Mary drank on the sly with her Irish mother or at the "hen parties" she hosted with women coworkers and friends like Frances Marion. But after their marriage, Mary and Doug held themselves aloof from the wider, and wilder, film colony, preferring to orchestrate their own socializing at home, where they always sat side by side and danced only with each other. (Fairbanks was known to be a very jealous man.) Nell was one of the few guests who approved of Fairbanks's stance against alcohol, joining a notable group of teetotalers who bucked the hard-drinking movie colony's habits. Given Nell's sad experience with Clayton, it is fair to say that it was not drinking per se, but rather drinking to excess, that troubled her so very much.[19]

"My Mary," as Nell called Pickford, really won her heart. "Mary is wonderful—a perfect hostess as though born to high company," she wrote her mother. Certainly the two women each had much to offer the other. Eager to learn the intricacies of the business, there was no better mentor than the woman whose "business and legal acumen" amazed Charlie Chaplin, leading him to dub his partner "Bank of America's Sweetheart." For her part, Pickford had grown concerned about keeping her more wholesome, "All-American" personality relevant to the raucous youth presently coming of age. She had shorn her famous long locks and begun experimenting with radically altering the kinds of parts she played. Madame Glyn, whatever her actual age, seemed to understand what the postwar generation wanted from the inside out.[20]

"That's Elinor Glyn, she's dining with us tonight," Fairbanks whispered to Samuel Goldwyn that summer when they came upon Nell one evening staring pensively into the sunset reflected in Pickfair's enormous swimming pool. Fairbanks's use of "Elinor" suggested a certain chill between them that comes across in Nell's letters, which linger on Pickford while never mentioning her ever-present husband. But his use of her first name also betrayed a wider pattern that showed up even among her closest friends in the movie colony, like Chaplin, Pickford, and actress Marion Davies. Few people from these years recall her as anything but "Elinor." The shift owed something to her more frequent opining in the press under the byline "Elinor Glyn," begun during the war. The regal Elinor, rather than the diminutive "Nell," also fit her advancing years and a stature she had earned. Still, the apparent failure to use Nell even by those she knew best in Los Angeles conveys a certain lack of intimacy in her relationships there.[21]

Dressed in a simple sea-green chiffon evening gown that made her eyes glow and her hair flame, Nell appeared to Samuel Goldwyn at their first meeting like the Greek sorceress Circe. All through dinner, and during the game of charades the couple often staged afterward if there was no movie to watch, Nell and Chaplin entertained the guests with outrageous stories. "Too amusing and attractive—the greatest wit and cynic and perfectly a gentleman," she described Chaplin to her mother.[22]

Madame Glyn intimidated many people in Los Angeles, even in Hollywood's most exclusive social circle. Most of her young friends knew so little of the world outside their make-believe bubbles. They had worked hard all their short lives at one thing, which had catapulted them suddenly into positions of wealth and fame. Nell was right—these kings and queens of make believe were fast becoming the heroines and heroes of a new more democratic age. Many had only just "risen from the gutter," as the elegant grande dame put it to her mother. And unlike Swanson, Pickford, and Fairbanks, some had only a passing interest (and at times none at all) in the opinions of outsiders. The choices made by these young and humbly sourced workers had taken them very far, very fast, after all.[23]

What was needed in American movies was not less sex, precisely, Nell came to see, but more glamour, more *class* in how the industry's actors went about communicating their desires. This dance along the tightrope of acceptability that could make previously ruinous erotic expression permissible was Madame Glyn's métier and trade, of course, and one the film folk needed desperately to learn.

But then suddenly all the merriment came to a screeching halt when news of the industry's first sex scandal broke. Broadcast as proof of Hollywood's Babylonian side, the scandal would test whether Madame Glyn's brand of eroticism could survive.

"S.F. BOOZE PARTY KILLS YOUNG ACTRESS" wailed a two-inch headline on the front page of William Randolph Hearst's *San Francisco Examiner*. "Virginia Rappe Dies after Being Guest at Party Given Here by 'Fatty' Arbuckle." "ARBUCKLE CHARGED WITH MURDER OF GIRL; ACTRESS' DYING WORDS CAUSE STAR'S ARREST," papers screamed the next day.[24]

A comedian second in popularity only to Charlie Chaplin, Roscoe "Fatty" Arbuckle had hosted a Labor Day party in a suite at the St. Francis, San Francisco's finest hotel, that transformed his five-foot-six, 266-pound body from comical to menacing overnight. At some point during an afternoon in which much drinking and dancing occurred, the slapstick star ended up alone in one of the suite's bedrooms with Virginia Rappe. Later, guests discovered the twenty-six-year-old actress in great pain, tearing at her clothes. When she died four days later of peritonitis, a female guest told reporters that Rappe had blamed Arbuckle for her condition. Newspapers could not use the word "rape," but they intimated he had done just that, rupturing her bladder in the process.[25]

It hurt that Arbuckle's party took place in Hearst's hometown of San Francisco, where he had turned his inheritance of the *Examiner* into a media empire by publishing the splashiest, most sensationally told stories by the best writers and editors he could hire. One newspaper had become forty-two, plus three magazines, by the time Hearst opened Cosmopolitan Pictures in 1918. "The Chief" was a study in contrasts: the tall, big-boned, energetic man had a small, tinny voice and surprisingly graceful dance moves. Hearst "could be ruthless and kind, calm and violent, during one single conference with him," Frances Marion recalled.[26]

"It's difficult to keep the news out of the newspapers," Hearst telegraphed Adolph Zukor after the studio boss entreated him to tone down his assault on Arbuckle before the facts were clear. Zukor had signed Arbuckle to make feature length comedies the year before—around the same time he agreed to distribute Hearst's Cosmopolitan Productions. But Hearst had become convinced that Zukor was sabotaging his mistress, Marion Davies, and therefore his own profits. He had grown "paranoiac" renegotiating his deal. Now he had the chance to show Zukor what he could do when crossed. Hearst branded the event as "Fatty's Orgy," and the press followed suit, launching a full-scale assault on a Babylonian movie industry exposed as imperiling the morality of young white women. Within weeks, Judge Sylvain Lazarus ruled that Arbuckle would stand trial for manslaughter, noting, "We are not trying the screen celebrity who has given joy and pleasure to all the world," he opined. "We are trying ourselves."[27]

As the "Victim of [the] Orgy," Virginia Rappe offered a grisly example of the fate said to await any ambitious single woman who went west to work in the movies. "What's Gone Wrong with [the] World Today?" demanded Annie Laurie, the pseudonym of one of Hearst's most popular columnists. Her answer? "Ten years ago, any girl who would go into a man's room in a hotel, party or no party, would have thrown away her good name the instant the fact of her visit was known." An editorial chorus quickly agreed the case proved the movie colony's moral standards were fast infecting the young.[28]

Rappe epitomized just the kind of free-spirited young woman said to distinguish Los Angeles's bohemian scene from those of the past. "The 'extra girl' type is the one impossible to ignore" among its bohemians, *Photoplay* had explained in the first article to use "Hollywood" to stand in for the industry as a whole. Like bohemians of yore, these young artists had traded routine, steady jobs for the chance to make a "masterpiece on celluloid." They were "odd, frank, sex-ful creatures. Worldly wise, cynical, well able to look after themselves." Their philosophy? "To succeed in the movies—and to have a good time. There is of course a great deal of 'sex' in Hollywood" and "the freedom between men and women is very great. Women can— and do—what they like." Another reporter wondered that while "in the old days the small boy" lit out for adventure, "now it is the girls who run away to emulate their favorites of the screen."[29]

The reports were not far off the mark. By 1920, talk about the fantastic opportunities awaiting women in the gold-rush business had made Los Angeles the first western American boom town in which single young women outnumbered men. "There are more women in Los Angeles than any other city in the world and it's the movies that bring them," was how one shopkeeper bluntly explained the situation.[30]

Days after the Arbuckle-Rappe scandal broke, Nell agreed to write a series of articles examining the conditions that had produced the trouble for Hearst's *Cosmopolitan* magazine. Then she set off on a lecture tour to publicize *The Elinor Glyn System of Writing* (1922) before landing in New York, where she would depart for Europe for the first time since arriving in the movie colony. Pickford, Fairbanks, and Pickford's mother, Charlotte, accompanied Nell on the Atlantic crossing, and she planned to give them an insider's tour of Paris once they arrived.[31]

The articles she wrote for Hearst spread the responsibility for the Arbuckle party across all segments of American society. The older generation had allowed "the pendulum . . . to swing too far" from Victorian hypocrisy and prudery. Too many young women used their sexual freedom merely to chase men for material gain. "My clairvoyant friend," she wrote, "tells me the question each woman asks her now is: 'Has he got money? Will he be rich?'" But American men were similarly obsessed with "business and the amassing of fortune." The value of glamour—the careful attraction of the *right* person— was nowhere. And everyone was drinking too much.[32]

Nell's sentiments seemed part genuine. Even after much of British society had ostracized her for describing their commonplace sexual habits, she continued to believe in the importance that the aristocratic code of conduct placed on outward decorum and restraint. Having seen the terrible effects of alcoholism before, she complained constantly in her letters about the new fashion of drinking to excess. She also well understood the dollar value that such opinions carried with *Cosmopolitan*'s market of middle-class mothers concerned about their modern young daughters' misbehavior. And it helped that Nell knew the teetotaler Hearst worried about the escapades his fun-loving girlfriend Marion Davies pursued when he was with his wife and five sons. Hearst had begun funding fulminations about how women's emancipation had gone far enough. His contemporary Madame Glyn suddenly seemed to agree—for now.[33]

The Hearst press articles were "having a colossal success" Nell crowed in a letter from New York. "That is good as the more publicity the better—vulgar as it is." Nell always appreciated the easy sociability of Americans, but she remained in many respects a social conservative and a snob who bristled at the seeming disinterest in formal graces, wider ideas, or even current events shown by most of the people she met in the movie colony. She was "always homesick for people with *brains*," she confessed. "I am fed up with the atmosphere of Western America. . . . How in one's soul one loathes common people, however worthy," she admitted in another. "One has to pretend democracy and equality with men clearing their throats and women behaving like barmaids. No time, no restraint, no distinction—No God but dollars—no individuality."[34]

And yet work, publicity, and dollars remained the chief preoccupations of this ever-industrious woman also. Hoping to capitalize on all her press in America, Nell had dashed off the four slim volumes that comprised *The Elinor Glyn System of Writing* during the time always spent waiting for a movie to get made. "I hope it will make me very rich," she wrote her mother before she left Los Angeles. "There is a tremendous demand for writers—writers of stories, of articles, of photoplays. Money is being spent like water by magazine publishing houses and photoplay companies," she wrote in one volume. Her "system" encouraged her assumedly female aspirants to have confidence that they could earn the freedom and fun that came from well-paid work. "Why should success be a thing others can attain and not she?" Nell wrote. "She has two good hands and a brain—she is intelligent, and though not a genius, surely, she tells herself, she can learn to write stories or photoplays as good as hundreds she has read and seen. Can she? Can she learn to write and get more joy out of life?"[35]

Although the *Elinor Glyn System of Writing* failed to make much money, it displayed the extraordinary distance she had traveled since arriving. Literary agencies were still relatively new, but literary agents who understood the complexities involved in adapting and selling an author's stories to multiple kinds of media outlets, including moving pictures, did not yet exist. Nell had stepped into this breach while encouraging ambitious young women to follow her lead.[36]

Once arrived in New York, Nell met with Tom McIlvaine, an old friend of the Glyn family from his days at Oxford who knew her well enough to call her "Mum." A descendant of a founding family of New Jersey, McIlvaine had returned to America and built an impressive career as a corporate lawyer at a white-shoe law firm. What Nell definitely did *not* know was that her daughter Juliet had already written to her old friend, asking Tom to help her to take her mother's affairs in hand. "We must not allow her to go on in the vague way she has been doing all this summer," Juliet fretted.

Awaiting the birth of her first child in London, Juliet had obtained copies of Nell's contracts from Hughes Massie & Co. and shared them with Tom. "He is very anxious to keep her business, and is consequently very willing to supply full information," she wrote, explaining why Nell's agent had furnished private details behind her back. "She had a great idea of breaking off with Massie with a view to forming an 'Elinor Glyn Company' to run all her books, films, and everything else, but I think this was completely in the air," Juliet worried. While she "has had no advice at all" she paid "Mr. Massie 10% of the contracts." And fresh with funds, Nell had reverted to her typically extravagant approach of spending most of the money she earned.[37]

A remarkably even-tempered man, Tom was genuinely fond of all the Glyns, seeming to enjoy their more glittering approach to life. Tom advised Nell when they met to sign nothing until she retained a local personal counsel in Los Angeles and recommended one there named Alan Ashburn, to straighten out the tax implications of her many addresses. "It is my opinion that you have exaggerated the difficulties and mysteries of the movie business and have come to believe that ordinary business principles do not apply," he calmly contended in a letter he wrote to her soon afterward. "You will never get your affairs properly straightened out until you do what you have been talking about and never done; that is take the advice of some one, responsible person in whose honesty, common sense and legal knowledge you have confidence." McIlvaine immediately wrote to Juliet to apprise her of his concerns. Where was Mum resident, he wondered. Britain? America? France? The contracts she sent him used a Los Angeles address. The answer had enormous tax implications, he warned, and caused him the most concern of all.[38]

No record exists of Nell's meeting with Tom in New York, but likely his tax concerns were responsible for her decision to not visit her family in England during this trip. If she docked in Southampton, an English tax collector might see her name in the papers and "pounce," she explained in a letter home.[39]

But Nell wanted to avoid her family for other reasons. "How does Juliet take it?" she asked her mother, referring to the arrival of her first grandchild, Glyn Rhys-Williams, born weeks later on November 1. Her daughter's pregnancy reminded Nell of her own difficult days of husband-hunting, marital adjustment, and child-birth. "Oh how divine to be past the age for such things. I look upon all that with absolute horror!" she averred to her mother. And she still seemed reluctant to embrace Juliet's much older husband, Rhys Rhys-Williams, as her son-in-law; the awkwardness of "Mum" and Rhys being the same age likely lingered.[40]

Returning to Paris, Nell wanted to look forward, not back. Her party sailed several hours early for Europe because so many young women mobbed the pier, hoping to get a glimpse of Mary Pickford. "We have all been so happy together," Nell wrote her mother. "Darling people whom you would love, including the clever, vulgar, kindhearted Pickford mother." Nell's surviving letters from this trip read like a celebrity reporter bent on detailing the comings and goings of her famous new friends. "Tomorrow Mary Pickford and the rest are to come out to lunch with Lucy and me. Then I am to take them onto Versailles and show them the chateau and the private rooms—we hope Charlie Chaplin is coming but we never can count upon him." Weeks earlier, Chaplin had been given a hero's reception in London when he returned to his hometown for the first time since the war for the opening of *The Kid*. His first feature-length film would become one of the highest-grossing of the decade.[41]

Nell made sure her friends got a taste of the gaiety associated with the "bright young people" who had burst onto the scene across Europe, too, survivors of the war's holocaust now bent on the pursuit of their pleasure. By this trip, much of the popular culture and fashions in Paris and London had American origins—everywhere they went they saw American movies and heard the sounds of jazz and Tin Pan Alley. Nell did not fail to notice how much of the glittering play with artifice on the surface of postwar culture papered over the trauma that lay beneath. An entire generation had been erased. And the peace she had witnessed at Versailles had proved wholly inadequate to the task of mending the wounds left when the guns ceased to fire.[42]

Many of those closest to Nell before her departure who remained in Europe—like Alfred Milner, Lucy, and Daisy, the Countess of Warwick—were so much poorer and further from the center of things than her new friends. Daisy paid her a short visit in Paris. She was widely known now as the Red Duchess for her decades-long, lavish commitment to Socialist politics, which had come into wider vogue as British society continued to democratize further. Daisy had lost everything except for what mattered most to her, Easton Lodge. Though it was gone to seed and damaged by fire, Daisy maintained Easton largely on sales from her letters and (ghostwritten) memoirs, while acting the patroness to her menagerie and left-wing activists like the writer H. G. Wells.[43]

Many nights, Nell dined with Lucy and her daughter Esmé. The sisters had not spent so much time together in decades. "She will miss me when I go," Nell predicted to their mother. After leading the way professionally and financially for years, Lucy had watched everything she had built blow away. A bitter restructuring of Lucile Ltd. had exposed to the public that other designers had drawn most of her styles for years. Then the company went bankrupt. Long estranged from Cosmo, Lucy had moved to Paris to make dresses for private clients from her home, returning exactly to where she began.[44]

However much Nell had wished over the years to curb Lucy's impetuous habits and dramatic temperament, she could not have enjoyed watching her sixty-year-old sister try to revive her career as a fashion trendsetter from scratch. Lucy was a cautionary tale about the difficulty of maintaining influence for an older woman. And after chasing each other's successes and scandals for so many years, it must have been unsettling for Nell to suddenly see her older sister fail so spectacularly in the unacknowledged competition between them.

While Nell enjoyed her first vacation since taking Hollywood by storm, Arbuckle's trial for manslaughter was playing out in the press. Even the more sober *New York Times* ran more than sixty headlines on the case. According to *Variety*, stock in Famous Players had plunged from $80 to $40. "Word comes from Los Angeles of the almost complete submergence of moviedom into the hands of Jews," Henry Ford's newspaper warned, noting the refusal of "two Jewish gentlemen" (Zukor and Lasky) to declare Arbuckle guilty before the trial "because he means a lot of money to them."

By year's end, thirty-two state legislators had introduced nearly one hundred censorship bills, and Zukor had shelved approximately $1 million worth of the actor's feature films. Newspapers praised producers' announcement that future contracts would contain a "morality clause" that promised termination for actors who did "anything to shock the community or outrage public morals."

But Hollywood's troubles worsened after Arbuckle's jury hit a deadlock. Judge Lazarus declared a mistrial and announced a new trial, ensuring the controversy would stretch into 1922. "If this keeps up there won't be any motion picture industry," Louis B. Mayer confided to director King Vidor.[45]

In the wake of the Arbuckle trial, the industry's leading producers wrote an extraordinary letter to William Hays, beseeching him to help win back "the confidence of the people of this country" that the film folk were not a bunch of Babylonian foreigners out to corrupt the nation's soul by leading its young women down the path of sin. Producer Lewis Selznick hand-delivered the letter asking Hays to serve as president of a new trade association, the Motion

Picture Producers and Distributors Association, for $100,000 a year. The MPPDA (or Hays Office, as it would be called), would include the industry's largest companies: Famous Players-Lasky; Loews; Fox; Warner Bros.; RKO; Universal; Columbia; and United Artists.[46]

"Why me?" wondered Hays, who did not look formidable enough to assume the role of "movie czar," as reporters would call him. Shorter than Zukor, Hays had enormous ears and the affable, nononsense air of "an unreconstructed Middle Westerner from 'the sticks.'" But Hays's down-home Indiana air was just what the immigrant producers needed. He was also well connected to the party in power and an early expert in public relations, having managed Warren Harding's presidential bid as the chairman of the Republican National Committee. And Hays genuinely preferred the "democratic concept of 'home-rule' and self-regulation" to censorship, "thinking of the parallel case of prohibition, which had by no means produced an era of national sobriety its proponents had contemplated." Hays accepted the job but first headed to Florida for a vacation.[47]

As Nell made her way back to California to begin work on *Beyond the Rocks*, she quickly penned another series of articles called "Justice" for *Motion Picture Magazine* that strengthened her image as Hollywood's new glamorous scold. If Heartland Hays presented the best possible political face for the industry, then the aristocratic Glyn offered the most imposing cultural one. *Motion Picture* reporter Gordon Gassaway adopted an awestruck pose, introducing "Madam Glyn, the industry's champion."

> Picture, if you will, a woman who has spent the greater part
> of her maturing life in and about the courts of Europe, inter-
> mingling with the keenest intellects of her day; achieving
> international prominence in the field of letters. Then imag-
> ine this woman suddenly transplanted into the very heart of
> a film colony—Imagine then—Elinor Glyn in Hollywood.[48]

With Hays out of the picture for several months, it would fall on Nell to see how much she could ameliorate the industry's reputation for moral debauchery without sacrificing its bohemian and very modern sex appeal.

◇ ◇ ◇

Madame Glyn had returned to lay her "firm white hand," as Gassaway put it, on the movie colony by teaching them how to express their scandalous desires with more elegance and finesse. The lesson that Lord Chesterfield had taught Nell at a tender age had never been more apt: only the right romantic key would permit the movie colony's bohemian players to express their desires without bringing down the wrath of the moral reformers. High-class settings and costumes, refined manners, and a smoldering intensity could transmute steamy erotic play into acceptable behavior that permitted the expression of women's sexual pleasure.

Before she began importing her aristocratic style to sex in *Beyond the Rocks*, Nell moved into the Ambassador Hotel. "The Ritz of this part of the world," she called it, was already her favorite place to dance and positioned her to claim an all-seeing eye on the situation spread out before her. She got a real suite this time, on the top floor of the hotel's main villa, complete with a terrace and a kitchen that Lasky had added at her request. Custom-decorated according to her wishes, the suite had gray walls and black floors, lavender and mauve upholstery, green lacquered furniture, and two tiger skin rugs. On the advice of her medium friend, she used the terrace as her bedroom, "sleeping under the stars completely restores me so that I wake the next morning completely fresh and vigorous again."[49]

No ordinary hotel, the Ambassador was an urban resort whose opening put into architectural form the arrival of Los Angeles as a new kind of metropolis whose "reckless, buoyant, sun-warmed, 'joie-de vivre'" promised to deliver residents a more pleasurable and passionate approach to life. Built in a Mediterranean-revival style laced with Art Deco elements on twenty-three acres, sited far back from the street behind an expanse of green, the hotel turned the stretch between downtown Los Angeles and Hollywood into prime real estate and Wilshire Boulevard into the city's Champs-Élysées. Guests approached the sprawling salmon-colored Italianate villa along a long pergola covered with vines. The grounds behind included a section of private cottages connected by more pergolas, retail stores, a post office, a health club, a miniature golf course, a bank, and a pool with a sandy beach. The Ambassador's Cocoanut Grove—an enormous Moorish-themed nightclub decorated with stuffed monkeys and silk palm trees from the *Sheik*—was quickly adopted as the movie colony's mecca. The Grove would host the earliest Academy Awards. While Nell lived at the Ambassador, the Polish siren Pola Negri (currently starring in *One Arabian Night*) walked her pet cheetah around the bungalows. Scott and Zelda Fitzgerald wandered the orange-blossom-scented grounds.[50]

"What a terrible storm about the poor movie world!" began Nell's first article for "Justice," which created a "furor" by seeming to admit that the deplorable stories about the colony were all true. But what did people really expect, Madame Glyn boldly asked?

> The temptations of the movie people are a hundred per cent greater than in any other vocation. Let loose any company of young, beautiful and healthy people, with no standard to live up to—no rules of conduct to obey—give them hard work—and constant strain on the emotions by the mingling of the two sexes: give them the excitement of the forbidden fruit of stimulants and then imagine what they would do! Poor, young, undisciplined, beautiful creatures. Most of them under twenty-five. . . . It is so easy for ugly old men and withered elderly spinsters, who seem to think they are the sole guardians of public morals, to thunder and denounce! [51]

The remarkably public and extravagant lives led by some movie folk simply made them the most visible—and often ostentatiously so, Nell thought—symbols of the younger generation's wildest aspects. The government's recent prohibitions against alcohol and "dope" (American slang for opium and its addictive friends heroin, morphine, and cocaine—all legal and widely used until the Harrison Narcotics Act of 1914) had sparked a wider embrace of lawlessness and intemperance as fashionable and fun. People drank *so much more* than when she had been to America last, and talk about rampant drug use (by stars like Wallace Reid) had reached her ears. "Girls of fifteen to twenty-five," she claimed were shockingly the main "patients at sanitariums suffering from dope addiction or alcohol."[52]

Nell had identified an unintended consequence of Prohibition: during the 1920s, women began to belly-up to the bar alongside the men in an atmosphere in which lawbreaking added an undeniable thrill. Prior to Prohibition, saloons had been all-male spaces, minus prostitutes, often segregated by class and race. If a reputable woman drank at all, she did so only moderately and at home. But after an initially precipitous fall, by 1921 the number of American drinkers began a steady upward climb, aided in no small part by women's unprecedented willingness to imbibe, and to make, alcohol. Women who would never have dreamed of setting foot in saloons trooped off to speakeasies. Well-heeled ladies competed over the best cocktail recipes, which became de rigueur before dinner. Youths armed with flasks of liquor drove off into the night in Henry Ford's Model-Ts as assembly-line techniques turned a luxury item into little more than a "house of prostitution on wheels," according to a juvenile-court judge.[53]

California was one of the wettest states from the start as liquor poured into the City of Angels on ships headed south from British Columbia and north from Mexico. The widespread use of addictive drugs for pleasure and pain relief was an open secret in the movie colony when Nell arrived. After the Arbuckle-Rappe scandal broke in the news, the general manager of Famous Players, Charles Eyton, had quietly invited the federal attorney in charge of alcohol and narcotics control for Los Angeles onto the lot.

The agency had no success ferreting out the source but later uncovered "palatial opium dens" maintained by "the 'millionaire' section of the city." Even sympathetic papers like Variety started carrying stories about the drug problem, warning that the secret was no longer possible to keep. "There is a dope ring on the Coast beyond a shadow of a question," Variety announced. "It is known that the wife of one of the most popular of the younger male stars has time and again had the peddlers of dope supplying her husband arrested, but she has been unable to get her husband to break his habit."[54]

The war on liquor and drugs unleashed a counter-plague of violence across the country, and the infection was immediate and acute in Los Angeles. "Queer murders, terrifying hold-ups, daring robberies, unexplained crimes of all sorts occurred continuously," Nell recalled of these years in which the biggest stars traveled with armed guards at night and employed private security to police their estates. An appalling crime wave swept the city the year after she arrived, and its homicide rate exceeded any other American city during her years there. The city's weak civic structures had not kept pace with its exploding population, and its police department was small and corrupt. In the 1920s, Los Angelenos experienced more burglaries than in Chicago, more hold-ups than in France, and more murders than in all of Great Britain. Guns were the instruments of choice for murderers who were overwhelmingly young, white American men who had moved there from somewhere else.

It all explained why Nell "never thought anything" about the violence around her, including a possible murder she stumbled upon with Chaplin and Davies late one night at the Ambassador that was quickly covered up.[55]

Living in an earthly paradise where the threat of violence crackled just around the corner gave Los Angeles its peculiar new Wild West flavor in this decade in which glamorous gangsters captivated the imagination of so many. It also was the price of doing business in Los Angeles, and business was booming for Nell and so many others as the American economy embarked on the dizzying upward climb that produced the decade's fabled prosperity. Andrew Mellon, the Pittsburgh industrialist who had become President Harding's secretary of the treasury, had just shepherded an extraordinary set of tax cuts through the Republican Congress that ensured the nation's new wealth would be enjoyed mostly by those at the very top—like Madame Glyn and her friends in Los Angeles.[56]

All Nell's hard work and focus on visualizing a fortune was finally paying off. "[Director] Sam Wood told me privately that the *Great Moment* had already netted the company 900,000 dollars and they think will make two million or more in the next year," she bragged to her mother. "This means that now I am of great commercial value to them and they will pay anything for the next play." After a lifetime of watching men call the shots, it would finally be her turn. "If I ordered the moon in the middle of the room for a table why there would not be a question." She would use this clout to claim even more control over her next picture.[57]

Knowing Madame Glyn's arrival would demand a shift in tone, the cast and crew of *Beyond the Rocks* let loose on Catalina Island before she joined them back on the studio lot. Chewing-gum magnate William Wrigley had bought the mountainous little island twenty-two miles off the coast in 1919, determined to make it a tourist destination that protected its natural charms.

Avid outdoor enthusiasts, Swanson and Valentino loved the setting and the respite from reporters. The pair had become friends during horseback rides in the Hollywood Hills when he was still an unknown actor and she a new leading lady, growing close enough to confide their marital woes. Rudy, as friends called him, won a divorce later that month, but not before being humiliated in the press. Hoping to pressure him into a larger settlement, his wife's lawyer publicized that the couple had never lived together or had sex and offered the court a nude photograph of him dressed like a faun wearing only full-body makeup and a nearly invisible leather jockstrap held in place by a tail (all staged by the gorgeous designer who became his next wife, Natacha Rambova).[58]

Not one to judge based on bad publicity, Nell found that she liked Valentino as much in person as on the screen. The two frequently lunched together "to discuss the psychology of his character" as she vainly struggled to gain more artistic control over the film. Just before her arrival, Sam Wood had shot the wedding scene between Theodora—the impoverished aristocratic heroine played by Swanson—and the elderly, gauche millionaire she marries to give her family a better life.[59]

"[He] was nervous that I shouldn't like the rushes (they are awful)," she wrote to Juliet. "Ye gods! The clothes," she yelped in another. "Full evening dress, bare arms, feathers and jewels in the hair of the ladies and feather fans. For a simple evening in a Swiss inn high up in the mountains amidst snow!" Nell thought Swanson particularly did not look her part. The film supports the view; often overdressed and wearing extremely heavy makeup, Swanson appears from a different world than the chic Valentino.[60]

Jesse Lasky knew the film's positive portrayal of the extramarital love affair between Theodora and the rakish earl played by Valentino would prompt howls from the moral reformers. So Lasky ordered Wood to shoot each love scene twice: a short one for the American market, a longer version for everyone else. "Poor Rudy could hardly get his nostrils flaring before the American version was over," Swanson laughed. The scenario department had added two hair-raising rescue scenes to replace the romantic excitement lost.[61]

But everyone knew the film's success depended on the love scenes. So Madame Glyn went to work teaching Swanson and Valentino to smolder by using an unhurried, more aesthetically elegant and passionate approach to expressing romantic love. Live violin music wafted across the set during the love scenes while Glyn read aloud from her novel to set the right tone: "My Darling! God, I love you so—beyond all words and sense—oh, let us be happy for this one night—we must pay for it afterwards I know—but just for tonight there can be no sin and no harm in being a little happy."[62]

She felt confident that this time she would make her influence felt onscreen. "The director and I direct it together. So we have got the most wonderful touches," she boasted a few weeks into the shoot. "I directed them to make really exquisite European love, he kissing all her fingers and the palm of her hand—too delicious!" she purred.

Rudolph Valentino, Gloria Swanson, and Nell "awaiting camera," *Beyond the Rocks* (1922)

As a "Latin," Valentino "readily fell into it and does it too beauti-fully." Watching the rushes "everyone gave a little gurgling murmur of joy when they saw the love-making. It was too amazing even the cameramen and property boys! The director and I did laugh but it shows what it will do for the public."[63]

Although she privately worried about the "extremely dark" actor playing her patrician earl ("We account for his darkness by an Italian grandmother," she wrote her mother), Nell believed Valentino was precisely the kind of hero she had come to find. He "is so full of 'it' he will get the audiences. He makes love *beautifully*! As no American *could*. All the little shop girls will throw fits of emotion when they see him. If you can take our Italian Hector and a vulgar but attractive Theodora you will see a real story with real emotion in it," she assured her mother shortly before the film wrapped.[64]

Madame Glyn believed Valentino's allure lay in his fusion of ste-reotypically masculine and feminine traits so that he appeared at once "masterful and tender" and "not to be teased with impunity." He looked "like he knew everything about love," she noted sim-ply. Madame Glyn explained this appeal in "Woman and Love," a *Photoplay* article she ghostwrote for him that blamed American men for the nation's soaring divorce rates.

"He cannot hold a woman" because "a woman can never have a happy love affair with a man unless he is her superior. I do not mean this in regard to intelligence, to education, even to position," Nell had him qualify. "I mean experience of life. Women don't want caveman techniques but finesse. It is only after you have won her love that you dare be master. . . . How ugly and cut-and-dry it has become—love. Either it must be marriage or it must be ugly scandal." S/he advised American women to study the art of love so they might "commit indiscretions that a vulgar puritan could never attempt."[65]

But Valentino's tender side—his love of dance, art, and roman-tic finesse—as well as his dark good looks, prompted hostility from most American men both inside and outside the movie colony that grew more intense with every movie that he made. Mary Pickford remarked that she had never seen her husband act so rudely, to anyone, when Nell once brought him to Pickfair. "All men hate Valentino," claimed Dick Dorgan in *Photoplay* after the film's release.

"I hate his oriental optics; I hate his classic nose; I hate his Roman face; I hate him because he dances too well." His list went on and on until concluding, "I hate him because he's the leading man for Gloria Swanson; I hate him because he's too good-looking."[66]

Days after *Beyond the Rocks* wrapped, the screams of Henry Peavey, the valet of the Anglo-Irish director William Desmond Taylor, woke the residents of Alvarado Court in fashionable Westlake after Peavey found his boss lying dead inside the door. Reporting on Taylor's death would again center on women's unruly, sexually liberated behavior in the bohemian movie colony by linking (the obviously innocent) stars Mary Miles Minter and Mabel Normand to the death.

Nell's favorite lovers: Valentino and Swanson in *Beyond the Rocks*

"I am glad it happened," a woman who hired female extras for jobs at the studios reportedly declared. If "the Arbuckle incident and the Taylor murder" stopped "the flow of women to Hollywood," then she believed that Virginia Rappe's sacrifice would not have been in vain.[67]

Dressed in bright golf pants and striped socks, Henry Peavey's style reflected the area's flourishing gay subculture where everyone who was anyone knew about the city's many "queer places" to enjoy. Days before the murder, Taylor had bailed Peavey out of jail for a vagrancy charge for cruising in Westlake Park, and the director himself had carried on "an affair of the heart, discreet but passionate" with his talented young production manager, George James Hopkins until his death. Same-sex couples threaded their way through the movie colony in this transitional period before homosexual identity became more fixed in the public eye and linked to other dangerous behavior.

The unwritten rules governing celebrity reporting also helped to keep same-sex preferences from the view of all but those in the know. "The people who get into the courts and coroners offices are responsible" for the fury brought down on their heads, Hearst had explained to Zukor when the Arbuckle news broke. This meant that if "queer" behavior remained discreet, reporters would hint at the same-sex preferences of stars like Alla Nazimova, Billy Haines, and Warren Kerrigan in ways that only sophisticated readers understood.[68]

Adolph Zukor personally managed the Taylor murder, perhaps explaining why it remains a cold case today. The most recent theory suggests that Famous Players-Lasky representatives, who arrived before the police, prevented news of Taylor's affairs with men and rampant drug use at the studio from leaking out. Better to let the press run amok with stories about heterosexual love triangles than to risk the exposure of Taylor's same-sex sexual preferences or the extent of drug use in the studios, the persuasive theory goes.[69]

Nell may have promoted more explicit expressions of sexual passion, but her constant complaining about excessive drinking and queenly censure of disorderly conduct intimidated coworkers into hiding these realities in her presence. Her example and lectures in the press exerted a policing effect that pointed producers toward the importance of finessing the publicity surrounding their workers by emphasizing a context of European-flavored, bohemian artistry and youthful rebellion rather than Babylonian moral ruin. This allowed Nell to thread the needle to create the more explicit romances that audiences yearned for while not inflaming the moralists too much.

Madame Glyn's view seemed vindicated as her first two protégés, Swanson and Valentino, rode out their bad publicity toward greater heights. And the enthusiasm of everyone over the rushes of *Beyond the Rocks* suggested she had been right in other ways too. Film fans wanted to see glamorously modern lovers enact more erotically daring love stories focused on women's sexual pleasure and power. And Nell knew how to give "It" to them.

Despite all her scolding, she felt happy in her new milieu and optimistic about the future. Long practiced at making her way among a pleasure-loving, hedonistically inclined crowd, she was in many respects in her element more than ever before. Unlike many aristocrats, the film folk were not an actual leisure class but people who liked and needed to work as much as she did. And here she often got to call the shots rather than observe.

"I really only get on with the aristocrats in all countries and the low classes who work. They are just as nice as aristocrats," Nell admitted to her mother. "I am in blooming health and have never looked or felt so vigorous and full of spirits. The hard work suits me provided I can have my dancing at night. At present, I do not want to marry *any man*, because I *love* freedom and believe I have a foot on the ladder of being really rich."[70]

CHAPTER 13

The Elinor Glyn Touch

The Twenties marked a high-water point for me. We made big pictures, made big money, and thought it would last forever. This was the decade in which everyone quoted Sigmund Freud and Tex Guinan's "Hello, sucker!" . . . Bootleggers and hijackers, gunfire in Chicago . . . Scott Fitzgerald's *This Side of Paradise* (1920) . . . bobbed hair . . . the flapper . . . the Leopold-Loeb murder . . . ouija boards . . . the Shimmy . . . scotch at $25 a bottle, gin at $18 . . . Babe Ruth's twenty-nine home runs . . . Sophie Tucker, "Last of the Red Hot Mamas" . . . Mary Pickford in *Daddy Long Legs* . . . Marion Davies in *When Knighthood Was in Flower* . . . Pola Negri . . . Elinor Glyn. . . .

—Mack Sennett[1]

If Hollywood hadn't existed Elinor Glyn would have had to invent it.

—Anita Loos[2]

Nothing focused Nell's mind like thoughts of her own motion-picture production company. In her daily meditations on her sleeping porch at the Ambassador Hotel, nothing acted as quite the same bright spot as the idea of having complete control over how her stories ended up looking and feeling on the screen. In Hollywood, Nell's stature as an elite, cosmopolitan woman of the world and celebrity author had given her the biggest stage yet to communicate her glamorous vision of romantic love and sexual passion. Here she had also managed to maintain elements of a more conservative public personality by performing the role of elegant grandmother to Hollywood's badly behaving stars. The combination fit Nell like one of Lucy's expertly tailored gowns and accounted for

the now-famous "Elinor Glyn touch" slipping a new kind of eroticism into the movies. Or, as director Cecil B. DeMille graciously
recalled: "Elinor Glyn deserves more credit than I do for inventing
sex appeal."[3]

She sailed out further than ever into the movie colony's social
whirl, looking for a new producer to help her create a motion-picture
company of her own. At "parties nearly every night" she swanned
around in one of her signature purple or black silk velvet evening
gowns with matching headdresses and velvet capes and voluminous fur wraps—depending on the weather. Nell danced most
nights—"until midnight and am daily growing younger," she said—
at some swanky club or one of the ever more lavish homes built to
reflect the personalities of Hollywood's first stars.[4]

Convinced *Beyond the Rocks* would surpass *The Great Moment*'s
success, Nell knew it was time to strike the kind of deal that no
other writer in Hollywood had yet to manage. She wanted the kind
of control that her friends Mary Pickford and Charlie Chaplin had
over the movies they made. The right to select a film's director and
stars, to control the look and style of the sets and costumes—these
would ensure that what emerged from the cutting room matched the
story she envisioned. And for all of her creative efforts, she wanted a
cut of the profits rather than a flat fee.[5]

She tried Zukor and Lasky first, but they were in no mood to
grant new liberties to the meddlesome Madame Glyn. Having built
Famous Players around stars like Mary Pickford, who then defected,
the two men were wary of the power that popularity conferred on
an individual with her savvy. All the scandal had also taken a financial toll, and morale was low at Famous Players as the company
retrenched. Zukor had remained in Los Angeles supervising the
situation. Like all the producers in the Motion Picture Producers'
Association, he wanted to rationalize business practices and curtail
competition as much as neutralize the moral reformers. That meant
giving individuals like Nell less artistic control, not more.

But Lasky still wanted the third story, as promised, and Nell
hoped the novel she had written during the war, *Man and Maid*,
would do. "I am sick of my life—The war has robbed it of all that a
young man can find of joy," the story opened. "I look at my mutilated

face," her hero mused, and believe "no woman can feel emotion for me again." Set in Paris, her story tracks two unlikeable characters—a cynical veteran and his arrogant secretary—overcoming their egotism for love. The novel was due out in April, and she knew how much a filmed version could boost its sales.[6]

For months Samuel Goldwyn had argued that his company would be a better fit for Madame Glyn's touch. Whenever she met the producer, he talked earnestly about his dreams of a new story from her and his hope of making a version of *Three Weeks* worthy of the novel. Goldwyn Pictures appeared like just the place to capture the sumptuously elegant settings her lovers needed to make glamorous sex. The year before, the company had taken over the Triangle's production lot founded by Thomas Ince, D. W. Griffith, and Mack Sennett in 1915. Now Goldwyn Pictures covered forty-six acres in Culver City that included six glass-walled stages, dozens of outdoor sets, administrative buildings, construction facilities, a swimming pool, and a restaurant. Hearst had left Zukor to make Cosmopolitan Pictures there instead.[7]

Appearances were deceptive. Suddenly Samuel Goldwyn was forced out of what was in fact a badly ailing company. He retreated to New York to plan his next move.

Nell's mood soured. "I am getting so fed up with everything here, the uncertainty, the delay about everything, the cheating and lying that I am going to just write stories and not bother to supervise anymore," she grumbled. "I'm only waiting to get the rest of my proofs of 'Man and Maid' which I am correcting then I am to see if Lasky will buy the picture rights and if so I will come to NY at once and write another *Cosmopolitan* article from there," she declared. "If he does not like it for a picture I must think of another story and as soon as this is delivered, I am leaving."[8]

She was homesick and had become a grandmother for the second time. It was likely no accident the delivery of a son months earlier by her longtime pet, Margot, drew her back to London. "I long to know my new grandson—who [is he] like? And how my Margot takes it?" she asked her mother. (Margot's son Geoffrey Davson became Nell's favorite grandchild, later renaming himself Anthony Glyn after becoming a professional author who wrote, among other things, a biography of his adored grandmother. There are no accidents, as Nell liked to say.)[9]

But life was as full of surprises as ever. That April, Lasky suddenly rejected *Man and Maid* and then released Nell from her contract. Next Arbuckle's third jury declared him innocent after six minutes. "Acquittal is not enough. We feel a great injustice has been done him," they declared to the press. The following day, Zukor announced he would release one Arbuckle feature, "for the purpose of gauging public sentiment." Crowds lined up in Chicago, New York, and Los Angeles to see *Gasoline Gus*. The industry's moral critics attacked. Even if technically innocent, Arbuckle's party—"an affair of disgusting debauchery and unspeakable licentiousness"—proved him unfit for adulation.[10]

Support and opposition worked a whiplash that left the industry reeling and led Zukor to call a meeting with William Hays, who had finally assumed his post as president of the MPPDA. The industry could not appear to condone outrageous bohemian behavior or pander to the lowest common denominator among fans with the Federal Trade Commission snooping around and so many censorship battles brewing. Zukor wanted Hays to announce Arbuckle's banishment so the moral reformers knew "the Association means business." And so Hays did just that—though for the record he later carefully held Zukor responsible. Then Hays beat back legislation to create a state censorship board in Massachusetts by calling it "antidemocratic" and "Un-American." This would become his winning formula for almost a decade. The industry was learning to manage its public relations better by exerting much more control over the face Hollywood presented to the world.[11]

For fans wanted their love stories, and the success of *Beyond the Rocks* in May 1923 proved that Nell knew how to deliver the goods. "Glyn's Story with Valentino Pulls Record for the Rivoli," reported the *Los Angeles Times* of the lines that snaked around the block. *Variety* reported the movie became a top box-office draw of the year. Reviewers noted that Glyn's name was as big a lure as the actors. "It is an established fact, recognized among theatre owners, that the magic name of Elinor Glyn is a wonderful stimulant to matinee attendance," wrote one exhibitor, using a euphemism for women patrons. "Elinor Glyn's Name Aids Attendance," agreed *Moving Picture World*.[12]

"The love scenes were the point," Nell admitted in a letter home. The glamorous magic of her touch had worked again. Attention to detail mattered in the sex scenes she orchestrated. Glyn's lovemaking technique demanded carefully choreographed caresses and lovers dripping with "It." The distance that accrued to her characters' upper-class milieu, settings far removed from ordinary life, and the mechanical reproduction of film itself counted too. Exquisite details and distance permitted her lovers more explicit expressions of passion without enraging the moral reformers.[13]

Before departing for England, she restarted negotiations with Abe Lehr at Goldwyn Pictures where his former boss had left off, signing a contract for her second original film scenario, *Six Days*, on identical terms to the ones with Famous Players. But Lehr promised a very different contract for the privilege of adapting *Three Weeks*.[14]

Nell had been working the movie colony's typical six-day workweeks and playing hard at night since she had arrived with only one short break. Likely determined to savor her own great moment, she left town with the matter of *Three Weeks* unresolved. She wagered that keeping Abe Lehr at Goldwyn Pictures waiting while she sought advice offered the best chance to strike the deal she wanted.

When Nell arrived in Europe that fall of 1923, the reception she met everywhere she traveled would have turned the head of a far less vain soul. She had three grandchildren to meet, finally holding in her arms Juliet's Glyn and Susan Rhys-Williams and Margot's Geoffrey Davson. Then one invitation led to another; a year would pass before she made the transatlantic crossing back to America. That she was turning fifty-nine in a few months made this warm reception all the sweeter. She had grown into a rare kind of woman, perhaps most visible among royalty: one whose power had increased with age.

The trip began in London, where it instantly became evident that she had become a widely recognized expert on the business that had taken the world by storm. She dined out on her Hollywood adventures with reporters eager to hear firsthand accounts from one of the industry's leading personalities. Requests from businessmen led to lunches to discuss partnerships that might begin to make the moving-picture business in Britain more viable. By 1924, Hollywood movies dominated the market everywhere in the world, but the British film industry had remained especially weak.[15]

Juliet actively began to try to take her mother's many business ventures in hand on this trip, armed with what she had learned from her friend Tom McIlvaine and the agent at Hughes Massie. Negotiations were ongoing over adapting *Three Weeks*, Nell's most valuable asset. Someone had to ensure Mum was not "eaten by the sharks" as Aunt Lucy had been, Juliet fretted to Tom. A tremendous dynamo like her mother, Juliet was right to worry. She had spent her childhood watching Nell's endless scramble to support her parents' habit of burning through serious cash.[16]

And unlike rich America, opportunities were exceptionally tight in Britain and throughout Europe, where runaway inflation was the norm. Rhys had found a job for £1,500 (about £84,000 today) a year

Nell and her mother, 192[?]

as a solicitor for the Great Western Railway. "It is not to be sneezed at and perhaps may lead to something else," Tom reassured his friend in his typically soothing manner. The year before, a terrible fire at Miskin Manor, the Williams family home in southern Wales, had left them with the tremendous expense of having to rebuild the Tudor-style house from the inside.

Later, Dame Juliet Evangeline Rhys-Williams would become a notable maternal health advocate and self-taught economist who worked during her long career in public service to finance the welfare state and promote an early vision of a European Union capable of partnering with the United States. But in the 1920s, Juliet was a young wife primarily concerned with tending to her rapidly growing family who knew her mother blew through amounts of money that would have kept her family of four in comfort and more.[17]

And Nell was getting old and had failed to set aside anything. The same was true of Juliet's husband, too, who was the same age as Nell. Born into a colorful and successful family of proud Welshmen, Rhys had gone to Eton and Oxford before being called to the bar in 1890, the same year Nell had wed Clayton. During the war, Rhys served as a military attaché in Tehran and then as assistant director general at the War Office, rising to the rank of lieutenant colonel. Rhys met Juliet in 1919 when the nineteen-year-old came to work as his private secretary at the Ministry of Transport, where he was working on demobilization. For his distinguished military record, Rhys was made a baronet, and began the process of changing his surname to the more patrician sounding Rhys-Williams. Like many older veterans, he had floundered professionally after the war while his expenses had only grown. About to turn sixty, Sir Rhys had his family seat, Miskin Manor, to rebuild and a very young wife and expanding family to keep in a certain style.[18]

Juliet convinced her mother to let Hughes Massie's agent in New York negotiate with the producers in Los Angeles and to allow Tom McIlvaine to review any contracts under consideration before she signed. Nell seems to have been worn down by her family's hectoring and from managing all the contractual details alone—on top of all the other creative work she had to do. She gave her daughter a power of attorney over the *Three Weeks* contract with Goldwyn Pictures

Juliet (née Glyn) Rhys-Williams in the   Margot (née Glyn) Davson in the 1920s
1920s

and then left in July to visit her apartment near Versailles, where she could find the peace she needed to write.[19]

In Paris, Nell began a series for her American readers in Hearst's newspapers called "Letters to X," that officially positioned her as "grandmother to all the young things in the world." Part travelogue, part advice column, part philosophizing about the meaning of life and love, the settings she described shifted along with its roving author. But the letters, fittingly, began where her story had started in many respects, with the passionate, erotic longings first stirred by Sarah Bernhardt onstage in the City of Light. "Floods may come and go, francs decrease in value. But Paris smiles through everything. It was like this all through the war," Nell opined.[20]

Her column suggested that she already missed America's less rigidly class-ordered society, as well as living and working on the movie colony's grand scale. "Have you ever been away from your home for a long time X, and come back to it again and been surprised at the change in your eye—so to speak—how your imagination has made the rooms larger than they really are—and how perhaps your taste has altered a little?" The view from Europe made freewheeling, fabulously rich America look better. "Europe is so old-fashioned, and still does think so much of class," she objected. "In free America, girls can have mop-head curls without being considered common or plebian."[21]

She also saw how "the gloom of unsettled conditions" cast a pall everywhere in Europe. On her first visit to Germany since the war she marveled that "there was not a trace of the old arrogance in the faces I saw in the streets. All looked poor and hungry." Seeing their suffering led her to support the move to renegotiate the enormous war reparations the country bore. What she witnessed led her to counsel "X" that "Americans ought to be more than ever grateful for their splendid prosperity, their riches, their youth, their chance to go ahead, their health and their beauty."[22]

Ever prolific, Nell used the column to try out ideas that she then funneled into her most successful book in a decade, *The Philosophy of Love* (1923), written over this year in Paris and while wandering around Europe. More than six months after she left, her agent sent Tom a proposed deal with Goldwyn Pictures that promised more of what she wanted. She would receive a $20,000 advance and 40 percent of the net profits if the production cost stayed at $175,000 or less. She had approval over the director and the use of a young set designer named Cedric Gibbons. The choice showed her impeccable taste. In 1924, Gibbons was just one of many in the still embryonic profession of set design. But handsome Gibbons would build and direct MGM's enormous art department over more than three decades, earning a record eleven Oscars for Best Production Design after designing the Oscar statuette itself in 1928. Nell's contract also stipulated the producers would "consult with the Author" on all other creative decisions. "Consult" was still too vague, but at least her supervisory role was a formal part of the deal.[23]

Having sent off the manuscript for *The Philosophy of Love*, Nell decided to accept an invitation from the Anglo-Swedish Literary Society to give a series of lectures taken from the book on the emancipation and education of women and changes in marriage. Long used to the sneers of literary types, she was amazed by her reception in Scandinavia. It struck her as ironic that "these calm-looking people, whose faces bore less trace of passion and emotion than those of any race which I had ever seen, should be the ones to show the greatest measure of appreciation for my romantic and supposedly very passionate books!" Lecturing on "Women's Place in Modern Civilization" was an ordeal, but she "felt deeply grateful and very much moved" to be treated as a woman of serious intellectual and creative consequence in Gothenburg, Stockholm, Oslo, and Copenhagen.[24]

The Scandinavian literary world's flattery, the regular opining in the press, the commercial success of her Hollywood films, and the contract for *Three Weeks* all encouraged Nell to feel on top of the world. Her vanity and creative spirits perhaps at an all-time high, she quickly wrote the scenario for *Three Weeks* when she returned to Paris. "I want to give you the best of my brain," she promised Abe Lehr while preparing to ship out for Los Angeles. In addition to the scenario, she sent him four copies of the novel—for the director, the art director, the continuity writer, and Lehr himself. "Read the book very carefully," she advised. "The awful play and worse film" made a decade earlier "gave a completely wrong impression to the public," she warned. If the film they made was "to have the huge success the book has had" then they would have to do better. *Three Weeks* must "hold as a tragedy as the 'The Four Horsemen' has done," she explained. "With one banal or false note, it could be a vulgar melodrama."[25]

Setting her sights on duplicating the success of the most critically acclaimed blockbuster film made since the Great War, Nell returned with her ambition and confidence soaring.

She used the days she always spent in New York to break up the journey between Europe and Los Angeles to, once again, try to shape the public's understanding of *Three Weeks* and how its adaptation *should* work. Confronted with one of the enduring challenges of her public life, this time she was determined to get it right. "The selection of the entire cast, director, *et al*, rests with me," she announced at a press reception at the Ambassador Hotel, slightly exaggerating her influence. If the producers reneged on this agreement, she predicted they would suffer the wrath of the moral reformers since only she could convey this was "a very, very great love story" and not just a sordid extramarital affair.

Many had missed this distinction over the years. "People branded my story, they read the isolated love passages and skipped the other parts." But understood as a whole, it became clear "Paul and the Lady had that blessed trinity of love . . . an intellectual bond, a physical bond, and a spiritual bond that gave them a love that was transcendental." This was Nell's chance to ensure the public finally saw *Three Weeks* as a tale of animal instinct ennobled by a higher bond since, good or bad, people usually watched a movie through to the end.[26]

Expectations everywhere ran high, especially about who would play the heroine who had blazed across the imaginations of so many millions of women and men for decades. "No feminine character of modern literature is so well known as *The Tiger Queen* of Elinor Glyn's famous 'Three Weeks,'" one of the reporters noted. "So once Goldwyn Pictures announced it would film the story under Elinor Glyn's personal supervision, everyone instantly demanded: 'and who is going to play *The Lady*?'"[27]

Finding the right actress to play her "despotic Slav" would prove a challenge once again, Nell expected. But nothing was more important, since the book's purpose was to show how beautiful a woman's fearless embrace of sexual passion could be. "The English women, the American women," were "terrified of passion" and consequently "ignorant of the art of bringing the love-light into a man's eyes." Her heroine demanded a seductress with "some of the attributes of a tiger. Of course, there are many who have said to me, 'Why write of tigers?' And to such people I say, 'Go on drinking your narcotic. And die without having lived.'"[28]

Silence met Madame Glyn's masterful performance.

Why not play the Tiger Queen herself? wondered the reporter who finally broke her spell. "I am young enough here," she replied, pointing to her heart, "but I am too old here," she said, gesturing to her brow and throat.[29]

This was the truth. However much she defied her age, Nell was far too old to play her Lady at sixty. Even few male actors could get away with playing the part of a man almost half their age. Yet there was also something uncharacteristically modest about the remark, or perhaps, more precisely, it was a kind of humble brag. For when she arrived in Los Angeles on a blazing June day, she looked every inch the impeccably elegant woman who could still turn admiring heads. Some of it was her skill in dressing in ways that flattered the aging body. Genetics and discipline over her diet and personal habits also helped. She had long practiced daily facial exercises that mimicked a facelift's effects to combat aging around the forehead and eyes. And in Los Angeles she had picked up a variety of new skincare tricks and routines, like rigorously exfoliating and stimulating circulation with a hairbrush. Then there were more esoteric practices like sleeping outside with the head pointing north, and mind exercises. "*Never* admit you are old," she wrote to her mother that year, as if that would do the trick.[30]

But it was more than this too. Around this time, according to family lore, Madame Glyn resorted to a more invasive medical intervention to refurbish the unlined face and jaw that amazed everyone she met. The procedure was so painful that for a week she slept with her arms restrained so as not to inadvertently tug at her healing skin. (This was almost certainly in Paris, an early center of cosmetic surgery, where she was often alone writing, or with Lucy, and could have healed before returning to Hollywood's glare.)

At the twentieth century's start, aesthetic surgery remained low in status and practiced mostly by doctors from marginal backgrounds, including some of Europe's first women physicians. The Great War had helped to change the practice by creating an unprecedented demand for fixing shattered faces. Simultaneously, cameras started to "shoot" movie actresses and others in the public eye in ever greater detail. The demand grew for surgical interventions to make faces match Western beauty ideals and to help women pass for younger than their years. By the 1920s, face lifts had become a well-practiced—if still socially stigmatized—procedure in American and European cities among the wealthy and socially ambitious that promised to rejuvenate women's spirits by rolling back the clock.[31]

For even if beauty was no longer part of Nell's power, no doubt it mattered that she still turned heads when Abe Lehr and writer Carey Wilson met her at the train station in Los Angeles. A dapper charmer with a waxed mustache, Wilson was called "a writer manipulator" by some for his ability to milk the brains of others and then claim the ideas as his own. He would turn Nell's scenario into a continuity (or shooting script, as they say today) and earn the final screenwriting credit. On the drive out to the studio in Culver City, they passed a new gigantic sign that blinked HOLLY-WOOD-LAND all night long. Harry Chandler, publisher of the *Los Angeles Times*, had built the sign (later shortened to HOLLYWOOD) to promote real estate in the area. Instantly iconic, it quickly symbolized the merging of the city with its leading industry, which had already taken place in the minds of many.[32]

Abe Lehr had heard about Madame Glyn's at times exasperating pickiness and worried that her supervisory duties might unleash an obsessive who would drive the director mad. When the trio arrived on the lot, Lehr showed the knack for soothing outsized personalities that had led him to become vice president of production after Samuel Goldwyn had been forced out. Lehr arranged for June Mathis—the adaptor of the *Four Horsemen* and now Goldwyn Pictures' editorial director—to act as the film's general producer, greet Nell at the studio, and conduct her welcome tour. A lady with a well-known temper, Mathis was a scenario writer, talent scout, producer, and walking symbol of what was possible for a woman in Hollywood. Mathis presented Nell with a dozen roses and then escorted her to her office, where the studio's publicity team snapped a picture of the group standing before a door emblazoned with her name. Everyone looks slightly wilted except for Nell, who stands regally, shoulders back, peering out from under the hat and gloves she unfailingly wore to protect her skin from the brutal sun.[33]

Nell quickly accepted Lehr's suggestion that Alan Crosland direct the picture. Crosland had already distinguished himself as an interpreter of modern morals with *The Flapper* (1920). A graduate of Dartmouth, he had started as a Shakespearean actor and possessed the well-educated manner Nell preferred. Here was a director who might respect her superior understanding of court culture and the deeper meaning of her stories about the importance of expressing animal instincts "civilized" by their aristocratic code of conduct. "He has all my ideas," she told her mother with relief.[34]

As might be expected from the past, casting the leads again started a simmer that Lehr worried might boil over. Remarkably, agreeing on the Tiger Queen proved easier than Paul. "Miss Pringle is a *beauty* and a *lady*! Quite remarkable!" Nell wrote her mother. Aileen Pringle's resemblance to a younger Nell likely helped her arrive at this assessment. ("Uncanny," she called it in a letter home, "Pringle is just me.") This likeness was crucial to why she accepted the actress—perhaps too crucial, given Pringle's eventual lackluster performance. Pringle's status as an unknown also appealed to producers eager to keep costs down. Her unusual upbringing offered Hollywood's publicity machine a story that Nell liked too. Born in San Francisco, Pringle boasted one wealthy English parent, one French, and had married the heir of Sir John Pringle, one of Jamaica's largest landholders. Finding the "life of gilded ease and rich comfort absolutely empty," Pringle sought "some purpose in the scheme of things" working in the movies.[35]

The struggle over which lucky actor would play the Tiger Lady's young lover, Paul, provided fodder for press and dinner-party gossip for months. Nell repeatedly insisted only a *real* Englishman—not one of the American "robot" men she complained about bitterly

Nell arrives at the Goldwyn Studio to make *Three Weeks*, with Abe Lehr, Carey Wilson, and June Mathis

in her letters home—could play the part. For her "splendid English young animal of the best class," as she described Paul in the novel, she wanted an unknown actor named Derek Glynne. "A perfect gentleman," she told to her mother, "so different from these dear, good people" and "very good looking" of course. Nell had him bleach his locks, but the actor failed his screen test.[36]

Goldwyn Pictures, in truth, did not yet possess an Anglo-American-looking leading man who sizzled on the screen. With fall closing in, Nell knew that further delays would only hurt everyone's profits, including her own. So, she capitulated and agreed to let Conrad Nagel play her "Sleeping Beauty," Paul. Nagel was another leading man most distinguished by his ability to pose as a blandly attractive mannequin who threw his leading lady's charms into relief. (His first featured role as Laurie in *Little Women* demonstrated the talent.)

Nell comforted herself that the talented Cedric Gibbons remained on board as art director. She had yet to meet anyone in Hollywood who so closely shared her aesthetic preferences and conviction that less was usually more when projecting style and wealth. Gibbons was a working-class Irish American New Yorker who played the part of a well-born Anglo-Irishman architect so well that he fooled even those who knew him best.

"It is my belief," Gibbons told the press, "we have been playing down to the public long enough. In the settings for *Three Weeks* I have eliminated all detail in design and have merely suggested the mood of the setting" by "working entirely in line, color and composition." Working together, the film exudes the gorgeously sleek modern-luxe style that Nell wanted and Gibbons made a hallmark of MGM's first house style. "The censor is our only worry now because the rules are so silly and so many," Nell wrote as the two-month shoot got under way in August.[37]

Her breakneck pace blurred the days, but she felt "younger and . . . less tired than when I was 18," Nell bragged. Up at six thirty a.m., she was on-set by nine, where she stayed until six p.m., six days a week. Evenings disappeared writing articles or going out, now frequently alongside actress Marion Davies, Hearst's twenty-six-year-old, Brooklyn-born mistress.

Alan Crosland, Nell, and Cedric Gibbons on the set of *Three Weeks* using a device that
turns the world into black and white

The free-spirited, former Ziegfeld Follies star had made her
screen debut modeling gowns by Lucy in a fashion newsreel of 1916
and was well known for her sense of humor and as "the only girl
in Hollywood who hasn't a single enemy." A brilliant mimic like
Nell and Charlie, Marion's hijinks set every party alight. Often
away from Davies, Hearst encouraged a friendship with Nell, hoping the glamorous grande dame would tame Davies's party-loving
habits. All the movie folk knew that getting drunk with Madame
Glyn was simply not allowed. But that did not mean sacrificing a
good time.[38]

It was easy for two women who loved dancing, parlor theatricals, and entertaining talk to keep company. Davies often partnered
with Chaplin that year; the couple's witty banter kept pace with
Nell's. A legendary charmer, the elfin Chaplin was "the real sheik
of Hollywood," as Grace Kingsley wrote in her *New York Daily News*
column. Chaplin had been forced into his second marriage that
year with Lita Grey, his co-star in *The Gold Rush*. Grey became his

second sixteen-year-old wife after the actress's parents threatened Chaplin with a lawsuit for impregnating the minor.

After the shotgun wedding, Chaplin had to suspend production on the film because of the pregnancy, but his partygoing with Glyn and Davies—with whom he carried on a not-so-discreet affair—did not miss a beat. Nell now had four different young men—"perfect dancers all"—to "exercise" her when needed. "A dynamo," people called her. "I have never in my life seen any vitality to compare," Charlie reportedly told Marion one night at the Cocoanut Grove. Nell and Charlie reportedly made quite a pair on the dance floor too.[39]

But during the day Nell's relationship with director Alan Crosland soured as she watched her supervisory powers erode again over the course of the shoot. Unable to convey the book's original focus on the lovers' shifting emotions, the movie created an elaborate storyline for the Lady's husband, showing the king's drunken orgies, disastrous rule, and plot to spy upon, and then murder, his wife. Crosland's "ideas about how people behave in palaces and how Kings act is simply grotesque," Nell fumed in a letter home. "Their answer to my protests is that these parts are not in my book and they must have them exaggerated to please the American public." What she did not mention, likely because she had so enthusiastically endorsed her look-alike, was that Pringle failed to capture the Tiger Queen's beguiling, dominatrix-like quality.[40]

Still, near the end of the shoot she concluded she could "not go on fighting especially as the love scenes are the real point of *Three Weeks* and these are very beautiful." Working with Gibbons, at least the film's mise-en-scène finally corresponded to her ideas. And Nell directed the love scenes. For the Lady's infamous scene on the tiger skin, Carey Wilson wrote in the film's continuity: "Better than describe this scene, I will simply mention that Mrs. Glyn will enact it for Mr. Crosland on the set. The Lady makes her decision to accept Paul as her lover."[41]

Magnanimity came more easily when each day watered her vanity evergreen. While shooting *Three Weeks*, *Six Days* opened. The film displayed Nell's ability to spin stories with more dramatic action. A couple spars their way across the Atlantic only to get trapped

Nell and Gibbons's "bed of roses" set for *Three Weeks* (1924)

in a wartime dugout in France for six days after the heroine sets off an unexploded bomb. There they languish, alternately trying to escape or making love until a rousing rescue gives way to an undercover mission. A "pot-boiler," Nell called her story that writer Ouida Bergère adapted for the screen, "but it will make a marvelous movie." Critics agreed, and the film became a hit.[42]

By the time *Three Weeks* wrapped in November, Madame Glyn had become simply "*the* authority on what makes the world go round," as a reviewer of *The Philosophy of Love* remarked after the book's publication earlier that fall. Ads promised "Startling Truths About Love and Marriage!" But the book was more bossy than bold, arguing that women's greater freedom and the acceptance of divorce meant that a successful marriage now required the effort of both spouses. "Once upon a time Marriage was not considered a 'problem.' It was the natural course of events," Nell wrote.

> But that was in the 'good old days' when a man was supreme master of his wife . . . simply because he was a man, a lord of creation, a superior being, and Woman was a chattel. Now all that has changed. Woman has asserted her independence, she is an individual. . . . With this development, this want of understanding between the sexes, no wonder modern marriage has become a problem!"[43]

And then lightning stuck when a series of earnest conversations with producer Irving Thalberg—the twenty-four-year-old "boy wonder" of Hollywood—resulted in the chance to make 1923 the most pivotal year yet in Nell's long career. Just before *Three Weeks* opened, the producer with the puppy-dog eyes offered Madame Glyn the opportunity of a lifetime: a fifty-fifty partnership making movies together.

Hollywood's most gifted head of production had not missed the crowds hanging on Madame Glyn's every word. And Nell knew that she needed a powerful insider in the insular, ever-shifting movie business to make her interests his own. This and more Thalberg promised. Although his reputation was not yet fully formed, the signs were clear that this "blue baby," who grew up knowing his

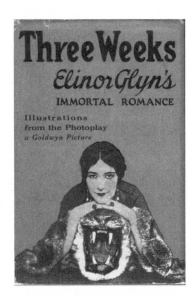

Reissue of the novel
Three Weeks to
capitalize on the
MGM film's release

heart would kill him early, would be the greatest producer of his age. Raised in middle-class Brooklyn, the sickly child had spent his adolescence like Nell: reading books inside. All those books had left him "knowledgeable when he discussed any subject, from movies to art to philosophy," and with an unusual regard for writers, as Frances Marion recalled. "Samuel Goldwyn had raised the writers' salaries, but Irving had elevated us to positions of considerable respect," she continued. "He withheld any criticism that might destroy our creative forces. 'I don't want to dictate what you're to write, or impose too many of my ideas on you. You're the creators, not I,'" explained the soft-spoken young man at one of the story conferences he was the first to organize at Carl Laemmle's Universal Pictures, where he began as a secretary in 1918.[44]

Within a year, Thalberg's memos detailing how to improve Universal's organization had made him the founder's right-hand man, and Laemmle brought him from New York to Universal City, his production studio in Los Angeles, before departing on a European vacation. A place where nepotism and mismanagement ruled, the studio was transformed within months after Thalberg designed practices that made a central producer the nerve center of the studio system of production. Invested with ultimate authority, a central producer oversaw multiple movies' story conferences—which put scripts through a series of meetings until approved to shoot—the firing of directors who ignored them, and the control over a film's final cut. ("Movies aren't made. They're re-made," Thalberg liked to say.) Thalberg knew how to exercise "the faculty of arbitrary decision" with cool polish, when necessary, as F. Scott Fitzgerald later observed admiringly of his boss. (Fitzgerald's hero in *The Last Tycoon* [1941] was modeled on him.)[45]

The year before he offered to partner with Nell, Thalberg had become vice president in charge of production for Louis B. Mayer Productions. Mayer's scrappy start resembled most of the other lightly read businessmen who had hired William Hays. Mayer's family had traded Russia's pogroms for Canada when he could barely walk. After moving to Massachusetts, he started in the salvage trade before deciding to sell motion pictures instead of junk. Loud, theatrical, and domineering, Mayer possessed an innate sense of the dramatic. "If a story makes me cry," he told one writer from behind his pince-nez glasses, "it's good."

Thalberg operated from his mind, but Mayer ruled from his heart, styling himself as everyone's blustering patriarch; lovingly devoted when respected, but a vindictive tyrant when crossed. His dome-shaped, balding head sat atop a barely visible neck attached to a stevedore's body encased in an immaculate suit. Not quite forty, Mayer became a father figure to Thalberg. The two were opposites except in their ambition to make the best movies in the world. "Spare nothing, neither expense, time, nor effort," he ordered Lois Weber, one of the first directors he hired. "Results only are what I'm after." Together they planned to knock Zukor and Lasky off their roost.[46]

Thalberg and Mayer also shared a belief in the ultimate importance of attracting women fans. "Wives and shop girls can always get their men to the movies they want to see," Thalberg told a group of screenwriters, "but a man can never get a woman to see one that doesn't interest her." Thalberg so valued "the women's angle," that he gave scripts written by men to women writers to check their work, remembered Frances Marion. Mayer Productions would assemble the most imposing array of women writers at one studio, including Marion, Lenore Coffee, Alice Miller, Adela Rogers St. Johns, and Bess Meredyth.[47]

Louis B. Mayer and Irving Thalberg in the 1920s

Madame Glyn's unparalleled touch with creating the kinds of lovers and romances that so many women wanted made her irresistible to this ambitious man with no time to waste. Convinced that Nell's "peculiar dramatic ability" had unequalled appeal, Thalberg assured her that with his guidance they would "make a fortune for them both."

Nell had learned that negotiating, always alone, with the men in charge had failed to earn her as much control as she wanted over what ended up on the screen. Cedric Gibbons had confidentially written to her that Frank Godsol—who had wrested the presidency away from Sam Goldwyn—believed that *Three Weeks* was the "best picture Goldwyn ever made. Mrs. Godsol wept" during a screening, Gibbons reported. But now Godsol planned to capitalize on what he believed would be the film's blockbuster success and have "another Glyn story done as quickly and cheaply as possible. Their notion is to reap more benefits from *Six Days* and *Three Weeks* at practically no cost. This will add no prestige to you," Gibbons warned.[48]

Before leaving for a Christmas visit home, Nell asked Alan

Ashburn, the Los Angeles lawyer Tom McIlvaine recommended, for advice about the deal. Thalberg "was one of the few men in the motion picture industry whose word was good and who can be depended upon to act in good faith," Ashburn advised. He was also "a young man distinctly on the rise" with "entrée to the biggest motion picture producers." Most important, Thalberg "possessed their confidence," giving him an enviable basis from which to negotiate the best deals possible while retaining the most creative control.[49]

So Nell took the plunge, signing a contract with Irving Thalberg to create Elinor Glyn Productions, Incorporated on the last day of November 1923. Nell insisted on completing the paperwork before she left on the long journey back to London. They had already decided to begin with an adaptation of her hit novel *His Hour*, her story about a repressed Englishwoman's sexual awakening in the Egyptian desert by a dashing and brutal Russian aristocrat modeled on her old flame in Cairo. She wanted funds to begin costume shopping while in Europe.[50]

But above all, Nell signed the paperwork before she left because she "did not desire to debate the matter" with Rhys and Juliet. They had no understanding of how this business worked. The film industry in Britain existed only in a primitive form. The lead in production capabilities and technological finesse that Hollywood had seized during the war had only increased with each passing year. And the couple was busy with their own problems and growing family, six thousand miles away. She feared their "over zealous interest on her behalf would fail to see the wood for the trees."[51]

The contract with Thalberg promised Nell the benefits of working with United Artists without the headaches—since Thalberg alone would be responsible for raising the money and arranging for the film's production and distribution. This was exactly the situation she had visualized and the good fortune that she had earned. "To those who believe in the logical theory of re-incarnation, that which is called 'bad luck' or 'good luck' is only the manifestation of the law of Karma—or the law of the boomerang. That which we send out returns to us again," she advised X in a column that appeared the day she signed the deal.[52]

Nell was elated about the prospects that lay ahead as she headed back to London. Perhaps America was the best place for her, after all. Americans had always most appreciated her work and persona, she had recognized that long ago. And the film industry had provided a medium perfectly suited to her talents and interests—and one in which a woman could deal with men almost as equals while making herself rich. She had gained a respect at the very highest levels in the movie colony that had eluded her in the literary world. The movie colony was also packed with adoring young men eager to curry favor. What was not to like? "I am on the train, X, on my way to New York," she wrote:

> it's just six months since I wrote to you from the train
> before, going to Los Angeles. And in those six months I
> have grown to know and love the Americans better than in
> all the years before. What strikes me as I review everything
> in perspective is the astonishing kindness and hospitality
> of the nation—so openhearted, so generous, so friendly, so
> intelligent—and so ready to learn. Old nations can't or will
> not learn things. . . .
>
> I am coming back to work here in the New Year when
> I am going to have an Elinor Glyn Corporation and make
> my own moving pictures. So I shall spend six months a year
> here for years to come I expect—and so you must not ever
> look upon me as a stranger, but as a fellow worker in your
> great country.[53]

When she returned to England, Nell showed Juliet and her son-in-law the contract, regally announcing that she had made a deal with Hollywood's "boy wonder" that promised to fulfill all her dreams at last. The partnership was daring, she coolly conceded, and still tentatively sketched. She had not shown it beforehand to Tom or the lawyer at her agency, C. D. Medley, as she had promised, because she knew they would disapprove.

But she had done instead what Tom had advised her to do months ago—gotten the local attorney he recommended, Alan Ashburn, to appraise the deal objectively on her behalf in the context of Hollywood's operations. She believed that Tom and the others so far away had failed to understand how making Hollywood movies worked. It took courage and technique and connections and patience and access to lots and lots of cash. Irving Thalberg had all of this and more—a contemplative, well-read air so different from most of the producers she met in Los Angeles. She had made the right choice, she knew, one that offered just the kind of power she wanted.[54]

An unnervingly quiet storm engulfed the family over the holidays. However carefully modulated, her family's hostility to her plan created an implacable force greater than she had feared. The charge was led by Sir Rhys-Williams, another man who, sadly, put his own interests first throughout this family drama. Once again, when confronted on intimate terms with a male authority, Nell would struggle to make her preferences heard above the din.

Who was this Irving Thalberg? Rhys wanted to know. What precisely were his resources? And what had possessed her to promise 50 percent of the profits from her stories to a glorified literary agent who should earn 10 percent at most? As one of the industry's many Jews, Thalberg's "racial characteristics" and "his training in the motion picture industry" meant he "was the sort of man who would be looking after his own pecuniary interests" alone. This made him at best "a rogue," at worst given to "cunning and dishonorable ways." Certainly, he was no gentleman. None would let a woman sign such a thing. They could not possibly let this Jewish charlatan take advantage of her this way. If Thalberg would not release her from this appalling arrangement, then they would sue, Sir Rhys-Williams concluded with the finality of a man who had recently been made a baronet.[55]

It was hardly surprising that Nell's family pressed the bruise of anti-Semitism that had worsened everywhere in the 1920s, but in a particularly pernicious form across the European Continent. After the war, rumors spread that an international cabal of Jewish bankers had orchestrated the conflict for their financial gain. But out of Germany an even more paranoid anti-Semitic vision blamed communists and Jews (often one in the same) for the Axis defeat. The "myth of the stab in the back" blamed the twinned disasters of the

Great War and Versailles on the Jews, saved the German generals' good names, and fueled the rise of Nazism when Hitler made it the central tenet of his political ideology while writing *Mein Kampf* that year in prison.[56]

The conviction of Rhys-Williams that the movie producers' "race," as Jews, made them a special danger to the family's interests was very much in line with the new kind of anti-Semitism spreading throughout Europe and Britain that increasingly viewed all Jewish people as an inherent threat to national interests. Until this point, Nell had not mentioned anyone's Jewishness in Los Angeles. But after the trouble erupted with her family over her proposed partnership with Thalberg, the subject would crop up regularly, prompting mounting alarm regarding whom she could trust.

Perhaps eager to soften the imperial stance of a son-in-law whom her mother hardly knew, Juliet wasted no time in gathering opinions that made her husband's view seem more reasonable. However, the lawyers consulted were not neutral arbiters, but agents who were already invested on the couple's behalf. "Deplorable" judged Tom McIlvaine and lawyers at the Society of Authors and a local literary agency. "Mr. Thalberg is a very young man . . . who has no financial resources and is contributing nothing very real to the enterprise." His services were "perhaps not even worth an agent's standard 10 percent." Yet, astoundingly, Nell was to give him total control and half of the profits.[57]

It is possible to see why from an Old World media perspective the merits of Nell's still sketchily arranged producing agreement with Thalberg struck her family as peculiar. Thalberg was indeed a very young man without much personal wealth. But everyone's constant refrain—Why is he asking more than 10 percent?—betrayed their fundamental ignorance of the matter at hand. At best, they had mistaken the movie industry for the publishing one. At worst, they were behaving like colonial aristocrats who failed to see that they no longer called all the shots.[58]

Unlike Nell's family, those like Alan Ashburn who knew the film business recognized that Thalberg's ability to secure the constellation of factors required for film production was in no way analogous to the contributions of a literary agent at that time. Producing required access to financing, to distributors, to theaters, to a well-equipped studio with experienced personnel and then the ability to shape a movie into a product with the best chance of commercial success. The Old World view was ignorant of the commercial innovations and creative complexity involved in making and marketing the kind of lavish feature films that Nell and Hollywood's global audience had come to expect. Never mind that independent production had become more fraught with each passing year as the consolidation of the American film business into the studio system's few large companies aimed to end it altogether.

Even though Tom and the other lawyers had been cherry-picked to approve the plan to scuttle the agreement, they nonetheless objected to Sir Rhys-Williams's threat of litigation against Irving Thalberg. Nell had consulted a personal lawyer, Alan Ashburn, whom Tom had recommended as an expert. Ashburn assured Tom that Nell was "not misled in any way" and, in fact, thought it "outrageous" for her "to repudiate the agreement now." While Tom claimed he could not understand Ashburn "having let any woman sign such a contract," he knew the lawyer was honest and, more crucially, that his opinion would doom any litigation. "But beyond all the legal questions," Tom cautioned Juliet and Rhys that an actual lawsuit against Thalberg would poison her relationships in Hollywood, marking her as "dangerous and difficult to deal with."[59]

"My dear friend," Thalberg wrote to Nell amidst the tempest in London, "that which was once made of dream fabric is now a practical reality with a very interesting future to anticipate." "After days when it looked very black and doubtful for us, and days of hope," he had convinced Marcus Loew and his lawyer, Robert Rubin, to back their plan. Loew Inc.—which controlled the largest chain of theaters in America, 150 and counting—desperately needed good product. Loew had just bought the ailing Metro Studio to meet the demand, but it was not up to the task. Thalberg had persuaded Loew and Rubin that they could help.

"The great fight was to make 'Elinor Glyn Productions, Inc.' a definite entity," he explained, by "allowing our productions on a definite series basis" to protect the "showman value" of her name. To do this, they had to sell their movies "individually and alone" rather than force exhibitors "to take other lesser pictures alongside" their jewels—a then commonplace monopolistic practice called block booking under investigation by the FTC.[60]

Nell knew that her family understood nothing about making movies or the cast of characters involved in their production in Hollywood. But her confidence flickered in the face of her family's withering opinions about her judgment and their often baldly anti-Semitic views of the man in whom she had placed her trust. She had let a juvenile Jewish American trick her, repeated everyone who knew her best—or, like her son-in-law, were assumed to know best.

Nell stalled, loath as ever to engage confrontation head-on. After ignoring several more telegrams, she replied with one so vague it is easy to understand why Thalberg continued to plow ahead. "Everything proceeding splendidly," he cabled two weeks later. "Ready start *His Hour* immediately your arrival hope you are working on continuity."[61]

Nell now made clear she wanted out. "I have formed myself into a company here in the hands of my son-in-law to deal with all my affairs, assigning to it all my rights," she wired back.

"I am certain your cable does not reflect your sincere wishes nor careful judgment," Thalberg replied, "but rather one of those impulsive motives inspired by your good nature and not too good business judgment, or perhaps your inability to properly explain the entire matter in a business way to those interested in your welfare." Avoid "a costly error," he admonished, and let him "make her on par with Fairbanks, Pickford and Chaplin"—the only creative talent to have succeeded operating independently outside of a major studio for long.[62]

Three Weeks opened the day after Thalberg's wire, its blockbuster box-office right out of the gate sharpening the struggle over controlling Madame Glyn's touch. Curiosity to see the "celluloid edition of a book that shocked us a generation ago" ran high. Pringle received praise for the hauteur, grace, and charm of her Queen. But as Nell predicted, Nagel was not the great lover fans hoped to see.

Reviews were surprisingly good, including a rave by the influential editor of the *Film Spectator*, Welford Beaton. "Mrs. Glyn made her own adaptation and the whole picture carried a suggestion of her

constant supervision. The screen being a simpler method of expression than literature I am of the opinion that the [1924] picture told
the story better than the book did," Beaton wrote, adding that he
hoped "there [would] be a place on the screen for a mind as brilliant
as Elinor Glyn's."[63]

While her adaptation of *Three Weeks* triumphed in America,
Nell lay wasting in bed in London. As was so often the case, she
became ill when things got too sticky and she could not exit the
scene. She contracted a serious case of the flu that seemed to signal her defeat, languishing in bed all of February while loyal Tom
McIlvaine doggedly hammered out a complicated three-picture
deal with Mayer Productions that simultaneously released her
from the contract with Thalberg. As wires shot between Rhys,
Tom, and the movie men, the woman in question withdrew to a
vanishing point.[64]

Movie-going was booming in Britain, too, and, like so many in
the 1920s, Juliet and Rhys could not understand why the comparatively impoverished and more culturally sophisticated British people
had failed to tap even the local market. Now Nell appeared like
a conduit to the riches contained in this weedlike industry dominated by a race of men whom many believed posed a special threat.
In marrying the daughter of Madame Glyn, it was as though Rhys-
Williams had hoped his mother-in-law would act as a conduit to
American cash.

Well practiced at taking charge, Rhys's daily telegrams sounded
authoritative despite his total ignorance about the movie business
and the fact that his mother-in-law's desirability was his only card. "I
have reason to doubt that Mayer has First National release. His business reputation here is bad," he instructed Tom. "Mayer now releases
through Metro. Consider Metro release and Mayer's business reputation satisfactory," patient Tom duly corrected. "Cannot accomplish
anything if instructions varied daily."[65]

While Nell lay in her sickbed, Tom, Juliet, and Rhys worked
feverishly to whip the company into shape to sign the contract. The
corporation's terms were spare and gave considerably more control
to its neophyte directors than Thalberg would have received, read-

ing almost as if written to protect the interests of someone with a serious mental incapacity. Nell would earn a modest £4,000 a year (far less than she was accustomed to spending, Juliet well knew), her expenses while traveling, and £1,000 to support her mother. The directors—Rhys and her cousin, Col. Geoffrey Glyn—would control all her future business dealings, decisions, and income. She would hold all but two of the shares.[66]

To comply with expectations about safeguarding a woman's "natural" ignorance, Tom advised hiring a lawyer to review the contract. The couple asked a rubber stamp: C. D. Medley, the Society of Authors lawyer who had advised them against the Thalberg contract. Medley only worried about the issue that had long bothered Tom—how incorporating in the U.K. would affect her tax liability there, in the United States and France. The question of tax liability caused the family no alarm.[67]

Nell hesitated. She worried that the trustees had the "absolute discretion to decide" how much more she could spend beyond her salary, Medley reported to her family. The prospects of having a virtual stranger—her daughter's husband—control her purse strings for the first time in decades must have prompted some concern. Her near silence throughout the affair spoke volumes about her likely overwhelmed state of mind while lying sick in bed.[68]

Meanwhile, everyone's ambitions galloped along about Nell's prospects in nurturing the fledgling British film industry. The couple hoped to arrange a deal with a new film company in London that would "establish Nell in the highest position in the British Film world," Rhys grandiosely announced to Tom. There was also talk of her representing the industry at the first British Empire Exhibition in April. "Try and leave terms open as regards future productions with Mayer," Rhys asked. "Glyn's value going up rapidly."[69]

Finally, Tom finalized the release and arranged the terms with Mayer. Then out of nowhere Rhys slipped in a new ask: "ten thousand for use of each story as offered by Thalberg." "Cannot propose this now," Tom fired back, in an unusual show of spine. "Please don't think we are trying to hamper you," Juliet interceded, perhaps sensing he was near a breaking point. "Settle whatever you like."[70]

But still Nell hesitated to sign away her future interests to her brilliant young daughter and the son-in-law she barely knew. "Dearest Mum, I don't think you need be nervous," assured Rhys. Hiring Medley was not the bad sign that she feared, he continued. They were so serious about defending her interests that the couple had decided to return to Los Angeles with her. This announcement seemed to steady Nell enough to make the deal, since one of her long-term objections had always been, quite reasonably, the difficulty of people managing her interests who were far away and without experience in the business. The couple agreed to come to Los Angeles and learn how things worked firsthand.[71]

"So relieved it's settled," Juliet wired Tom in March, as the "British Film proposal is off—partly because we've held it up too long, and partly because of the rumor that went round that the Censor refused to pass any of her works over here."

The rumor was false, but the reaction of the British Board of Film Censors betrayed the notorious aura there that still suffused *Three Weeks* (and Nell's reputation because of it). The board promised, "No film subject will be passed that is not clear and wholesome and absolutely above suspicion." Now confronted with the scandalous *Three Weeks*, the board felt trapped. "Most right-minded people" would protest passing it; but rejecting it would set off a "campaign against Mrs. Grundy" (a figurative name for a priggish person).

After deliberating for weeks, the board steered to the middle. The title would be changed to *The Romance of a Queen*. The board also demanded cuts—including the birth of Paul and the Lady's illegitimate child—to emphasize how her actions brought only disaster. They also insisted the movie end with the Tiger Queen's death, to show "retribution as overtaking the woman." The struggle had made it impossible for Nell to represent the British Film Industry.[72]

What no one in London knew was that developments in Hollywood were about to change everything for Nell's future prospects. Louis B. Mayer and Marcus Loew had just closed a deal to create MGM, the biggest vertically integrated movie company the industry had yet to spawn. Four companies contributed pieces to the combination that put production, distribution, and exhibition under the same giant corporate roof. Metro contributed a well-designed pipeline to Loew's very many theaters. Goldwyn had a huge physical plant full of talented directors, writers, actors, and technicians, as well as a tie to the Hearst press to publicize it all. Mayer Productions contributed what would always be the least appreciated part of making movies: the leadership ability to keep it running, to hold the pieces together in a way that produced the stream of hits that paid for it all. The faith that Mayer and Thalberg had in each other at this time was another invaluable resource. When Marcus Loew, the man who financed it all, tried to replace Irving with his son, Mayer threatened to quit.[73]

"Want you to know only have friendliest and highest regard for yourself," Thalberg cabled Nell the day McIlvaine signed the contract between Mayer Productions and Elinor Glyn Ltd. No record exists of Thalberg's reaction to losing control over Madame Glyn's touch. But this astute judge of popular tastes knew that *Three Weeks* was one of the very few movies inherited from Goldwyn Pictures making money for MGM. He recognized that Madame Glyn exuded a romantic, sophisticated glamour loved by many and that her way with actors produced the kind of love scenes that so many wanted to see.[74]

And no one could miss that Nell's name appeared everywhere one turned in America by 1924: on the credits before her films packing the theaters; on the cover of the "novelizations" of her movies that ran in *Motion Picture Magazine*; in the bylines for her stories in the Hearst press; and on the copies of *The Philosophy of Love* flying off bookstore shelves. Thalberg believed that these qualities and fans were the special sauce needed to make MGM Hollywood's new powerhouse.

But as Juliet and Nell embarked for California—Rhys would take a holiday before joining them later—Alan Ashburn insinuated that trouble lay ahead for Madame Glyn. They had made a serious mistake toying with a key player in the tight-knit cast of producers who ran the studios, the Los Angeles lawyer believed. He knew Irving Thalberg, and after meeting him recently, warned that Nell would suffer for her choices. "I tell you that by your conduct you have destroyed the confidence of Mr. Thalberg," he cautioned (and by extension all who trusted him as well?) by robbing "the arrangement of its essential feature, namely mutual confidence and joint efforts for joint profit."[75]

Would "Elinor Glyn Ltd." best leverage Nell's magic touch into the kind of creative control she wanted? Or was Alan Ashburn right, and had Elinor's family convinced her to squander the professional opportunity of a lifetime?

CHAPTER 14

Family Fortunes

Whatever will bring in the most money will happen.

—Elinor Glyn

Juliet and Nell arrived in Los Angeles in April 1924, and things got off to a marvelous start. The difficult reception *Three Weeks* had met in the U.K. had reinforced how much more respect Nell had won inside the movie colony and more broadly among audiences in the United States. No doubt Madame Glyn appeared eccentric to many. But here her international standing, queenly bearing, and carefully well-maintained elegance created a glamorous persona who disarmed much of the public into accepting her promotion of sexual passion onscreen. Her stature as the impossibly elegant grandmother to all the young things in the world also helped, allowing her to talk about sexual desire and romantic love in the abstract and with the wisdom that only comes with hindsight. Certainly, the female fans on whom the industry had set its sights seemed unable to get enough of Madame Glyn's approach to depicting erotic bliss. (And "Remember the Ladies!" might have been the new MGM's motto.)

Mother and daughter settled into the Ambassador Hotel, where Juliet, ever the quick study, realized that "the chief cause of Mum's troubles at Goldwyn's and Lasky's" had been that she "had not recognized up to now the need for a proper continuity, thinking they could shoot from her scenario." But since the continuity the director used always differed dramatically from what "Mum had in her mind," Juliet explained, "the struggle began when everything was ready on the set and actors waiting. Naturally the time wasted was incredible, and the wrangling must have been ghastly." So brilliant

Juliet decided to write the continuity herself. She knew it sounded "rather a joke for me to do it after a week's experience, but I have picked up their jargon and formulas, and am cramming Mum's ideas into them, and if I can succeed, I think half the trouble will be solved," she wrote hopefully to Tom while Rhys was still on vacation. "Carey Wilson got $3000 for the continuity of *Three Weeks*, which was hardly followed at all, as it was quite different to Mum's ideas."[1]

Nell's very smart daughter was right. After three intensive weeks working with her mother and a so-called script girl who knew the technical side, they delivered a continuity that Mayer and Thalberg called perfect.

Juliet believed they had outmaneuvered the movie men. Thalberg was "gushing and I should say all the better for being kicked. I am not anxious about him at all," she assured her friend of the young producer she had recently met. Mayer she "rather liked at least if it is possible to like an unshaved Jew! I think he is probably the best of the lot of producers here and certainly very successful at the moment—the Goldwyn merger deal has raised him sky high." Juliet's fixation on the producers' Jewishness suggested that she had arrived armed with a distinct idea of the threat they posed to the family's interests. Still, she agreed with Mayer's idea to have her mother work for the company on a salary basis. It "would be to her advantage as she will give her advice anyhow—she cannot help it, if she sees something wrong—and might as well get paid for doing so."[2]

Shooting on *His Hour* began in May, and things had never gone so brilliantly. Nell had delightedly approved the cast assembled, though technically she had no right. Aileen Pringle would star again, this time as her repressed English widow and a talented newcomer named John Gilbert would play the hero, Gritzko, the Russian Cossack noble modeled on the Grand Duke who swept Nell off her feet at Khedive Abbas's ball in Cairo. With flashing dark eyes and black hair, Gilbert looked the part of the hero who forcefully awakens the widow's slumbering passion. This would be Gilbert's first starring vehicle at Metro, and Thalberg believed he could become a romantic leading man in the Valentino mold—the kind that the studio badly needed.

"Ah—behold the black stallion," Nell purred when the two

Nell laughing on the studio lot

met. At last, here was an American leading man whose "It" rivaled Valentino's. Glyn's reaction reportedly embarrassed Gilbert, who struggled with his typecasting onscreen even as he acted the wild lover inside the movie colony. Before meeting Nell, Gilbert called the story "trash," but he trusted Thalberg's instinct. After meeting Madame Glyn, he realized like so many others that she was smart, perceptive, and would work her magic—however strange it appeared—to ensure he shone in his first starring role.[3]

A short tussle ensued over the choice of director until Thalberg suggested another exceptionally talented relative newcomer, King Vidor, who would have one of Hollywood's longest, most successful careers. "Swathed in long, flowing pastel veils," the Englishwoman had "distinction," the unfailingly polite Southerner admitted, though he could "not think why she was called 'Madame,' unless it was due to the novels she wrote." When Nell learned Vidor had never read *His Hour*, she insisted he visit her at the Ambassador, where she recited her story while reclining on a chaise draped with a tiger skin. ("A wonderful cloth imitation," she explained, noticing Vidor's shock. "She would be happy to tell us where it could be purchased.")[4]

A raffish Texan whose unassuming manner belied a powerful creative drive, Vidor hid his initial discomfort with this passionate love story and its unusual author. Worried that he was "expected to top all the provocative values" of *Three Weeks*, Vidor pressed on, accepting Madame Glyn's suggestions about royal etiquette and romantic conduct with unblinking calm. Vidor, Thalberg, and Gilbert all became friends; this would be the first of five films in which the producer paired Gilbert with the director. "When we all began at MGM, after the big merger," Gilbert recalled, "we worked together during working hours. We played together after working hours. We were afire. We had tremendous things ahead of us. We went, all of us, higher and higher." One of the hardest drinkers in the movie colony's hard-drinking crowd, Gilbert recalled that "as we sky-rocketed we drifted apart. We began to be too stupidly successful. Or I did."[5]

True to the novel, they shot one love scene in an enormous Russian sleigh, with Pringle lying next to Gilbert in a low-cut, sleeveless velvet gown. The lovers embrace until Gilbert tunnels under their bearskin rugs to find and kiss her fingers. A close-up follows the journey of his lips up her arm, shoulder, and neck until he finally reaches her face, where he pauses to caress her cheek with the tips of his eyelashes. Much of the smoldering scene would be cut after objections from the Hays Office, but what remains conveys the kind of sensuality and erotic longing associated with Madame Glyn's touch. When Vidor fell ill, she took over and directed the wedding sequence. The rushes are "too beautiful," she wrote her mother, "a real romance, perfect in story and sense of reality." Everything was going swimmingly. This would be her triumph, she was sure.[6]

Her son-in-law had finally joined them at the Ambassador, and it appeared like all their efforts were working beautifully. "I am still overcome with the brains of Juliet," Nell wrote to Gran shortly after Rhys arrived. "She has mastered all the techniques which it takes ordinary mortals years to learn." The praise heaped upon her daughter by her coworkers stimulated her typically dormant maternal side, particularly weak with respect to Juliet, who had long played the plain, clever sister to Margot's pretty, sweet one. "Everyone in

America thinks her perfectly lovely and more intelligent than they can say," Nell boasted. "She ranks as a sort of goddess here. Mary Pickford told me that since she arrived everyone tells her about Juliet not being painted and being so simple and modest and yet *so* clever. It is quite delightful to hear it all, the love. . . . Rhys also will soon have discovered everything that there is to know in the business end," she added. Then Nell's surviving correspondence falls silent, likely because of the long six-day workweeks.[7]

But a letter Juliet wrote to Tom in her capacity as Elinor Glyn Ltd.'s secretary blithefully mentioned a plan at work that threatened everything Nell had achieved. They had arranged for the accounting firm Wales & Wales to audit MGM's production costs for *Three Weeks* and *His Hour*, she reported. Then she warned her old friend that Rhys had started "a game of bluff" with Mayer. "He is here on the spot, feeling the undercurrents, and taking an infinity of trouble," she assured Tom. However strange his instructions might sound, she implored him as the company's lawyer to "please back him up. . . . It is all a game, very like poker, and quite amusing!" she added. "The people here are awfully kind to us, and I get on with them all well, and so does Rhys."[8]

The next day, Rhys asked Mayer and Thalberg to pay Juliet $10,000 for the continuity that she wrote with Nell and the script girl ("who knew the technical side"). Having just arrived, this was likely Rhys's first solo meeting with the men. Rhys likely considered this a paltry figure, given the vast sums visibly coursing through Los Angeles. Compared to Europe, America appeared so rich, and the inhabitants of the movie colony exhibited the nation's new standards of conspicuous consumption like no one else. An older gentleman long practiced at having his opinions accepted without debate, Rhys likely expected the producers would happily pay the sum, given that he had already outmaneuvered them and everything was going so splendidly.

Nell's family could not have been more wrong. The baronet's high-handed request, out of the blue, for an amount the couple knew to be exorbitant (given Juliet's comments about Carey Wilson, one of the best in the business, getting $3,000 for writing the continuity of *Three Weeks*) was bad enough. They missed how to the producers this demand exploded like a third strike, coming on the heels of Nell's shenanigans over the Thalberg contract followed by the hiring of auditors to aggressively monitor their films' production costs. Juliet and Rhys—still embedded in a more elitist and anti-Semitic culture than Nell had become accustomed to—had also confused the humble origins of these uneducated, "unshaved Jews" with a lack of intelligence and assumed their race made them a special threat. The couple seemed to fail entirely to appreciate that these men were ruthless empire builders of another kind whom they had now provoked.

Thalberg and Mayer would show the family who was in charge around Hollywood. "Mayer's attitude hitherto friendly now completely altered," Rhys wired Tom immediately after the meeting. "At interview here today he stated Glyn supervision was valueless and that he was willing to dispense with it for the next two pictures." *His Hour* was "going splendidly and Director delighted. See no reason for change of attitude except our request for payment for continuity."

Mayer admitted it was "a mistake not to have continuities written by Glyn," but insisted that "paying the price asked is a breach of his principle which is apparently not to pay for anything if he can help it. Great dissatisfaction being expressed throughout studio trouble brewing all around." Immediately after the meeting, Rhys wrote to Mayer demanding an apology, Nell's release from the contract, and $10,000 for the continuity, again.[9]

"My dear Sir Rhys, I am afraid it is going to be useless to try and harmonize our views unless you are willing to see two sides to every question," Mayer replied, clearly relishing playing poker with the baronet. Why did he think it fair that Glyn's trust should employ a man "to watch and question all our expenditures" and yet was "hurt and resentful that we don't accept a charge that we don't see as fair?" If they did not "appreciate and admire Mrs. Glyn's ability and services" why would they "split profits with her and consult her as we do?" They enjoyed their "very happy and cordial" relationship and would not release her to make deals with other companies.[10]

But "Sir Rhys," as Mayer persistently called him, had not become a baronet by conceding the field so fast. "You appear to have forgotten your words," he replied after insisting again that Mayer owed him an apology. "Your words were: 'We don't want any more of her supervision—we don't consider her supervision of any value—a vase here and a vase there and a bunch of flowers here.'" Rhys's quote certainly sounded like Mayer, a ferocious negotiator who said what was necessary to win his point, which now was to teach Nell's family that they could not trifle with MGM.[11]

Dismissing the significance of his words, Mayer replied that all their "attitude and actions" proved they only wanted Nell to do "her most brilliant work for them." He reminded the baronet again that MGM had patiently endured "the red tape of having every one of their moves watched with suspicion" by the family's auditors because of the value they "placed upon her supervision in the development of stories, continuities, the shooting of the picture, cutting and titling." Then he accused Rhys of trying to poison Nell against them to explain his failure "to secure exaggerated and unbusinesslike advantages," concluding, "you are the person from whom an apology is due."[12]

Rhys wrote one sentence to Louis B. Mayer the next day: "I have received your pathetic letter and can only say that you are living up to your reputation." Then the couple left for New York to ship out on the *Mauretania* for England.

"This Mayer contract is a millstone round our necks. How I wish we could get it cancelled and be free once more," he wrote Nell from on board before thanking her for giving Juliet 10 percent of the company's shares for her efforts in Los Angeles. "We were quite ready to do our best to help you in every way without reward."[13]

Left to her own devices in Los Angeles, Nell tried to patch things over with the producers by demonstrating her willingness to work for the common good. She quickly agreed when Marcus Loew "implored" her to be his guest at the opening of the new Loew's State Theatre in St. Louis, where *Three Weeks* would be the debut film. Loew wanted Nell to make a speech, since the "censors of the Middle West were very venomous to Three Weeks." He hoped that if "they hear me speak it will disarm them as it always has before," she wrote her mother.[14]

Designed by Thomas Lamb, who made a fortune dreaming up opulent theaters in the 1920s, the State Theatre cost $1.2 million to build and featured a black marble ticket booth that contrasted dramatically with its white marble rotunda-shaped lobby. A central chandelier with one thousand crystals glittered above the main auditorium where Madame Glyn would defend the morality of *Three Weeks*. She had to endure the special brew of Mississippi River Valley heat St. Louis dripped in late summer. It was "105 in the shade," she reported to her mother, but it was an "adventure," and seeing "these queer solid people" gave "her real insight into middle western psychology."[15]

She returned to Los Angeles determined to put the dispute behind her and focus on cutting and titling the film. Nell was "very happy with everything pertaining to her picture," Mayer reported to Tom McIlvaine. She believed that his remarks about her supervision had been made in a fit of temper over her son-in-law's demand. Like a good lawyer, Tom tried to convince Juliet that her mother's conciliatory approach was right. "If we try to get the very last penny we are more likely to make less net money," he warned. "These long drawn out negotiations cost time and money and dissatisfy the producers. While we have probably the very best goods in the market nevertheless if we prove too difficult to deal with the value of our stock is lessened."[16]

Most worrisome, Elinor Glyn Ltd.'s interminable squabbling with Thalberg and Mayer was gaining Nell less, not more, leverage in Hollywood. Dogged Tom tried to persuade Juliet of this view in several very long letters. "Mum wants to supervise and to some extent I think that we must humor her. I do not believe that the policy of having her write scenarios exclusively would work; I think before long she would go off the handle." He also advised negotiating for cash payments, rather than percentages of profits, in the future to avoid the awful wrangling over costs. As the trust's main go-between with the producers, he was "spending a lot of time on this," but feared "we are gradually falling deeper and deeper into the mire."[17]

But Rhys's idea of the best way forward was completely different from Madame Glyn's or Tom's. Determined to regain control, that very day he had Tom request immediate payment for the continuity yet again. When no reply came that week, Rhys served Mayer

Productions with a summons over a lawsuit filed to recover $10,000 that MGM had never agreed to pay.[18]

Entirely ignorant of this plan, the news exploded in Los Angeles and New York, where it was almost possible to hear Tom's exhausted groan. Nell saw red, fearing that everything she had built in Hollywood was headed for a smash-up unless she put an end to her family's meddling at once.

Tom immediately wired Rhys from New York to London on hearing the news of the lawsuit. He would be "a good solider and 'march to the guns,'" but he described in lengthy detail all the reasons he thought the lawsuit would fail. Experienced continuity writers only made several hundred dollars. Juliet was a novice at the job. Nell was a partner who had assumed no financial risk in an enterprise whose success would only benefit her.[19]

Not to worry, the lawsuit was merely "a ruse" to get a better deal from Mayer, or to get out of the contract, Rhys wired back. But Rhys feared that Nell was nearing a breakdown over the negotiations and would not stay the course he had prescribed. He asked Tom to convince her to come to New York—or better yet, London—until he finished the job. Joseph Schenck was close to taking over their deal, he explained. "I reported all this to Mrs. Glyn and warned her that although Schenck was being extraordinarily kind and helpful still he was a Jew and would try to get some advantage for himself out of the transactions."[20]

Days later, Schenck obtained a release for her from MGM largely on Rhys's terms, but secured only $5,000 for the continuity. This Rhys could not accept. The detestable Mayer had impugned his name. Now Schenck became "antagonized" by the baronet.

"Things at a complete deadlock," Tom reported with another almost audible despairing sigh.[21]

One by one the big men were circling their wagons out west. They held Nell inside their ring and turned implacable faces to the family that wanted her freed to better enclose her themselves. In the middle of it all, Tom seemed increasingly exasperated with his role. Schenck was "in a grouch," and no longer wanted to work with them. "He said we had changed our minds too often and that he really did not know what we wanted or how to deal with us." Loew's lawyer, Robert Rubin, had also concluded he could not "deal with Sir Rhys as there is too much an air of finality in what he says." In reporting the producers' opinions of Sir Rhys, Tom likely hoped that he might back off and let him do the negotiating.[22]

Rhys immediately dashed his hopes. "I am getting tired of being accused of antagonizing everyone," he retorted. It was hard to miss the hypocrisy, and prejudice, behind Rhys's attitude, as he complained about the producers' cunningly greedy ways while he barreled ahead trying to secure every last penny for his wife.[23]

Nell's family was far from alone in assuming that Jewish people posed a particular threat to gentiles' interests in Europe. Nor was America immune to the rise in anti-Semitism in the interwar period; one popular editor called it "one of the most curious specimens" of "all the dirty spawn germinated in the refuse left by the Great War." A postwar congressional report that justified the new ethnic-origins quota acts Congress passed in 1921 and 1924 grossly exaggerated the number of Jewish immigrants, calling them "abnormally twisted, unassimilable, and filthy, un-American, and often dangerous in their habits." The new restrictions stopped the flow of people from southern and eastern Europe and the "Orient" while leaving the numbers from northern and western Europe untouched.[24]

In the United States, the industrialist-hero Henry Ford distributed a version of *The Protocols of the Elders of Zion*, a fabricated text first published in Russia in 1903 that described a plan for global domination by Jewish leaders. Ford emphasized Jewish leaders' resolve to use their influence in key industries, including the press, publishing, the theatre, and the movies, to corrupt "the very heart of American life." More polite versions made their way into the arguments of leading film-censorship activists who argued only federal oversight of the industry could stop the spread of the dangerous "Sex Pictures" favored by "perverse," "degenerate" "Hebrew" producers. But historians of anti-Semitism conclude that such arguments stopped short of employing the kind of racialist logic becoming prevalent in Europe, which perceived all Jewish people as permanent outsiders who were inherently threatening to the nations in which they lived. In the

United States, anti-Semitism was also embedded in a larger nativist and racial context in which Jewish Americans were only one threatening group among many other new immigrant ethnic types and the so-called New Negroes who began moving into cities outside the South in the 1920s in larger numbers than ever before.[25]

Part of Madame Glyn's special touch lay in her ability to toss a glamorous, upper-class, Anglo-Saxon cloak around the sex pictures that she made. As Marcus Loew's request to help with the moral reformers in the St. Louis revealed, the producers knew that, much like William Hays, Nell presented a far better face, voice, and manner to show the world than their own. It is also clear that Nell would not have risen so far, so fast in the movie business had she openly displayed the kind of racial superiority that at least in part motivated her family's conduct. The producers had already established an unwillingness to tolerate obvious prejudice in their midst.[26]

Nell's private correspondence also suggested that she had come to know Jewish people at least a bit beyond their stereotypes while working and playing with them six days a week. She knew that far from being cheap, the producers generously spent whatever was needed to do a job right. "I am simply to have the sun, moon, and stars for the next picture if I want. Such is success with the Jews!" she wrote to her mother. "Blatant, kind hearted, shrewd, nefarious good fellows!" was another way she characterized the "Jewish race" in this most race-conscious age. Ever the snob, like most everyone she met in the movie colony, she considered the Jewish producers almost "unbearably common," but her choice of words was less harsh than other literary figures. "The minds of Hollywood producers seem to have the characteristics of the minds of chimpanzees," quipped Aldous Huxley, "agitated and infinitely distractable." While Joseph Conrad wrote that in selling his book there, he "felt exactly like a merchant selling glass beads to African natives."[27]

Nell's family may have kindled her own more submerged anti-Semitic ideas, but she also knew well who was in charge in Hollywood. She saw that her family's behavior threatened the special value she offered the producers and jeopardized all of her hard work to master the business. The situation had passed the point of reconciliation. She would have to choose a side.

Nell dropped work editing *His Hour* and left for New York, where she met Tom for dinner in a cold fury the night she arrived. She had never dreamed that the company would give her "no voice in her own affairs. It was outrageous to begin a suit in her name of which she disapproved and without consulting her." She appreciated that they had her best interests at heart. But the company's dealings with the producers had brought nothing but trouble, and after three months of constant bickering "her future in the moving picture world was being ruined." Now they had botched the attempt to transfer the contract to Schenck. Continuing to quarrel with Mayer would turn "the whole picture community against her," she railed. The wisest course now was to drop the entire matter and allow her to finish the contract as best as she could in peace.[28]

Then she hammered home the most essential point: She was sixty and being "treated like a child" rather than the successful self-made woman that she was. This she could no longer abide. The trust must go, or she would "smash the trust." She refused to linger in New York or go to England, as Rhys wanted. Her contract required she remain in Culver City until the picture was cut and titled. She would return at once to finish this important work.[29]

"In my opinion the situation is very dangerous," Tom wrote Juliet. "I see she feels like a trapped animal and consider it unwise and dangerous to press her further. If you insist on controlling her I apprehend a family row." Like a good lawyer, he drew a picture of where things could go. "If Mum got independent advice from somebody who was not interested in preserving amicable family relations a very awkward situation might be created."

After all, the company was made "at the solicitation of those in confidential relations to her and, above all," Nell had received "no independent legal advice." All the uproar over the Thalberg contract and her flu would give an unfriendly lawyer grounds to reasonably claim that they had forced her hand at a vulnerable moment. They should remember that she was alone in California. "If too tight a rein is kept," Tom believed that "sooner or later Mum will jump over the traces and scratch the fellow on the box seat, and there will be nothing but law suits, family scandal, and business disaster."[30]

Tom knew the English well enough to know that he had uttered the magic word. The risk of scandal was the surest way to force a British gentleman into retreat.

Moreover, Mayer had just threatened a countersuit for breach of contract, since Nell had left Culver City before finishing *His Hour*. Days later, Tom discontinued the suit against Mayer Productions, but things had already gone too far. "All I have from Mayer are telegrams to the effect that the contract is broken," Tom wrote Juliet.[31]

After her dinner with Tom, Nell immediately returned to Los Angeles to help finish cutting *His Hour*. After being self-sufficient for almost two decades, her fortunes had suddenly become hostage to powerful men again. While negotiations dragged on she was largely without pay, since Mayer had stopped her salary as soon as she left for New York.

The trust was proving a stingy manager, as she had feared. "I am not the least impatient about the contract," she disingenuously wrote Tom a few weeks later, "but absolutely at the end of my tether regarding my ambiguous financial position. The present situation is grotesque and impossible, I have never received my salary regularly; only sums doled out now and then, so that I don't know where I am or if I ought to economize or can spend it," she wrote him.[32]

She hoped her "masterpiece" might repair the damage to her reputation in the movie colony. Pickford, Fairbanks, and Chaplin were "all unanimous in declaring that it is the best picture of its kind (that is of romantic modern society) that has ever been made" after screening *His Hour* at Pickfair's theater one night before the premiere, she told her mother. Everyone predicted a great success, though William Hays had warned that the publicity for it must be as clean as possible. Her Hollywood friends believed "her value after this as a maker of pictures not only as an author" would shoot to stratospheric heights.[33]

Tom finally restruck a deal with MGM in October that included an additional $1,700 for each continuity in their three-picture deal and an agreement to pay Nell $3,000 in back salary. He believed they could have gotten more before and possibly even finished another picture "during the time that has been lost." But this was the best he could do now.[34]

Shortly after Rhys conceded that Old World superiority had

failed in the contest against New World corporate smarts, the company fired Tom for having been duped by Nell's "play acting" into sabotaging their strategy.

"I am not going into all the various points you raise in your letters over the settlement with Mayer—for better or worse—that's finished. Life is not long enough to argue with one's lawyer," Juliet wrote, suddenly reducing their relationship to a purely professional one.[35]

Tom would remain Nell's personal lawyer, tellingly, and sounded equal parts defensive and relieved when he got the news. "If I was deceived in thinking that a smash up was a possibility, that surely is the fault of my intelligence and not of my heart," he assured Rhys. But he likely also felt relief knowing he would be spared the fearsome quarreling over calculating the production costs to determine Nell's share of the profits from her last two films.[36]

A letter to the London *Times* that Nell wrote suggested why she had picked the American producers' professionalism and production values over the approach to making movies back home. "American producers realized about ten years ago that if it was necessary to spend a million dollars to obtain a certain result, the million must be risked." They saw that "high salaries must be paid to the best brains in the country in every department of the business" and that "the psychology of the public taste must be studied." The result was "that American picture methods improve year by year" while "the whole British manner of presentation is amateurish."

Nell was not exaggerating the extent to which Hollywood films dominated the U.K. market; by that year more than 95 percent of films shown there were American-made.[37]

She would not let even her family ruin her Hollywood love affair. Hollywood had appreciated her talent more than other any creative community she had encountered before and had the resources and experience necessary to make the kind of lavish movies she liked. The so-called Jewish characteristic Nell most feared was their tribalism, their willingness to band together to win the bigger point—a quality that, ironically, resembled all the other successful imperialists she had known. Now she believed that "the clannish nest of Jews which compose the moving picture business" had, "however unjustly," developed "a deep prejudice against Elinor Glyn Ltd."[38]

She had regained control of her fate but had been left to wonder if she could trust the producers at all.

Pickford and Chaplin were correct about *His Hour*. Within weeks, the enthusiastic crowds at the largest, most lucrative first-run theaters indicated that its box office would likely surpass *Three Weeks*. And Madame Glyn was right about Gilbert; the film launched him as an American actor whose allure rivaled Valentino's. Madame Glyn was again the toast of the town. With its much lower production cost, the film's profit would equal that of *Three Weeks*; both were among the most profitable films that MGM released in its early years.[39]

While fans lined up to see her "personally supervised" film, the Author's Press released a set of ten of her novels, highlighting the ones that appeared onscreen. "10 GREAT $2.00 novels by Elinor Glyn NOW YOURS—All For Only $2.98 If You Act Now," promised a full-page ad in *Photoplay* each month that offered a teasing, and conveniently timed, selection from one of her books.

"'Doushka,'" whispered Gritzko (from *His Hour*) in an advertisement the month the movie opened. "'Life is so short. Let us taste it while we may!' and the princely stranger who had suddenly appeared out of the soft shadow of the warm, sensuous Egyptian night, bent and kissed her lips."[40]

Nell had indisputably shown the value her supervision added but seemed further than ever from making her next deal reflect this clout. After all the negotiations, and renegotiations, with Thalberg and Mayer, Elinor Glyn Ltd.'s audit of the production costs continued into the next year. There were disputes over the charges and questions about what constituted a "net profit." The lack of trust among all parties made reaching consensus very hard.[41]

Knowing Nell was looking for a new studio, Mary Pickford began recruiting her to join United Artists once her deal ended. UA desperately needed more profitable products. Artists frequently took too long and spent too lavishly on their work, it turned out. They also tended to focus on their projects rather than the survival of the company as a whole. Tied up with previous commitments, Chaplin only started making movies for the company in 1923. Now his jewels would each take two or more years to make. Griffith had been a much greater disappointment; he worked slowly *and* spent so much that even his successes failed to turn much profit.

Only Pickford and Fairbanks reliably completed movies that made money for the new company. As the 1920s roared on, the remarkably athletic Fairbanks had made the transition from comedy to swashbuckling roles like *The Thief of Bagdad* (1924), which made Anna Mae Wong the first Chinese American Hollywood star.[42]

The most business-minded of the original partners, Pickford had tried to stay relevant to postwar audiences too, bringing the great German director, Ernst Lubitsch, to Hollywood to modernize her appeal. The celebrated director of *Passion* was known for directing urbane comedies of manners that managed to make a joke out of sex. Lubitsch decided to make *Rosita* (1923), featuring Pickford as a sexy, impoverished Spanish singer.

Nell had approved the choice, and *Rosita* was an enormous critical and commercial success, but then Pickford suddenly repudiated the film. (Later she destroyed all its prints.) She worried about reports that small-town audiences disliked the movie, but there was more at work. At thirty-three, Pickford realized that she could, or would, not adapt to the new kinds of heroines that the rising generation wanted. "Now of course, [Lubitsch] understood Pola Negri or Gloria Swanson, that type of actress, but he did not understand me because I am of course a purely American type," she explained later. By 1924, the producer in Pickford knew people like Madame Glyn would have to join her company if United Artists was to survive.[43]

As 1925 approached, the parties in Hollywood grew ever more dazzling and Nell was at the center of the "greatest, gaudiest spree in history" even if the company's control over her finances had made money a real source of stress for the first time since Clayton's death. Some 1,200 guests packed the Cocoanut Grove for a feast thrown for Marion Davies one night. Chaos erupted when a thousand toy monkeys attached to balloons suddenly rained down from the ceiling. Davies and Hearst (when he was not with his wife) now reigned supreme as Hollywood's most lavish hosts. Their parties always had "the best bands and the dancing goes on until 2am after the richest dinner is served off silver and gold plate," Nell wrote home.[44]

On several weekends she traveled up the coast and along "miles of winding road where deer, antelope, bison, giraffe, and zebra roamed" to visit San Simeon, the faux "feudal castle right out of Arabian Nights" that Hearst and architect Julia Morgan would build and rebuild until his death. At San Simeon's "cosmopolitan parties the World and his wife—and often his mistress—met formally, or informally, according to one's personal taste and interests," writer Frances Marion recalled. Decorated with interiors bought from aristocrats impoverished by the Great War, the estate appeared like a series of "exquisitely engineered stage sets for hedonism."

Parties there were like the Countess of Warwick's Saturday to Mondays at Easton reflected through a carnival mirror. Nell was not one to judge about the sexual shenanigans of her friends even if she wanted all the beautiful young things lolling beside the one-hundred-foot-long Neptune pool to drink a lot less. "So much joy and laughter keeps me young," she wrote home. "Then on my off night I dine with my beloved Mary and have home and peace."[45]

But then scandal threatened the movie colony, again, because of a party Hearst and Davies threw in November on his magnificent yacht, the *Oneida*, for the forty-third birthday of Thomas Ince. A pioneering producer and director, Ince had founded Inceville, the first vertically integrated film company, and later Triangle Pictures with D. W. Griffith and Mack Sennett in 1915. By 1924, the Triangle Studio in Culver City had become MGM and Ince was an independent producer struggling to regain his stature in the emerging studio system by arranging a co-production deal with Hearst.[46]

Nell was one of the few guests who later admitted to being aboard the *Oneida*, but other definite attendees included Charlie Chaplin, actress Seena Owens, various Hearst executives, and Margaret Livingston, rumored to be Ince's mistress. After missing the cast-off, Ince had joined them in San Diego, where Davies greeted him wearing a jaunty sailor suit and holding a huge bouquet of helium balloons in each hand. But the party took a sudden tragic turn when Ince fell ill late that night. Taken off the boat the next morning in San Diego, the hard-drinking, heavy smoker died at home of heart failure, at least according to his doctor and the district attorney.[47]

"This will put a stop to all gaiety for a time," Nell speculated to her mother. She was wrong.

Like the nation's economic prosperity, the movie colony's penchant for partying seemed only to be gathering speed with Hays's better PR management in place. Worried about his relationship with Davies and flagrant violation of Prohibition making the news, Hearst succeeded in mostly keeping their party out of the press concerning Ince's death. But the local rumor mill quickly went into overdrive: the most pervasive rumor whispered the tycoon had shot at Chaplin in a jealous rage but hit Ince instead.[48]

Wanting to capitalize on the scarlet flush surrounding her name and finish her deal with MGM, Nell had dashed off the scenario and continuity (like "child's play now") for *Man and Maid*. "A real artist" she called director Victor Schertzinger, who had a storied career as a concert violinist before getting his start in the movies when Ince asked him to compose an original score for *Civilization* (1916). Silent films, of course, were never silent; theaters had almost always featured at least a piano player. But during the extravagant 1920s, the nicest ones began to feature full orchestras.

Set in Paris, the French actress Renée Adorée played the courtesan who tempts the war-scarred, cynical hero, played by the perfectly cast Lew Cody. Adorée resembled Margot. "It's uncanny how I seem to draw these family types," she wrote her mother. Harriet Hammond played the secretary who wins his heart. Work on *Man and Maid* (1925), a lost film, again went so well that a visitor to the studio would never have guessed that there was any trouble between Nell and the producers.[49]

On the set, Madame Glyn continued her quest to turn actresses into glamorous ladies, renovating Hammond's style by "patiently showing her every move and look. Before I took her she 'jazzed' her walk, shoulders up to ears, and a silly mincing smile all the time—what is known here as the 'Sennett bathing girl style.' Now she is quite a gentle lady," Nell proudly wrote home. "The people here have said, 'If Elinor Glyn can make the dumb beauty act she certainly is a wizard!'" She was working fourteen-hour days, overseeing every detail. Even more than *His Hour*, she felt "everything is left to me. I do the sets and the furnishings and the costumes and even the smallest trifles," she wrote, "then somebody actually explains my orders to the actors." She loved "seeing the scenes grow under your eyes." They finished the picture at top speed; by the end of January it was cut, titled, and ready to send to theaters.[50]

If image had ruled in the first act of her life and storytelling in the second, Nell's third act making movies let her marry image and story. No wonder she felt more creatively fulfilled than ever. Filmmaking was "the most intrusive hard work anyone can do but so interesting now that I have absolute control. I would rather do it than anything else—it is like living thrilling love stories instead of writing them."[51]

But her experience with *Man and Maid* again made her long to assume total creative control. "If I had *no* director and could direct entirely alone I would get the characterizations much finer and the groupings better and the 'tempo' faster," she believed. For even Schertzinger, "absolutely obedient as he appears, somehow" got the actors "to overact in places although he really meant to carry out my orders." As soon as this contract was over, she wanted nothing "but a good assistant with me." This was precisely the working arrangement that Irving Thalberg had proposed under the partnership that her family had nixed.[52]

The only thing she missed were people capable of "intellectual conversations." In the movie colony, it was always talk of parties, pranks, work, and diets.

Surrounded by "stars as beautiful as angels and as ignorant as savages," she began a salon in 1925 composed of other European expatriates and "no common 'movie' people." The only Americans were those like Schertzinger and Cedric Gibbons, who possessed the kind of cultural clout that translated in European terms. "The joy to have the companionship of one's own class in this weird country is great," she wrote home. "No Jews, no vulgarities, or common ways and no familiarities. We get on splendidly." The salon was well populated with a bevy of beautiful young men who paid court to an aging beauty bent on keeping her vanity well fluffed, reported a disgusted Lady Diana Manners Cooper after attending one such gathering while visiting Los Angeles on tour. Many considered Lady Diana Britain's most beautiful socialite of the interwar era, much as Nell had been more than a generation earlier. Cooper was amazed to find Nell looking twenty-five and surrounded by "a cluster of beautiful young men" hanging on her every word.[53]

One handsome young man at Nell's salon quickly separated himself from the pack. Within weeks of meeting John Wynn, she began having him attend to her fan mail, "which came by the hundreds a day," she boasted. "A tall, slim young man, fully six feet," Wynn had "the air of an English gentleman"—educated just like Rhys at Eton and Oxford, Nell said. But her gentleman was of course decades younger and had "very dark hair, practically black, violet eyes and traces of a light brown moustache." The adoring John Wynn was an excellent dancer too. When her old friend and Daisy Greville's half-sister, Lady Millicent, Duchess of Sutherland, came to visit, she had Wynn and a friend squire them around town. "Two grandmothers, both really rather attractive," she wrote to her mother, "with two of the very best-looking young men you ever saw, too enchanted to be with us and in years young enough to be our sons!"[54]

The pleasure of finding a dashing young man who made her welfare his sole purpose must have been comforting after so many years of going solo or tangling with men who always put their own needs first. If anything deeper developed with the younger men she kept company with in Hollywood, Wynn was definitely the one. And conveniently he appeared in her life just at the moment when she most needed a kind of male proxy to help her better regain control of her affairs. Although possibly a scoundrel, John Wynn was without a doubt a tall and distinguished-looking British man who tended to her every wish.

Determined to show the producers how efficiently she could work, she threw herself into supervising her last film for MGM, *The Only Thing* (1925), with director Jack Conway, a newcomer at the job. It was hard to miss that the directors Thalberg assigned to her grew successively less distinguished. Drawing on her past successes, this lost film returns to a Balkan kingdom threatened by revolutionaries and ruled by an old, unattractive king and his beautiful young queen, played by Eleanor Boardman. After they kill the king, the revolutionaries imprison the queen and the duke of Chevenix, a handsome British diplomat played by Conrad Nagel.

"Any motion-picture set is a melting pot, but even more so than usual" was "Elinor Glyn's production of 'The Only Thing,'" the press noted. On the set she assembled a former Russian general and prince, several important Frenchmen and "English colonials," Spaniards, Scandinavians, Austrians, Argentinians, and "a real Italian countess." The mob scenes and the lovers' daring escape—from a sinking ship where they are lashed together—showed how much Nell had learned about the screen's demand for action.[55]

But the budget for such effects (the sinking ship, the five hundred extras for the revolutionary mob), plus the royal setting and costumes, ran high. The production costs for this movie surpassed all of her previous ones, including *Three Weeks*. Allowing such runaway production costs was unlike Thalberg, perhaps a telltale of more complicated, even retributive, motives at work.[56]

Nell kept herself glamorously visible while supervising the film, promising to "Give the Public What It Expects." "The public has always associated my work with flame and passion and in this next picture I assure you they are going to get what they expect," she told a group of reporters in her office at MGM. Dressed all in cream except for an electric-blue chiffon headscarf wrapped around "her auburn tresses," the increasingly thick-in-the-middle Nell frugally lunched on "warm milk and crackers."[57]

Everywhere the press touted her magic touch with actors. "Madam Glyn has, as is well known in Hollywood, a passion for selecting her actors and actresses and then redoing them with her own ideas," reminded one. "There is always much interest manifested each time a Glyn production is begun at the Metro-Goldwyn-Mayer studios, for new faces appear on the screen and new personalities are discovered," wrote another. Reporters described her influence over actresses in ways usually reserved for male impresarios. "She is trusted and respected as a director," particularly among "the girl stars" who felt the power of "her fascination and believe that her influence upon them doesn't end when their work together ends." Gloria Swanson's marriage that year to Henry de La Falaise, a French marquis, delightfully proved the point.[58]

Nell had decided to live permanently in the New World, she announced that summer when the film was over, now praising

Americans' virtues. "'America, I adore it,' says Madam Glyn. 'I never would live anywhere else permanently. Europe is of the past. America is the future, the place where one can do things. America is youth.'"[59]

She reported to her family that John Wynn was the partner she needed to advance her interests in Hollywood. He has "the brains of Thalberg only honest," she assured Juliet and Rhys, in a comment that reflected Irving was still her gold standard. Nell and Wynn had decided that "a totally new policy must be inaugurated" for her future contracts that would give her absolute creative control. To do this meant formalizing his role as her manager, for which she wanted the company to pay him $300 a week and 20 percent of whatever contracts he negotiated.[60]

Her family was aghast, this time with better reason. Like Thalberg, John Wynn was a very young man. But unlike Thalberg, Wynn had no experience or connections in the industry—and no one to vouch for him. The "prime minister does not get such a salary," Juliet replied before Rhys retorted in a cable: "Only an adventurer trading on your credulity would ask such terms."

Tom and Juliet patched things over to neutralize this "new horror," as she called Wynn. "I should think he is about the same caliber as the rest of the young hangers on, who are perpetually besieging her," Juliet worried. Her daughter believed the two were romantically involved. "Paying for his advice is simply hush money, but what else could I do in the face of her cable," she told Tom. Nell had also confidentially asked Tom how to disband the trust so she might control her own affairs again. "She intends to live the rest of her life in California and wants to buy a house. I am at a loss to know what to do."[61]

In the end, Nell's family offered John Wynn $100 a week and 10 percent of her contracts, but Nell flashed her claws. "I am cabling friendly," but feared the attempt "to be managed by laymen 6000 miles away is hopeless."[62]

When Nell sent Wynn to New York to strike a deal with the men in charge of the money to let her direct her next movie, Juliet asked Tom to speak to the handsome young man. "He is not especially Jewish looking though I have seen many Jews who look like him," Tom wrote after their meeting. "I think he is a Jew, probably of Austrian descent from a mixed breed." Meanwhile Juliet had been researching Wynn. "We have looked him up in the Eton records and find that he was never there—at least not under the name Weiner which I understand is his name. So he is clearly an impostor," she wrote.[63]

Tom had learned from Bernard Merivale, Nell's agent at Hughes Massie after the founder's death, that Wynn had met with Walter Wanger, a new producer at Famous Players, who said Nell wanted to return, but they worried she was overexposed and on the "downgrade." Next Wynn tried to restart negotiations with MGM, but the family's conviction that the studio was shortchanging Nell on royalties short-circuited the attempt. MGM's lawyer-producer, Robert Rubin, "seemed disgusted" and now believed she "was trying to hold an auction sale and that they would not bid against one another." When Wynn left, Tom reported they were "finished with MGM forever."[64]

Disgruntled and shut out of the dealings, the family used their control over Nell's purse strings to reassert control. "Please accept one month's notice termination of your contract salary," read a telegram sent to Nell's violet-eyed friend. "No travelling or hotel expenses will be refunded."[65]

When MGM released *The Only Thing* that fall, its poor performance seemed to illustrate Wanger's point that perhaps Madame Glyn had become overexposed. Reviews were mostly good. "In its appeal to the eye, Elinor Glyn's new picture is a gorgeous and beautiful thing," wrote a common tribute. And Madame Glyn had worked her magic again, coaxing "a sparkle never discerned before" from Conrad Nagel. "We might even say that Mr. Nagel possesses 'it' (Mrs. Glyn's pronoun) to a marked degree." But early receipts indicated this would be Nell's first film to lose money. After the lackluster performance of *Man and Maid*, this smelled of trouble.[66]

The bickering over production costs dragged on all summer, and by fall Nell had enough: "Elinor Glyn Ltd." would have to go. Cannot "understand this arbitrary dismissal and refuse sanction," she wired. A longer letter followed. "The object of the company has been achieved," she diplomatically began. With £100,000 already invested, they had ensured sufficient funds for her retirement. But

Nell returned to the point she had made so often before when dealing with her difficult husband and the mother who cosseted him. All the drama was killing her ability to do the work on which everyone depended. (And her daughter Juliet, perhaps unwittingly, like her mother had chosen to tend another man's wounded pride and self-interest over her own.)[67]

The family fortune they all sought to protect was at stake, Nell emphasized. "When I am worried, hampered, or unhappy my imagination does not work—that is my chief reason for asking the company to be wound up," she explained in a sadly familiar refrain. "Over and over again, different producers have said they cannot bother dealing with the Company in London." This reluctance had "been the cause of negotiations becoming lukewarm, when I have said I am powerless to make any decisions and they must refer to the Co."[68]

Now Nell and Wynn were negotiating a 50/50 partnership deal with Joseph Schenck, who was about to become United Artists' new chairman of the board. Much like Thalberg, Schenck blended artistic sensitivity with hardheaded business smarts and had been approached to save the ailing company. Times were so desperate at UA that Pickford was in production on *Little Annie Rooney*, her first little urchin girl role in years. But Schenck was "prejudiced against McIlvaine and the Company's ignorance of the movie business and will only sign with me direct," Nell claimed.

Treating her like a tantrummy toddler, her family ignored her demands. They were acting like "a small town mayor demanding off Mussolini," Nell shot back, warning their "childish and ridiculous" approach "would end the whole magnificent thing."[69]

So Nell started playing poker herself, signing a new contract and then announcing her plans as a fait accompli. Schenck was suddenly so busy trying to merge with MGM that he could not manage Nell's productions for several months. But he had arranged to loan her out to Mayer, a common practice, to quickly make what Nell called her "pot boiler," *Love's Blindness* on excellent terms. The speed and lucrative nature of the deal that came together suggested Hollywood was not yet finished with Madame Glyn—provided her family stayed out of her affairs.[70]

"Wynn has entirely justified my faith in him as I knew he would if given time," Nell gloated, even though Schenck had made the arrangements. "He has secured for me immediate cash and finest prize the industry can offer me by affiliation with United Artists. Please immediately commence taking steps to dissolve Company now," she reiterated. "If this worry goes on how can I make *Love's Blindness* a success, or have energy enough to continue working? I am like a dog with a kettle on his tail and leg tied up." Better to put these difficulties behind them and "be happy friends freed from business." When no word came, Nell pressed McIlvaine to share details with her about the E. G. Ltd.'s assets and discovered that it already contained more than $100,000, which would generate "an annuity that would surely be ample for anyone." With that matter settled, she wanted "to dissolve the Company immediately and . . . so that I am entirely free and responsible myself."[71]

Then Nell started making more deals, betting that her family would be powerless to stop her. The Hughes Massie literary agency reported feeling "quite helpless at the moment because all the film companies now go direct to Mrs. Glyn." Having sold "some of the Company's property (*Love's Blindness*)" without their permission she had made "the situation impossible," Rhys conceded. "The only thing they could do is a law suit against her, which is, of course, out of the question."

"The truth is that mum is making it impossible to work for her," Juliet confessed to Tom. "As we have amassed sufficient money to invest in an annuity to bring her in a sufficient income for any old lady, we do not feel called upon to struggle any longer." The situation was insulting, but they would put the best face possible on it, as Nell had taught them. "Mum thinks she is going to make an enormous fortune, now that she has the handling of her affairs unhampered by your and our stupidities! I hope to goodness she will but think it unlikely," her daughter wrote.[72]

While Nell may have forced her family out of her professional life, she remained very much rooted in their old world as much as her new one—as all the very long letters she continued to write almost weekly to her mother attested. Ties of blood and kinship were deep even if lightly observed for Nell.

And it was hard to miss how all her struggles with the producers had left her prospects more elusive and harder to visualize than
since she had arrived in the movie colony. Her trust had been deeply
shaken. Increasingly she would spend more of her time dancing alone
in her room at the Ambassador when the long day's work was done.[73]

CHAPTER 15

The It Girl

Sweet Santa Claus, give me *him*.

—Clara Bow in *It* (1927)

Six days a week Nell rose at five thirty a.m. on her sleeping balcony made of glass at the Ambassador Hotel. The view looked out over Wilshire Boulevard toward Hollywood and the mountains beyond. Although she had been hunting for a permanent home in Los Angeles, Nell still preferred hotels for their unusual combination of on-demand sociability or seclusion and distant staff.

After glancing at the newspapers, she took a heavy black pencil and a pad of plain foolscap paper back to bed and began writing: articles, correspondence, magazine stories, or a chapter in one of the novelizations of her movies, like the one of *Love's Blindness* that she published that year. She had learned long before that she could never write so productively with the distraction of another person in the room.

Next she began her toilette with her dressmaker, Ann Morgan. That took an hour or much more, depending. By that time her secretary had arrived and she passed her the day's work; then John Wynn drove her to the MGM lot in Culver City where she arrived by nine a.m., usually staying until nine p.m. or later.[1]

After the poor performances of *Man and Maid* and *The Only Thing*, Nell knew *Love's Blindness*—her last movie at MGM, regardless—counted quite a lot. She had written a novella that had begun serialization in Hearst's *Cosmopolitan* about the kind of American hero with "It" that she had come to find, but no company had taken an interest in the idea. What came next, she did not know.[2]

The set of *Love's Blindness* already bustled with activity by the time she arrived. Another unoriginal story, this lost film featured an earl whose debts force him to marry a "luscious Jewess," played by Pauline Starke, to obtain a loan from her moneylender father. Unaware that her father has forced the earl's hand, "the marriage takes place, and then Glyn's love plot begins to work, for the girl is in love and the man isn't." The decision to tell a story about the successful intermarriage of a Jewish woman to an aristocrat was an interesting choice for Nell, Mayer, and Thalberg's last venture together. Turning the stereotypically Spanish-looking actor Antonio Moreno into a convincingly passionate English lord would be her biggest challenge, Nell knew. Irving Thalberg had assigned director John Francis Dillon to the picture. Dillon had established himself as the go-to man to capture the spirit of the age with *Flaming Youth* (1923), an enormous hit starring flapper actress Colleen Moore.[3]

It was 1926, and there seemed to be no limit to America's acceleration of the rate of change. Transformations that verged on miraculous abounded. Several years of unparalleled "Coolidge Prosperity" (the Vermont lawyer became president when Harding had died in office in 1923) promised economic growth without end.

As towns like Los Angeles ballooned into metropolises, the United States became more urban than rural for the first time. Henry Ford's mass-produced Model T's clogged the National Road that recently stretched from coast to coast. Out of the ether, broadcasts squawked through radio sets, making radio another wonder of the modern world and galvanizing the growth of the music recording industry. Even though most of the nation's new wealth went only to those at the very top, the recent development of mass credit fueled the growth of a new consumer economy of abundance whose point was to teach people to buy more than they needed; mass credit meant that a majority of Americans—many living just at the edge of poverty—would own a radio set by the decade's end.[4]

The public's taste in heroines had shifted decisively toward female stars who not only fit this modern landscape but whose glittering participation made its dramas whirl: independent women of the world like Gloria Swanson and Norma Shearer; foreign sophisticates like Pola Negri, and the twenty-year-old Swedish newcomer,

Greta Garbo; free-spirited, "All-American" flappers like Colleen Moore, Clara Bow, and Joan Crawford (whose first speaking role was in Nell's *The Only Thing*).

Gossip that Madame Glyn's famous touch might no longer fit the times emerged like smoke and then evaporated. But the vapors left behind made the ever-sensitive Nell aware that some questioned whether her aristocratic sensibility, coupled with her tendency to renege on negotiations, was still a package worth producing.

Perhaps this accounted for why her deal at United Artists did not materialize. UA's failed merger with MGM might also have played a role. Charlie Chaplin had scotched the attempt, unwilling to join the kind of behemoth that the partners had escaped. The picture business was consolidating into enormous, vertically integrated companies that controlled the industry from beginning to end. Chaplin wanted to protect the last strongholds for independent production as so many others disappeared for good.

Nell's surviving correspondence is silent on why she failed to join UA. Not wishing to risk a war between the partners, Schenck had abandoned the merger with MGM and brought in more star-producers to make the films the company needed to survive. Swanson, Valentino, Goldwyn, and Schenck's wife, Norma Talmadge, sister-in-law Constance, and brother-in-law Buster Keaton all joined. But not Madame Glyn. Schenck had free rein about such decisions; he may have bet that Glyn's fading touch, and reputation for being difficult in business dealings, no longer justified giving her so much control.[5]

As temperatures soared across the country that summer, Madame Glyn's and every flapper's favorite actor was due to appear in the most highly anticipated sequel Hollywood had ever made: *Son of the Sheik*, featuring Rudolph Valentino as both the original lover and his headstrong son. At thirty-one, Valentino was weary of wearing the mantle of the screen's greatest lover. "Heaven knows I am no sheik! Look at 'this sleek black hair.' Getting a little thin about the temples, isn't it?" he had recently told a reporter. The expectations the role created in women ("'Let's see you excite *me*,' they say.") had worn him out. "The whole thing is false and artificial. You can't go on and on with it," he complained. Onscreen "one appears to be what others desire, not what one is in reality."[6]

But since audiences desired most to see Valentino again as the sheik, the actor acquiesced to Schenck's request that he make the picture. After a two-year-long strike at Paramount to get a higher salary and more control, Valentino had returned to the screen in 1924 to make a series of moderately successful films plagued by troubles partially resulting from his wife's, designer Natacha Rambova's, artistic demands on the set. He endured a painful divorce after barring her from his future sets. Terribly in debt, he needed to fill his own coffers as much as UA's. "FLAPPERS, gaze! Rudy, the Sheik, is back!" beckoned *Photoplay* beneath a photograph of Valentino dressed for the role.[7]

On his way to the film's premiere in New York, the *Chicago Tribune* ran an editorial that blamed Nell for crafting the emasculated ideal Valentino embodied and that was idolized throughout America. "Down with Decatur; Up with Elinor Glyn. Hollywood is a national school of masculinity. Rudy, the beautiful gardener's boy, is the prototype of the American male," declared the unsigned editorial, "Pink Powder Puffs." Valentino's taste for "masculine cosmetics, sheiks, floppy pants, and slave bracelets," had produced the unimaginable: facial powder dispensers in men's public washrooms. "Why didn't someone quietly drown Rudolph Guglielmo [*sic*], alias Valentino, years ago?" the writer fumed. "It is time for a matriarchy if the male of the species allows such a thing to exist. Better a rule by masculine women than by effeminate men." En route, Valentino called the editorialist "a contemptible coward" and demanded to settle "in American fashion" who was the best man in a boxing ring. The editorialist did not respond.[8]

On *Son of the Sheik*'s opening night, a double line of fans stretched for two blocks in 98-degree heat. Similar scenes unfolded across the country. Weeks later, the hard-drinking, heavy smoker collapsed at a club and was taken to the hospital, where doctors performed a double operation for acute appendicitis and perforated gastric ulcers. "Did I behave like a pink powder puff or like a man?" he asked when he woke up. Peritonitis—an inflammation of the membrane that lines the walls of the abdominal cavity—had set in. The infection spread quickly in this pre-antibiotic era.[9]

Valentino died on August 23, 1926; an estimated 100,000 people tried to view his body over the two days it lay in a Midtown funeral home. On the first day mounted police tried to control the frustrated crowds. Rioting erupted after it began to pour. Store windows were smashed, injuring more than a hundred people. The chief of police said he had never seen such a large, unruly crowd. Many claimed, then and since, that hysterical women dominated the mob. But overhead photographs of the scene show roughly an equal number of men's hats.

It is easy to imagine that the city's large immigrant population, and the many younger men who imitated his dress and style, felt differently from their elders about the death of Madame Glyn's friend and protégé, Rudolph Valentino. "It was not so much a motion picture actor who lay dead, as Pan or Apollo," was how journalist Heywood Broun described the passing of the Roaring Twenties' greatest screen lover.[10]

Very soon, few would doubt that the death of this silent-film god marked the beginning of the end of early Hollywood itself.

Nell and five hundred other Hollywood notables celebrated

Rudolph Valentino's casket in New York City, 1926

Valentino's second High Mass in Beverly Hills on September 7. She attended with George Curzon's eldest daughter, Irene, and then carried on with a long-planned welcome dinner party for her guest, telling herself that party-loving Valentino would have wished it so. Irene was Lady Ravensdale now, Curzon having died the year before, estranged from his second wife entirely. Before his death, he had arranged for Irene to inherit his subsidiary title. Unmarried and unchanged, Irene spent her time hunting, shopping, gambling, traveling, and falling in and out of love. A bad end to a tumultuous affair with a married man had sent her on a cruise that ended with a long stay at the Ambassador to be near the closest thing to a mother she had.[11]

Nell felt her familiar worry that Irene exhibited the lack of purpose too common among patricians but did her best to show her guest a good time. The day after Valentino's funeral and Irene's dinner, they attended King Vidor's wedding to actress Eleanor Boardman, who had starred the year before in Nell's *The Only Thing*. The splashy affair was held at the sprawling Mediterranean-style estate that William Randolph Hearst and Marion Davies had just bought on 3.5 acres in the heart of Beverly Hills. Other guests included Louis Mayer; his wife, Margaret, and daughters, Edie and Irene; Thalberg; Goldwyn; actor William Haines; and John Gilbert, whose new lover, Greta Garbo, failed to show up.

Gilbert and Garbo had fallen passionately in love making *Flesh and the Devil*. "It was the damnedest thing you ever saw. It was the sort of thing Elinor Glyn used to write about," recalled director Clarence Brown. "When they got into that first love scene, well, nobody else was even there." But Garbo was like a skittish colt, impossible to corral, and her absence coupled with the "sight of his friends' happiness threw John Gilbert into a fine frenzy of despair." Gilbert's misery poisoned the wedding and displayed the cracks emerging in the partnerships among the cohort who first put MGM on the map.[12]

The two women also attended intimate dinners with John Wynn, Chaplin, and Goldwyn, and a big party at Jesse Lasky's beach house that signaled Nell's new relationship with her first producers at the newly renamed Paramount Studio. Shortly before Irene Curzon's

arrival, producer Budd Schulberg had approached Nell with a proposition. Young Schulberg had got his start as Adolph Zukor's publi-
cist, famously coining Mary Pickford's marquee-defining nickname,
"America's Sweetheart." He remained a publicity man at heart. The
year before, he had tried to promote his biggest property, actress Clara
Bow, as the "Brooklyn Bonfire," but the trademark did not take.

Like everyone else, Schulberg had heard Madame Glyn wax on
for years about that "strange magnetism that attracts both sexes"
called "It." He had noticed her unsuccessful attempt earlier that year
to promote Conrad Nagel as a bearer of the quality. "Many complained of the difficulty of finding American actors who exuded what
Elinor Glyn calls 'it,'" sighed one fan magazine writer. Schulberg's
proposition was simple: would Nell fashion a scenario for Clara Bow
illustrating the concept and then proclaim her as *the* "It Girl" of
Hollywood? For this service, Paramount would pay her a $50,000
advance and royalties of 25 percent of the film's net income in excess
of three times the negative cost.[13]

Instantly intrigued, Nell asked to meet Clara. Nell had already
written a novella that she now called *It* for *Cosmopolitan* that depicted
the hero she had been dreaming about for years: a commanding, self-
made businessman, likely modeled on William Randolph Hearst,
who fell in love with his impoverished but well-born secretary that
was set in an urban American environment entirely different from
her typical aristocratic, European ones. According to Schulberg,
Madame Glyn agreed unconditionally at once.

However she got there, days later Nell met Bow on a break the
actress took from shooting *Wings*, a Great War movie that would
win the first Academy Award for Best Picture. She knew Clara Bow
as Hollywood's second-best flapper, following Colleen Moore.

But the movie colony largely shunned the twenty-one-year-old
actress socially for her unwillingness to hide her rough-and-ready
ways. "Her Brooklyn accent and dreadful manners would reproach
them with their common origin, making her presence an insulting
reminder of their uneasy position in 'high society,'" observed actress
Louise Brooks, a raven-haired, ex-Follies girl from Kansas, whose
husband at the time refused to invite Clara to a dinner party. "Oh,

no, we can't have *her*," he said, according to Brooks. "We don't know what she'd *do*. She's from Brooklyn, you know" (so were Marion Davies, Thalberg, and many other pillars of the movie colony).[14]

Unlike those other Brooklynites, open scandal constantly nipped at Clara's heels. Her recent negotiation with Paramount had made her contract the only one without the morals clause that had become standard after Arbuckle's disgrace. This unique privilege seemed to admit tacitly that her playing "the reckless generation— on and off the screen," as *Photoplay* put it, was good for business. "Little Clara Bow got her name in the papers recently when Robert Savage, untamed Yale student, tried to kill himself because Clara wouldn't marry him," *Photoplay* continued. "In the subsequent trial . . . Robert testified that Clara kissed him so fervently that he was laid up with a sore jaw for two days. Now Clara says that the more she sees of men, the better she likes dogs." The gossip appeared beneath a photograph of Clara with one of her Chow-Chows, whose hair had been dyed to match her own shade of red.[15]

Clara's charm dazzled Nell when they met in Schulberg's office the first time. She arrived "hatless, her flaming head tied up with some kind of scarf. She was frightfully dressed," Nell recalled a few years later. "But in spite of the shocking clothes and ridiculous scarf, Clara exuded immense attraction. Her large, lovely eyes flashed with life, and her tiny figure seemed all-alive with desire to go." Clara "talked in the toughest vocabulary I had ever heard in the film colony! But it was apt and very funny. She was perfectly genuine, and did not pretend to have come from anywhere grand, but just from the poorest class. This naturalness drew me at once."[16]

Madame Glyn had found an American woman whose "It" was plain for all to see. "You are my medium child," she gravely announced. " 'It' is an inner magic, an animal magnetism," she told her. "Valentino possessed this certain magic. So do John Gilbert and Rex," (a stallion made famous by western films).

"I was awful confused about the horse," Clara reportedly said later, "but if she thought he had 'It,' then I figured he must be quite an animal." And with the partnership sealed between Hollywood's most famous redheads, Clara went back to work.[17]

"Elinor Glyn's famous definition of 'It' is to be explained on the screen," Schulberg announced, "with Clara Bow in the leading feminine role. This will be the first of a series of Glyn pictures with Madame Glyn in charge of production." By the time Irene Curzon visited, Nell had a new office at Paramount and had passed her scenario off to screenwriters Hope Loring and Louis D. Lighton. Filming would begin the second week of October and "Madame Glyn is going to play a role in her own story, 'It.'"[18]

She had found a way to stay relevant. Now she would make the best of it.

"It was an age of miracles, it was an age of art, it was an age of excess, and it was an age of satire," wrote F. Scott Fitzgerald in "Echoes of the Jazz Age."[19]

Thanks to Madame Glyn, the 1920s was also the age of Clara Bow. "She danced even when her feet were not moving," said Adolph Zukor of the first great star at his newly renamed Paramount Pictures. "Some part of her was always in motion, if only her great rolling eyes." After Nell met Bow, she became "the it girl, the girl for whose services every studio was in violent completion. This girl was the real thing, someone to stir every pulse in the nation."[20]

Underneath her madcap surface, the "incandescent symbol of the flapper" was a very old soul whose relationship to the movies illustrated why so many young women saw Hollywood as the pot of gold at the rainbow's end. Clara with the "too black eyes, and too red hair" had made her long, stormy entrance into the world during a heat wave in July of 1905. The Bows were "ghetto nomads," moving almost every year and always "scrimping the corners" for food and coal in the wintertime. Her mother, Sarah, had as many as three seizures a day. A nervous disease, the doctor said. Generous Clara called her father unlucky, but others remembered Robert Bow as a shiftless drunk who possibly sexually abused his only child.[21]

When Clara was a child people usually thought she was a boy, which suited her fine. She never had any use for girls and their sissy games. "Carrot top" and "tomboy," they called her on a good day. But Clara was fast and strong and played with the boys until the year she turned thirteen and Sarah had "an usually long spell of being almost herself," perhaps because Robert had found his first steady job. Sarah made Clara her first pretty dress, she wore it to school, and suddenly she was no longer a pal but someone the boys wanted to kiss. Horrified, Clara quit school, got a job, and felt utterly alone.[22]

Except when she went to the movies, where she spent every extra cent looking for the kind of beautiful, romantic adventures that Madame Glyn had come to Hollywood to make. Just as Nell had hoped when she had headed to Los Angeles to spread her ideals to a larger audience, Clara learned at the picture show "there was beauty in the world." There in the dark she saw "distant lands, serene, lovely homes, romance, nobility, glamour," as she told writer Adela Rogers St. Johns in an unusually candid biography *Photoplay* published in 1928. Bow fell in love with "everything the magic silver sheet" signified to a "lonely, starved, unhappy child."

And though no one had ever called her pretty, a grand ambition unfolded in her heart. She would be a movie actress—"not for the fame or money or anything like that" but to share "how beautiful it all was." She would be an instrument of motion-picture magic and "do for others what the pictures did for her."

The year Clara turned sixteen she took a picture with a precious dollar to enter a "Fame and Fortune" contest in *Motion Picture Magazine*. The red tint of her wild mop was unmistakable even in black and white, creating a dramatic counterpoint to her enormous dark, sad eyes and serious mouth. It was January of 1921, just months after Nell arrived in Los Angeles.

In September, Clara received a letter asking her to take a screen test. At the Brewster office, each girl was given the same task: walk into the room, pick up a telephone, laugh, look worried, then terrified. "She is plastic, quick, alert, young and lovely," wrote Brewster's judges. "The rapidity of her improvement is scarcely credible." Clara Bow became Brewster Publications' "Fame and Fortune Contest Winner of 1921." "You are going straight to hell," Sarah said at the news. After Clara landed her first part, she woke to find her mother standing above her with a butcher's knife. Robust Clara fended off the attack, and Robert committed his wife to an asylum where she died a year later having been diagnosed with psychotic epilepsy.[23]

Even before Madame Glyn worked her magic, Clara Bow was a very sexy-looking girl. "She just jumped right off the screen," recalled her first boyfriend, Arthur Jacobson, who filmed her first screen test. "And her eyes—all she had to do was lift those lids and she was flirting." Just the type producer B. P. Schulberg liked. Connecticut-raised and college-educated, Schulberg believed himself a bit better than the older, immigrant generation of producers that came before him. He had started Preferred Pictures in 1919 after a merger at Famous Players had forced him out.

But the company floundered until Clara signed a contract for $50 a week and went to Los Angeles just shy of her eighteenth birthday in 1923. Schulberg's "organization was the cheapest and his reputation for the sexual abuse of young actresses who worked for him was the worst in Hollywood," said Louise Brooks, who joined the company at the same time. "Coming from the Brooklyn slums to work for Ben [B. P. Schulberg] automatically labeled Clara as a 'cheap little whore,'" Brooks claimed. "She came from Brooklyn, she looked cheap," agreed Sam Jaffe, a producer Clara dated. Like someone "men wanted to screw."[24]

Over the next two years, Clara made over twenty films. Even working at this pace, she collected raves. Her success in *The Plastic Age*—based on a bestselling novel by a Brown professor about sex and school spirit—crystallized her appeal as a woman whose libido was plain for all to see while tempting a college boy into joining her dancing to "the jungle rhythm of jazz." Bow's services netted Schulberg $3,000 a week on loan out to other film companies (a common practice under long-term contracts); he paid her $750 of the fee he collected. Paramount needed new stars, and *The Plastic Age* convinced Zukor that Bow was the one.

Zukor could feel the competition coming for him. "More Stars Than There Are in Heaven," MGM's ads beckoned, and Thalberg and Mayer had made this true in just two years. To get Bow, Zukor convinced Schulberg to rejoin his fold, swallowing Preferred Pictures and making him an independent producer.[25]

And then Clara Bow went to work with Madame Glyn, and nothing was the same for either woman again.

When she arrived on the set of *It*, "The Playgirl of Hollywood" was publicly on her second engagement that year, a tacit admission a couple was likely having sex. But Clara was in no rush. "Marriage ain't a woman's only job no more," she told Hearst columnist Dorothy Manners. How could "a girl whose [sic] worked hard and earned her place be satisfied as a wife only?" She wondered. "I know this. I wouldn't give up my work for marriage. I think a modern girl's capable of keeping a job and a husband."

As was obvious to all, Hollywood's many other working women agreed. Public-opinion polls by the 1930s registered how the film industry's women workers' intimate arrangements and romantic attitudes often placed them in the vanguard of progressive ideas about white women's proper roles. Well into the 1960s, most Americans disapproved of women's work after marriage and children except in case of dire need. And like so many in the movie colony, Clara played as hard as she worked. She stayed up late and drank too much and dressed exactly as she pleased. She swore good-naturedly, chewed gum constantly, and always dropped her g's. She kept a string of beaus waiting while she whizzed down Sunset Boulevard in her red convertible Kissel Speedster with her seven chows.[26]

Thoroughly a cat person, Nell detested the wild drives she took with Clara and her dogs, but she did not own a car and needed to be seen out and about with her protégée. All those redheads glinting in the Southern California sunshine must have been a sight.

Despite being strongly discouraged by almost everyone she knew, Nell invited Bow to a dinner party she hosted shortly after they met and found the treatment Clara received appalling. "No one was kind to her except Marion Davies, whose golden heart is always kind to everyone," Nell recalled. She would quickly learn firsthand that Bow was not just uncontrollable but possessed a style that would absorb and outstrip her own.[27]

Nell also appears to have been swept up in her promotion of Clara Bow to unprecedented degree. Remarkably, the publicity savvy Madame Glyn would say a lot of things promoting her It Girl that she later regretted. Everywhere Madame Glyn told reporters that Clara Bow was one of the *very* few people in Hollywood who deserved membership in her "Exclusive 'IT' Society." *Photoplay* announced just before *It*'s premiere:

At last, Elinor Glyn has given out an official list of screen luminaries possessing IT. Here it is: Clara Bow, Jack Gilbert, Greta Garbo, Pola Negri, Wallace Beery, Emil Jannings, Doug Fairbanks, and Gary Cooper. She said that Gloria Swanson and Tom Mix once had IT. Not now though. However, she declares that Mary Pickford, Lillian Gish, Ramon Navarro, Ronald Colman and Williams Haines are IT-less. . . . So that question is settled for all time.[28]

All the talk attributed to Glyn during this publicity spree alien-ated some of her closest friends in the business—particularly the women who had first believed in her magic, like Pickford, Pringle, and Gloria Swanson, the latter of whom was in New York producing her first film for United Artists, *The Loves of Sunya* (1927).[29]

The press gave Madame Glyn full credit for *It*'s screenplay, applauding her having finally "sidestepped her famous royal char-acters and given us a story of the everyday working girl." But Nell's story had been significantly revised by Hope Loring and Louis D. Lighton, a husband-and-wife team at Paramount, who created in the character of Betty-Lou the kind of uninhibited, working-class flap-per that Bow played best.

The scenario is a Cinderella story with feminist undertones and sex-positive overtones: Waltham Department Store clerk Betty-Lou spies her boss, Cyrus Waltham Jr., wants him, and uses her "It" to get him. Along the way, she teaches Waltham to question the sexual double standard (while officially maintaining it) and to have fun. Set in New York, most of the film's settings—Coney Island, a Lower East Side tenement, and Waltham's Department Store itself—were as foreign to Nell as an English country house to Clara.[30]

Like everyone who worked with Bow, Nell realized that when the cameras started rolling the best thing to do was nothing. Having just supervised Anthony Moreno in *Love's Blindness*, she also knew there was no chance of improving his appeal. On the set, she caught glimpses of Clara's "unhappy, comfortless past, utterly neglected as far as training in any domestic virtues went." So the grandmother to all the world's young things stepped into the breach.[31]

But Hollywood's most freewheeling flapper had no intention of

Clara Bow with other shop girls ogling the boss in *It* (1927)

Clara Bow and Glyn promoting *It*

Nell playfully chastises Bow

sawing the edges off her mannerisms or changing her style to suit anyone's idea of a lady. Bow's rebellious attitude indicated how much women like Madame Glyn had already licensed a freer sexual mode and emotional register that modern young girls now took for granted. Legend has it that when word got back to Nell that Bow had called her "that shithead," she quit trying to influence the actress at all. "Clara is the complete nonconformist," Nell later cautioned screenwriter and journalist Adela Rogers St. John when Adela tried to mentor Clara. "She has a big heart, a remarkable brain, and the most utter contempt for the world in general. You'll fail as I did."[32]

Still, the illustrious Madame Glyn's promotion of Clara Bow as the It Girl of her dreams sanctioned the actress's sexually assertive appeal by lending her image the touch of glamour she needed to become a superstar. Becoming the celebrated bearer of Madame Glyn's magic (if not her actual protégée) also gave Clara confidence. And confidence was the essential ingredient in glamour that so many young women lacked, particularly young women from the kind of background out of which Clara had climbed.

"Once Elinor Glyn called her 'The It Girl' it changed Clara completely," agreed actor Buddy Rogers, Clara's co-star in *Wings*. "She had always put on this act because she was so shy and insecure. Now Clara believed she was 'The It Girl.'"

Bow eventually became grateful for this, explaining Madame Glyn "taught me to bring out my personality" by concentrating "her great word 'IT' upon me." She also later remarked that Nell was only one of two people in Hollywood who ever tried to help her at all.[33]

Certainly, Madame Glyn presides over *It* as the film's spiritual guide, flooding viewers with her presence in the opening twenty minutes. After announcing *Clara Bow in an Elinor Glyn—Clarence Badger Production* (Badger was one of the film's two directors), Glyn received credit for the story, adaptation, and playing herself. Then a title card flashes a definition above her signature: "'IT' is that quality possessed by some which draws all others with its magnetic force. With 'IT' you win all men if you are a woman—and all women if you are man. 'IT' can be a quality of the mind as well as a physical attraction." Cut to the film's first scene, featuring Waltham's best friend, a "pansy" character named Monty who acts to shore up Moreno's lackluster sexual dynamism. While visiting Waltham, Monty spies a copy of *Cosmopolitan*, reads Glyn's story, "IT," and sets off in search of someone with this magical quality. Enter Betty-Lou, who has already identified her new boss as the man she wants. After learning that Waltham will be at the Ritz, she maneuvers Monty into asking her to dinner there.[34]

"Of course you are reading Elinor Glyn's latest story, 'IT'?" enquires Waltham's It-less society lady date that evening. "Monty was raving about it today. What *is* this IT?" he asks. Before his date can reply, all eyes turn to the dining room's entrance, where Nell makes a regal entrance on a gentleman's arm. "Here's Elinor Glyn herself!" Waltham exclaims. "Let's ask her to tell us something about 'It.'" Nell obliges: "Self-confidence and indifference as to whether you are pleasing or not—and something in you that gives the impression that you are not all cold."[35]

It's opening week indicated the film had struck gold, with Glyn and Bow sharing space as if they were co-stars in most reviews. "Clara Bow gets off to a running start in her first starring picture, 'It,'" hav-

Nell as she regally appeared in the movie *It*

ing established "once and for all the fact that she is brimming over with that Elinor Glyn quality." Theater owners wrote ecstatic letters about how the crowds required holding the picture over an extra week. Within the year, *It*'s box office surpassed any other movie on which Nell worked.[36]

Some reviewers found Nell's appearance in the film vulgar, to use one of her favorite words. "The only response evoked in the breast of this moderately literate observer was a slight contempt for the not-too-subtle advertising methods of the author," sniffed the influential film critic Richard Watts at the *Herald Tribune* in "Saying Some Unkind Things about Madame Elinor Glyn." "Did Paramount ask Madame Elinor Glyn to appear in the picture called 'It' or did she volunteer?" wondered Harriette Underhill, before conceding that Nell had worked her magic on Bow again. "To give Mrs. Glyn her due—and we consider her an unusually canny person," she "is noted for making players over to suit her fancy. And when she gets through with them, they usually suit ours."[37]

Some critics worried that Glyn giving her seal of approval to a "sexy ingénue given to having cinematic affairs with young men and otherwise behaving in the manner which the reformers say all flappers behave" would encourage others to emulate Bow's ways. They were right. Glyn's glamorous touch smoothed the acceptance of the open eroticism of a single young working-class woman. That year exhibitors named Bow the top box-office draw of 1927, displacing "gentle" flapper Colleen Moore.

Nell felt no remorse. "It is true that we have been going through a great period of looseness, and perhaps of license, since the War," Madame Glyn conceded while making the film. "But along the sex lines, the world has progressed. Frankness and honesty about sex matters of all kinds is the result of our present education . . . and the great facts of life are rightly and beautifully explained and understood, instead of being barbarously concealed and distorted."[38]

When Paramount released *Ritzy* months later, the film barely turned a profit, so the studio returned to *It*'s formula with *Red Hair* and *Three Weekends* (1928), two more lost films that are no longer in existence—like the vast majority of silent films. Heavily advertised as Bow-Glyn-Badger productions, both romantic comedies were hits. *Red Hair* included a scene shot in Technicolor to highlight the hue of Clara's curls and performed almost as well as *It*. "Bow Scintillates as Gold-Digger," playing Bubbles, a "poor manicurist whose flirtations with three elderly gentlemen cause lots of trouble when the right young man comes along." One of her gentlemen friends tells her: "Elinor Glyn says a red haired girl can get anything she wants in the world," as if there was any doubt. By the time *Three Weekends* (1928) appeared, ads simply declared: "'IT' GIRL IN GLYN STORY," and people turned out in droves. In these films, Bow did as much for a new type of revealing lingerie called the step-in as Brigitte Bardot did for the bikini thirty years later. Or, as one film critic mocked: "Bow plus Glyn equals underwear." The postmaster of Los Angeles announced his office processed 33,727 fan letters a month to Bow, many simply addressed to "The 'It' Girl, Hollywood, USA."[39]

In her walk-on in *It*, Nell looked like the strikingly elegant, heavier-set middle-aged woman she had become. However good a face she put on, though, it must have been difficult to be a vain sixty-four-year-old former society beauty living in an era and a place consumed with the exploits of flaming, stunning youth. *The Wrinkle Book, or How to Keep Looking Young*—published as *It* flickered on screens across the country—testified to that challenge. Oddly, and perhaps because of the ever more complicated tax troubles Nell continued to ignore, she returned to her roots to bring out the book, publishing it with Duckworth in March of 1927 as the press chattered on about Clara Bow and Madame Glyn.

The *Wrinkle Book* prescribed scrubbing one's face with a dry nailbrush until it burned red, sleeping with the head always pointing toward magnetic north, and daily facial exercises to combat the sag of time. Once again, Nell was too direct for British tastes and too avant-garde in general, since the vast majority of women her age, everywhere, had not yet gone Hollywood enough to obsess over the methods of maintaining an unlined face. The book sank like stone, leaving virtually no trace anywhere. Luckily, she did not need the money, having made the fortune she had come to Hollywood to find.[40]

Nell's spectacular success promoting the first It Girl was all the sweeter because *Love's Blindness*—the very last film she supervised in Hollywood—performed poorly at the box office. The movie fared better than *The Only Thing* but failed to turn a profit despite all her hard work. "Written, supervised, and dominated by Elinor Glyn," wrote a *Photoplay* reviewer, the heroine had been "groomed to Glyn's style of London society" and the story "was the same as every other Glynish affair." Luckily, *It* appeared on screens just weeks after *Love's Blindness* and Madame Glyn was back on top of the movie colony's pecking order because of the megawatt success of her barnstorming with Clara Bow. "MANY OF FILMDOM'S PLUMS NOW

ARE FALLING TO WOMEN," the *Baltimore Sun* announced, describing the exalted positions occupied by Nell and five other women at Paramount Studios alone.[41]

But Madame Glyn was in reality headed for a tumble like so many of the women still poised near Hollywood's top. All three of Madame Glyn's movies at Paramount had required the significant creative reinvention of other hands in ways that none of her previous movies had. With *Three Weekends* and *Red Hair*, the magic of Madame Glyn's touch had become detached entirely from the details of her ideas. As with royalty, it was enough for her spirit to sanction the proceedings. In these more democratic times, the allure of the kind of aristocratic, European settings about which Nell always wrote would dramatically diminish, ebbing from the height of interest and the center of the drama to a fascinating side story featuring slightly exotic types. And, as Walter Wanger had predicted, she had become overexposed since the fallout with Thalberg and Mayer. It is almost impossible to believe that her ever-observant novelist's eye had missed that the times were changing and that a dramatic shift hovered in the air.

"*IT* appeared as two eras were drawing to a close," Adolph Zukor remarked in retrospect. "One was the Jazz Age itself. The other was that of silent film." Just weeks after *It*'s premiere, forty-year-old Sam Warner died of a heart attack the day before his great experiment, *The Jazz Singer*, opened. Making the movie killed him, his brother Jack said. The first feature-length movie with synchronized music and dialogue, *The Jazz Singer* was a biopic about the Americanization of Al Jolson, the Russian-born son of a cantor who became the "World's Greatest Entertainer" as a blackface performer on Broadway, starring Jolson as himself. The film was a sensation.[42]

It would take more than two years for the movie colony to accept that the talkies were not just another passing fad. By that time, the 1920s' roaring prosperity had come crashing down, along with the star of the first official It Girl. At the height of her fame, Clara Bow traded Hollywood for a Nevada ranch with western actor Rex Bell in 1931, driven out by overwork and the mounting scandal surrounding her personal life because of her pursuit of a good time like one of the boys. "My life in Hollywood contained plenty of uproar," Bow reflected after returning to the screen in 1932 to make two movies to fund her permanent retirement. "I'm sorry for a lot of it but not awfully sorry. I never did anything to hurt anyone else. I made a place for myself on the screen and you can't do that by being Mrs. Alcott's idea of a Little Woman."[43]

Clara and many others learned the hard way what Nell had cautioned them about through so many different mediums: Any woman who forged an independent life, who chased her desires where they led, teetered along a tightrope that balanced the public's fascination against their outrage over her evasion of her traditional role. The balance became easier for some of the luckiest white women like Nell, in important respects, during the early decades of the twentieth century, before it got harder again during and after the Great Depression.

But pursuing the kind of personal, professional, and sexual liberation that Nell attained over decades to become an avatar of the modern woman required courage, careful strategizing, and always came at a cost. It also often proved as evanescent as youth. Youth was prized everywhere in modern culture, but nowhere more punishingly so than among women, which Nell's own increasingly masklike face and her heroines illustrated every time—every time except for her Tiger Queen. As people's lives continued to lengthen over the twentieth century the struggle would get more intense and extreme as so many women (and men) fought to keep back the creep of time.

It's release was also timed to the close of a third era that Adolph Zukor failed to note: the end of women's unusual influence in early Hollywood. The fluid industrial landscape in which Madame Glyn had amassed so much power was waning rapidly and would not be repeated after the "Big Five" and the "Little Three" emerged as the eight vertically integrated companies that controlled the studio system which made about 90 percent of American movies.

The industry's corporate consolidation by the early 1930s followed the founders' pursuit first of cultural acceptability and then of financial legitimacy after the Great War. The first phase gave ambitious white women—because of their perceived influence over cultural matters and art—more institutional clout and latitude in the American film industry then in any other. This period, from the teens through the 1920s, coincided with the silent film era itself, and made Madame Glyn its cultural arbiter par excellence.[44]

But having attained an at least tenuous cultural acceptability and brought politically savvy William Hays into the fold, the movie men with the most clout next grasped for the imprimatur of Wall Street's bankers. The enormous cost of converting to sound, much of which coincided with the onset of the Depression, and the ever-expanding distribution networks needed to deliver their product to a global audience also abetted Hollywood's search for funds in the citadel of American capitalism. And Wall Street expected white men, alone, to be in charge.

The move to make Hollywood a boys' club, like every other big business of the time, began internally first with the trade associations for directors, cinematographers, camera operators, and the like. Organized as fraternal orders, they excluded the participation of women and most non-white workers. Accordingly, the number of women deemed capable of calling the shots in the industry began a steep decline after the early 1920s.

When Lois Weber was asked in 1927 to advise women eager to follow in her footsteps, the director widely lionized as one of early "Hollywood's Three Great Minds," (along with Griffith and DeMille) warned: "Don't try it. You'll never get away with it." Dorothy Arzner—who directed Clara Bow in *Get Your Man* (1927) and Paramount's first sound film, *The Wild Party* (1929)—got her start working under Weber, making her a second-generation woman filmmaker. But Arzner would soon become Hollywood's only female director from 1927 until her early retirement in 1943.[45]

All that came before disappeared from film history (if not the archive) and public memory. By the 1930s, Arzner's press portrayed her as the *first* woman director when in fact she was the *last* in a long line (for a long time). As actresses signed iron-clad, long-term contracts with the major studios, the ability of the savviest to leverage their celebrity into more control ended everywhere but at United Artists (until the "seven-year rule" from actress Olivia de Havilland's 1943 lawsuit helped to reverse the trend again).[46]

When the movies started to talk, Hollywood's most powerful insiders believed estimates that reported that women occupied more than 75 percent of movie seats. "Now one thing never to be lost sight of in considering the cinema is that it exists for the purpose of pleasing women," wrote film critic, and later the Museum of Modern Art's first film curator, Iris Barry, in *The Public's Pleasure* (1926). But by the time *It* appeared, producers felt more secure in the loyalty of their flapper fans; consequently, there was less concern about needing women writers to appeal to them.[47]

The talkie takeover hastened the process of making women less welcome in Hollywood's writers' rooms. Screenwriting—long the creative branch most heavily populated with influential women like Madame Glyn—began to shed its female workforce even at MGM. Frances Marion, long the industry's highest paid screenwriter, male or female, wrote the critically acclaimed *The Scarlet Letter* (1928) and *The Wind* (1929) for Lillian Gish and went on to win back-to-back Oscars at MGM for her original screenplays for *The Big House* (1931) and *The Champ* (1932). But by then even Thalberg had begun to favor the kind of hard-drinking men from New York thought to excel at writing the hard-boiled characters who populated even the comedies of Depression-era Hollywood. Although veterans like Bess Meredyth, Anita Loos, and Marion continued to advise on "virtually every script MGM produced in the 1930s," they began to carry their scripts about in "unmarked plain covers" because of growing complaints about "the tyranny of the woman writer," Marion recalled. After Thalberg's death in 1936, things got worse.[48]

Sensing the greater changes on the horizon, and her contract with Paramount finished, Nell's next move astonished most, but proved her intuition as sharp as ever: she left Hollywood in 1928 at the height of her fame.

Afterlives of a Tiger Queen

T he final decision to live no more in America came during one of Nell's annual visits home in the summer of 1929, when the tax troubles about which Tom McIlvaine, still Nell's personal lawyer, had long worried became impossible to ignore any longer. If she returned to the United States, the townhouse that she had so recently bought (and redecorated from top to bottom) in the Georgetown area of Washington, DC, would become subject to seizure by the IRS for unpaid back taxes; she might even face criminal charges, Tom warned.[1]

She had no choice but to make her future in London, where relations with her family remained strained but intact. This turnabout seemed foretold when, once back for good, plans quickly came together to revive Elinor Glyn Productions so that Nell could direct and produce two films, *Knowing Men* and *The Price of Things*. Having put her Hollywood ambitions behind her, she had suddenly attained her dream—total control over her pictures.

"Elinor Glyn—the exotic authoress of *Three Weeks* and the discoverer of 'It' has now decided to make pictures for herself," announced Ernest Freedman in his weekly letter from London.[2]

These movies would be a family affair and would significantly warm things up after the last few frosty years. Juliet wrote the continuities and helped to edit, Rhys organized the contacts, Lucy made all the costumes. Their confidence that Nell could make her own movies, and raise film production in the U.K. to a higher level while

378

doing so, was a balm for her ego. Nell directed, wrote the stories, and financed it all from her bank account.

When *Knowing Men* appeared in September 1930, the reviews ranged from scathing to dismissive and especially detested Nell's delivery of a prologue and presentation of men as "polygamous animals." Coauthor Edward Knoblock sued to prevent distribution of the slow-paced musical comedy, arguing it would hurt his reputation. The judge quickly ruled in Nell's favor, but after calling her the author of immoral books refused to force Knoblock to pay the legal costs. Next, Australia banned the movie for no stated reason, but likely because of the odor of impropriety still hovering around the Glyn name throughout the Commonwealth.

Her second effort, *The Price of Things*, was much more polished, but the box office and reception fared no better. Critics called it "too Mayfair" and "the most old fashioned hokum."[3]

Her autobiography (somewhat justifiably) blamed the British press, once again, for its too-harsh criticism and "extraordinary allegations of immorality." She also held producer Joseph Schenck partially accountable for the failures of her films.

"I know you believe in my power of knowing what the ladies (who make up the largest part of most audiences) require to make their hearts beat! And hold the hands of their boyfriends in the dark," she had written to Schenck after completing *Knowing Men*. "This film means *romance*, which always brings in the dollars," she continued. "Do not let anyone, dear Mr. Schenck, put you off 'Knowing Men' for any reason of the male mind! *I know what women want*." No evidence suggests that Schenck replied, and Nell failed to secure an American distributor to tap the enormous market that she had cultivated in the United States for so long, so well.[4]

She lost most of the fortune that she had made in Hollywood producing the two movies in London. Nowhere extant did Nell ever betray any bitterness over the fact that those closest to her had participated in assisting her down the wrong path professionally. Family would be maintained above all, even if the family's fortunes were greatly diminished like so many others in Britain by the 1930s after new taxes, inflation, and unemployment sent so many great London townhomes to the wrecking ball. The trust fund established by Juliet and Rhys in 1925 remained. To this Nell added the various sums she earned writing the articles and books she continued to publish until just three years before her death in 1943.[5]

As the Great Depression deepened across the world, Nell repented of her money-mad, fame-obsessed ways, holding Hollywood's atmosphere during the Jazz Age partially to blame. She believed the global Depression illustrated "the law of the boomerang" and as the clouds of war gathered across the Channel, again, she thought atonement the order of the day.[6]

Nell's modest earnings and the small fortune tucked away by far-sighted Juliet funded her last years in a series of elegant apartments filled with eighteenth-century French antiques and tall vases of fresh flowers mostly in London, fittingly. Conquering London society was where it all began, where Nell had celebrated her marriage to Clayton and Lucy had staged the fashion industry's first "mannequin parades." And, so, she closed the circle, spending her last years living with her two beautiful, tawny-haired Russian cats, Zadig and Candide. Once, in 1939, the Tiger Queen wore Candide as a stole around her neck to speak at a literary luncheon. The cat behaved beautifully. "Great success," she wrote in her diary.[7]

The losses of those she knew best made a regular rhythm, fitting the mood of the times. After a short illness, Lucy died at a nearby hospital of breast cancer in 1935, four years to the day after her estranged husband, Cosmo. During the six months of her illness, Nell regularly visited the bedside of the sister she put on her list of the "World's 20 Most Influential Women." "I do not think that, on the whole, it is good for a woman to have temperament," Lucy had confessed on the first page her memoir, *Discretions and Indiscretions* (1932), just a few years earlier. "It is much better for [her] to be a vegetable and certainly much safer, but I never had the choice." Their mother, Elinor Kennedy, died two years after her elder daughter, at the age of ninety-six. Countess Daisy Greville, well-known at the end as the Red Duchess for her socialist politics, followed the next year in 1938.[8]

Nell took up the story of her own life in these years as the Nazi Party began hammering out an ever-larger ring of terror after Hitler became chancellor in 1933. Written with the help of Juliet in 1934

Nell's London apartment, 1934

and 1935, *Romantic Adventure* is a solid, largely factual account of an eventful life that left out as much as it said, unlike the author's novels. The book's greatest surprise—though less so when one considers her daughter's intimate involvement with the project—is how light and fast it skims over the astonishing successes of her Hollywood years. The producing debacle in London merits less than two pages.

In treating the last great act of Nell's life so casually, *Romantic Adventure* makes plain what the avant-garde element of the author's modernism and all her success in America obscured: her historical context, the emotional sensibility and playing field, the people who shaped her experiences and mind, who composed the meat of her life, were of the late Victorian British world. The influence and purchase of that culture had ebbed dramatically after the First World War— her triumph in the 1920s' greatest mass medium notwithstanding— and was now fading fast as the next war approached.

Beverly Nichols, one of Nell's many young fans during the 1930s, memorably recounted learning this lesson about her temporal moorings, to his astonishment, during one of their many luncheons at the London Ritz. "After she had been served with a huge portion of smoked salmon, she 'drew herself up' and fixed me with a glistening eye," Nichols recalled with gusto, "and said, '*Tell your readers that sex has never touched the hem of my garment!*' It was the most wonderful sentence and it made my luncheon," recalled the English writer, gay bon vivant, gardener extraordinaire, and fellow Spiritualist. "As I walked home, I tried to put it in its historical context," Nichols continued. "It did not belong to the twenties or thirties, nor even to the Edwardians; it was firmly late Victorian."[9]

The romantic fantasies and sexual desires that so much of Anglo-American Victorian culture aimed to erase from the page, repress on the stage, or to make unsayable, particularly for women, had always been Nell's subject, driving her to create heroines who were not always Ms. Alcott's idea of good little women, to paraphrase Clara Bow, but whose daring and style made them blaze across the imaginations of millions. With good reason, then, she positioned her reputation for posterity in *Romantic Adventure* as a sex radical: "a member of the band of pioneers in the cause of feminine emancipation." She and the movement's other "social pioneers" had "labored so earnestly—almost too successfully—to free the souls and bodies of women from the heavy age-old trammels of custom and convention."[10]

Nell understood that the Tiger Queen had become not just a touchtone of sexual liberation for two earlier generations but the reigning empress of "High Camp" to many of the "bright young people" of the current interwar one. Too young to have participated in the Great War, yet too old to have escaped its near obliterating significance, this cohort of socialites, artists, and aristocrats experimented with modes of outrageous, playful, personal, and creative expression that made "camp" widely glamorous for the first time. "The hallmark of Camp is the spirit of extravagance," Susan Sontag wrote in her seminal essay that tried to pin down the notoriously hard-to-capture sensibility the OED first defined as "ostentatious, exaggerated, affected, theatrical; effeminate or homosexual" in 1909.[11]

The bright young person par excellence, and their greatest visual chronicler, Cecil Beaton, carried a torch for the empress from when he got his start as a society portraitist and *Vogue* photographer in the 1920s until decades after Nell died. In 1930, the "queer" taste-maker dressed as Nell for the birthday party of the famous American hostess Elsa Maxwell (who invented the scavenger hunt, among other follies). Everyone had to appear as a personality well known to Parisian society. Beaton came as Madame Glyn, all blasé intensity, slinky velvet, tiger skins, and holding an impossibly long strand of pearls that dangled a cross to add a humorously transgressive *oomph*.

Cecil Beaton dressed as Nell for Elsa Maxwell's party, Paris 1930

In 1934, Beaton had photographed Nell and then, much later still, he wrote the introduction for a 1974 reissue of *Three Weeks*, issuing an homage to "The World of Elinor Glyn," just before the novel's republication that credited her with "breaking down much of the remaining Victorian hypocrisy" about sex. Beaton emphasized that Nell was smart ("the friend of intellectual university dons") and no prude ("There is no doubt that lives of historical prostitutes fascinated her as did all forms of eroticism").

Beaton also knew that she was dead serious—the heart of true camp lay in a joyous commitment to going all-out, after all—about the morality of her very passionate and well-appointed illicit love story. More than a half century after the Tiger Queen of *Three Weeks* had first captivated him as a boy at Harrow, Beaton still burned over how the author had been branded a "scarlet woman and outlawed in Society by all but a few loyal friends" because she had the audacity to "give explicit descriptions of the most private thoughts and behavior" that everyone imagined, or wish they did—the kinds of feelings and acts that after World War II so many writers became free to express in ever greater detail, if they wished.[12]

By the time of his homage, Sir Cecil Beaton was an old man, knighted for his many artistic contributions to the British realm and beyond. As a photographer he had captured over decades the greatest personalities of the age as well as the ordinary tragedies and triumphs of Britons on the home front during World War II. Beaton had also won two Academy Awards for set design and costumes (*My Fair Lady* and *Gigi*), and was widely accepted as having perhaps the century's greatest eye.

Beaton's homage wanted Glyn seen as not only the writer who had the courage to put sexual passion into the novel but also as the woman who became "the reigning queen of the early film world" after "Hollywood lured her" to Los Angeles. With the talent for friendship that followed her everywhere, Glyn was "amused by and delighted with that extraordinary community," he reported. Awestruck by her style, the producers "soon asked her to direct." Ultimately, Beaton credited Glyn with achieving "the paradox of bringing not only 'good taste' to the colony, but also 'sex appeal.'"

Like Nell, Beaton knew that true style emerged from disrupting the expected and required courage and the intensive labor of art and artifice more than the ephemera of beauty or what got called sex appeal once Madame Glyn worked her magic and exited the stage. Near the end of his life, Sir Beaton knew more than ever what he saw to be true even as a young man: power inhered in the style that emerged with the mature Madame Glyn whose cosmetic efforts increasingly gave her face a mask-like quality rather than the red-headed beauty who'd won Clayton's heart. "With her chalk white complexion, emerald, kohl-rimmed eyes with unplucked eyebrows, she appeared as a Huysmans figure in her long, black velvet gowns with fur to match her hair. Among the corny peroxide blondes with their plucked eyebrows, and drab pink and blue frocks, she appeared like some Ruritanian Empress," Beaton wrote wistfully.

Nell seemed content in those last London years to have passed largely into the ether of popular consciousness through its absorption of her outrageous glamour and the concept of her modern It Girls who knew how to attract the best kinds of attention while chasing their desires wherever they led. One of the last essays stored in her eventual archive at Reading University exhorted her older readers as war came again to Britain to remember they no longer counted and *never* to grumble; they'd had their day!

For a time, after the war started in 1939 and Germany began to bomb Britain in earnest, Juliet persuaded her mother to evacuate to Miskin Manor in Wales along with the grandchildren. Nell very much enjoyed her grandchildren in doses; they fondly recall her telling stories during air raids in the cellar and staging picnics. She formed a particular bond with Margot's eldest boy, Anthony, who would grow up to be another romantic novelist, marry Juliet's daughter, and spend their days together in the South of France.[13]

But Nell could not sit out the war in Wales, and she quickly headed back to London to be at the center of the action, where she had always liked it best, even if she was now almost blind. She spent the Blitz in her apartment, a figure of bravura who followed all the details of the war's progression. Still believing firmly in her psychic gifts, her last official prediction in 1940 was that Britain "would survive the holocaust and win through to complete and final victory" though she would not live to see it—at least in her current form.

Nell with her last cats, Candide and Zadig, 1935

She was right. After the publication of her last book, *The Third Eye* (1940), she faded steadily but peacefully, dying of natural causes in a London nursing home after a short illness in 1943.[14]

Still, the little girl with the bright-red hair and the spooky green eyes who began dreaming it all up in her stepfather's library had lived to see the expression of her desires spread out far beyond the island of Jersey. Though many others would try, she had done her part to let loose the genie of women's sexual liberation, and it would not be stuffed back into the bottle again.

The End

ACKNOWLEDGMENTS

This book was more than ten years in the making, but its origins go back much further: to my dissertation on the sexual politics of early Hollywood, where I first encountered Elinor Glyn and learned that her life was in fact even more dramatic and interesting than her publicity in the 1920s had claimed.

But I would never have undertaken this project without the generosity of EG's and LDG's descendants, who, on my first research trip to the United Kingdom a decade ago, shared family stories and brought me into their homes in London to photograph EG's voluminous correspondence, remaining journals, and LDG's *Titanic*-related materials. I am especially grateful to Miranda Rhys-Williams, Evie Soames, Will Duff-Gordon, and Susan Glyn in this regard. My heartful thanks in London also go out to: Katherine Field at the Philip de László Archive Trust for access to materials there and for allowing me to reproduce *gratis* his stunning painting of EG; to Marc Bryan-Brown, from the estate of Paul Tanqueray, for the use of Tanqueray's matchless portrait, and to the artist Richard Harpum for sharing his beautiful painting of Sheering Hall.

Over the last decade, I have received funding and research support that helped finance travel to archives and—even more crucially for this working mother of two—time to write. My deepest thanks in this regard go to the New York Public Library's Cullman Center for Writers and Scholars. I can say with certainty that this book is undoubtedly better for the congenial company and inspiration of my fellow fellows, Jean Strouse, and all the people who make the Cullman Center and the library such an utterly delightful place to work. This book would also *still* not be finished without that break from my regular professional responsibilities. As with all scholarship, the help of librarians and archivists at several other libraries was also invaluable to collecting research, including particularly the Special Collections Department at the University of Reading; the Margaret Herrick Library at the Academy of Motion Pictures Arts and Sciences (especially Kristine Krueger); and the Wellington County Museum and Archives, Ontario. I am also grateful for the financial assistance of the Lenfest Junior Faculty Award and the History Department's Junior Faculty Award at Columbia University.

My colleagues at Columbia University provided essential encouragement as I simultaneously tried to write this book and navigate the tenure process. My deepest appreciation in this regard go to Alice Kessler-Harris, Karl Jacoby, Eric Foner, George Chauncey, Ron Gregg, David Stone, Mae Ngai, Jane Gaines, Casey Blake, Rebecca Kobrin, Natasha Lightfoot, Line Lillevik, Eileen Gillooly, Dan Polin, Carl Wennerlind, and Monica Miller. Many colleagues who work on women and film have listened to me try out my ideas about Elinor and early Hollywood in numerous scholarly venues over the years and I send particular thanks to Shelley Stamp, Lois Banner, Linda Williams, and Christine Gledhill. Richard Register and Nan Riley listened to me talk about old Hollywood with unfailing enthusiasm. Robin Aronson—anyone's ideal of the "educated idiot" reader—read the manuscript and gave me feedback that kept me going in a moment of grave doubt. We were incredibly lucky that during the pandemic, our family's extraordinary neighbors (and great readers all) in New York and Vermont supported our spirits in ways that made the final push revising this manuscript possible; my thanks especially to Kate Schaal, Jim Fox, Tyrone and Michiru Brown, and the Philip-Ness, Wyman-Bradley, Bradford-Kirkpatrick, Coyne-Hammerschlag, and Resilient Thompson family clans.

I have been blessed with the help of numerous diligent and creative research assistants at Columbia, among them Douglas Kronaizl, Thalia Ertman, Monique Kil, Matthew Joseph, Tessa McGowan, and Donna Casella were particularly helpful. Aisha Dejelid, at the University of Reading, finished copying materials there when I could not manage to return to Reading again myself. At the last minute, Kathleen Karcher stepped in to help me manage image permissions, and her assistance and good humor saved my sanity with the process.

David Nasaw read the very first iteration of my book proposal and told me that I should write this as a trade book. After the incomparable redhead Tina Bennett became my agent, she did the most to turn that suggestion into a reality, patiently guiding me through the process of imagining this as a history that could translate beyond the academy. Without Tina's faith and help in this project, I doubt I would have had the courage to undertake writing it in this way at all.

At Liveright-Norton publishing, Katie Adams believed in this project even before it landed there because I hoped that working with her would be a delight. I was not wrong. Katie's wit, patience, and insight as an editor (who carefully read multiple drafts) ensured that this is the very best book that I could write. Once Katie left Liveright, editor Gina Iaquinta stepped in with grace and good humor to make valuable suggestions and guide me through the last stages of the book's production. My thanks also to Zeba Arora, for help with the production process, to Rachelle Mandik for her expert copyediting, to Steve Attardo, for creating a cover that exceeded my expectations and imagination in every way, and to Nick Curley and Cordelia Calvert for their efforts to get the word out about Elinor Glyn again!

This is a book, in part, about two extra-ordinary sisters, and I thank my own extraordinary sisterhood's partner, Kaitlin Hallett-Pugh, and her incredible family Andy, Griffith, Lillian, Jennifer, and Charlie. Greg Metz, Jocelin Saks, Todd Edelman, and Robert and Yvonne Stella have my thanks for their enduring support. My mother, Kathryn Hallett, did not live to see this book's completion, but I know that she would have approved of Elinor Glyn with all her heart. What a babe, she would have said.

Above all, my thanks go to my husband, Christopher L. Brown, our family's true Anglophile. This book would still be far from finished, and would be much weaker, without his help. On too many occasions over the last decade, Chris took time from his own scholarship to handle innumerable domestic details to give me time to research and to write. He also shared his brilliant historical mind with me whenever I needed it most, reading drafts and helping me to surface ideas and dynamics that otherwise would have remained too buried. I spent too many days with EG rather than with my two wonderful sons, Miles and Jackson. They have grown up hearing more about Elinor Glyn than they ever wanted to know. To my sons and their father, I again dedicate this book and everything else I have.

NOTES

Please note: all newspaper and periodical research for this book was done online via: British Periodicals; British Library Newspapers; ProQuest Historical Newspapers and Periodicals; and Chronicling America.

PROLOGUE: ON FLAPPERS AND THEIR PHILOSOPHERS

1. "Creator of 'It' Dies at 78," *Irish Times*, September 24, 1943. See also "Elinor Glyn, Author of Romances," *Times* (London), September 24, 1943; "Elinor Glyn Dies; Novelist, Aged 78, Self-Styled 'High Priestess of God of Love' Shocked Many Readers on 2 Continents; GAVE 'IT' NEW MEANING," *NYT*, September 24, 1943.

2. On this "Basic Story" of Hollywood's founding in standard accounts, see David Bordwell, *On the History of Film Style* (Cambridge, MA: Harvard University Press, 1997), ch. 1; Kevin Starr, *Inventing the Dream: California through the Progressive Era* (New York: Oxford University Press, 1985), chs. 8–9; Neal Gabler, *An Empire of Their Own: How the Jews Invented Hollywood* (New York: Doubleday, 1998). Although outside this book's scope, Black women blues singers were also central to the development of the American recording industry in the 1920s, see Daphne Harrison, *Black Pearls: Blues Queens of the 1920s* (New Brunswick, NJ: Rutgers University Press, 1990). The scholarship on white women's roles in early Hollywood and the era's sexual politics has grown extensive. Key texts include Anthony Slide, *The Silent Feminists: America's First Women Directors* (Lantham, MD: Scarecrow Press, 1996); Shelley Stamp, *Movie-Struck Girls* (Princeton, NJ: Princeton University Press, 2000); Karen Ward Mahar, *Women Filmmakers in Early Hollywood* (Baltimore: Johns Hopkins University Press, 2008); Hilary Hallett, *Go West, Young Women! The Rise of Early Hollywood* (Berkeley: University of California Press, 2013); Shelley Stamp, *Lois Weber in Early Hollywood* (Berkeley: University of California Press, 2015); Jane Gaines, *Pink-Slipped: What Happened to Women in the Silent Film Industries?* (Urbana: University of Illinois Press, 2018). Within this literature, this book has benefited from a concurrent recognition of EG's role in the film industry, see Anne Morey, "Elinor Glyn as Hollywood Labourer," *Film History* 18 (2006): 110–118; Anette Kuhn, "The Trouble with Elinor Glyn," *Historical Journal of Film, Radio and Television* 28, no. 1 (March 2008): 23–35; Laura Horak, "'Would You Like to Sin with Elinor Glyn?' Film as a Vehicle of Sensual Education," *Camera Obscura* 74, no. 25.2 (2010): 75–117. On EG's invention of sex appeal, see Cecil Beaton, "The World of Elinor Glyn," *The Times Saturday Review*, October 26, 1974, 8–9; Samuel Goldwyn, *Behind the Screen* (New York: George H. Doran and Co., 1923), 245–248; Joseph Roach, *It* (Ann Arbor: University of Michigan Press, 2009), 4–7, 21–27, 60–81, and 89–92. Martin Francis, "Cecil Beaton's Romantic Toryism and the Symbolic Economy of Wartime Britain," *Journal of British Studies* 45, no. 1 (2006): 90–117.

3. "Free love" ideals rejected the conventional legal and religious basis of marriage, instead defining it as one characterized by love. The approach accepted divorce and espoused women's sexual passion, placing it on the radical fringe of Anglo-American culture, see George Robb, "The Way of All Flesh: Degeneration, Eugenics, and the Gospel of Free Love," *Journal of the History of Sexuality* 6, no. 4 (April 1996): 589–603. "Bestseller" denoted both popularity and cultural visibility and circulated first around the astounding popularity of writers like Ouida Bergère and Marie Corelli in 1890s. By 1900, the British press defined a bestseller as selling over 100,000 copies. The comparable figure in the United States was 750,000. Sales figures of the era are unreliable, but it was reportedly one of twenty novels in the United States to have reached that benchmark by World War I, see Frank Luther Mott, *Golden Multitudes: The Story of Best Sellers in the United States* (New York and London: R.R. Bowker Co., 1947), 312. For Britain, see Desmond Flower, *A Century of Best-Sellers, 1830–1930* (London: National Book Council, 1934), 17. Glyn was one of the few simultaneously to appear on both British and American "bestseller" lists, see Phillip Waller, *Writers, Readers and Reputations:*

Literary Life in Britain, 1870–1918 (Oxford: Oxford University Press, 2006), 638, 947, 639ff, and 646ff. Beginning with Leo Markun, *Mrs. Grundy* (London and New York: D. Appleton and Company, 1930), historians of Anglo-American literature note, but fail to explore, how *Three Weeks'* commercial success set new standards for writing about sex in Anglo-American print. See also Mott, *Golden Multitudes*, 244–252, 249; Paul S. Boyer, *Purity in Print: The Vice Society Movement and Book Censorship in America* (New York: Charles Scribner's Sons, 1968), 33–35; David Trotter, *The English Novel in History, 1895–1920* (London: Routledge, 1993), 182; Peter Keating, *The Haunted Study: A Social History of the English Novel* (London: Secker & Warburg, 1989), 210. Glyn's books were translated into French, Swedish, and Czech from the beginning, but *Three Weeks* was also translated into Spanish, Italian, Norwegian, Danish, German, and Russian. Vincent Barnett and Alexis Weedon, *Elinor Glyn as Novelist, Moviemaker, Glamour Icon, and Businesswoman* (Farnham, Ashgate: 2014), 56–58. Adaptations do not include the many parodies made of the novel in literary, filmic, and theatrical form. James Card, *Seductive Cinema: The Art of Silent Film* (New York: Knopf, 1994), 202; Victor Neuburg, *The Popular Press Companion to Popular Literature* (Madison: University of Wisconsin Press, 1983), 123.

4. Cartland called EG "the first instigator of the romantic novel" and became her protégée in the 1930s, see Barbara Cartland, *I Search for Rainbows* (London: Hutchinson, 1967), 194–195. A prominent society hostess noted for her daring parties, Cartland's early plays such as *Blood Money* (1926) were banned by the Lord Chamberlain before she went on to sell an estimated 2 billion books. Between 1977 and 1979, her "Library of Love" reissued EG's *Six Days, His Hour, The Reason Why, Vicissitudes of Evangeline, The Great Moment, The Sequence, The Price of Things, It,* and *Man and Maid,* but notably not *Three Weeks.* See Cecil Beaton, introduction to *Three Weeks,* by Elinor Glyn (London: Duckworth, 1974); Sally Beauman, introduction to *Three Weeks,* by Elinor Glyn (London: Virago Modern Classics, 1996).

5. On "sex novels," see Billie Melman, *Women and the Popular Imagination in the Twenties* (London: Macmillan, 1988), 41–51; Trotter, *English Novel,* 198–211; Keating, *Haunted Study,* 208–216. I view the modern popular romance as more focused on women's sexual pleasure and the part it plays in identifying "true love." These books' interest in emotional psychology and sexual feeling meant the hero often played a bigger role than in the past. See Pamela Regis, *A Short History of the Romance Novel* (Philadelphia: University of Pennsylvania Press, 2003), 11–12. On the genre's sales, see Clive Bloom, *Bestsellers: Popular Fiction since 1900* (London: Palgrave Macmillan, 2008), 34–36. On EG's role in romance, see Martin Hipsky, *Modernism and the Popular Romance in Britain, 1885–1925* (Athens: Ohio University Press, 2001), 319–329; Hilary Hallett, "A Mother to the Modern Girl: Elinor Glyn and *Three Weeks* (1907)," *Journal of Women's History* 30, no. 3 (2018): 12–37. Cookson was the pen name of Catherine McMullen, see UK RED, record number 1026, Catherine McMullen, 1926.

6. Beaton, "World of Elinor Glyn," 8.

7. This biography is the first to combine archival research and scholarly expertise in a style aimed at a non-scholarly audience. For past biographies, see Anthony Glyn, *Elinor Glyn: A Biography* (Garden City, NY: Doubleday, 1955); Meredith Etherington-Smith and Jeremy Pilcher, *The "It" Girls: Lucy, Lady Duff-Gordon, the Couturiere "Lucile," and Elinor Glyn, Romantic Novelist* (San Diego: Harcourt Brace Jovanovich, 1986); Joan Hardwick, *Addicted to Romance: the Life and Adventures of Elinor Glyn* (London: Andrew Deutsch, 1994); Barnett and Weedon, *Elinor Glyn.*

8. "Famous Novelist Dead," *Times of India,* September 24, 1943; Andrew Lycett, *Ian Fleming* (New York: St. Martin's Press, 1995), 85.

9. F. Scott Fitzgerald to Adelaide Neal 1937, in *Correspondence of F. Scott Fitzgerald,* ed. Matthew J. Bruccoli, Margaret Duggan, Susan Walker (New York: Random House, 1980), 472. On EG's influence on *The Great Gatsby,* see Nigel Brooks, "Fitzgerald's *The Great Gatsby* and Glyn's *Three Weeks,*" *Explicator* 54, no. 4 (1996): 233–236.

CHAPTER 1: IN THE LIBRARY, JERSEY, THE CHANNEL ISLANDS, 1880

1. Virginia Woolf to Vita Sackville-West, December 29, 1929, quoted in Hermione Lee, *Body Parts: Essays in Life Writing* (London: Chatto & Windus, 2005), 45. Lee notes the importance of reading in the paternal library to many middle- and upper-class Anglo future female writers in this era who were so often informally educated.

2. This opening scenario is based on several accounts and means. EG described these years—the loneliness, the dog walks, the library, and the books she read—in great detail in EG, *Romantic Adventure: Being the Autobiography of Elinor Glyn* (E. P. Dutton & Co., 1937), 29–41. See also her description of the library in Glady Hall and Adele Whitely Fletcher, "We Interview Elinor Glyn," *Motion Picture Magazine*, October 1923, 21–22. I visited the house in Jersey and retraced the only path that existed along the coast from St. Helier. One assumption stems from the belief that no fastidious middle-class Victorian mother would let a dog through the front door.

3. Hall and Fletcher, "We Interview Elinor Glyn," 21.

4. EG, *RA*, 11–13.

5. EG, *RA*, 5–9; Lady Duff-Gordon, *Discretions and Indiscretions* (London: Jarrolds Ltd., 1932), 12.

6. EG, *RA*, 23; LDG, *DI*, 11–12.

7. EG, *RA*, 13.

8. LDG, *DI*, 23; EG, *RA*, 16.

9. EG, *RA*, 16–17; LDG, *DI*, 18.

10. EG, *RA*, 25. 36. Lenore Davidoff and Catherine Hall, *Family Fortunes: Men and Women of the English Middle Class, 1780–1850* (Chicago: University of Chicago Press, 1987).

11. "Mrs. Glyn's Life When Young" by A.L. [Ada Lloyd?] (1914), Box 6, Reading.

12. LDG, *DI*, 16.

13. "Mrs. Glyn's Life When Young" Reading. Wilkie Collins, *I Say No* (Floating Press, 2010 [1884]), 317. Red hair is in only 2 percent of the population). See Emily Cameron Walker, *Sirens and Scapegoats: The Gendered Rhetoric of Red Hair*, M.A. diss., University of Southern Indiana, 2021; LDG, *DI*, 13, 21.

14. Jennifer Allen, "Discovering Lillie Langtry: Aestheticism and the Development of a Transatlantic Market in Beauty, 1880–1927," PhD diss., University of Texas, 2005.

15. EG, *RA*, 31; LDG, *DI*, 25.

16. LDG, *DI*, 19.

17. EG, *RA*, 36.

18. EG, *RA*, 24–25.

19. "Glamour" was from the old Scots "glammer." See Stephen Gundle, *Glamour: A History* (Oxford: Oxford University Press, 2008), 7, 17, 20, 35–48; Carol Dyhouse, *Glamour: Women, History, and Feminism* (London: Zed Books, 2010). I follow the idea that "Romance and Novel are not one, but neither are they two," Margaret Doody, *The True History of the Novel* (New Brunswick, NJ: Rutgers University Press, 1996), 15. See also Ian Duncan, *Modern Romance and Transformations of the Novel* (Cambridge: Cambridge University Press, 1992), 59. On the contrast between licensed and unlicensed reading, see Kate Flint, *The Woman Reader* (Oxford: Oxford University Press, 1993); Helen Small, Jams Raven, and Naomi Tadmor, eds., *The Practice and Representation on Reading in England* (Cambridge: Cambridge University Press, 1996).

20. Dryden quoted in John Buchan, *Some Eighteenth Century Byways and Other Essays* (Edinburgh: W. Blackwood & Sons, 1908), 109. EG compared her memoir to Pepys's and impossibly claimed to have read "an early, unexpurgated edition," suggesting she enjoyed the more robustly smutty, but still bowdlerized printing of 1874, EG, *RA*, 2. Christopher Hill, "Samuel Pepys," in *The Collected Essays of Christopher Hill* (Brighton: Harvester Press Limited, 1985), 259–273. Claire Tomalin, *Samuel Pepys: The Unequaled Self* (New York: Random House, 2002). Sophie Tomlinson, *Women on Stage in Stuart Drama* (Cambridge: Cambridge University Press, 2005); Jacob Abbot, *Charles II* (New York: Harper & Brothers, 1877), 243–281; Osmund Airy, *Charles II* (New York: Charles

Scribner's Sons, 1901); A.C.A. Brett, *Charles II and His Court* (London: Methuen & Co., 1910); Tim Harris, *Politics under the Later Stuarts* (London: Longman, 1993).

21. Arthur H. Scouten and Robert D. Hume, "'Restoration Comedy' and Its Audiences 1660–1776," in *The Rakish Stage: Studies in English Drama, 1660–1800*, ed. Robert Hume (Carbondale: University of Southern Illinois Press, 1983), 46–81; Pat Gill, "Gender, Sexuality and Marriage," in *The Cambridge Companion to English Restoration Theatre*, ed. Deborah Payne Fisk (Cambridge: Cambridge University Press, 2000), 191–208. Clifford Bax, *Pretty Witty Nell* (New York: Benjamin Bloom, 1969 [1932]). Quote from Marie de Rabutin-Chantal, *Letters from the Marchioness de Sevigné to her daughter the Countess de Grignan*, volume 2 (London: N. Blanford, 1727), 73.

22. EG, *Three Weeks* (New York: Duffield & Co., 1907), 193.

23. EG, *RA*, 24. EG, *The Career of Katherine Bush* (New York: D. Appleton & Company, 1916), 211.

24. Jorge Arditi, "Hegemony and Etiquette: An Exploration of the Transformation of Practice and Power in Eighteenth-Century England," *British Journal of Sociology* 45, no. 2 (June 1994): 177–193; Georges Lamoine, "Lord Chesterfield's Letters as Conduct Books," in *The Crises of Courtesy: Studies in the Conduct-Book in Britain, 1600–1900*, ed. Jaques Carré (New York: E. J. Brill, 1994); C. Dallett Hemphill, "Manners and Class in the Revolutionary Era: A Transatlantic Comparison," *William and Mary Quarterly* 63, no. 2 (April 2006): 345–372. Quotes from Earl of Chesterfield, *Letters to His Son on the Art of Becoming a Man of the World and a Gentleman Vol 1* (New York: The Chesterfield Press, 1917), 2, 245.

25. Chesterfield, *Letters*, 107–108. Joan Perkin, *Women and Marriage in Nineteenth-Century England* (London: Routledge, 1989).

26. Robert Lougy, "Vision and Satire: The Warped Looking Glass in Vanity Fair," *PMLA* 90, no. 10 (1975): 258–260. William Makepeace Thackeray, *Vanity Fair: A Novel without a Hero* (New York: E. P. Dutton & Co., 1927), 504.

27. Dorthy Van Ghent, *The English Novel: Form and Function* (New York: Harper, 1961), 686.

28. Thackeray, *Vanity Fair*, 578,

29. Sharon Fiske, *Heretical Hellenism* (Athens: Ohio University Press, 2008). Glyn, *RA*, 22, 129. Joseph Kestner, "Edward Burne-Jones and Nineteenth Century Fear of Women," *Biography* 7, no. 2 (1984): 104–105.

30. See EG, Chronicle 1888, on being a "too vain girl."

31. EG, *RA*, 42.

CHAPTER 2: A GENTLEMAN'S WIFE

1. EG, *RA*, 57–58.

2. Frances Evelyn Greville, Countess of Warwick, *Afterthoughts* (London: Cassell, 1931), 158; Jessica Girard, *Country House Life: Family and Servants, 1815–1914* (Oxford: Blackwell, 1994), 6–10. Girard argues for the group's inclusion with patricians because of the "unifying forces which forged all levels into one class self-consciously distinguishing itself from the rest of rural society," 7. "Clayton Glyn July 13, 1857–November 10, 1915," *Burke's Peerage and Baronetage*, 106th ed., vol. 1 (London: Burke's Peerage, 1999), 1161. Clayton descended from Sir Richard Carr Glyn, Lord Mayor of London in the eighteenth century.

3. "Records of Manor of Sheering Hall," Estate and Family Records, Essex Record Office, UK.

4. "Harlow Laborers' Friend Society," *Chelmsford Chronicle*, October 6, 1865; "Obituary," *Essex County Chronicle*, January 6, 1888. All British newspapers accessed online via *British Library Newspapers, Part III: 1741–1950*.

5. "Shocking Harvest Fatality at Sheering," *Essex County Chronicle*, September 14, 1888. "Alarming Accident to Mrs. Glyn at Harlow," *Essex Newsman*, November 17, 1888;

"The Accident to Mrs. Glyn," *Essex Newsman*, November 24, 1888; "Death of Mrs. Glyn," *Essex County Chronicle*, November 23, 1888.

6. David Cannadine, *The Decline and Fall of the British Aristocracy* (New Haven, CT: Yale University Press, 1990), 8–31.

7. John W. Young, *Britain and the World in the Twentieth Century* (London: Arnold, 1997).

8. Lenore Davidoff, *The Best Circles: Society Etiquette and the Season* (London: Croom Helm, 1973). Churchill quoted in Keith Aldritt, *Churchill the Writer: His Life as a Man of Letters* (London: Hutchinson, 1992), 164–165; Consuelo Vanderbilt Balsan, *The Glitter and the Gold* (New York: Harper, 1953), 29. Statistic cited in Angela Lambert, *Unquiet Souls: The Indian Summer of the British Aristocracy* (London: Macmillan, 1984), 7.

9. Cannadine, *Decline and Fall*, 35–139. In the previous fifty years they were less than 10 percent of new lords. Queen quoted in Davidoff, *Best Circles*, 62.

10. Davidoff, "Change and Decline" in *Best Circles*; Pamela Horn, *High Society* (London: Alan Sutton, 1992), 1–23. W. T. Stead's *Pall Mall Gazette* was a major driver in Britain of the investigative and scandal-oriented "new journalism." See Perry Curtis, *Jack the Ripper and the London Press* (New Haven, CT: Yale University Press, 2008).

11. Margaret Blunden, *The Countess of Warwick* (London: Cassell, 1967), 46. *Manners of the Aristocracy by One of Themselves* (London: Ward, Lock, and Co., Warwick House, 1881?).

12. Mrs. George Corwallis-West, *The Reminiscences of Lady Randolph Churchill* (New York: The Century Co., 1908), 51; C.F.G. Masterman, *The Condition of England* (London: Methuen & Co., 1911), 45–46.

13. EG, *RA*, 63.

14. Greville, *Afterthoughts*, 163.

15. Aldritt, *Churchill the Writer*, 164–165; EG, *RA*, 68–69.

16. LDG, *DI*, 22–25.

17. EG to Mr. Roberts, October 25, 1940, RBTS 2/14, Churchill Archives Centre; L. G. Pine, *The New Extinct Peerage, 1884–1971* (Baltimore: Genealogical Pub. Co., 1973), 125–126; EG, *RA*, 43–44. On his father, see "Berkeley, Maurice Frederick Fitzhardinge, first Baron Fitzhardinge of Bristol," *Oxford Dictionary of National Biography* (online ed.). Oxford University Press. doi:10.1093/ref:odnb/2219.

18. Between 1870 and 1914, 102 American women married peers or the sons of peers, and by the early 1900s they accounted for nearly 1 in 10 of all peers' marriages. See Maureen Montgomery, *Gilded Prostitution: Status, Money and Transatlantic Marriages* (London: Routledge, 1989), 65; Jessica Gerard, *Country House Life: Family and Servants, 1815–1914* (Oxford: Blackwell, 1994), 86; Davidoff, *Best Circles*, 54; Gail MacColl and Carol McD. Wallace, *To Marry an English Lord* (New York: Workman Publishing, 1989).

19. Quoted in Jennifer Phegley, *Courtship and Marriage in Victorian England* (St. Barbara: Praeger, 2002), 2. David Turner, *Fashioning Adultery: Gender, Sex, and Civility in England, 1660–1740* (Cambridge: Cambridge University Press, 2002).

20. Stephanie Coontz, *Marriage, A History: From Obedience to Intimacy, or How Love Conquered Marriage* (New York: Viking, 2005), 167.

21. The trend toward more outward morality for women began in earnest in the eighteenth century. Donna T. Andrews, *Aristocratic Vice: The Attack on Dueling, Suicide, Adultery, and Gambling in the Eighteenth Century* (New Haven, CT: Yale University Press, 2013), 128–169; Coontz, *Marriage*, 177; Harry Cocks, "The Cost of Marriage and The Matrimonial Agency in Late Victorian Britain," *Social History* 38, no. 1 (2013): 66–88.

22. MWPA gave women sole possession of their earnings and inheritances before or after marriage for the first time. Lawrence Stone, *Family, Sex, and Marriage in England, 1500–1800* (New York: Harper and Row, 1979), 43. Gerard, *Country House*, 105, 140. EG, *RA*, 131.

23. EG, *RA*, 45–46. See "Biography of Henry Pelham Archibald Douglas Pelham-Clinton, 7th Duke," University of Nottingham Special Collections, https://www.nottingham.ac.uk/manuscriptsandspecialcollections/collectionsindepth/

family/newcastle/biographies/biographyofhenrypelhamarchibalddouglaspelham-clinton,7thduke(1864-1928).aspx.

24. Mary Sperling McAuliffe, *Dawn of the Belle Epoque* (Lanham: Rowman & Littlefield, 2011), 5–16.

25. Descriptions of her time in Paris taken from EG, Chronicle 1888; Journal 1889; Souvenir 1891.

26. Mary Louise Roberts, "Making the Modern Girl French," in *The Modern Girl around the World: Consumption, Modernity, and Globalization* (Durham: Duke University Press, 2008), 92, 78; Rosalind Williams, *Dream Worlds: Mass Consumption in Late Nineteenth-Century France* (Berkeley: University of California Press, 1982), 12. Lenard Berlanstein, "Historicizing and Gendering Celebrity Culture," *Journal of Women's History* 16, no. 4 (2004): 65–91; Mary Louise Roberts, *Disruptive Acts: The New Woman in Fin-de-Siècle France* (Chicago: University of Chicago Press, 2002), 49–72, 165–221.

27. Quoted in Robert Gottlieb, *Sarah: The Life of Sarah Bernhardt* (New Haven, CT: Yale University Press, 2010), 81. Diana Holmes and Carrie Tarr, "New Republic, New Women?" in *A 'Belle Epoque'? Women and Feminism in French Society, 1890–1914*, ed. Diana Holmes and Carrie Tarr (New York: Berghan Books, 2006), 17. David McWhirter, *Henry James in Context* (Cambridge: Cambridge University Press, 2010).

28. Holmes and Tarr, "New Republic, New Women," 18. Mounet quoted in Gottleib, *Sarah*, 96.

29. EG, Heather Wood 1910, 24–25. See also in *RA*, 111–112.

30. EG, *RA*, 41.

31. EG, Chronicle 1888; EG, Journal 1889.

32. EG, Journal 1889. Quoted in Philippe Perrot, *Fashioning the Bourgeoisie: A History of Clothing in the Nineteenth Century* (Princeton, NJ: Princeton University Press, 1994), 18. The "Freedom of Dress" (1793) did not pertain to women's ability to wear trousers (transvestism).

33. EG, Chronicle 1888; Perrot, *Fashioning the Bourgeoisie*, 15–25.

34. Quoted in Coontz, *Marriage*, 147. See also Marion Kaplan, introduction to *The Marriage Bargain*, ed. Marion Kaplan (New York: Haworth Press, 1985), 6–7; Bonnie G. Smith, *Ladies of the Leisure Class* (Princeton, NJ: Princeton University Press, 1981), 57–63; Beatrice Gottlieb, *The Family in the Western World from the Black Death to the Industrial Age* (New York: Oxford University Press, 1993), ch. 7.

35. EG, "Dora," in Chronicle 1888.

36. EG, Chronicle 1888; Journal 1889.

37. EG, Journal 1889.

38. EG, Souvenir 1891.

39. EG, Heather Wood 1910, 13. Rebecca Sprang, *The Invention of the Restaurant: Paris and Modern Gastronomic Culture* (Cambridge, MA: Harvard University Press, 2020).

40. EG, Souvenir 1891.

41. EG, Souvenir 1891.

42. Kathryn Levitan, "Redundancy, the 'Surplus Woman' Problem, and the British Census, 1851–1861," *Women's History Review* 17, no. 3 (2008): 359–376.

43. Levitan, "Redundancy," 359. Barbara Caine, *Victorian Feminism* (Oxford: Oxford University Press, 1992); Jane Rendall, *The Origins of Modern Feminism: Women in Britain, France and the United States* (London: Macmillan, 1985); Nancy Cott, *The Grounding of Modern Feminism* (New Haven, CT: Yale University Press, 1987).

44. Austen quoted in Coontz, *Marriage*, 185; Carol Dyhouse, *Girls Growing Up in Late Victorian and Edwardian England* (London: Routledge and Kegan Paul, 1981), 3–5, 44–47; Davidoff and Hall, *Family Fortunes*; Martha Vicinus, *Independent Women* (Chicago: University of Chicago Press, 1985). Alice Kessler-Harris, *In Pursuit of Equity: Women, Men, and the Quest for Economic Citizenship in 20th Century America* (Oxford: Oxford University Press, 2003).

45. Beaton, "World of Elinor Glyn." EG, *The Vicissitudes of Evangeline* (New York: Harper and Brothers, 1905, aka *Red Hair*), 3, 6.

46. EG, *RA*, 54–56, 61.
47. Jeffrey Weeks, *Sex, Politics and Society*, 2nd ed. (London: Longman, 1989), 25. "She Changed Eve's Dress," *London Daily Sketch* (April 22, 1935), 2.
48. EG, *RA*, 47; LDG, *DI*, 35.
49. On the custom, see Phillis Cunnington & Catherine Lucas, *Costume for Births, Marriages, and Deaths* (New York: Harper & Row, 1972), 70–71.
50. Helena Michie, *Victorian Honeymoons* (Cambridge: Cambridge University Press, 2006).
51. Kara Blakley, "Domesticating Orientalism: Chinoiserie and the Pagodas of the Royal Pavilion, Brighton," *Australian and New Zealand Journal of Art* 18, no. 2 (2018): 206–223; John Dinkel, *The Royal Pavilion, Brighton* (New York: Vendome Press, 1983).
52. EG, *RA*, 59. EG, *The Point of View* (New York: D. Appleton & Company, 1913), 108.
53. EG, *The Reflections of Ambrosine, A Novel* (New York: Duffield & Co., 1902, aka *The Seventh Commandment*), 66; EG, *Beyond the Rocks, A Love Story* (New York: The Macaulay Co., 1906
54. EG, *RA*, 59–60.

CHAPTER 3: IN SICKNESS AND IN HEALTH

1. Vanderbilt Balsan, *Glitter and the Gold*, 49.
2. "Mrs. Glyn's Life When Young," Reading.
3. EG, *RA*, 62–63.
4. EG, *RA*, 62–63, 87.
5. LDG, *DI*, 15–21.
6. Helena Mitchie, *Victorian Honeymoons: Journeys to the Conjugal* (Cambridge: Cambridge University Press, 2006), 1–22. Blunden, *Countess of Warwick*, 48. Will Pavia, "Fairies Stop Developers in their Tracks," *Times* (London) November 21, 2005; "St Fillans," Undiscovered Scotland, http://www.undiscoveredscotland.co.uk/stfillans/stfillans/, accessed September 20, 2016.
7. EG to EK, September 10, 1892, COR.
8. EG to EK, September 10, 1892, COR.
9. Cooper quoted in Philip Ziegler, *Diana Cooper* (London: Hamilton, 1981), 26.
10. EG to EK, September 10, 1892, COR.
11. EG, *RA*, 63; Greville, *Afterthoughts*, 158.
12. Blunden, *Countess of Warwick*, 92–94. Frances Evelyn Maynard Greville, Countess of Warwick, *Discretions* (New York: C. Scribner's Sons, 1931), 163. Frances, Countess of Warwick, *Life's Ebb and Flow* (New York: William Morrow & Co., 1929), 3; EG, *RA*, 74. EG also notes Daisy was the model for Lady Tilchester in *Ambrosine*, *RA*, 75.
13. *Manners and tone of good society; or, solecisms to be avoided: by a member of the aristocracy, third edition* (London: Frederick Warne and Co., 1879), 43. *Manners of the Aristocracy* (London: Ward Lock Warwick House, 1881), 25. Italics in the original.
14. Warwick, *Life's Ebb and Flow*, 205.
15. Blunden, *Countess of Warwick*, 32–33; Gerard, *Country House Life*, chs. 4–5; Davidoff, *Best Circles*.
16. EG, *RA*, 78; Warwick, *Life's Ebb and Flow*, 178.
17. Queen Victoria quoted in Perkin, *Women and Marriage in Nineteenth-Century England*, 92. EG, *RA*, 78.
18. Ruth Hall, ed., *Dear Dr. Stopes: Sex in the 1920s* (New York: Penguin, 1981); Maria Stopes, *Married Love, or Love in Marriage* (New York: The Critic and Guide, 1918); Melanie Lantham, *Regulating Reproduction: A Century of Conflict in Britain and France* (Manchester: University of Manchester Press, 2002); Lesley Hoggart, *Feminist Campaigns for Birth Control and Abortion Rights in Britain* (Lewiston: Edwin Mellen Press, 2003); Angus McLaren, *A History of Contraception: From Antiquity to the Present* (Oxford: Oxford University Press, 1990). There is dispute over Stopes, I follow Leslie Hall, "Uniting Science and Sensibility: Marie Stopes and the Narrative

of Marriage in the 1920s," in *Rediscovering Forgotten Radicals: British Women Writers, 1889–1939*, ed. Angela Ingram and Daphne Patai (Chapel Hill: University of North Carolina Press, 1993); Claire Debenham, *Marie Stopes' Sexual Revolution and the Birth Control Movement* (Manchester: Palgrave, 2018); Peter Neushul, "Maria C. Stopes and the Popularization of Birth Control Technology," *Technology and Culture* 39, no. 2 (1998): 245–273. On the prevalence of withdrawal and abortion, see Kate Fisher and Simon Zzreter, "They Prefer Withdrawal: The Choice of Birth Control in Britain, 1918–1950," *Journal of Interdisciplinary History* 54, no. 2 (2002): 263–291. On fertility's relationship to the repression of female sexuality, I follow Hera Cook, "Sexuality and Contraception in Modern England," *Journal of Social History* (2007): 915–1932; Hera Cook, *The Long Sexual Revolution: English Women, Sex, and Contraception, 1800–1975* (Oxford: Oxford University Press, 2004).

19. EG, *The Visits of Elizabeth* (London: Duckworth, 1900).
20. Susan Tweedsmuir, *The Edwardian Lady* (London: Gerald Duckworth and Co., 1966), 44.
21. Blunden, *Countess of Warwick*, 79–83. On her politics, see K. D. Reynolds, "Frances Greville," *Oxford Dictionary of National Biography*, accessed September 9, 2016, http://www.oxforddnb.com.ezproxy.cul.columbia.edu/view/article/33567?docPos; Pamela Horn, *High Society* (Avon, UK: Bath Press, 1992), 47–48; *Country Life*, September 18, 1897, 286, BLN; Lady Augusta Fane, *Chit-Chat* (London: T. Butterworth, Ltd., 1926), 261.
22. Queen Victoria quoted in Jane Ridley, *Bertie: A Life of Edward VII* (London: Chatto & Windus, 2012), 79, 62–65.
23. Diana Souhami, *Mrs. Keppel and Her Daughter* (New York: Harper Collins, 1996), 33–35; Montgomery, *Gilded Prostitution*. MacColl and Wallace, *To Marry an English Lord*, 36–104.
24. EG, *RA*, 79. Italics in the original.
25. *A Book of Edwardian Etiquette; being a facsimile reprint of etiquette for women: a book of modern modes and manners by "one of the aristocracy"* (London: George Allen & Unwin, 1983 [reprint 1902]), 111. See also *Manners and Tone*; *Manners of the Aristocracy*, 7; *Manners and rules of good Society: by a member of the aristocracy*, 31st edition (London: Frederick Warne and Co. 1910), 12.
26. Souhami, *Mrs. Keppel and Her Daughter*; Elizabeth Hamilton, *The Warwickshire Scandal* (London: Michael Russell, 1999).
27. Lady Angela St Clair-Erskine Forbes, *Memories and Base Details* (London: Hutchinson, 1921), 78–79.
28. Daisy quoted in Gerard, *Country House Life*, 133. Blunden, *Countess of Warwick*, 83. Fane, *Chit-Chat*, 261–262.
29. Fane, *Chit-Chat*, 261. EG, *RA*, 67.
30. Souhami, *Mrs. Keppel and Her Daughter*.
31. EG, *RA*, 136.
32. EG, *RA*, 79, 71, italics in the original.
33. EG, *RA*, 71. Italics in the original.
34. "Birth," *Essex County Chronicle*, June 9, 1893, BLN.
35. Roger Fulford, *Dearest Child: Letters between Queen Victoria to Princess Royal, 1858–1861* (New York: Hold Rinehart, Winston, 2008), 343.
36. See Madeline Riley, *Brought to Bed* (South Brunswick: A. S. Barnes and Company, 1968), 3. Daniel Defoe, *The Life of Colonel Jack*, ed. Gabriel Cervantes and Geoffrey Still (Peterborough, ON: Broadview Press, 2016 [1738]), 246; Henry Fielding, *The Adventures of Joseph Andrews*, vol. 2 (London: Gay and Bird, 1903 [1742]), 156.
37. Charles Dickens, *Our Mutual Friend* (Chicago: Belford Park, 1884 [rpt. 1864–5]), 332. George Eliot, *Scenes of Clerical Life*, vol. 2 (Edinburgh: William Blackwell and Sons, 1854), 40.
38. Irvine Loudon, *Childbed Fever: A Documentary History* (New York: Garland Publishers, 1995), xxxvi. Lister's technique of antisepsis was first used in surgery in 1860 and in mid-

wifery in 1880s, but did not become routine until 1920s. T. R. Forbes, "The Regulation of English Midwives in the Sixteenth and Seventeenth Century," *Medical History* 7 (1964): 235–243; R. L. Petrelli, "The Regulation of French Midwifery during the Ancien Regime," *Journal of the History of Medicine* 26 (1971): 276–292. Irvine Loudon, *Death in Childbirth: An International Study of Maternal Care and Maternal Mortality, 1800–1950* (Oxford: Clarendon Press, 1992), 166–172. William Farr, *Vital Statistics: A Memorial Volume of Sections*, ed. Noel A. Humphreys (London: Edward Stanford, 1885), 279. On maternal mortality in the period, 270–281. Donald Caton, MD, *What a Blessing She Had Chloroform* (New Haven, CT: Yale University Press, 1999), 71.

39. Doctor quoted in Loudon, *Death in Childbirth*, 35; See also xlix–lii, 36–37.

40. Loudon, *Childbed Fever*, xxii–xxxvi.

41. Description based on Loudon, *Death in Childbirth*, 185–187. Janet Oppenheim, *"Shattered Nerves": Doctors, Patients, and Depression in Victorian England* (London: Oxford University Press, 1991), 226–227.

42. S. W. Mitchell, "Civilization and Pain," *Journal of the American Medical Association* 18, no. 4 (1892): 108. Loudon, *Death in Childbirth*, 13–15.

43. EG, RA, 86. Riley, *Brought to Bed*, 12–13.

44. EG, "'The Pen Portrait of a Great Man. By one who knows the greatness of his soul' by Elinor Glyn," August 1915, Marquess Curzon of Kedleston Papers (F 0287/2), BLIO.

45. H. Harold Scott, *Some Notable Epidemics* (London: Edward Arnold & Co., 1934), 91–92; Anne Hardy, "Typhoid," in *The Epidemic Streets: Infectious Diseases and the Rise of Preventive Medicine, 1856–1900* (Oxford: Oxford University Press, 1993): 151–220.

46. EG, RA, 86. Gerard, *Country House Life*, ch. 2.

47. EG, RA, 87. This is the only mention of this woman; while her autobiography left much out to protect the living what is there mostly tells the truth as she understood it, I have found.

48. On Costebelle, see George John Romanes, *The Life and Letters of George John Romanes* (London: Longmans, Green, and Co., 1896), 330–342; *A Handbook for Travellers in France, Part 2* (London: John Murray, 1884), 177–179. George F. Shrady, AM, MD, ed., *Medical Record: A Weekly Journal of Medicine and Surgery* 41 (1892): 79.

49. EG to EK, October 27, 1894, Hôtel de L'Hermitage, Costebelle, COR.

50. EG to EK, October ? 1894, Hôtel de L'Hermitage, Costebelle, COR.

51. George Beard, *American Nervousness* (New York: Putnam's, 1881), vi. George Cheyne, *The English Malady: or, A Treatise of Nervous Diseases* (1733), quoted in Roy Porter, "Nervousness, Eighteenth and Nineteenth Century Style," 32 and Chandak Sengoopta, "'A Mob of Incoherent Symptoms'? Neurasthenia in British Medical Discourse, 1860–1920," 87, both in Marigike Gijswijt-Hofstra, ed., *Cultures of Neurasthenia: From Beard to the First World War* (New York: Brill, 2001). Oppenheim, *Shattered Nerves*, 10–15.

52. Hilary Maland, "Uterine Mischief," 129, in Gijswijt-Hofstra, *Cultures of Neurasthenia*; Oppenheim, *Shattered Nerves*, 181, 226–227.

53. EG to EK "Wed Oct" 1894, COR. Suzanne Poirier, "The Weir Mitchell Rest Cure: Doctor and Patients," *Women's Studies* 10 (1983): 20–23, 30; Barbara Sicherman, "The Uses of a Diagnosis: Doctors, Patients, and Neurasthenia," in *Sickness and Health in America: Readings in the History of Medicine and Public Health*, ed. Judith Walzer Leavitt and Ronald L. Numbers (Madison: University of Wisconsin Press, 1978), 33.

54. EG, RA, 87–89.

55. EG, *Vicissitudes of Evangeline*, 105. Italics in the original. *The Book of Common Prayer*; *The Protestant Episcopal Church* (London: Eyre and Spottiswoode, 1892), 278.

56. Anthony Glyn, *Elinor Glyn*, 145; Sarah Lyall, "Sir Anthony Glyn," *NYT*, January 28, 1998.

57. EG, RA, 82–85; EG, *The Philosophy of Love* (Auburn, NY: Author's Press, 1923), 10.

58. Montgomery, *Gilded Prostitution*, 22–24; Marie-Claire Baroness von Alvensleben, *Absolutely! Everything about Cowes* (West Island, 2001).

59. EG, RA, 98–102.

60. Etherington-Smith and Pilcher, *The It Girls*, 55. On Lucy's career, see also Valerie

Mendes, *Lucile: A Great English Couturiere* (London: Victoria and Albert Museum, 1985); Victoria Steele, *The Fashion Stages of Lucile, Lady Duff Gordon* (Los Angeles: University of Southern California Press, 2000); Randy Bryan Bigham, *Lucile, Her Life by Design: Sex, Style, and the Fusion of Theatre and Couture* (New York: MacEvie Press Group, 2012). EG to EK, n.d., 1895, Rome Grand Hotel; EG to EK, January 28, 1896, Rome, Grand Hotel, COR.

61. EG to EK, January 28, 1895, Rome, Grand Hotel; EG to EK February 19, 1895, Cannes, COR.

62. Davidoff, *Best Circles*, 25, 51–52,

63. EG, *RA*, 89–90. "Essex Ladies at the Drawing Room," *Essex County Chronicle*, May 22, 1896.

64. Francis Harry St. Clair-Erskine, *My Gamble with Life, by the Earl of Rosslyn* (New York: J. H. Sears and Co., 1928), 137–139; EG, *RA*, 91.

65. "Their Royal Highnesses Present at 'Diplomacy,'" *Morning Post*, May 18, 1893; Joel H. Kaplan, *Theatre and Fashion: From Oscar Wilde to the Suffragettes* (London: Cambridge University Press, 1995), 39–44; St. Clair-Erskine Forbes, *Memories and Base Details*, 78–79.

66. Jonathan Conlin, *Tales of Two Cities: Paris, London and the Birth of the Modern City* (London: Atlantic Books, 2013), 129–133.

67. Neil McKenna, *The Secret Life of Oscar Wilde* (New York: Basic Books, 2005).

68. *Ten Days at Monte Carlo: At the Bank's Expense by V.B.* (London: William Heinemann, 1898); Vanderbilt Balsan, *The Glitter and the Gold*, 52–53.

69. EG, *RA*, 92.

70. Jeffrey Griffiths et al., *Public Health and Infectious Disease* (Oxford, UK: Academic Press, 2010), 177–78. Current estimates claim this happens in about 75 percent of patients; rheumatic heart disease occurs in 30 percent.

CHAPTER 4: MARRY THE LIFE, NOT THE MAN

1. EG, *RA*, 213.

2. EG, *RA*, 90–93, 130.

3. Quoted in Anthony Glyn, *Elinor Glyn*, 78–79. *Scottish Life* ran between 1898 and 1900; her grandson Anthony Glyn surmised that she "forgot" this earlier effort.

4. EG, *Visits of Elizabeth*, 8.

5. EG, *Visits of Elizabeth*, 3.

6. Anthony Glyn and Dasiy Greville have slightly different stories about the book's publication. See Alexis Easley, "Imagining the Mass-Market Woman Reader," in *The News of the World and the British Press, 1843–2001* (London: Palgrave Macmillan, 2016), 92–95, J. Wiener, "How New Was the New Journalism?" in J. Wiener, ed., *Papers for the Millions: The New Journalism in Britain, 1850s to 1914* (New York: Greenwood Press, 1988).

7. Greville, *Afterthoughts*, 159

8. "Mrs. Glyn's Life When Young," Box 6, Reading.

9. "People Who Write," *Tatler*, July 31, 1901; "Some Authors and Some 'Breaks,'" *Bookman* (NY) 14, no. 2 (October 1901): 17, 19.

10. St. Clair-Erskine Forbes, *Memories and Base Details*, 79.

11. The other four were Lady Mary Sackville, Baroness D'Erlanger, Mrs. Penn Curzon, and Lady St. Oswald.

12. "The Guard's Entertainment: Tableaux and Masque," *The Standard*, February 14, 1900; Ridley, *Bertie*, 338–339.

13. Quoted in E. Phillips Oppenheim, *The Pool of Memory* (London: Hodder & Stoughton Ltd., 1941), np., http://freeread.com.au/@RGLibrary/EPOppenheim/NonFiction/ThePoolOfMemory.html#ch22; Geraldine Beare, "Duckworth, Gerald L'Étang," *Oxford Dictionary of National Biography*.

14. "Advertisements & Notices," *Pall Mall Gazette*, November 7, 1900, 7, BLN.

15. George Bullock, *Marie Corelli: The Life and Death of a Best-Seller* (London: Constable &

Co., 1940); Natalie Schroeder, *Ouida the Phenomenon* (Newark: University of Delaware Press, 2008). See also footnote 3. *Elizabeth* was on the "high demand" *Bookman* lists in London and New York for six months, see "Eastern Letter," *Bookman* 13, no. 4 (June 1901): 392–393; "Eastern Letter," *Bookman* 13, no. 5 (July 1901): 505–506; "Eastern Letter," *Bookman* 13, no. 6 (August 1901): 618; "Eastern Letter," *Bookman* 14, no. 1 (September 1901): 99–100; "Eastern Letter," *Bookman* 14, no. 2 (October 1901): 197; "Eastern Letter," *Bookman* 14, no. 3 (November 1901): 308; "Popular Fiction of 1901; The Year in England," *Bookman* (January 1902): 454–455; J. M. Bulloch, "The Literary News in England," *Book Buyer* 22, no. 4 (May 1901): 321; "The Visits of Elizabeth," *Athenaeum*, 3816 (December 15, 1900): 790. All AP. It had 18 editions in English, https://openlibrary.org/works/OL5439948W/The_Visits_Of_Elizabeth.

16. William Moton Payne, "Recent Fiction," *Dial* 30, no. 356 (April 16, 1901); W. G. Robinson, "Harvest of a Quiet Eye," *Town and Country*, August 13, 1904.

17. "A Success That Is a Problem," *Overland Monthly* 38, no. 4 (October 1901): 319–319; "The Visits of Elizabeth," *Literary World* 32, no. 5 (May 1901): 67.

18. Elsa D'Esterre-Keeling, "What to Read," *Womanhood* 6, no. 32 (1901): 139; "A Libel on 'Elizabeth,'" *Saturday Review of Politics, Literature, Science and Art*, August 10, 1901, 180. *The Letters of Her Mother to Elizabeth* (London: T. Fisher Unwin, 1901). The parody landed on the NY *Bookman's* bestseller list for two months and news of William R. H. Trowbridge's authorship spread slowly, see Bulloch, "Literary News."

19. Greville, *Afterthoughts*, 159.

20. "Some Authors and Some 'Breaks,'" 17, 19; "A Success That Is a Problem."

21. LDG to EK, July 1910, COR. J. M. Bulloch, "Literary News."

22. Celebrity's claims—"born at the moment private life became a tradable, public commodity"—on the public were more "limited and earthbound" than fame's and emerged around the sexual scandal of performing women, see Stella Tillyard, "Celebrity in Eighteenth Century London," *History Today* 5, no. 6 (2005): 21; Martin Postle, ed., *Joshua Reynolds and the Creation of Celebrity* (Tate Publishing, 2005); Heather McPherson, "Siddons Rediviva," in *Romanticism and Celebrity Culture*, ed. Tom Mole (Cambridge: Cambridge University Press, 2009), 120–140; Mary Louise Roberts, "Rethinking Female Celebrity," in *Constructing Charisma*, ed. Edward Berenson and Eva Giloi (New York: Berghahn Books, 2010), 108. On fame's implicit rooting in the masculine, see Leo Braudy, *The Frenzy of Renown* (Cambridge, MA: Harvard University Press, 1986); Joshua Gamson, *Claims to Fame* (Berkley: University of California Press, 1994); Fred Inglis, *A Short History of Celebrity* (Princeton, NJ: Princeton University Press, 2010).

23. Steele, *Fashion Stages of Lucile.*

24. Elsie Kings, *Saturday Evening Post*, February 19, 1927, quoted in Bingham, *Lucile*, 55.

25. J. M. Bulloch, "The Literary News in England," *Book Buyer* 22, no. 4 (May 1901): 321.

26. "Some Authors and Some 'Breaks,'" 17, 19.

27. Teresa Mangum, *Married, Middlebrow, and Militant: Sarah Grand and the New Woman Novel* (Ann Arbor: University of Michigan Press), 84–93; Sos Eltis, *Acts of Desire: Women and Sex on Stage* (Oxford: Oxford University Press, 2013), 115–117.

28. Sarah Grand, "The New Aspect of the Woman Question," *North American Review* (March 1894): 270, 272. Grand debated Ouida, who used a slur to attack Grand in her May article. See also Ruth Brandon, *The New Women and the Old Men* (London: Seeker and Warburg, 1990).

29. Eliza Lynn Linton, "The Partisans of the Wild Woman," *Nineteenth Century* 31 (1892): 463, quoted in Sally Ledger, "The New Woman and the Crisis of Victorianism," in Ledger and Scott McCracken, eds., *Cultural Politics at the Fin de Siècle* (Cambridge: Cambridge University Press, 1998), 22–44. Elaine Showalter, *Sexual Anarchy* (London: Bloomsbury, 1991); Elaine Showalter, *Daughters of Decadence* (New Brunswick, NJ: Rutgers University Press, 1993); Bram Dijkstra, *Idols of Perversity: Fantasies of Feminine Evil in Fin-de-Siècle Culture* (New York: Oxford University Press, 1988).

30. Hansson quoted in Karen M. Offen, *European Feminisms, 1700–1950* (Palo Alto: Stanford University Press, 2000) 190, 203.

31. Roberts, "Making the Modern Girl French," in *Modern Girl around the World*, 80, 86–89; EG, *RA*, 130–131.

32. On Edward's central role, see John Wolffe, *Great Deaths* (New York: Oxford University Press, 2000), 233–235. Gladstone quoted in David Cannadine, "The Context, Performance, and Meaning of Ritual: The British Monarch and the 'Invention of Tradition' c. 1820–1977," in *The Invention of Tradition*, ed. Eric Hobsbawm and Terence Ranger (London: Cambridge University Press, 1982), 101–164.

33. Edward quoted in Stanley Weintraub, *Edward the Caresser* (New York: The Free Press, 2001), 222, 223, 240.

34. J. Perkins, *The Coronation Book* (London, 1911) quoted in Cannadine, "Context and Performance," 125; Sir Frederick Ponsonby, *Recollections of Three Reigns* (London: Eyre & Spottiswoode, 1951), 82; J. Morris, *Farewell the Trumpets* (London: Faber and Faber, 1978); Young, *Britain and the World*. Others considered these "invented traditions" and the Boer War a sign of the decline of the British Empire. See Samuel Hynes, *Edwardian Turn of Mind* (Princeton, NJ: Princeton University Press, 1968).

35. "Queen Victoria's Funeral as I Saw It," *Leamington-Spa Courier and Warwickshire Standard*, February 8, 1901.

36. Morris, *Farewell the Trumpets*, 49; EG, *RA*, 97–98.

37. Ledger, "The New Woman and the Crisis of Victorianism," 35; Mary Ann Fay, *Unveiling the Harem* (New York: Syracuse University Press, 2012), 24–25.

38. EG, *RA*, 99.

39. Statistic cited in Matthew Rubery, *The Novelty of Newspapers: Victorian Fiction after the Invention of the News* (New York: Oxford University Press, 2009), 168; Young, *Britain and the World*, 18–20.

40. Morris, *Farewell the Trumpets*, 28–30.

41. On the obsession with the decline of empires and the unfitness of British men during the Boer War, see Hynes, *Edwardian Turn of Mind*, 24–30.

42. EG, Heather Wood 1910, 25.

43. EG, *RA*, 99.

CHAPTER 5: UNDER FOREIGN SKIES

1. E. A. Wallis Budge, *Cook's Handbook for Egypt and the Egyptian Sudan* (London: T. Cook, 1905), 35.

2. Nightingale quoted in Derek Gregory, "Performing Cairo," in *Making Cairo Medieval*, ed. Nezar AlSayyad et al. (Oxford: Lexington Books, 2005), 77, 69–83. On the well-established link between Orientalist fantasy and sexual license in the colonial imagination, see also Edward Said, *Orientalism* (New York: Pantheon, 1978); 186–190; Mary Roberts, *Intimate Insiders: The Harem in Ottoman and Orientalist Art and Travel Literature* (Durham: Duke University Press, 2007); James Canton, *From Cairo to Baghdad: British Travellers in Arabia* (London: I. B. Tauris, 2011). Other primary sources consulted by colonials on "oriental Cairo" in this era: William Merton Fullerton, *In Cairo* (London: Macmillan, 1891); R. L. Devonshire, *Rambles in Cairo* (Cairo: Sphinx Printing Press, 1917); A. O. Lamplough, *Cairo and Its Environs* (London: Sir J. Causton, 1909); Douglas Sladen, *Oriental Cairo, the City of the "Arabian Nights"* (Philadelphia: Lippincott, 1911); Gerard de Nerval, *The Women of Cairo: Scenes of Life in the Orient* (London: G. Routledge & Sons, 1929). Mary Hall, *A Woman's Trek from the Cape to Cairo* (London: Methuen & Co., 1907); John Murray, *A Handbook for travellers in Egypt; including descriptions of the course of the Nile through Egypt and Nubia, Alexandria, Cairo, the pyramids, and Thebes, the Suez Canal* (London: J. Murray, 1875).

3. Edward Berenson, *Heroes of Empire: Five Charismatic Men and the Conquest of Africa* (Berkeley: University of California Press, 2011), 1–48.

4. EG, *RA*, 107.

5. Quoted in Eugene Rogan, *The Arabs: A History* (London: Allen Lane, 2009), 101.

6. EG, *RA*, 109.

7. EG, *RA*, 108.

8. EG, *His Hour* (New York: D. Appleton & Co., 1910), 1. Originally *When the Hour Came* in the UK.

9. Anthony Glyn, *Elinor Glyn*, 94.

10. On her embarrassing faithfulness, see EG, *RA*, 78–81, 127.

11. EG, *RA*, 99.

12. B. Bosworth Smith, MA, *Life of Lord Lawrence, Vol. 2* (London: Smith, Elder and Co., 1883), 2. Some argue that the superiority complex that grew out of the success of the British Empire made the diverse group within the UK "British," see Paul Ward, *Britishness since 1870* (London: Routledge, 2004); Berenson, *Heroes of Empire:* Morris, *Farewell the Trumpets.*

13. See particularly, EG, *Vicissitudes of Evangeline* and *Katherine Bush.*

14. EG, *RA*, 110.

15. EG, *RA*, 111.

16. EG, Heather Wood 1910, 24; Elena Boeck, "Archaeology of Decadence: Uncovering Byzantium in Victorien Sardou's Theodora," in *Byzantium/Modernism*, ed. Roland Betancourt and Maria Taroutina (New York: Brill, 2015), 102–133.

17. EG, Heather Wood 1910, 25.

18. EG, *RA*, 110–112. By the time of *RA*, EG had befriended the philosopher and Spiritualist F. H. Bradley.

19. EG, *RA*, 101.

20. EG, *His Hour*, 28.

21. EG, *RA*, 107. Catherine Radzwill quoted in Julia Gelardi, *From Splendor to Revolution: The Romanov Women, 1847–1928* (London: St. Martin's Publishing Group, 2011), 211. Other quote, David Chavchavadze, *The Grand Dukes* (London: Atlantic, 1989), 235.

22. EG, *RA*, 107; EG, *His Hour*, 28. Anthony Glyn, in *Elinor Glyn*, says he was modeled on Prince Gritzko Wittgenstein, 96. But EG identified him as the son of her patron, the Grand Duchess Maria Pavlovna.

23. Stacey, *Red*, 134–135.

24. EG, *RA*, 104.

25. Anthony Glyn, *Elinor Glyn*, 100. EG, *Ambrosine*, 53, 58, 153, 238, 111, 240, 53.

26. EG, *Ambrosine*, 10, 192

27. EG, *Ambrosine*, 293, 96.

28. "Library Reports on Popular Books," *The Critic* 42, no. 2 (February 1903). A long, thoughtful review of her picture of society's morals, see Arthur Pendenys, *The Critic* 42, no. 2 (February 1903); "Books of the Week," *Outlook* November 29, 1902; *Current Literature* (Apr 1903); *Town and Country*, January 4, 1903.

29. EG to EK, April 24, 1902, Rome, Grand Hotel, COR; "Waldo Story," *The Graphic*, November 19, 1921.

30. Elinor Glyn to Maude Story, undated, Story Family Collection (MS-O4065), 5.13, HRC.

31. EG, *RA*, 125.

32. Munthe quoted in Bengt Jangfeldt, *Axel Munthe: The Road to San Michele* (London: Bloomsbury, 2008), 167.

33. Foucault's work has notably argued for the explosion of talk about sex that occurred during the nineteenth century among elite colonial men who used sex as one main axis to separate the "civilized" from the "barbarous." See Charles Michel Foucault, *The History of Sexuality I* (1978), 146–147. But Foucault also noted the period was distinguished by the "hysterization" of women, which involved "a thorough medicalization of their bodies and sex" and the regulation of their sexuality and reproduction in the name of protecting the family and nation. It is possible to agree with Foucault while arguing, as I do here, that average people in Great Britain and the United States in this era encountered a society characterized by increasing censorship of the subject of sex and control over women's sexuality, making it more of a taboo.

34. Dijkstra, *Idols of Perversity*, 44–46.

35. George Fredrick Drinka quoted in Nina Auerbach, *Private Theatricals: The Lives of the Victorians* (Cambridge, MA: Harvard University Press, 1990), 81.
36. Axel Munthe, *The Story of San Michele* (London: J. Murray, 1933).
37. All quotes above, EG, *RA*, 127–129.
38. On Carlsbad, see Emil Kleen, MD, *Carlsbad: A Medico-Practical Guide* (New York: G. P. Putnam's Sons, 1893); "The 'Cure' at Carlsbad," *Chamber's Journal of Popular Literature, Science, and Arts* 14, no. 686 (1897): 118–120; James Tyson, MD, "A Physician's Holiday at Karlsbad," *The Philadelphia Medical Journal* 7 (January 1901): 26–29.
39. Elizabeth Crawford and Kate Parry Frye, *The Great War: The People's Story—Kate Parry Frye: The Long Life of an Edwardian Actress and Suffragette*. London: ITV, 2014; EG to EK, "Karlsbad" no date, COR.
40. EG to EK, "Karlsbad" no date, COR.
41. *The Critic* 42, no. 2 (February 1903); *Town and Country*, January 4, 1903.
42. Morris, *Farewell the Trumpets*, ch. 6; EG, *RA*, 132–133.
43. J. Lee Thompson, *Forgotten Patriot: A Life of Alfred, Viscount Milner of St James's and Cape Town, 1854–1925* (Madison, NJ: Fairleigh Dickinson University Press, 2007), 228–229, 258–259. No letters between them survive in Milner's papers; Nell's only show respect and affection.
44. EG, *Damsel and the Sage: A Woman's Whimsies* (London: Duckworth, 1903), 80.
45. Ridley, *Bertie*, 228–229. Vanderbilt quoted in Montgomery, *Gilded Prostitution*, 22–23.
46. Elinor Glyn to Waldo Story, undated, Story Family Collection (MS-O4065), 5.13, HRC.
47. EG, *Vicissitudes of Evangeline*, 19, 268. Arthur Pendenys, "Books of To-day," *The Critic*, 46, no. 4 (April 1905): 373; Stacey, *Red*, 134–135.
48. EG, *RA*, 65; Anthony Glyn, *Elinor Glyn*, 112, 137, 214; EG, *Beyond the Rocks*, 7; "Smart Society: 'Beyond the Rocks' by the Author of 'The Visits of Elizabeth,'" *NYT*, November 24, 1906.
49. EG, *Beyond the Rocks*, 19.
50. EG, *Beyond the Rocks*, 20–21.
51. On sales in the UK, see W. T. Stead, "Leading Books of the Month," *Review of Reviews*, 33, no. 198 (June 1906); London *Bookman* 3, no. 178 (July 1906); "Most Successful Books of the Season," *Academy*, November 10, 1906. All BP. Bad reviews include "Our Table," *Zion's Herald*, January 9, 1907; AP; "New Novels," *Manchester Guardian*, June 6, 1906; "Prolific Elinor Glyn," *Sun*, June 14, 1908; "Beyond the Rocks," *Athenaeum*, May 26, 1906; "Beyond the Rocks," *Academy*, May 26, 1906. An exception was "Beyond the Rocks," *Saturday Review* (London), June 2, 1906.

CHAPTER 6: WRITING *THREE WEEKS*

1. To mark this novel's significance, EG wrote a chapter entitled "The Writing of 'Three Weeks'" in *RA*, devoting more attention to it than any other by far.
2. EG, Heather Wood 1910, 3.
3. EG, Heather Wood 1910, 3.
4. EG, Heather Wood 1910, 3; EG, "Why I Wrote *Three Weeks*," *Grand Magazine* 37, no. 181 (March 1920), Box 9A, Reading. All quotations in italics are from EG, *Three Weeks*, 80.
5. Caroline Heilbrun suggests that deep into the twentieth century, women had to experience a kind of "symbolic fall" that freed them from the demands of class and society to achieve outside the home. See Heilbrun, *Reinventing Womanhood*. On the romance genre's popularity, see Regis, *Natural History of the Romance Novel*, 108–109; Bloom, *Bestsellers*, 4–5.
6. EG, *Three Weeks*, 2.
7. EG, *Three Weeks*, 115, 48, 189.
8. EG, *Three Weeks*, iii, 65–66.
9. EG, *Three Weeks*, 25, 6.

10. EG, *Three Weeks*, 73, 11.
11. EG, *Three Weeks*, 48, 20, 38.
12. Burton quoted in Deborah Lutz, *Pleasure Bound: Victorian Sex Rebels and the New Eroticism* (New York: Norton, 2001), 248.
13. Dane Kennedy, *The Highly Civilized Man: Richard Burton and the Victorian World* (Cambridge, MA: Harvard University Press, 2007), 232–236.
14. EG, "Why I Wrote *Three Weeks*."
15. EG, *RA*, 129, 134. On the popularization of Freud, see Nathan Hale, *Freud and the Americans* (New York: Oxford University Press, 1971).
16. EG, *Three Weeks*, 73, 36–38.
17. EG, *Three Weeks*, 76–77.
18. EG, *Three Weeks*, 76.
19. EG, *Three Weeks*, 80.
20. EG, *Three Weeks*, 123. "Elinor Glyn's List of the World's 20 Greatest Women," Box 28, Reading; Clea Kore, *Decadence and the Feminine: The Case of Leopold Von Sacher-Masoch* (Stanford University Press, 1983).
21. EG, *Three Weeks*, 113–114, 146.
22. EG, *Three Weeks*, 179.
23. Richard von Krafft-Ebing, *Psychopathia Sexualis* (New York: G. P. Putnam's Sons, 1965 [1886]), 33, 55. Scholars concur that women were often considered the lustier sex in Western civilization through the seventeenth century and that lust was viewed as a universal temptation. The view that women were weaker in body, morals, and mind led to the assumption that they were less able to control their lustful urges. Thomas Lequeur, *Making Sex: Gender and the Body from Aristotle to Freud* (Cambridge, MA: Harvard University Press, 1990); Faramerz Dabhoiwala, *Origins of Sex: A History of the First Sexual Revolution* (London: Oxford University Press, 2012). On the rising commitment to the sexual double standard during the nineteenth century, see Nancy Cott, "Passionlessness: An Interpretation of Victorian Sexual Ideology," *Signs* 21 (1978): 219–236; Cook, *Long Sexual Revolution*, 63–121.
24. Over the nineteenth century, practices associated with birth control were criminalized and ideas common until the early modern period that tied female sexual pleasure to reproduction were reversed. Public discourse also focused on problems associated with sex such as prostitution, confirming that Victorians were most comfortable discussing sex in relationship to immorality and making women's open engagement with sexual pleasure a mark of deviance. See Roy Porter and Leslie Hall, *The Facts of Life: The Creation of Sexual Knowledge in Britain, 1650–1950* (New Haven, CT: Yale University, 1995), 8–11, 125–177; Barbara Welter, "The Cult of True Womanhood, 1820–1860," *American Quarterly* 2 (1966): 151–174; Carol Smith-Rosenberg, 'The Hysterical Woman: Sex Roles and Conflict in Nineteenth Century America,' *Social Research* 39 (1972): 653–678; Rachel Maines, *The Technology of Orgasm: "Hysteria," the Vibrator, and Women's Sexual Satisfaction* (Baltimore: Johns Hopkins University Press, 1999), 48–67.
25. Jack Lynch, *You Could Look It Up: The Reference Shelf from Ancient Babylon to Wikipedia* (London: Bloomsbury Publishing, 2016), 231.
26. Correspondence with servicemen, Box 6, Reading.
27. EG, *RA*, 131.

CHAPTER 7: TRASH

1. Richard Burton, "A Few Unvarnished Truths about Elinor Glyn's 'Three Weeks,'" *St. Paul Bellman*, October 5, 1907.
2. Advertisement, *Academy*, April 27, 1907; "Special Announcement," *Athenaeum*, May 18, 1907.
3. *Athenaeum*, June 1, 1907.

4. "Country Life: A Notice of Sheering Hall's Sale to Guy Bilbey," *Daily Telegraph*, August 23, 1907.

5. See Hall and Davidoff, *Family Fortunes*, 13–35. Wanting to seem aristocratic, both EG and Clayton ignored money matters.

6. Elinor Glyn to Waldo Story, undated, Story Family Collection (MS-O4065), 5.13, HRC.

7. UK RED, record number 5602, Anthony Glyn.

8. EG, *Three Weeks*, 11; Advertisement, *Athenaeum*, June 15, 1907.

9. "Reviewers Shocked Again," *Bystander*, June 19, 1907.

10. "Fleshly School of Fiction," 33 (October 1907): 25–27. More than a dozen letters— from the likes of Marie Corelli, Robert Hichens, and Arthur Pinero—were published in the *Bookman* over the next two months. Most agreed that women were the worst offenders, and Hichens and Pinero referred to the problem of *Three Weeks*. See "The Reader: 'The Fleshly School of Fiction,'" *Bookman* 33 (November 1908): 70, 77–80; "'The Fleshly School of Fiction' Further Correspondence, and a Reply by 'A Man of Letters,'" *Bookman* 33 (December 1907): 127–128. "Three Weeks," *Academy*, June 29, 1907; "Three Weeks," *Liverpool Courier*, June 14, 1907.

11. Davidoff, *Best Circles*, 40–41, 80.

12. Nancy Cunard, Glyn's huge fan, reported the king's reaction, Anita Leslie, *Edwardians in Love* (Ann Arbor: University of Michigan Press, 1972), 301; Anthony Glyn, *Elinor Glyn*, 127.

13. EG to Ralph D. Blumenfeld, undated, Ralph D. Blumenfeld Collection (MS-0425), HRC.

14. EG to Blumenfeld; Stephen Colclough, "Purifying the Sources of Amusement and Information?" *Publishing History* 56 (2004): 27–51; Paul Rooney, "Conduits of Culture and 'Food for the Mind,'" *Publishing History* online [Cambridge] January 1, 2016, 25.

15. EG, *RA*, 136.

16. Cecil Beaton, introduction to *Three Weeks* (London: Duckworth, 1977), xii–xiii; Nancy Cunard, *GM: Memories of George Moore* (London: Hart-Davis, 1956), 56–57.

17. Goldman quoted in *St. Louis Post-Dispatch*, November 1, 1908, in Candace Falk, ed., *Emma Goldman: A Documentary History of the American Years—Making Speech Free, 1902–1909*, vol. 2 (University of Illinois Press, 2008), 388–389; EG to Ben Reitman, April 14, 1909, COR. On how Russian anarchists like Goldman infused America's native "meagre free-love tradition," see Christine Stansell, *American Moderns: Bohemian New York and the Creation of a New Century* (New York: Metropolitan Books, 2000), 279–281, 294–297.

18. "Three Weeks," *Dublin Express*, June 17, 1907; Leslie, *Edwardians in Love*, 300–302.

19. Such fears date to the rise of the novel, became pronounced in Britain, Europe, and America by the mid-nineteenth century, and complemented patriarchal assumptions in the era's medical discourse about the need to protect the weaker, illogical female brain from harmful texts. On the Anglo-American context, see Bloom, *Bestsellers*, 2–13, 31–38, 60–61; Flint, *Woman Reader*, chs. 2 and 3; Scott Black, "Romance Redivivus," in *The Cambridge History of the English Novel*, ed. Robert L. Caserio and Clement Hawes (Cambridge: Cambridge University Press, 2012), 246–261; Belinda Elizabeth Jack, *The Woman Reader* (New Haven, CT: Yale University Press, 2021), 186–275; Cathy Davidson, *Revolution and the Word: The Rise of the Novel in America* (New York: Oxford University Press, 1986), 109–115; Carl F. Kaestle et al., eds., *Literacy in the United States* (New Haven, CT: Yale University Press, 1991), 22–31, 123–4, 197–199. On the French, see Martyn Lyons, *Readers and Society in Nineteenth-Century France: Workers, Women, Peasants* (New York: Palgrave, 2001), chs. 1, 4, 5, 7.

20. Hawthorne quoted in Mott, *Golden Multitudes*, 122.

21. Bloom, *Bestsellers*, 34–36; Keating, *Haunted Study*, 176.

22. My own account of the hegemonic Victorian literary code in Anglo-America presupposes that it was both more repressive about the public expression of white female sexuality while at the same time fostering an explosion of discussion on the topic to which

EG contributed. Michael Mason, *The Making of Victorian Sexuality* (London: Oxford University Press, 1994), 8–20. On the NVA, see particularly Edward Bristow, *Vice and Vigilance: Purity Movements in Britain since 1700* (London: Gill and Macmillan, 1977), chs. 5, 6; Alec Craig, *Banned Books of England* (London: G. Allen & Unwin, Ltd., 1937). On the NYSSV, see John D'Emilio and Estelle Freedman, *Intimate Matters: A History of Sexuality in America* (New York: Harper and Row, 1988), ch. 9; Boyer, *Purity in Print*, chs. 1, 2. On the shared genteel literary standards of Anglo-Americans from David Hollinger, "Literary Culture," in *The United States in the Twentieth Century*, vol. 4, ed. Stanley Kutler et al. (New York: Scribners, 1996), 1435; Henry F. May, *The End of American Innocence* (1959), ch. 1; Keating, *Haunted Study*, 152–238, Waller, *Writers, Readers, and Reputations*, 175–232, 975–1001. Michael Winship, "The Transatlantic Book Trade and Anglo-American Literary Culture," in *Reciprocal Influences*, ed. Steven Fink and Susan S. Williams (Columbus: Ohio State University, 1999), 98–122. The United States' extension of protection to foreign authors with the American Copyright Act of 1891 helped, see Waller, *Writers, Readers, and Reputations*, 575–631; Helmut Lehmann-Haupt, *The Book in America: A History of Making and Selling Books in the United States* (New York: R.R. Bowker Company, 1951), 322–332.

23. Keating, *Haunted Study*, 247, 451, ch. 4; Boyer, *Purity in Print*, ch. 1; Helen Lefkowitz Horowitz, *Rereading Sex: Battles over Sexual Knowledge and Suppression in Nineteenth-Century America* (New York: Knopf, 2002), chs. 14, 15.

24. Both the British and American book markets doubled between 1890 and 1910s. See Lehmann-Haupt, *Book in America*, 318–322; Alexis Weedon, *Victorian Publishing* (Aldershot: Ashgate, 2003), 55. John Tebbel, *Between Covers: The Rise and Transformation of Book Publishing in America* (New York: Oxford University Press, 1987), 178–179. Martin Hipsky, *Modernism and the Women's Popular Romance* (Athens: Ohio University Press, 2011), 55–62.

25. On sex novels, see Melman, *Women and the Popular Imagination*, 41–51; Trotter, *English Novel in History*, 198–211; Keating, *Haunted Study*, 208–216. In key ways, *Three Weeks* fit the modern definition of pornography, including the naming of parts and sensations to stimulate sexual response; describing a self-contained, hedonistic world of self-gratification cut off from any higher moral authority; positing a physical, sexual reality in order to expose hypocritical social conventions. See Allison Pease, *Modernism, Mass Culture, and the Aesthetics of Obscenity* (Cambridge: Cambridge University Press, 2000), 4–5.

26. Percival Pollard quoted in "Three Weeks," *Current Literature* (December 1907): 694. See also "Miss Glyn's New Novel," *Birmingham Post*, June 14, 1907.

27. Other noteworthy "sex novels" include Somerset Maugham, *Mrs. Craddock* (1903); May Sinclair, *The Helpmate* (1907); Henry de Vere Stacpoole, *The Blue Lagoon* (1908); H. G. Wells, *Anne Veronica* (1909); Hubert Wales, *The Yoke* (1908); Cicely Thompson, *Just to Get Married* (1911); Victoria Cross, *The Greater Law* (1914).

28. "Fleshly School of Fiction," *Bookman* 33 (October 1907): 25–27. Robert S. Lynd and Helen Merrell Lynd, *Middletown: A Study in Modern American Culture* (New York: Harcourt Brace & Company, 1957 [1929]), 232–234. "Novelized" quoted in Edward de Grazia, *Girls Lean Back Everywhere: The Law of Obscenity and the Assault on Genius* (New York: Random House, 1992), 18. Tebbel, *Between Covers*, 179–183; Keating, *Haunted Study*, 175–87.

29. "The Best Books of 1907," *The Bystander*, January 8, 1908, 92.

30. On the cheap edition, Waller, *Writers, Readers, and Reputations*, 947.

31. EG to CG, no date, 1907, COR.

32. EG to CG, October 3, 1907, COR.

33. EG, RA, 168–170.

34. EG to CG, September 7, 1907, COR. Douglas Sladen, *Who's Who: An Annual Biographical Dictionary* (London: A.C. Black, 1897).

35. "Novel about Our Smart Set," *NYT*, September 29, 1907. EG to CG, no date, 1907, COR.

36. EG to CG, September 7, 1907, COR.

37. EG, *RA*, 137–139; Bernard DeVoto, ed., *Mark Twain in Eruption* (New York: Harper, 1940), 315.

38. Berenson, *Heroes of Empire*, 25–31.

39. EG, "How New York City Appears to Elinor Glyn," *NYT*, October 13, 1907.

40. "Elinor Glyn Talks about Her American Critics," *NYT*, October 6, 1907.

41. "Mrs. Glyn Reaches New York," *Chicago Daily Tribune*, October 5, 1907; "American Men Just So Nice," *LAT*, October 6, 1907; "Heroine's Views Not My Views, Says Elinor Glyn, Author of 'Three Weeks,'" *St. Louis Post-Dispatch*, October 6, 1907; "Critics Idiots—Mrs. Glyn, but the Author of 'Three Weeks' Finds American Reporters Charming," *NYT* November 17, 1907.

42. EG, *Three Weeks*, i. Italics in the original.

43. "Three Weeks," *Current Literature* 43, no. 6 (December 1907); "Elinor Glyn Outdoes Herself in the Line of Audacious Fiction," *Chicago Tribune*, September 14, 1907; "Elinor Glyn," editorial, *Chicago Daily News*, October 1, 1907; "Elinor Glyn's Three Weeks," *Brooklyn Eagle* October 5; "The Visit of Elinor Glyn," *Philadelphia Inquirer*, October 9, 1907; "Three Weeks,"_Boston Transcript*, October 2, 1907; "Prurient and Worse Yet—Dull," *NYT*, September 28, 1907; "Three Weeks," *The Saturday Review*, June 15, 1907; "Three Weeks," *LIFE*, October 10, 1907, 428; "Women Running Neck-and-Neck with Men in 'Best Seller' Race," *NYT*, October 20, 1907.

44. "Elinor Glyn's Remarkable Book," *Louisville Courier Journal*, September 28, 1907. See also "Elinor Glyn," *San Francisco Argonaut*, October 5, 1907; "Mrs. Elinor Glyn: The Woman—and Her Work," *Washington Post*, January 8, 1908. On French romanticism, see Sylvana Tomaselli, "Sensibility," in *The Blackwell Companion to the Enlightenment*, ed. John W. Yolton (Oxford: Blackwell, 1991); John Mullan, "Sensibility and Literary Criticism," in *The Cambridge History of Literary Criticism, vol. 4, The Eighteenth Century*, ed. H. B. Nisbet and Claude Rawson (Cambridge: Cambridge University Press, 2005); Robert Darnton, *The Forbidden Bestsellers of Pre-Revolutionary France* (New York: W. W. Norton, 1996), 64–68, 112–114.

45. "The French Novel and the American Public," *NYT*, September 28, 1907; George Jean Nathan, "The-Girl-Alone-in-the-City Novels," *Bookman* 33 (1911): 202.

46. "Found Mrs. Glyn Charming," *Baltimore Sun*, October 16, 1907; James Donahue, "Latest Gossip of the Big Metropolis," *San Francisco Chronicle*, February 2, 1908; "Critics Idiots—Mrs. Glyn."

47. "Elinor Glyn, the Author Talks about her Husband and Heroines," *Washington Post*, December 20, 1907. See also "Mrs. Glyn Here in Search of a Man," *New York World*, October 5, 1907; "Women Shiver as Love Is Defined by Novelist," *St. Louis Post-Dispatch*, December 18, 1907; "Love Analyzed by Mrs. Glyn," *Chicago Daily Tribune*, December 18, 1907.

48. Peter Bailey, "The Victorian Barmaid as Cultural Prototype," in *Popular Culture and Performance in the Victorian City* (Cambridge: Cambridge University Press, 1998), 156, 151; Stephen Grundle, *Glamour* (New York: Oxford University Press, 2008), 4–6. See also Virginia Postrel, *The Power of Glamour: Longing and the Art of Visual Persuasion* (New York: Simon & Schuster, 2013).

49. "Mrs. Elinor Glyn Gives Advice to Married Women," *Niagara Falls Gazette*, October 14, 1907. See also "Women Cannot Rebel against Social Law," *Syracuse Journal*, October 5, 1907; "From 'Very Free Love' Elinor Glyn Draws Back," *Atlanta Constitution*, August 4, 1907; "Mrs. Glyn Reaches New York, Denies Favoring Free Love," *Chicago Daily Tribune* October 5, 1907; "Elinor Glyn, Novelist, and Children, 'Most Beautiful Girls in All of England,'" *New York Evening Journal*, October 9, 1907. Despite the still relative rarity of using photographs, other stories that featured pictures of "Lady" Glyn and her daughters included Alice Rohe, "Marriage May Be the Union of Two Creatures Who Hate Each Other, Says EG, the Clever and Daring Author of 'Three Weeks,'" *Washington Post*, October 9, 1907; "Author of 'Three Weeks' Here; Mrs. Glyn Says Her Critics Won't Understand," *Washington Times*, January 7, 1908; "Novelist Wants American Hero," *Hawaiian Star*, November 9, 1907; "A Pair of Eyes," *New York Globe*,

September 21, 1907. This contradictory representational style first promoted women theatrical stars during the nineteenth century; see Hilary Hallett, *Go West, Young Women: The Rise of Hollywood* (Berkeley: University of California Press, 2013), ch. 1; Lenard Berlanstein, *Daughters of Eve: French Theater Women from the Old Regime to the Fin de Siècle* (Cambridge, MA: Harvard University Press, 2001); Lenard R. Berlanstein, "Historicizing and Gendering Celebrity Culture: Famous Women in Nineteenth-Century France," *Journal of Women's History* 16, no. 4 (2004): 65–91; Mary Jean Corbett, "Performing Identities; Actresses and Autobiography," *Biographies* 24, no. 1 (Winter: 2001): 15–23.

50. EG to EK, November 4, 1907, COR.
51. EG to EK, Nov 4, 1907, COR; Mark Neider, ed., *The Autobiography of Mark Twain* (New York: Harper & Row, 1959), 353; De Voto, *Mark Twain in Eruption*, 315. Albert B. Paine, ed., *Mark Twain Letters vol. 2.* (New York: Harper, 1917), 809; Elinor Glyn, "Mark Twain on 'Three Weeks,'" Box 29, Reading.
52. EG to EK, November 4, 1907, COR.
53. LDG, *DI*, 86–88.
54. "Too Hot for Their Presses?" *Nashville Tennessean*, January 5, 1908.
55. Donahue, "Latest Gossip of the Big Metropolis"; "Lady Duff Gordon Sees Chinatown," *NYT*, December 23, 1907, 9.
56. EG to EK, November 4, 1907, COR; See also EG, *RA*, 139.
57. "Puritanical Puritans," *NYT*, December 22, 1907; "Won't Let Mrs. Glyn Speak," *Chicago Daily Tribune*, December 22, 1907.
58. "Pilgrim Mothers Cold to Mrs. Glyn," *NYT*, December 22, 1907; "Pilgrim Mothers Amused Mrs. Glyn," *NYT*, December 23, 1907; "Old England and New," *Nashville American*, December 26, 1907, 4. "ONLY FRUMPS ARE ENGLISH," *Chicago Daily Tribune*, December 24, 1907, 1. "Reply to Mrs. Glyn: 'Coarse,' the Pilgrim Mothers Say of Authoress," *Washington Post*, December 24, 1907; "MRS. GLYN'S FIRE UNCOVERS OPPONENT," *NYT*, December 24, 1907. "Mrs. Glyn Demands Apology," *St. Louis Post-Dispatch*, December 27, 1907; "ELINOR GLYN, THE NOVELIST WHO HAS UPSET NEW YORK," *Nashville Tennessean*, December 30, 1907.
59. "Woman's Book May Be Branded Obscene," *LAT*, January 1, 1908; "For the Year 1907–1908," *New England Watch and Ward Society* (1908): 9; "Sex Novel Banned," *NYT*, Dec 30, 1907; "Puritanical Puritans: After Perusing 'Three Weeks' 'Turn Down' Mrs Glyn," *New York Tribune*, December 22, 1907; "'Coarse' the Pilgrim Mothers Say," "HITS MRS. GLYN'S BOOK; Comstock Refers Her 'Three Weeks' to Prosecutor," *Washington Post*, December 29, 1907, 12; "'Three Weeks,' Called Obscene, Will Be Barred from Mails," *St. Louis Post-Dispatch*, January 7, 1908.
60. "Mrs. Glyn Sails Away," *NYT*, February 9, 1908; "Elinor Glyn Sails Away," *Washington Post*, February 9, 1908. EG to EK, n.d., "Salt Lake," COR.
61. LDG, *DI*, 107.
62. "Elinor Glyn: The Woman—and Her Work," *Washington Post*, January 9, 1908.
63. "Country Homes," *NYT*, April 18, 1908; "London Waits for 'Three Weeks,'" *Chicago Daily Tribune*, April 12, 1908.
64. EG to CG, February 27, 1908, COR.
65. "ELINOR GLYN, A WOMAN OF RAVISHING BEAUTY ELUCIDATES," *Detroit Free Press*, April 26, 1908; "Bound for California," *LAT*, April 18, 1908; EG to EK, May 12, 1908, COR.
66. "Here for a Day, Not Three Weeks," *Detroit Free Press*, April 25, 1908.
67. EG, "Why I Am Misunderstood," *Chicago Daily Tribune*, July 12 1908.
68. "ELINOR GLYN, A WOMAN OF RAVISHING BEAUTY."
69. "Calls Chicago Happy," *NYT*, April 27, 1908; "What Shall I Read?" *Tatler*, May 27, 1908; "Tells about 'Three Weeks': Mrs Elinor Glyn, Authoress of Passion, Arrives in Chicago," *Chicago Daily Tribune*, April 26, 1908; "Mrs. Glyn Lauds Divorce," *Chicago Daily Tribune*, April 27, 1908.
70. London quoted in Cecelia Tichi, *Jack London: A Writer's Fight for a Better America* (Chapel Hill: University of North Carolina Press, 2015), 82.

71. "Society," *San Francisco Chronicle*, May 8, 1908, 11; EG, *RA*, 163. On the Grahams, see Michael Redmon, "Question: Wasn't There Another Mansion Where Clark Estate Is Today?" *Santa Barbara Independent*, October 25, 2007.

72. Walter S. Trumbull, "SERVED HER RIGHT," *Lippincott's Monthly Magazine* (May 1908): 696.

73. Henry Sheldon, *Theosophy and New Thought* (New York: Abington Press, 1916); Ferenc Szasz, "'New Thought' and the American West," *Journal of the West* 23 (1984): 83–90.

74. EG, *RA*, 154–155. Her letters home from California describe her new interest at length. "Incaculable harm is done by our loved ones fearing thoughts, drawing the current of things feared upon us," EG to Glyn Family, May 17, 1908, Santa Barbara, COR.

75. "Mrs. Glyn's Land of Promise," *Louisville Courier*, April 22, 1908. See also "Hackett Comes Now to Produce 'Three Weeks,'" *St. Louis Post-Dispatch*, July 30, 1908; EG to EK, April 21, 1908, COR.

76. "Elinor Plays Faro," *NYT*, May 29, 1908; EG, *RA*, 165. EG to Glyn Family, May 31, 1908, Salt Lake City, COR.

77. "EG Plays Faro," *NYT*. "'One Night' in Rawhide Beats 'Three Weeks,'" *St. Louis Post-Dispatch*, May 29, 1908.

78. EG to Glyn Family, May 3, 1908, Salt Lake, COR; "Mrs. Glyn Is Back," *NYT*, June 14, 1908.

79. "Declares Marriage Vow Is an Insult to God," *LAT*, May 3, 1908.

80. EG to EK, May 2, 1908, Salt Lake, COR.

CHAPTER 8: THE WORD BECAME FLESH

1. EG to EK, July, n.d., COR.

2. Todd Endelman, *The Jews of Britain, 1656–2000* (Berkeley: University of California Press, 2002), 150–165, 171–172.

3. EG to EK, April 21, 1908, COR. EG, *RA*, 174; Greville, *Afterthoughts*, 159.

4. EG to EK, February 26, London Ritz; EG to EK, April 21, 1908, COR.

5. EG, Heather Wood 1910, 11.

6. *Commonwealth v. Buckley*, 200 Mass. 346, 86 N.E 910 (1909). "For the Year 1907–1908," *New England Watch and Ward Society* (1908): 9; Arthur E. Bostwick, "The Librarian as Censor," *Library Journal* 33 (July 1908): 264. These included Mudie, W. H. Smith, Boots, Day's Cawthorn & Hutt, and the Times Book Club. Nicholas Hiley, "'Can't You Find Me Something Nasty?': Circulating Libraries and Literary Censorship in Britain from the 1890s to the 1910s," in *Censorship and the Control of Print in England and France, 1600–1910*, ed. Robin Myers and Michael Harris (Winchester, UK: St. Paul's Bibliographies, 1992), 130. "'Three Weeks' Abandoned: Hackett Will Not Play Dramatization of Book," *St. Louis Post-Dispatch*, August 21, 1908.

7. Curtis Brown, *Contracts* (London: Cassell, 1935), 11; Barnett and Weedon, *Elinor Glyn*, 25–39.

8. Her plea to the censors emphasized how her Lady "must pay a great price" for her actions, contradicting much of her recent publicity, and blamed the king for the Lady's decision to "go get an heir." See Victoria and Albert Theatre Museum, reference THM/14/7, April 6, 1908.

9. "Russian for 'Three Weeks': Mrs. Glyn Finds Actress in Paris to Match the Tiger Skin," *NYT*, July 7, 1908.

10. Quoted in Anthony Glyn, *Elinor Glyn*, 78. Pavlovna's biographer says the quote rings true, Charlotte Zeepvat, *Romanov Autumn* (New York: St. Martin's Publishing, 2000), 162.

11. "Elinor Glyn Has a Long Second Toe," *St. Louis Post-Dispatch*, July 26, 1908.

12. EG to EK, July 14, 1908, COR.

13. In 1900, seven-room flats built in the best suburbs with electric light and tennis courts could be rented for £50 a year. R. J. Minney, *The Edwardian Age* (Cassell London, 1964), 128.

14. EG to EK, n.d., COR.
15. Joseph Roach, *It* (Ann Arbor: University of Michigan Press, 2007), 25.
16. "All London Society Sees Mrs. Glyn's Play; 'Everybody One's Seen Every Day for Years,'" *NYT*, July 26, 1908; "Mrs. Glyn's Play Social Hit: Purple Performance Admirably Put On before Noted Audience," *Chicago Daily Tribune*, July 26, 1908. See also "Elinor Glyn on Stage: Author of 'Three Weeks' Appears in Role of the Queen," *Washington Post*, July 25, 1908; "'Three Weeks' on Stage in London," *Christian Science Monitor*, August 7, 1908.
17. "All London Society Sees Mrs. Glyn's Play."
18. Keppel quoted in Soulami, *Mrs. Keppel and Her Daughter*, 4. Nancy Cunard also reported the King's reaction, Leslie, *Edwardians in Love*, 301.
19. Hobsbawm and Ranger, eds., *The Invention of Tradition*.
20. "'Three Weeks' Too 'Tame' for British Playgoers: Mrs. Glyn's Dramatic Version Falls Flat," *NYT*, August 2, 1908; "Elinor Glyn Feels Hurt at Critics of 'Three Weeks,'" *Atlanta Constitution*, August 23, 1908; EG, *RA*, 209.
21. Anthony Glyn, *Elinor Glyn*, 124.
22. EG, "Pen Portrait," 33, BLIO; Nayana Goradia, *Lord Curzon: The Last of the British Moghuls* (Oxford: Oxford University Press, 1993), 154.
23. Curzon quoted in David Gilmour, *Curzon: Imperial Statesman* (New York: Farrar Straus & Giroux, 2003), 1.
24. Curzon quoted in Gilmour, *Imperial Statesman*, 7,
25. Quoted in Gilmour, *Imperial Statesman*, 30.
26. Quoted in Lambert, *Unquiet Souls*, 113.
27. EG, "Pen Portrait," 61, BLIO. Curzon quoted in Gilmour, *Imperial Statesmen*, 360.
28. Krishna Dutta, *Calcutta: A Cultural and Literary History* (New York: Signal Books, 2003), 124–135. Dutta calls him "the most articulate, passionate, arrogant, effective and most important of all the viceroys."
29. Gilmour, *Imperial Statesmen*, 468.
30. EG, "Pen Portrait," 63, 85, BLIO.
31. EG, "Pen Portrait," 11, 71, 34, BLIO.
32. EG, "Pen Portrait," 73, 51, 49, BLIO; Beaton, "World of Elinor Glyn."
33. Cragie quoted in Gilmour, *Imperial Statesman*, 464; EG, "Pen Portrait," 52, BLIO.
34. Quoted in Lambert, *Unquiet Souls*, 3. Gilmour, *Imperial Statesmen*, 111.
35. EG, "Pen Portrait," 58–59, 53, BLIO.
36. EG, "Pen Portrait," 8, BLIO.
37. EG, "Pen Portrait," 57, BLIO.
38. EG, "Pen Portrait," 63, BLIO.
39. EG, "Pen Portrait," 53, 80, BLIO.
40. "Naughty Gritzko and Tempted Tamara," *Academy*, October 29, 1910.
41. EG, Heather Wood 1910, 32, 26.
42. EG, Heather Wood 1910, 23.
43. EG, Heather Wood 1910, 20.
44. EG, Heather Wood 1910, 11.
45. EG to CG, April 21, 1908; EG to EK, August 17, 1909, Karlsbad; EG to EK, n.d. She pled with her mother in this letter to see that there "was not the slightest chance of saving C. unless he can save himself," noting Lucy agreed, COR.
46. EG to CG, January 22, 1909[?]; EG to CG, January 5, 1910, COR.
47. EG to EK, December 27, 1909, Saint Petersburg, COR. As usual while traveling, she wrote very long letters home and almost daily on this trip. On Margot, see EG to EK, June 10, 1909, Hotel Minerva, COR.
48. EG to Glyn family, December 28–January 10, 1910; Gelardi, *From Splendor to Revolution*, 48–49, 100–105, 153–155, 289–90.
49. EG to EK, February 1910, COR.
50. EG to CG, January 9, 1909; EG to CG, March 1910; EG to Glyn family, April 25, 1910, COR.

51. "Women of the Week," *Tatler*, October 19, 1910; Arnold Bennett, *Books and Persons: Being Comments on a Past Epoch, 1909–1911* (New York: George H. Doran Company, 1917), 271–277; "Mr. Arnold Bennett and Criticism," *Saturday Review*, July 21, 1917.
52. "His Hour," *The Sketch*, November 2, 1910, xii.
53. "Naughty Gritzko and Tempted Tamara."
54. Minney, *Edwardian Age*, 86–87.
55. EG, Heather Wood 1910, 40–42. Nell complained to her mother about Curzon's reports of the valet letter reader, EG to EK, January 30, 1910, Saint Petersburg, COR.
56. EG, Heather Wood 1910, 40.
57. EG, Heather Wood 1910, 37.
58. EG, Heather Wood 1910, 38.
59. EG, Heather Wood 1910, 36–37.
60. EG, Heather Wood 1910, 43–44; "Francis Herbert Bradley," *Stanford Encyclopedia of Philosophy*, https://plato.stanford.edu/contents.html#b/.
61. UK RED record number 3232, unknown academic; EG, RA, [??].
62. EG, Heather Wood 1910, 41.
63. EG to EK, May 1911, COR.
64. EG, RA, 174–175.
65. EG to EK, Feb 1912?, COR.
66. EG to EK; EG, Heather Wood 1910.
67. Anne de Courcy, *The Viceroy's Daughters: The Lives of the Curzon Sisters* (New York: William Morrow, 2000), 18–26.
68. Lord Curzon to László, July 23, 1913, DLA, 135–0005. On the painting's provenance, see de László Archive Trust: https://www.delaszlocatalogueraisonne.com/catalogue/the-catalogue/glyn-elinor-nee-sutherland-married-name-mrs-clayton-glyn–5361/search/keywords:glyn/page/6; Sandra de László et al., eds., *De László, A Brush with Grandeur* (London: Paul Holberton Publishing, 2004), 9.
69. EG to László, October 13, 1914, 123–0005; EG to László, undated, 123–0007, DLA. De László quoted in Owen Rutter, *Portrait of a Painter* (London: Hodder and Stoughton, 1939), 298–299; "A Very Much Discussed Painting: 'Elinor Glyn,'" *Sketch* 90, no. 1160 (April 21, 1915): 55.
70. EG, RA, 216–217.

CHAPTER 9: SURVIVING THE WORST

1. EG, RA, 2; LDG, DI, 12–13.
2. Victor Hugo, *The Man Who Laughs* (Grosset & Dunlap, 1950 [1869]), 97; EG, RA, 27–28
3. "A Legacy Redeemed, Sir Cosmo Edmund Duff Gordon," *In the House!* 2, no. 2 (May 2008): 18–19. LDG, DI, 129. A lifeboat drill was canceled the day before the accident. Most sailors aboard had not manned lifeboats before.
4. LDG to family, April 19, 1912, Ritz Carlton, New York. "Angry Letter from *Titanic* Survivor, Lady Duff-Gordon, Goes to Auction," *Fine Books & Collections*, January 14, 2015.
5. LDG, DI, 134–135.
6. LDG to family, April 19, 1912, Ritz Carlton, copy in possession of the author.
7. EG to EK, no date, COR; EG's report of her premonition, see "DUFF-GORDONS IN LIST OF NOTABLES," *Chicago Daily Tribune*, April 17, 1912; Tellingly, EG made no mention of the *Titanic* in RA.
8. "LADY DUFF GORDON GOT SOUVENIR NAMES ON HER LIFE BELT," *St. Louis Post-Dispatch*, May 18, 1912, 2.
9. "TALE OF 'THE MONEY BOAT,'" *New York Tribune*, May 10, 1912, 6.
10. "RESCUE STOPPED BY DUFF-GORDONS," *Atlanta Constitution*, May 18, 1912, 2; "SIR COSMO OPPOSED SEA RESCUE," *NYT*, May 10, 1912, 6; "Rescue Stopped by Sir Cosmo," *St. Louis Post-Dispatch*, May 10, 1912, 2.

11. Symons at the British inquiry: "British Wreck Commissioner's Inquiry, Day 10," Titanic Inquiry Project, http://www.titanicinquiry.org/BOTInq/BOTInq10Symons02 .php, accessed October 28, 2021; "British Wreck Commissioner's Inquiry, Day 10," Titanic Inquiry Project, http://www.titanicinquiry.org/BOTInq/BOTInq10Symons04 .php, accessed October 28, 2021.

12. Among the male passengers, 32 percent of first class, 8 percent of second class, and 13 percent of steerage passengers survived.

13. Lowe testimony at British inquiry, see "United States Senate Inquiry, Day 5," Titanic Inquiry Project, http://www.titanicinquiry.org/USInq/AmInq05Lowe06.php, accessed October 28, 2021.

14. Laura Francatelli to Mary Ann Taylor, April 28, 1912, National Maritime Museum, Greenwich, London.

15. Andrew Wilson, *Shadow of the Titanic* (New York: Atria Books, 2012), 145, 173, 174.

16. LDG, *DI*, 1.

17. *New Yorker* quoted in Yvonne McEwen and Fiona Fisken, eds., *War, Journalism, and History* (Bern: Peter Lang Inc, 2012), 3. "WOMEN OF THE TITANIC; Why the Drowning Were Not Rescued," *Daily Mail*, May 10, 1912.

18. LDG to Esmé Wallace quoted in Etherington-Smith and Pilcher, *It Girls*, 187.

19. LDG to Glyn family, May 27, 1912, captured from auction, "Angry Letter from *Titanic* Survivor."

20. Quoted in "Calais Is Scene of Torture," *NYT*, May 21, 1912, 4. See also the archive of the inquiry: "British Wreck Commissioner's Inquiry, Day 10, Testimony of Sir Cosmo Duff-Gordon," http://www.titanicinquiry.org/BOTInq/BOTInq10Duff-Gordon01.php, accessed October 28, 2021.

21. LDG, *DI*, 148.

22. See Cannadine, *Decline and Fall of the British Aristocracy*, 73–83.

23. EG, Heather Wood 1910, 37. EG, "America Has Revived the Spirit of France," *Shanghai Times*, October 30, 1917. Nell wrote her mother, "she has 'found herself' and loves America, it is exactly her affair and she means to live there," EG to EK, n.d., 1915, COR.

24. EG to EK, no date. In one of her very long letters, EG describes at length the financial turmoil, reviewing Clayton's many loans from LDG and Curzon, her pawning of jewels. This letter indicates Clayton is too sick to be trusted and that Walters will put him on allowance, making him dependent on her "like a child."

25. EG to EK, "Sunday Night," no date, COR.

26. My account of the context and origins of the war relies on Christopher Clark, *The Sleepwalkers: How Europe Went to War in 1914* (New York: Harper, 2013), 375, 381.

27. Margaret MacMillan, *Paris, 1919: Six Months That Changed the World* (New York: Vintage, 2001), 44.

28. Hunt Tooley, *The Great War: The Western Front and the Home Front* (London: Palgrave Macmillan, 2003).

29. EG, *RA*, 222; *Gil-Blas*, July 15, 1914, 36th year, nr. 18605, page 4.

30. LDG's syndicated column went back to 1910 and always included pictures of LDG, see "Lady Duff-Gordon ('Lucile'): The Oriental Touch," *Nashville Tennessean*, April 10, 1910; "Lady Duff-Gordon Greatest Creator of Fashions in the World," *Nashville Tennessean*, January 30, 1910; Etherington-Smith and Pilcher, 171–180.

31. Chris Dubbs, *American Journalists in the Great War: Rewriting the Rules of Reporting* (Lincoln: University of Nebraska Press), 13.

32. Young, *Britain and the World*, 57–59, quoted in Dubbs, *American Journalists*, 21; David French, "Spy Fever in Britain, 1900–1915," *The Historical Journal* 21, no. 2 (1978): 355–370.

33. Martin Pugh, *Women and the Women's Movement in Britain* (New York: Macmillan, 1992),19.

34. "Women Writers Appeal," *NYT*, October 1, 1914; EG, *RA*, 228.

35. Dr. J. Pratt to EG on behalf of the 39th DAC division of the BEF, April 14, 1917, Box 6, Reading.

36. EG, *Three Things* (New York: Hearst International Library, 1915), 1, 42, 70. On her growing magazine work and Duckworth's lower royalties for the book, see Barnett and Weedon, *Elinor Glyn*, 32–33, 44–47.

37. EG to Juliet and Margot Glyn, October 7, 1915, COR.

38. Alfred Harmsworth to EG, October 12, 1915, Corresp. with Society of Authors (Add. MS 56710), BL.

39. Northcliffe quoted in MacMillan, *Paris, 1919*, 163; Dubbs, *American Journalists*, 64–67. J. Winter, "British National Identity and the First World War," in *The Boundaries of the State in Modern Britain*, ed. S.J.D. Green and R. C. Whiting (Cambridge: Cambridge University Press, 1996), 266.

40. Quoted in McEwen and Fisken, eds., *War, Journalism, and History*, 3.

41. John Baxter, *Paris at the End of the World: The City of Light during the Great War* (New York: Harper, 2014), 30, 49–56, 102.

42. MacMillan, *Paris, 1919*, 148.

43. Dubbs, *American Journalists*, 99–101

44. Dubbs, *American Journalists*, 49–51, 108–109.

45. MG to EG, Nov 11, 1915, COR.

46. EG to CG's sister "Nellie," November 14, 1915, COR.

47. *Glyn v. Weston Feature Film Company Limited* (1916) 1 ch. 261. The burlesque was *Pimple's Three Weeks (Without the Option)* (Piccadilly Film Productions, 1915).

48. EG to Margot Glyn, November 1915; EG to Margot Glyn, May 24, 1916, COR.

49. EG, *Katherine Bush*, 12. Serialized in Britain in *Nash's and Pall Mall Magazine*, October 1916–July 1917. On Long, see David Nasaw, *The Chief: The Life of William Randolph Hearst* (New York: Houghton Mifflin, 2000), 345, 372.

50. "Editor's note; The Career of Katherine Bush," *Cosmopolitan*, March 1916, 465.

51. "Current Literature," *Daily Telegraph*, April 20, 1917; "To Begin in October, The Career of Katherine Bush," *Nash's and Pall Mall Magazine*, September 1916; "New Novels," *Times Literary Supplement*, April 12, 1917; "New Novels," *Illustrated London News*, June 2, 1917.

52. Pugh, *Women and the Women's Movement in Britain*, 19; Susan R. Grayzel, *Women and the First World War* (London: Pearson Education, 2002), 28–29.

53. EG, Heather Wood 1910, 13.

54. De Courcy, *Viceroy's Daughters*, 25–26, 31, 36–37, 54.

55. Grace Duggan quoted in Gilmour, *Imperial Statesman*, 464.

56. H.C.G. Matthew, "Asquith, Herbert Henry, first early of Oxford and Asquith," *Oxford Dictionary of National Biography* online.

57. Gilmour, *Imperial Statesman*, 469–470.

58. LDG to Esmé Wallace quoted in Etherington-Smith and Pilcher, *It Girls*, 187.

CHAPTER 10: WORLD SPLIT IN TWO

1. Beverly Nichols, "Celebrities in Undress: LXXV—Elinor Glyn," *The Sketch*, August 31, 1927, 398.

2. Woodrow Wilson speech before Congress, April 2, 1917, Woodrow Wilson, *War Messages*, 65th Cong., 1st Sess. Senate Doc. No. 5, Serial No. 7264, Washington, DC, 1917, https://wwi.lib.byu.edu/index.php/Wilson%27s_War_Message_to_Congress, accessed October 28, 2021.

3. David M. Kennedy, *Over Here: The First World War and American Society* (Oxford: Oxford University Press, 1980), 10–14.

4. MacMillan, *Paris, 1919*, 159. When the armistice came, 6 of 10 Frenchmen between the ages of eighteen and twenty-eight were dead or permanently maimed; the nation lost more than twice the number of men mobilized for Great Britain and all its dominions.

5. Elizabeth Greenhalgh, *The French Army and the First World War* (Cambridge: Cambridge University Press, 2014), 201–206.

6. EG, *RA*, 232; EG quoted in MacMillan, *Paris, 1919*, 146.

7. Deborah Thom, *Nice Girls and Rude Girls: Women Workers in World War I* (London: I. B. Tauris, 1998), 17; Nicoletta Gullace, "*The Blood of Our Sons*," *Men, Women, and the Renegotiation of Citizenship during the Great War* (New York: Palgrave Macmillian, 2002), 9–10.

8. Grayzel, *Women and the First World War*, 56–62; Allison Fell, "Female War Icons," *L'Homme* 29, no. 3: 35–53.

9. EG, *RA*, 232–233; Margaret Darrow, *French Women and the First World War* (New York University Press, 2001); Joanna Shearer, "Dressing Up for War," *Minerva* 1, no. 2 (2008): 66–76; Judith Wishnia,"Women and the Anti-War Movement in World War I," *Proceedings of the Western Society for French History* (1989): 339–344.

10. "EG Says War Means End of Snobs," *Pittsburgh Press*, June 5, 1917.

11. McEwen and Fisken, eds., *War, Journalism, and History*, 5.

12. Caroline Edy, *The Woman War Correspondent, the U.S. Military, and the Press* (Lanham, MD: Lexington Books, 2016), 39. Martin Pugh, *Women and the Women's Movement in Britain since 1914*, 3rd ed. (London: Palgrave, 2015). "A Special Letter from Elinor Glyn on Her Series for the Atlanta Constitution," *Atlanta Constitution*, May 5, 1918. "Nell Glyn Writes of Visit to Western Front; Famous Author of 'Three Weeks' Describes Conditions in Noyons, Chauny and Other Places Recently Recaptured by the Germans," *Idaho Daily Statesman*, May 5, 1918, 1. "In the Track of the Barbarous Hun," *Atlanta Constitution*, May 12, 1918.

13. "Woman Paints Pen Pictures of Hun Horror," *Detroit Free Press*, May 5, 1918, C1; "Sinister Trail of Germans Followed by Elinor Glyn," *San Francisco Chronicle*, May 5, 1918, N5. "Glimpses of a German-Made Hell," *Atlanta Constitution*, May 5, 1918, 24. "Elinor Glyn Tells of Outrages against Womanhood," *San Francisco Chronicle*, May 12, 1918, NB4. "Elinor Glyn at the Front Tells How It Seems to Be under Fire," *Boston Globe*, May 26, 1918, 45. "In the Track of the Barbarous Hun." "Where Battle and Outrage Swept Along, Elinor Glyn Writes of German Outrages in France," *Detroit Free Press*, May 12, 1912, E4. EG, *RA*, 237.

14. "Where Battle and Outrage Swept Along."

15. EG, *RA*, 240. EG to William Randolph Hearst, n.d., "On behalf of 'peasants' in war-torn France, (1917)," Box 7, Reading.

16. "Elinor Glyn Tells of Horrors Where Germans Have Passed," *Boston Globe*, June 2, 1918, 47.

17. EG, *RA*, 240; LDG, *DI*, 266, 274; "Fashion Display at Palace: Lady Duff-Gordon Appears for a War Charity," *NYT*, December 4, 1917, 11; "Lady Duff-Gordon to Make Debut in Fashion Sketch," *Boston Herald*, December 16, 1917. "Lady Duff Gordon, Le Grande Dame of Fashion, to Present Her Regal Fashion Revue This Week," *Buffalo Times*, February 24, 1918, 345; "Fleurette's Dream at Peronne," *Baltimore Evening Sun*, May 1, 1918, 8.

18. *Wood v. Lucy, Lady Duff-Gordon*, N.Y.S. 576 and 222 N.Y. 88, 118 N.E. 214 (1917); Marlis Schweitzer, "Patriotic Acts of Consumption," *Theatre Journal* 60, no. 4 (2008): 585–608.

19. EG, *RA*, 242.

20. EG to EK, May 28, 1918.

21. EG, "Speech made to American soldiers of the S.O.S. at Nevers, on 27 June 1918," COR.

22. EG, "America Has Revived the Spirit of France," *Shanghai Times*, October 30, 1918; EG, "Despite Bestial Hun Brutality France Is Enjoying New Spirit Due to Arrival of the Americans, says Novelist Elinor Glyn," *NYT*, September 17, 1918; EG, "France Wrecked by German Deviltry; Bestial Hun Brutality Contrasted with Wonderful Spirit of America," *Atlanta Constitution*, September 19, 1918.

23. EG, *RA*, 257–258.

24. "CC" to EG, August 7, 1917, "Buckingham Palace," Box 6, Reading.
25. Pugh, *Women and the Women's Movement in Britain*, 63–78; Grayzel, *Women and the First World War*, 27–29, 43–56, 101–105; Thom, *Nice Girls and Rude Girls*, 17–20.
26. MacMillan, *Paris, 1919*, 157.
27. EG, "When Our Men Come Home," *Cosmopolitan*, September 1918, 50–51, 114–115.
28. MacMillan, *Paris, 1919*, 145–146.
29. Gilmour, *Imperial Statesman*, 491, 528, 575–578, 594–595.
30. George Allardice Riddell Baron Riddell, *Lord Riddell's Intimate Diary of the Peace Conference and After, 1918–1923* (London: Reynal & Hitchcock, 1933), 92–93.
31. Sir William Orpen, *An Onlooker in France, 1917–1919* (London: Williams and Norgate, 1921), 115.
32. EG, *RA*, 258.
33. Riddell, *Lord Riddell's Intimate Diary*. Wilson quoted in MacMillan, *Paris, 1919*, 474–75.
34. Cyril Bainbridge, *The News of the World Story* (New York: Harper Collins, 2010), 55–56.
35. EG, "No Prussian Pride; Five Plebian Men Sign for Germany," *News of the World*, June 28, 1919. Riddell had the article in the *World* and another EG wrote in the *Ladies' Field* bound together as a special "Souvenir of the Signing of Peace at Versailles," from Lord Riddell to Mrs. Elinor Glyn, Box 13, Reading.
36. Frances Stevenson quoted in MacMillan, *Paris, 1919*, 476; EG, "Paris—A Letter to My Friend X," *Ladies' Field*, July 12, 1919.
37. EG, "No Prussian Pride."
38. Quoted in MacMillan, *Paris, 1919*, 491.
39. EG, "Paris—A Letter to My Friend X."
40. "Elinor Glyn Creates Sensation in Cairo," *Washington Post*, April 18, 1920, 41.
41. Letter from Alfred Milner to EG, reproduced in EG, *RA*, 278.
42. See EG, *RA*; EG, "Mrs. Elinor Glyn in Spain," *Ladies' Field*, May 29, 1920; EG, "The Visit to Spain" (1920), unpublished essay that she later funneled into her book, Box 11, Reading.
43. EG, *RA*, 242.
44. "E.G. and Famous Players Film Co. Copy of Agreement and correspondence regarding E.G.'s visit to American in October 1920 and payment for the visit," Box 25, Reading. According to the CPI, see https://www.measuringworth.com/. On her dressmaker, Ann Morgan, see Marian Fowler, *The Way She Looks Tonight: Five Women of Style* (Toronto: Random House Canada, 1997), 99–101.
45. EG, *RA*, 293–293.

CHAPTER 11: AT THE HOLLYWOOD HOTEL

1. Quoted in A. Scott Berg, *Goldwyn: A Biography* (New York: Knopf, 1989), 105.
2. Cecil Blount DeMille, *The Autobiography of Cecil B. DeMille* (New York: Garland, 1959), 153; Jesse L. Lasky, *I Blow My Own Horn* (New York: Doubleday, 1957), 141.
3. Lasky, *I Blow My Own Horn*, 141; Gloria Swanson, *Swanson on Swanson: An Autobiography* (New York: Random House, 1980), 154.
4. Isabel Ross, "Wives Too Egotistic; EG on Problems that Confront the Women of This Country," *NYT*, November 7, 1920.
5. EG, *RA*, 293–294.
6. Ross, "Wives Too Egotistic."
7. Eileen Bowser, *The Transformation of Cinema, 1907–1915* (Berkeley: University of California Press, 1990); David Bordwell, Janet Staiger, and Kristin Thompson, *The Classical Hollywood Cinema: Film Style and Mode of Production to 1960* (New York: Columbia University Press, 1985); Charles Musser, *Before the Nickelodeon* (Berkeley: University of California Press, 1991).
8. Adolph Zukor, with Dale Kramer, *The Public Is Never Wrong: The Autobiography of Adolph Zukor* (New York: Putnam, 1953), 59. In 1922, the first year for which reliable

statistics exist, the industry sold 40 million tickets every week to a population of 100 million. By the time EG left Los Angeles in 1928, 64 million tickets changed hands each week, Richard Koszarski, *An Evening's Entertainment: The Age of the Silent Picture, 1918–1928* (Berkeley: University of California Press, 1994), 26; Shelley Stamp, *Movie-Struck Girls: Women and Motion Picture Culture after the Nickelodeon* (Princeton, NJ: Princeton University Press, 2000), 3–45.

9. Richard deCordova, *Picture Personalities: The Emergence of the Star System in America* (Champagne: University of Illinois Press, 1990), 72; Zukor, *The Public Is Never Wrong*, 4.

10. The claim that the movies were the fourth or fifth largest industry in the U.S.A. became widespread after WWI. See *Exhibitors Herald*, October 22, 1921, 41; "The 'Movie' as an Industry," *Literary Digest*, October 16, 1921, 55; "The Jazzy, Money-Mad Spot Where Movies Are Made," *Literary Digest*, March 6, 1921, 71–72. Including theaters, it was close to the mark, see Richard Maltby and Ian Craven, *Hollywood Cinema* (Oxford: Blackwell, 1995), 60; Ruth Vasey, *The World According to Hollywood, 1918–1939* (Madison: University of Wisconsin Press, 1997), 14–15.

11. "Sex O'Clock in America," *Current Opinion* 55 (August 1913): 113–114; Agnes Repplier, "The Repeal of Reticence," *Atlantic Monthly* 113 (March 1914): 297–304. Susan Glenn, *Female Spectacle: The Theatrical Roots of Modern Feminism* (Cambridge, MA: Harvard University Press, 2000); Kathy Peiss, *Cheap Amusements: Working Women and Leisure in Turn-of-the-Century New York* (Philadelphia: Temple University Press, 1986); Jacqueline Najuma Stewart, *Migrating the Movies: Cinema and Black Urban Modernity* (Berkeley: University of California Press, 2005); Saidiya Hartman, *Wayward Lives, Beautiful Experiments: Intimate Histories of Riotous Black Girls, Troublesome Women, and Queer Radicals* (New York: W. W. Norton, 2021).

12. Charles Pettijohn quoted in *Wid's Year Book 1920* (New York: Wid's Films), 333, 217–225. The five states with censorship boards were Kansas, Maryland, Pennsylvania, Ohio, and New York. The rate of premarital intercourse jumped to almost 50 percent of women coming of age, see D'Emilio and Freedman, *Intimate Matters*, 246; Daniel Scott and Michael Hindus, "Premarital Pregnancy in America," *Journal of Interdisciplinary History* 5, no. 4 (1975): 537–70. The term "sex picture" came into use as a category for reformers after the war. See Ellis Paxson Oberholtzer, PhD, *The Morals of the Movie: For Six Years a Member of the Pennsylvania State Board of Censors* (Philadelphia: The Penn Publishing Company, 1922), ch 11, "Sex Pictures," 31–52; Zukor, *The Public Is Never Wrong*, 202. Between 1919 and 1921, state censorship boards rejected these films at a rate of three times that of other kinds of pictures, see *Wid's Year Book 1921*, 217; William H. Short, *A Generation of Motion Pictures* (New York: National Committee for the Study of Social Values in Motion Pictures, 1978 [1928]), 13, Censorship Collection, MHL; *Report of the Pennsylvania State Board of Censors* (Philadelphia: J.L.L. Kuhn, 1919).

13. Oberholtzer, *The Morals of the Movie*, 31. "We shall have a care for what costs three dollars on Broadway, but infinitely more concern for what is simultaneously shown for a few cents in a thousand places . . . in all parts of the land," he explained. "Reform Agitation Extends to all Parts of the Country," *Exhibitors Herald*, February 12, 1921, 42.

14. Frances Marion, *Off with Their Heads? A Serio-Comic Tale of Hollywood* (New York: Macmillan, 1972), 64–68. On her early career, see Cari Beauchamp, *Without Lying Down: Frances Marion and the Powerful Women of Early Hollywood* (Berkeley: University of California Press, 1997).

15. F. Scott Fitzgerald, *This Side of Paradise* (New York: Vintage Books, 2009 [1920]), 58, 163; "What a 'Flapper Novelist' Thinks of His Wife," *Courier-Journal* (Louisville), September 30, 1923; Paula Fass, *The Beautiful and the Damned: American Youth in the 1920s* (New York: Oxford University Press, 1979); Catherine Gourley, *Flappers and the New American Women* (New York: Twenty-First Century Books, 2008); Judith Mackrell, *Flappers: Six Women of a Dangerous Generation* (New York: Farrar, Straus and Giroux, 2013).

16. Marion, *Off with Their Heads*, 65; "OLIVE THOMAS' DEATH INQUIRY BARES ORGIES," *San Francisco Chronicle*, September 12, 1920, 1. *The Flapper* (Selznick/ Select, 1920).

17. Grace Kingsley, "When Hollywood Was a Pasture," *Photoplay*, June 1927, 140.

18. On L.A.'s early myth-making, see William Deverell, *Whitewashed Adobe: The Rise of Los Angeles and the Remaking of Its Mexican Past* (Berkeley: University of California Press, 2005); Kevin Starr, *Inventing the Dream: California through the Progressive Era* (New York: Oxford University Press, 1985), 54–74, 75–98; Carey McWilliams, *Southern California Country: An Island on the Land* (New York: Solan and Perce, 1946); David Fine, *Imagining Los Angeles, A City in Fiction* (Albuquerque: University of New Mexico Press, 2000); Hilary Hallett, "Based on a True Story: New Western Women and the Birth of Hollywood," *Pacific Historical Review* 80, no. 2 (May 2011): 177–185.

19. Berg, *Goldwyn*, 38–78; Mark Garrett Cooper, *Universal Women: Filmmaking and Institutional Change in Early Hollywood* (Urbana: University of Illinois Press, 2010).

20. Six thousand new building permits changed hands in 1918; when the building boom peaked five years later the number had soared to 62,548. See Kevin Starr, *Material Dreams: Southern California through the 1920s* (New York: Oxford University Press, 1990), 69–70. Marion, *Off with Their Heads*, 6.

21. Starr, *Material Dreams*, 98; Marion, *Off with Their Heads*, 2; Charles Chaplin, *My Autobiography* (New York: Simon & Schuster, 1964), 202.

22. EG to EK, October 6, 1921, COR; EG, *RA*, 293–294.

23. "The Marrying of Elinor Glyn's Two Daughters," *The Sketch*, March 3, 1921, 322. See also "Edward Davson: Death Notice," *Times* (London), August 9, 1937.

24. EG to EK, October 6, 1921.

25. Chaplin, *My Autobiography*, 202; Vidor quoted in Berg, *Goldwyn*, 105; John Baxter, *The Hollywood Exiles* (New York: Taplinger Publishing, 1976), 93–94.

26. Goldwyn, *Behind the Screen*, 235–263. Louella Parsons, "Eminent Authors Active," July 23, 1919, Louella Parsons Scrapbook #3, MHL. Another was Gertrude Atherton.

27. Goldwyn, *Behind the Screen*, 235–36; Lasky, *I Blow My Own Horn*, 141.

28. "Sir Gilbert Parker and His Studio Activity," *Exhibitors Herald*, January 15, 1921, 1940; EG, *RA*, 294; Lasky, *I Blow My Own Horn*, 141.

29. DeMille, *Autobiography*, 231; EG, *RA*, 295; Charles Higham, *Cecil B. DeMille* (New York: Scribner, 1973), 110.

30. Goldwyn, *Behind the Screen*, 239; Lasky, *I Blow My Own Horn*, 142–143; Swanson, *Swanson on Swanson*, 9; EG to EK, Jan. 29, 1922, COR.

31. Description of her rooms from Chaplin, *My Autobiography*, 202–203; Swanson, *Swanson on Swanson*, 159–160; Delight Evans, "Tiger Skins and Temperament: EG Reaches America," *Photoplay*, January 1921, 70, 120.

32. Swanson, *Swanson on Swanson*, 161.

33. Swanson, *Swanson on Swanson*, 63; Mack Sennett and Cameron Shipp, *King of Comedy* (New York: Doubleday, 1954), 171–173.

34. See the prologue, endnote 2, for a good place to start.

35. Louella Parsons, "In and Out of Focus: Josephine Quirk; She Is Following Horace Greeley's Advice and Going West," November 21, 1920, Louella Parsons Scrapbook #4, MHL; Hallett, "Based on a True Story"; Samantha Barbas, *The First Lady of Hollywood: A Biography of Louella Parsons* (Berkeley: University of California Press, 2006).

36. Louella Parsons, "Jeannie McPherson Signs Contract with DeMille," June 26, 1920, Louella Parsons Scrapbook #4, MHL; Lasky to DeMille, January 6, 1917, quoted in Sumiko Higashi, "The New Woman and Consumer Culture," in *A Feminist Reader in Early Cinema*, ed. Jennifer Bean and Diane Negra (Durham: Duke University Press, 2002), 301; Lizzie Franke, *Script Girls* (London: British Film Institute, 1994), 13–15.

37. Swanson, *Swanson on Swanson*, 166.

38. EG, *RA*, 299; Goldwyn, *Behind the Screen*, 247; Swanson, *Swanson on Swanson*, 159–60.

39. "Elinor—The Tiger," *Photoplay*, June 1921, 24.

40. EG, *RA*, 155–156, 305–307; Ferenc Szasz, "'New Thought' and the American West," *Journal of the West* 23, no. 1 (January 1984): 83–90.
41. Swanson, *Swanson on Swanson*, 160.
42. Gloria Swanson, "The Confessions of a Modern Woman: The Mysterious Star's Startling Philosophy," *Photoplay*, February 1922, 20–21. See also Faith Service, "A Sunday Afternoon with Mrs. Falaise: The Most Human Story Ever Written about Gloria Swanson (April 1927): 30; "Gloria Swanson Greets You from Her Drawing Room Just Before Leaving Paris," *Motion Picture Magazine*, April 1925, 59; "A Glorified Gloria," *Motion Picture Magazine*, September 1924, 26.
43. Swanson, *Swanson on Swanson*, 160.
44. EG, *RA*, 295.
45. Waitress quoted in Goldwyn, *Behind the Screen*, 249; Anita Loos, *A Girl Like I* (New York: Viking Press, 1963), 118–119.
46. Goldwyn, *Behind the Screen*, 239–240, 249; Chaplin, *My Autobiography*, 202.
47. EG to Mr. Massie, December 20, 1920, Box 32, Reading.
48. EG to Massie, Reading.
49. Anthony Glyn, *Elinor Glyn*; *Exhibitors Herald*, August 6, 1921. William Nicoll, "Williams, Dame Juliet Evangeline Rhys," *Oxford Dictionary of National Biography*.
50. EG to Massie, Reading.
51. Evans, "Tiger Skins and Temperament"; EG, "In Filmdom's Boudoir; The Sister of 'Lucile' Inspects Our Actresses" *Photoplay* (March 1921): 29; EG, *RA*, 139, 299; Lasky, *I Blow My Own Horn*, 142.
52. "What They Think about Marriage: The Stars Reply to Elinor Glyn's Charge," *Photoplay*, April 1921, 20–22.
53. Swanson, *Swanson on Swanson*, 161.
54. Quoted in Goldwyn, *Behind the Screen*, 246.
55. EG to EK, December 18, 1921, COR; EG, *RA*, 294.
56. EG, *RA*, 296–297; Lasky, *I Blow My Own Horn*, 142.
57. Goldwyn, *Behind the Screen*, 243; Edward Knoblock quoted in Selina Hastings, *The Secret Lives of Somerset Maugham: A Biography* (New York: Arcade Publishing, 2009), 254.
58. *Exhibitors Herald*, July 9, 1921; *Exhibitors Herald*, July 29, 1921; *Exhibitors Herald*, August 6, 1921.
59. "Sex and the Photoplay," *Motion Picture Magazine*, June 1921, 21. By 1920, the six leading fan magazines had circulations of almost a half a million each, Tino Balio, *Grand Designs: Hollywood as Modern Business Enterprise, 1930–1939* (Berkeley: University of California Press, 1995), 170. See Hallett, *Go West, Young Woman*, 69–102.
60. *The Great Moment* (Paramount 1921); "'The Great Moment' Hit at Alhambra," *Los Angeles Daily Times*, October 5, 1921; "The Great Moment," *Exhibitors Herald*, August 6, 1921. *Exhibitors* noted its success with the ladies, see March 11, 1922; March 25, 1922; April 1, 1922; April 15, 1921; August 6, 1921.
61. EG to EK, August 8, 1921, COR; Edwin Schallert, "The Great Moment," *LAT*, August 8, 1921.
62. Robert Sherwood, "The Silent Drama," *LIFE*, August 25, 1921.

CHAPTER 12: BABYLON OR BOHEMIA?

1. Mary Winship, "Oh, Hollywood! A Ramble in Bohemia," *Photoplay*, May 1921, 20–22, 112.
2. Swanson, *Swanson on Swanson*, 103; EG to EK, February 19, 1922, "Ambassador," COR.
3. Lizzie Franke, *Script Girls*, 5–8; Vincent Barnett, "The Novelist as Hollywood Star: Author Royalties and Studio Income in the 1920s," *Film History* 20 (2008): 280–293; Morey, "Elinor Glyn as Hollywood Labourer."
4. See also Hallett, *Go West, Young Women*, ch. 3 "Hollywood Bohemia"; Jerrold Seigel, *Bohemian Paris: Culture, Politics, and the Boundaries of Bourgeois Life, 1830–1930*

(Baltimore: Johns Hopkins Press, 1999); Edward Soja, *Thirdspace: Journeys to Los Angeles and Other Real and Imagined Spaces* (Malden, MA: Wiley-Blackwell, 1996), 3, 77, 97–98; Colin Campbell, "Understanding Traditional and Modern Practices of Consumption," in *Consumption and the World of Goods*, ed. John Brewer and Roy Porter (New York: Routledge, 1993), 40–57.

5. John Emerson and Anita Loos, *Breaking Into the Movies* (New York: James McCann Co., 1921); Pearl Gaddis, "He, She Or It: When the Pretty Ladies of the Screen Don Breeches and the Men Don Skirts," *Motion Picture World* 13, no. 4 (1917), 27–28; for "clannish," see Winship, "Oh, Hollywood!," 111; for "on the edge," see "The Jazzy, Money-Mad Spot," 71. Valeria Belletti to Irma Prina, all in Cari Beauchamp, ed., *Adventures of a Hollywood Secretary: Her Private Letters from Inside the Studios of the 1920s* (Berkeley: University of California Press, 2006), 119, 34, 19, 52, 24–25, 167, 32–33, 44–47, 69–70.

6. Swanson, *Swanson on Swanson*, 170.

7. Swanson, *Swanson on Swanson*, 164; Diana Manners Cooper, *The Light of Common Day* (New York: Random House, 1959), 281–284; JRW to TM, February 24, 1925, Box 44, Reading.

8. On how anti-Semitism shaped censorship drives and the larger discourse surrounding the Hollywood's emergence, see Hallett, *Go West, Young Woman*, 154–179. On the revival of the KKK and shifts in nativism, see John Higham, *Strangers in the Land: Patterns of American Nativism* (New Brunswick, NJ: Rutgers University Press, 1955); Mae Ngai, *Impossible Subjects: Illegal Aliens and the Making of Modern America* (Princeton, NJ: Princeton University Press, 2004); Nancy MacLean, *Behind the Mask of Chivalry: The Making of the Second Ku Klux Klan* (New York: Oxford University Press, 1995); Matthew Frye Jacobson, *Whiteness of a Different Color: European Immigrants and the Alchemy of Race* (Cambridge, MA: Harvard University Press, 1998).

9. Klaus Kreimeir, *The UFA Story: A History of Germany's Greatest Film Company, 1918–1945* (Berkeley: University of California Press, 1992), 145–155; John Trumpbour, *Selling Hollywood to the World: U.S. and European Struggles for Mastery of the Global Film Industry* (Cambridge, MA: Cambridge University Press, 207), iv., 1–62.

10. Harry Carr, "The Fight for the Crown—the Fight for Supremacy between Gloria and Pola," *Motion Picture Magazine*, September 1925, 34–35; Kristin Thompson, *Herr Lubitsch Goes to Hollywood: German and American Film After World War I* (Amsterdam University Press, 2005), 13, 20–22, 43–46, 60–63.

11. Marion, *Off with Their Heads*, 83–84. Key works on Valentino include Emily Leider, *Dark Lover: The Life and Death of Rudolph Valentino* (New York: Farrar, Straus and Giroux, 2003); Miriam Hansen, *Babel and Babylon: Spectatorship in American Silent Film* (Cambridge, MA: Harvard University Press, 1991); Gaylyn Studlar, *This Mad Masquerade: Stardom and Masculinity in the Jazz Age* (New York: Columbia University Press, 1996), 150–198.

12. "We Discover Who Discovered Valentino; Gladys Hall and Adele Whitely Fletcher Pose as Twentieth Century Columbuses," *Motion Picture Magazine*, June 1923, 20; Joan Jordan, "Confessions of a Modern Don Juan," *Photoplay*, May 1921, 46; Rudolph Valentino, "Women and Love," *Photoplay*, March 1922, 48, 106; Gordon Gassaway, "The Erstwhile Landscape Gardner: Rudolph Valentino's Career," *Motion Picture Magazine*, July 1921, 40–41; "The Vogue of Valentino," *Motion Picture Magazine*, February 1923, 27; "Four Horsemen," *Baltimore Sun*, October 22, 1920; Lasky, *I Blow My Own Horn*; Leider, *Dark Lover*, 171, 188; Swanson, *Swanson on Swanson*, 158. The three-year contract still paid him $500 a week; Swanson earned $2,500 a week that year.

13. All quotes from *The Sheik* (Famous Players, 1921). On Hull, see Hipsky, *Modernism and the Popular Romance*,175–181, 286–288; Melman, *Women and the Popular Imagination*, 45–50.

14. Cartland, *I Search for Rainbows*, 194–195; "The Motion Picture Autobiographies,"

Cases 9 and Case 1 compiled by Herbert Blumer, in Garth Jowett, Ian Jarvie, and Kathryn Fuller, eds., *Children and the Movies: Media Influence and the Payne Fund Controversy* (Cambridge: Cambridge University Press, 1996), 245, 275–276; "The Sheik," *Variety*, November 11, 1921, 37; "What the Picture Did for Me," *Exhibitors Herald*, April 8, 1922.

15. "*Beyond the Rocks* agreement between E.G. and Famous Players Lasky (1921)," Box 25, Reading.
16. Eileen Whitfield, *Pickford: The Woman Who Made Hollywood* (Lexington: University of Kentucky, 1997), 190–193.
17. "Greeted Like Royalty," *Marlborough Express*, July 9, 1920; Whitfield, *Pickford*, 200–210.
18. Chaplin quoted in Whitfield, *Pickford*, 219. On the Pickford and Fairbanks marriage, see Lary May, *Screening Out the Past: The Birth of Mass Culture and the Motion Picture Industry* (Oxford: Oxford University Press, 1983).
19. Whitfield, *Pickford*, 152–160; Beauchamp, *Without Lying Down*, 221–225.
20. EG regularly referred to Pickford in her letters as "my" or "darling" Mary. EG to EK, October 11, n.d., "Ambassador," COR Chaplin, *My Autobiography*, 223–224; "Mary Pickford Core Clipping File," MHL.
21. Fairbanks quoted in Goldwyn, *Behind the Screen*, 237.
22. Chaplin, *My Autobiography*, 307, 317–319, EG, *RA*, 301–303; EG to EK, February 19, 1922[?], "Ambassador," COR.
23. EG to EK, no date, "Ambassador," COR.
24. "S.F. Booze Party Kills Young Actress," *San Francisco Examiner*, September 10, 1921. "Arbuckle Is Charged with Murder of Girl: Actress' Dying Words Cause Star's Arrest," *San Francisco Examiner*, September 11, 1921. See also "Nurse Relates Last Words of Dying Actress," *New York American*, September 12, 1921.
25. For more on how the Arbuckle-Rappe event became scandalous because of pre-existing concerns about Hollywood's liberalizing effect on sexual politics, see Hallett, *Go West, Young Women*, 180–212.
26. Marion, *Off with Their Heads*, 139–140; Nasaw, *Chief*, 67–125.
27. Nasaw, *Chief*, 312–314; "Fatty's Orgy," *New York American*, September 17, 1921.
28. "Victim of Orgy," *New York American*, September 14, 1921, 3. "Hope for Fame Lured Actress to Her Death," *New York American*, September 14, 1921, 3. See also "Another Girl Was Attacked at Fatal Arbuckle Party," *Brooklyn Daily Eagle*, September 13, 1921, 1; "Falstaff of the Movies and Victim of the 'Party,'" *Chicago Herald Examiner*, September 14, 2, 1921. Annie Laurie, "Old Rules for Girls Supplanted by New Now: What's a Little Pitch among Friends?" *San Francisco American*, September 14, 1921, 2; Winifred Black, "Orgy Menace Is Grave, Says Winifred Black," *New York American* September 15, 1921, 2; "Rappe Death Held as Warning to Girls; God Is Speaking through Lips of the Dead Actress, says Dr. L. Gordon," *San Francisco Examiner*, September 19, 1921, 3.
29. Winship, "Oh, Hollywood!," 20, 21.
30. Suzette Booth, "Breaking into the Movies," *Motion Picture Magazine*, June 1917, 76. In 1920, the city's sex ratio was 97.8 to 100, See Warren S. Thompson, *Growth and Changes in California's Population* (Los Angeles: The Haynes Foundation, 1955), 16–17, 48–51, 88–89; Frank L. Beach, "The Effects of Westward Movement on California's Development, 1900–1920," *International Migration Review* 3 (1969): 25.
31. EG, *Elinor Glyn System of Writing* (New York: The Author's Press, 1922). EG to EK, September [?], 1921, Olympic, COR.
32. "Elinor Glyn Asks: What's the Matter with You American Women?" *Cosmopolitan*, November 1920; "What's the Matter with You American Parents? Asks Elinor Glyn," *Cosmopolitan*, December 1920; "Elinor Glyn Says—You Americans Are Making Beasts of Yourselves," *Cosmopolitan*, January 1922.
33. Adela Rogers St. Johns, *The Honeycomb* (New York: Doubleday, 1969), 17–19.
34. EG to EK, February 19, 1922, "Ambassador"; EG to EK, March 23, 1922 "Ambassador," COR.

35. EG to EK, August 8, "Hollywood," 1921, COR. EG, *System of Writing*, vol. 2, 195, vol. 3, 356. On the pioneering nature of this cross-media emphasis, see Barnett and Weedon, *Elinor Glyn*, 182–184.

36. TM to JRW, May 29, 1924, Box //, Reading.

37. JRW to TM, July 20, 1921; Massie Co. to JRW, July 18, 1921, Box 24, Reading.

38. TM to EG, August 3, 1921; TM to JRW, August 3, 1921, Box 24, Reading.

39. EG to EK, October 6[?], 1921, COR.

40. EG to EK, October 6[?], 1921, COR. Later she wrote, "I do hope they won't have any more for a couple of years," EG to EK, February 19, 1922, "Ambassador," COR.

41. "Olympic Leads Seven Departing Lines," *NYT*, September 25, 1921. EG to EK, October 6, 1921, COR; Charles Maland, *Chaplin and American Culture* (Princeton, NJ: Princeton University Press, 1989), 60–70.

42. D. J. Taylor, *Bright Young People: The Lost Generation of London's Jazz Age* (New York: Farrar, Straus and Giroux, 2007); Mary McAuliffe, *When Paris Sizzled* (Lanham: Rowman & Littlefield, 2016).

43. Sushila Anand, *Daisy: The Life and Loves of the Countess of Warwick* (Bloomington: University of Illinois Press, 2008), 189–248. Likely after this visit, Elinor mentioned that she was going "to ask Hearst at a good moment to let her write again in his papers—she could live on this without Lucile," EG to EK, October 11, n.d., "Ambassador," COR.

44. EG to EK, October 12[?], 1921, COR.

45. Mayer quoted in Berg, *Goldwyn*, 106. "Society Leaders' Millions to Back Better Pictures," *Variety*, September 16, 1921, 1, 44. "Jewish Supremacy in Motion Picture World," *International Jew* 2, no. 134 (January 12, 1921). "Exhibitors Withdraw Arbuckle Comedies Awaiting Court Action on Murder Charges," *Moving Picture World*, September 24, 1921, 382; "Arbuckle Dragged Rappe Girl to Room, Woman Testifies," *NYT*, September 13, 1921; "Fatty Arbuckle Involved in Orgies in Los Angeles, Says Official," *San Francisco Chronicle* September 13, 1921; "Mistrial Results in Arbuckle Case, *Washington Post*, December 5, 1921.

46. "New Organization of Distributors and Producers Planned—Will Hays Offered Presidency," *Wid's Daily*, December 9, 1921, 1–2; "Says Hays Accepts," *Wid's Daily*, December 21, 1921, 1; "Hays Accepts Offer to Head Producer-Distributor Alliance," *Exhibitors Herald*, January 28, 1922.

47. William H. Hays, *The Memoirs of Hays* (New York: Doubleday, 1955), 359. Ellis Hawley, *The Great War and the Search for a Modern Order* (New York: St. Martin's Press, 1992), 44–49; Michael McGerr, *The Decline of Popular Politics* (New York: Oxford University Press, 1986), 169–171; John Braeman, "American Politics in the Age of Normalcy," 17–18, in *Calvin Coolidge and the Coolidge Era*, ed. John Earl Haynes (Washington, DC: Library of Congress, 1998); Hays, *Memoirs*, 326.

48. Gordon Gassaway, "The Altar of Alcohol: Elinor Glyn and Her Impression of Hollywood," *Motion Picture Magazine*, December 1921, 20; EG to EK, December 18, 1921 "Ambassador Hotel," COR.

49. "Elinor Glyn Rather Chary in Giving Memberships to Exclusive 'IT' Society," *LAT*, January 16, 1925.

50. Allen Cambell, "Bohemia in Los Angles," unpublished pamphlet, n.d., n.p., Huntington Library, San Marino.

51. EG, "Justice," *Motion Picture Magazine*, January 1922, 21.

52. EG, "Justice," *Motion Picture Magazine*, February 1922, 21. See also EG, "Justice," *Motion Picture Magazine*, March 1922, 21. David F. Musto, *The American Disease: The Origins of Narcotic Control* (New York: Oxford University Press, 1999), 54–68.

53. Judge quoted in Lynd and Lynd, *Middletown*, 114. Lisa McGirr, *The War on Alcohol: Prohibition and the Rise of the American State* (New York: Norton, 2015), 52–53, 95–100; Daniel Okrent, *Last Call: The Rise and Fall of Prohibition* (New York: Scribner, 2010), 13–16, 23–30, 197, 207–213; Mark Edward Lender and James Kirby Martin, *Drinking in America: A History* (New York: Simon & Schuster, 1982), 177–178, 653.

54. Variety, "Trouble," September 23, 1921; Kenneth Rose, "Los Angeles and Its Liquor Problem," *Southern California Quarterly* 69, no. 1 (1987): 60.

55. EG, *RA* 307. Homicide records have been kept continuously in L.A. since 1827, see Eric Monkkonen, "Homicide in LA, 1827–2002," *Journal of Interdisciplinary History* 36, no. 2 (2005): 167–183; Eric Monkkonen, "Homicide in New York, Los Angeles, and Chicago," *Journal of Criminal Law and Criminology* 92, no. 3 (2002): 809–822.

56. John Witte, *The Politics and Development of the Federal Income Tax* (Madison: University of Wisconsin Press, 1985), 88. Maximum tax rates fell from a wartime high of 77 to 24 percent; lower rates were set for capital gains, and excess profit taxes eliminated.

57. EG to EK, December 18, 1921, COR.

58. Russell Ball, "Mr. and Mrs.," *Motion Picture Magazine*, July 1923, 24; "The Valentinos," *Motion Picture Magazine*, August 1923, cover; "Mrs. Rudolph Valentino: A Woman of Many Talents," *Motion Picture Magazine*, September 1924, 45. Leider, *Dark Lover*, 22–23, 107–108, 184–187.

59. EG to EK, December/January 1921–1922, COR.

60. EG to EK, "Xmas Day, 1921," COR.

61. Swanson, *Swanson on Swanson*, 170–174.

62. *Beyond the Rocks* (Famous Players, 1922).

63. EG to EK, January 29, 1922, COR.

64. EG to EK, December 18, 1921, COR.

65. Valentino, "Women in Love," 106; Valentino's biographer agrees that Glyn likely ghost-wrote this for him, see Leider, *Dark Lover*, 191–195; EG, *RA*, 299–300.

66. Quoted in Whitfield, *Pickford*, 221; Dick Dorgan, "A Song of Hate," *Photoplay*, July 1922, 27. Dorgan was likely a pseudonym.

67. *San Francisco Chronicle*, February 6, 1922; "Movie Kings Act to Quiet Scandal," *Atlanta Constitution*, February 9, 1922.

68. William J. Mann, *Tinseltown: Murder, Morphine, and Madness at the Dawn of Hollywood* (New York: Harper, 2014), 4–8, 86–87, 111, 130, 173, 200, 240; William Randolph Hearst to Adolph Zukor, September 21, 1921, Zukor Correspondence, File 4, MHL.

69. Mann, *Tinseltown*, 251.

70. EG to EK, February 19, 1922, "Ambassador," COR.

CHAPTER 13: THE ELINOR GLYN TOUCH

1. Sennett and Shipp, *King of Comedy*, 217.

2. Loos, *A Girl Called I*, 119.

3. DeMille, *Autobiography*, 231.

4. EG to EK, February 19, 1922, COR. On these estates, see May, *Screening Out the Past*, 22, 44–53; Eve Golden, *John Gilbert: Last of the Silent Film Stars* (Lexington: University of Kentucky Press, 2013), 99–102.

5. EG to EK, no date [March 1923?], "Ambassador," COR.

6. EG, *Man and Maid* (New York: Lippincott, 2004 [1922]), 4.

7. Berg, *Goldwyn*, 103–108.

8. EG to EK, no date [March 1923?], "Ambassador," COR.

9. EG to EK, March 13, 1922, COR; "Sir Anthony Glyn," *NYT*, January 28, 1998.

10. "Acquit Arbuckle within 6 Minutes; Victim of Injustice Acquittal Not Enough," *Washington Post*, April 13, 1922; "Censors Here Will Not Bar Arbuckle Films," *Chicago Daily Tribune*, April 14, 1922; "Ban Put on Arbuckle: Hays Stops All Picture; Big Boss Makes First Move toward Cleaning Up Film Industry," *LAT*, April 19, 1922. Berg, *Goldwyn*, 103–109, 112; Mann, *Tinseltown*, 27.

11. Hays, *Memoirs*, 360–361.

12. Quoted in Leider, *Dark Lover*, 191, 196.

13. EG to EK, November 5, 1923, COR.

14. "Agreement between EG and Goldwyn Pictures regarding *Six Days*," Box 18, Reading.

She received $10,000 and had forty-five days to submit a synopsis that the studio could change.

15. Beverly Nichols, *The Unforgiving Minute: Some Confessions from Childhood to the Outbreak of the Second World War* (London: W. H. Auden, 1978), 195–196; Stuart Hansen, *From Silent Screen to Multi Screen* (Manchester: U of Manchester Press), 41–45; "Leslie Stuart's Scheme for Setting Up a British Film Company," Box 25, Reading, COR; Trumpbour, *Selling Hollywood to the World*, 60–66, 77–79, 92–4; Richard Maltby and Andrew Higson, eds., *"Film Europe" and "Film America": Cinema, Commerce, and Cultural Exchange, 1920–1939* (Ann Arbor: University of Michigan Press, 1999).

16. JRW to TM, March 8, 1924, Box 45, COR. See also Edmund Cook, Massie & Co. to JRW, July 18, 1921, Box 25, Reading.

17. Nicoll, "Williams, Dame Juliet Evangeline Rhys," *Oxford Dictionary of National Biography.*

18. TM to JRW, February 16, 1923, Box 25, Reading. She estimated Nell spent $1,200 a month in Los Angeles.

19. "Power of attorney given by EG to Lady Juliet Williams with regard to Agreement with Goldwyn Pictures to Film Three Weeks (1923)," Box 18, Reading.

20. EG, "Letters to X, No 1," Box, 24, Reading. She had written these letters previously from time to time, but now began to regularly.

21. EG, "Letters to X, No 1," Box, 24, Reading.

22. EG, *RA*, 312; "Letter to X; 73," Box 24, Reading.

23. "Draft Agree re: 'THREE WEEKS,'" n.d., Box 25, Reading.

24. EG, *RA*, 313–314.

25. EG to Lehr, May 8, 1923, Box 25, Reading.

26. Gladys Hall and Adele Whitely Fletcher, "We Interview Elinor Glyn and Discover Why She Wrote 'Three Weeks,'" *Motion Picture Magazine*, October 1923, 20–22.

27. Mary Winship, "The Tiger Queen," *Photoplay* (Jan. 1924), 45.

28. Hall and Fletcher, "We Interview Elinor Glyn," 20–22.

29. Hall and Fletcher, "We Interview Elinor Glyn," 20–22.

30. EG to EK, September 17, 1924, COR. This letter details these practices and her belief in New Thought's ability to stem aging.

31. Anthony Glyn, *Elinor Glyn*, 304. Family lore recalls Nell had a surgical treatment around this time so painful she needed her arms restrained while she slept for a week to prevent her from clawing at her face. Ann Japenga, "Face-Lift City: Palm Springs, California," *Health* 7 (March 1993): 46, 73; Sander Gilman, *Making the Body Beautiful: A Cultural History of Aesthetic Surgery* (Princeton, NJ: Princeton University Press, 1999).

32. Frederica Sagor Maas, *The Shocking Miss Pilgrim: A Writer in Early Hollywood* (Lexington: University of Kentucky Press, 2010), 62, 73–74, 84.

33. Maas, *Shocking Miss Pilgrim*, 17, 26–35.

34. EG to EK, no date, 1924, COR.

35. EG to EK, July 4, 1924, "Los Angeles," COR; Winship, "The Tiger Queen," 45.

36. EG to EK, July 30, 1924, COR; "Glyn and Glynne: Madame Elinor Picked Derek for the Role of Paul in 'Three Weeks' Only to Have Her Choice Vetoed," *Photoplay*, May 1924, 53, 223; Janet Reid, "Three Weeks: A Novelization of the Famous Elinor Glyn Novel," *Motion Picture Magazine*, April 1924, 26.

37. EG to EK, July 30, 1924 "Studio," COR. Gibbons quoted in Howard Gutner, *MGM Style: Cedric Gibbons and the Art of the Golden Age of Hollywood* (New York: Lyons Press, 2019), 52–53.

38. "The Girl on the Cover: Marion Davies," *Photoplay*, September 1926, 94; Nasaw, *Chief*, 348–9, 372; EG to EK, July 30, 1924, "Studio," COR.

39. Quoted in Nasaw, *Chief*, 343; EG to EK, August 14, 1924, COR.

40. EG to EK, August 14, 1924, COR.

41. "Screenplay by Carey Wilson, August 15, 1923," Box 9A, Reading.

42. *Six Days* (Goldwyn Picture, 1923); EG to EK, February 14, 1925, COR. She called *Love's Blindness* this too.

43. EG, *The Philosophy of Love* (New York: Author's Press, 1923), 47. "The Six Best Sellers," *New York Tribune*, November 25, 1923; *New York Herald*, "The Season's Best Sellers," June 21, 1925. By June of 1924, the *Retail Bookseller*—which aimed to compile actual counts of copies sold—listed it as among the top twelve nonfiction sellers for the first half of the year, see *New York Herald*, "The Season's Six Best Sellers," June 29, 1924.

44. Mark Vieira, *Irving Thalberg: Boy Wonder to Producer Prince* (Berkeley: University of California Press, 2010), 17–34; Marion, *Off with Their Heads*, 145–146;

45. Lenore Coffee quoted in Patrick McGilligan, ed., *Backstory: Interviews with Screenwriters from Hollywood's Golden Age* (Berkeley: University of California Press, 1986), 137; F. Scott Fitzgerald, Matthew Bruccoli, *The Love of the Last Tycoon: A Western* (Cambridge: Cambridge University Press, 2014 [1941]), 141. Fitzgerald modeled his movie producer hero on Thalberg.

46. Vieira, *Thalberg*, 18; Scott Eyman, *Lion of Hollywood: The Life and Legend of Louis B. Mayer* (New York: Simon & Schuster, 2005), 56.

47. Vieira, *Thalberg*, 142–143.

48. Cedric Gibbons to EG, December 8, 1923, Box 44, Reading; Will Cuppy, "Have a Heart," *New York Tribune*, September 30, 1923.

49. Ashburn to TM, March 19, 1924, Box 25, Reading.

50. "Agreement between EG and Irving Thalberg regarding forming an organization to make films (November 1923)," Box 44, Reading.

51. Ashburn to TM, March 19, 1924, Box 25, Reading. See the "Thalberg Contract," November 30, 1923, Box 44, Reading.

52. EG, "Letters to X," no. 60 (November 30, 1923), Box 24, Reading.

53. EG, "Letters to X" no. 62 (December 13, 1923), Box 24, Reading.

54. Ashburn to TM, March 19, 1924, Box 25, Reading. Letter contains a long description of meeting with EG.

55. TM to JRW, February 19, 1924; "Mrs. EG and Irving Thalberg Agreement Dated November 30, 1923, Opinion,"; "Notes on present position Re: Thalberg,"; TM to JRW, February 19, 1924, which discusses the importance of her relying upon "one man, and that man one who is an Anglo-Saxon," Box 44, Reading. See also JRW to TM, April 1, 1924, Box 45, Reading.

56. See for instance, "Jewry at the End of the War," *Nation*, May 4, 1921; James Quirk, "Oh, Henry!" *Photoplay*, June 1921, 44. For more on anti-Semitic stereotypes and their rise after WWI, see Albert S. Lindemann, *Anti-Semitism before the Holocaust* (Edinburgh Gate, UK: Pearson Education, 2000), ch. 4.

57. Mr. Medley, Society of Authors, to JRW, February 1, 1924.

58. TM to Ashburn, March 6, 1924, Box 25, Reading. TM made the family's position explicit to Ashburn: "I cannot see that under the contract he could be required to do much more than a literary agent, who markets an author's works and gets no more than 10 percent."

59. Ashburn to TM, March 19, 1924, Box 25, Reading.

60. Thalberg to EG, December 20, 1923, Box 44, Reading.

61. Thalberg to EG, January 6, 1924, Box 44, Reading.

62. Thalberg to EG, February 6, 1925, Box 44, Reading.

63. "Elinor Glyn Named Her as Queen," *Motion Picture Magazine*, February 1924, 59. On its box office, see Vieira, *Thalberg*, 37; Barnett and Weedon, *Elinor Glyn*, 123–125. Beaton quoted in Morey, "Elinor Glyn as Hollywood Laborer," 114.

64. On EG's illness, see JW to TM, February 24, 1924; RW to TM February 20, 1924, Box 44, Reading. For more details on the negotiations, see "Thalberg correspondence, 1923–1924," Box 44, Reading; Vincent L. Barnett, "Picturization Partners: EG and the Thalberg Contract Affair," *Film History* 19 (2007): 319–329. Our assessments differ.

65. RW to TM, February 25, 1924; TM to FR, February 25, 1924, Box 24, Reading.

66. "Elinor Glyn LTD. Memorandum and Articles of Association (1924)," Box 2, Reading.

67. Medley to JRW, February 1, 1924; Linklater to RW, February 25, 1924; EG to Medley, February 28, 1924, Box 44, Reading.
68. Reported on in Medley to EG, March 4, 1924, Box 44, Reading.
69. RW to TM, cables, February 8, February 9, 1924; Box 44, Reading.
70. TM to RW, March 1, 1924, Box 44, Reading. Nell was guaranteed a minimum $40,000 for each of the first two films, regardless of their box office, and then a royalty of 33.3 percent of the net profits minus the advance. She earned $300 per week for her role as supervisor and her advisers—her family—earned a flat fee of $2,500. The conditions for the third picture were left open. The full details can be found in "ELINOR GLYN LTD., Memorandum and Articles of Association, 1924," Box 2, Reading.
71. RW to EG, March 4, 1924, Box 44, Reading.
72. JRW to TM, Feb 28, 1924, Box 44; Kuhn, "The Trouble with Elinor Glyn," 28; British Board of Film Censors to Mr. S. W. Harris, Home Office, March 24, 1924, HO 45/200045.
73. Vieira, *Thalberg*, 30; Eyman, *Lion of Hollywood*, 111–117.
74. Thalberg to EG, February 27, 1924, Box 44, Reading.
75. Ashburn to TM, March 19, 1924, Box 25, Reading.

CHAPTER 14: FAMILY FORTUNES

1. JRW to TM, April 1, 1924, Box 45, Reading. JRW received $250 a week for her role as supervisor.
2. JRW to TM, April 1, 1924, Box 45, Reading.
3. Vieira, *Thalberg*, 38; Golden, *John Gilbert*, 97–99.
4. King Vidor, *A Tree Is a Tree* (New York: S. French, 1989), 107–110.
5. Golden, *Gilbert*, 104–105.
6. EG to EK, June 6, 1924, COR.
7. EG to EK, n.d., 1924, COR.
8. JRW to TM, April 17, 1924, Box 44, Reading.
9. RW to TM, May 25, 1925; RW to Mayer, May 24, 1925, Box 44, Reading.
10. Mayer to RW, June 2, 1924, Box 44, Reading.
11. RW to Mayer, June 3, 1924, Box 44, Reading.
12. Mayer to RW, June 4, 1924, Box 45, Reading.
13. RW to LB, June 4, 1924; RW to EG, June 24, 1924, Box 45, Reading.
14. EG to EK, August 19, 1924, COR. TM repeatedly reported to RW that EG was "entirely happy" and that MGM's lawyer Robert Rubin believed she was taking their advice not his. See TM to RW, June 3, 1924; Mayer to TM, June 25, 1924, Box 45, Reading.
15. EG to EK, August 19, 1924, COR. Katheen Drowne, Patrick Huber, Fitzhugh Mullan, *The 1920s* (Westport, CT: Greenwood Publishing, 2004), 85.
16. TM to JRW, July 10, 1924, Box 45, Reading.
17. TM to JRW, July 7, 1924, Box 45, Reading.
18. RW to TM, July 7, 1924; TM to Mayer, July 7, 1924. See also *EG Ltd. v. Louis B. Mayer Productions*, Box 45, Reading.
19. TM to RW, July 18, 1924, Box 45, Reading.
20. RW to TM, July 18; RW to TM, July 19, 1924, Box 45, Reading.
21. Schenck to RW, July 23, 1924, Box 45, Reading.
22. TM to RW, August 14, 1924, Box 45, Reading.
23. RW to TM, August 14, 1924, Box 45, Reading.
24. Frank Crane, "The Jew," *Current Opinion* (May 1921): 596; report quoted in Higham, *Strangers in the Land*, 309.
25. See "Trailing the New Anti-Semitism to Its Russian Lair," *Current Opinion* (April 1921); Henry Ford drew upon the *Protocols* for articles run in his *Dearborn Independent* and then republished them in four volumes as *The International Jew, the World's Foremost Problem* (Dearborn: Dearborn Publishing Co., 1920–1922), hereafter, "*The International Jew.*" His campaign emphasized the prominence of Jewish people in the

"cultural regions," see "Jewish Supremacy in Motion Picture World," (February 19, 1921) *International Jew*, vol. 2, 102. Neil Baldwin, *Henry Ford and the Jews: The Mass Production of Hate* (New York: Public Affairs, 2001); Albert Lee, *Henry Ford and the Jews* (New York: Stein and Day, 1980); Esther Webman, ed., *The Global Impact of the Protocols of Elders of Zion: A Century Old Myth* (New York: Routledge, 2011).

26. Eyman, *Lion of Hollywood*, 49, 63, 96, 152, 163, 335, 342–342; Vieira, *Thalberg*, 74, 218, 235, 264, 356.
27. EG to EK, August 8, 1921; EG to EK, July 26, 1924; EG to EK January 6, 1925, COR; Huxley and Conrad quoted in Baxter, *Hollywood Exiles*, 97.
28. TM to JRW, July 23, 1924; EG to TM, September 14, 1924, Box 45, Reading. Tom routinely wrote letters that were six to twelve pages long to the directors in this period and two extraordinarily long ones written immediately after meeting with Nell.
29. TM to JRW, July 23, 1924; EG to TM, September 14, 1924, Box 45, Reading.
30. TM to Rubin, June 12, 1924; TM to JRW, July 31, 1924, Box 45, Reading.
31. The trustees had also suggested *The Man and the Moment* as picture number two without telling the producers that a British film company had adapted it years before. Both actions explicitly violated their deal with MGM.
32. EG to TM & Director E. G. Ltd, September 14, 1924, Box 45, Reading.
33. EG to EK, n.d., "Ambassador," COR.
34. TM to RW, October 3, 1924, Box 45, Reading. They would substitute *Man and Maid* for the second picture using the same terms as before, but would negotiate over *The Reason Why* once the box office on the first two films came in. Schenck had negotiated $5,000 weeks earlier for the continuity.
35. JRW to TM, October 31, 1924, Box 45, Reading.
36. TM to RW, August 14, 1924, Box 45, Reading.
37. For a copy of the letter, see EG, "English Relations with America: The Influence of Film," Box 13, Reading. Michael Chanan, "State Protection of a Beleaguered Industry," in *British Cinema History*, ed. James Curran and Vincent Porter (London: Weidenfeld & Nicolson, 1983), 59–73.
38. EG to Directors EG Ltd., November 5, 1924, Box 45, Reading.
39. Vieira, *Thalberg*, 37–39.
40. Ad for Author's Press Series, "His Hour," *Photoplay*, May 1924, 13.
41. For the voluminous correspondence on the audits, see "*Three Weeks* (film) Agreements with Goldwyn Pictures and correspondence with Wales & Wales (1923–4)" Box 25; "His Hour: Audit on behalf of E.G. of the MGM accounts," Box, 4, Reading.
42. On UA's fortunes, see Peter Kramer et al., eds., *United Artists* (London: Routledge, 2020), 1–4. Nell wrote about the "scheme" to EK, February 14, 1924.
43. Whitfield, *Pickford*, 237–238; "Pickford Oral History Transcript: 2733–2743" Butler Library, Columbia University.
44. F. Scott Fitzgerald, *The Crack-Up* (New York: Charles Scribner's Sons, 1931), 87. EG to EK, August 14, 1924, COR.
45. Marion, *Off with Their Heads*, 136–137.
46. Brian Taves, *Thomas Ince: Hollywood's Independent Pioneer* (Lexington: University Press of Kentucky, 2012), 247–270.
47. "Death of Ince Brings Story of Rum Party," *New York Herald-Tribune*, December 11, 1934; "Thomas Ince Dies, Was Stricken aboard Yacht," *Chicago Daily Tribune*, November 20, 1924. These reports were the only ones to mention the location of the party aboard "Davies's yacht." The idea that Hearst shot Ince defies both common sense and all the known facts, see Nasaw, *Chief*, 344–345.
48. EG to EK, November 19, 1924, COR.
49. EG to EK, November 24, 1924, COR.
50. EG to EK, November 24, 1924, COR.
51. EG to EK, November 24, 1924, COR.
52. EG to EK, January 6, 1925, COR.
53. EG to EK, January 6, 1925, COR; Manners, *Light of Common Day*, 281–284.

54. EG to EK, February 14, 1925; EG to EK, April 26, 1925. Description of Wynn, TM to JRW, March 30, 1924, Box 45, Reading.

55. "FILM SET REAL MELTING POT," *LAT*, June 1, 1925.

56. On its box office, see Barnett and Weedon, *Elinor Glyn*, 115.

57. Rosalind Shaffer, "Give the Public What It Expects, Is EG's Aim," *Chicago Daily Tribune*, May 24, 1925.

58. "Elinor Glyn Introduces New Talent," *LAT*, June 15, 1925. On her effect on "girl stars," see Fowler, *The Way She Looks Tonight*, 97.

59. Rosalind Shaffer, "Give the Public What It Expects." TM also reported this, TM to JRW, October 5, 1925, Box 44, Reading.

60. EG to JRW, Feb 19, 1925, Box 44, Reading.

61. JRW to EG, Mar 4, 1925; RW to EG, 1925, Box 44, Reading.

62. EG to EG Ltd., February 19, 1925, Box 44, Reading.

63. JRW to TM, April 8, 1925; TM to JRW, March 30, 1925, Box 44, Reading.

64. TM to JRW, March 30, 1925; TM to JRW, April 10, 1925, Box 44, Reading.

65. RW to EG, October 17, 1925; Box 45, Reading.

66. "Elinor Glyn's Picture a Feast for the Eyes," *Chicago Daily Tribune*, November 24, 1925; "Elinor Glyn's Vivid and Stirring Love Story at the New Douglas," *New York Amsterdam News*, January 27, 1926; "'The Only Thing,' at the Capitol, Romantic Thriller, by Elinor Glyn," *New York Herald Tribune*, November 24, 1925; *The Only Thing* (MGM, 1925).

67. EG to EG Ltd., October 15, 1925; EG to EG Ltd., November 5, 1925, Box 44, Reading.

68. EG to EG Ltd., November 5, 1925, Box 44, Reading.

69. E.G. Ltd. Directors, November 11, 1925; EG to RW, November 17, 1925, Box 44, Reading. Whitfield, *Pickford*, 239–240; Peter Kramer, "One of the United Artists," in *United Artists*, 19–37.

70. EG to EK, February 14, 1925; "MGM regarding Love's Blindness (1925)," Box 20, Reading. Schenck wanted to orchestrate a partial merger with MGM to give UA a bigger financial base and pipeline to theaters. Schenck secured an enormous $50,000 advance and the same percentage of the profits recouped over that amount minus the production's costs.

71. EG to Chairman and Directors of EG Ltd., December 5 and December 18, 1925, Box 44, Reading.

72. JRW to TM, December 18, 1925; Bernard Merivale at Hughes Massie to E.G. Ltd., January 5, 1926; E.G. Ltd. to Merivale at Hughes Massie, December 18, 1925, Box 44, Reading.

73. EG mentioned this new trend in EG to EK, January 6, 1926; January 27, 1926; March 1926; COR.

CHAPTER 15: THE IT GIRL

1. "Elinor Glyn Rather Chary," *LAT*; "Elinor Glyn Hard Worker," *Washington Post*, December 26, 1926; "He's Consistent in His Taste," *LAT*, July 11, 1926; EG to EK, n.d., COR.

2. On the film's performance, see Barnett and Weedon, *Elinor Glyn*, 115. On the end of the relationship with MGM, see "Differ on Why She Quit," *LAT*, October 13, 1925.

3. "Elinor Glyn Play Again," *Austin American*, December 19, 1926.

4. Michael J. O'Neal, *America in the 1920s* (New York: Facts on File, 2006), 84. Lynn Dumenil, *Modern Temper: American Culture and Society in the 1920s* (New York: Hill and Wang, 1995), 140. Fredrick Lewis Allen, *Only Yesterday: An Informal History of the 1920s* (New York: Open Road, 2015); Roland Marchand, *Advertising the American Dream: Making Way for Modernity* (Berkeley: University of California Press, 1985).

5. Maltby, *Hollywood Cinema*, 34–63; Kramer, "One of the United Artists."

6. Quoted in Leider, *Dark Lover*, 365.

7. "Valentino—The Son of the Sheik," *Photoplay*, June 1926, 36.

8. "Pink Powder Puffs," *Chicago Tribune*, July 18, 1926; Valentino quoted in Leider, *Dark Lover*, 374–390.

9. Valentino quoted in Leider, *Dark Lover*, 381.

10. "EG Rather Chary," *LAT*.

11. De Courcy, *Viceroy's Daughters*, 108–110, 185; Eugene Brewster, "The Passing of Rudolph Valentino"; Faith Baldwin, "In Memoriam to Rudolph Valentino," both: *Motion Picture Magazine*, November 1926, 5, 47.

12. EG to EK, December 1925, COR; Golden, *Gilbert*, 151–154,

13. EG to EK, "1925," COR; de Courcy, *Viceroy's Daughters*, 108–111; EG, "In Filmdom's Boudoir," *Photoplay*, March 1921, 29; "Attributes of Ideal Man as Told by Elinor Glyn," *LAT*, March 14, 1926; Lasky, *I Blow My Own Horn*, 143; "Paramount Famous Lasky Corp. Regarding IT, Ritzy, and Red Hair," Box 20, Reading.

14. Louise Brooks in Kevin Brownlow, *Hollywood: The Pioneers* (New York: Knopf, 1979), 178–179.

15. "Clara Bow," *Photoplay*, September 1926, 84; David Stenn, *Clara Bow: Runnin' Wild* (New York: Cooper Square Press, 2000), 70–72.

16. EG, "In Defense of Clara Bow," Box 13, Reading. The article was never published, presumably because no one wanted to hear a defense.

17. Quoted in Stenn, *Clara Bow*, 82.

18. "Stage and Screen," *Hartford Courant*, August 10, 1926; Grace Kingsley, "Author on Screen," *LAT*, October 5, 1926.

19. F. Scott Fitzgerald, "Echoes of the Jazz Age," *Scribner's Magazine*, November 1931.

20. Zukor, *Public Is Never Wrong*, 245; F. Scott Fitzgerald, "A Patriotic Short," *Esquire*, December 1940. This was the twelfth of *The Pat Hobby Stories*. Pat Hobby is a Hollywood screenwriter that Fitzgerald used for seventeen stories in *Esquire* between January 1940 and May 1941.

21. "Sex Symbol of the Roaring 20s: Silent movies 'It' Girl Clara Bow Dies at 60," *Austin Statesman*, September 27, 1965; "My Life Story as Told to Adela Rogers St. Johns: Pt. 1," *Photoplay*, February 1928, 30–32, 106–108. Adela Rogers St. Johns, Hearst journalist turned "Hollywood's Mother Confessor," was likely the other person in Hollywood to try to mentor Bow, see Adela Rogers St. Johns, *Love, Laughter and Tears: My Hollywood Story* (New York: Doubleday, 1978), 218–228.

22. "My Life Story as Told to Adela Rogers St. Johns: Pt. 1."

23. Quoted in Stenn, *Clara Bow*, 18; Clara Bow, "My Life Story: Second Installment of a Touching Narrative as Told to Adela Rogers St. Johns, Pt. 2," *Photoplay*, 38–39, 11.

24. Quoted in Stenn, *Clara Bow*, 28–29. Although the term "sexual abuse" is clearly modern and Stenn's evidence is unclear, everyone remarked on her dysfunctional relationship with her father.

25. Liberty Theater manager quoted in *The Reel Journal*, July 10, 1926; *Time*, August 2, 1926. Few reliable statistics exist, but most commentators agree that the industry viewed women as its "ideal," most "fanatic" members between the 1920s and 1940s. My interest is this widespread perception. See Benjamin Hampton, *A History of the Movies: From Its Beginnings to 1931* (New York: Covici Friede, 1970 [1931]), 224–226; Leo Rosten, *Hollywood: The Movie Colony, The Movie Makers* (New York: Harcourt Brace, 1941), 12–15, Appendix H, "Fan Mail"; Stamp, *Movie-Struck Girls*, 10–40; Gaylyn Studlar, "The Perils of Pleasure? Fan Magazine Discourse as Women's Commodified Culture in the 1920s," *Wide Angle* 13 (January 1991): 6–33; Rabinovitz, *For the Love of Pleasure*; Hansen, *Babel and Babylon*, 245–268; Melvyn Stokes, "The Female Audience of the 1920s and early 1930s," in *Identifying Hollywood's Audiences: Cultural Identity and the Movies*, ed. Stokes and Richard Maltby (London, 1999), 42–60; Richard Abel, "Fan Discourse in the Heartland" *Film History* 18.2 (2006): 140–153.

26. Manners quoted in Stenn, *Clara Bow*, 105, 117; Adela Rogers St. Johns, "The Playgirl of Hollywood," *Liberty*, August 3, 1929. On how America viewed Hollywood's women as in the vanguard of women's roles, see Hallett, *Go West, Young Women*; Elaine Tyler May, *Homeward Bound: American Families in the Cold War Era* (New York: Perseus, 1988), 42–49, 66, 95.

27. EG, "In Defense of Clara Bow."

28. "Marion's Six Questions: What recent EG story has been brought to the screen by MGM?" *Photoplay*, January 1927, 11; "Studio News and Gossip," *Photoplay*, February 1927. "IT is going to be the name of a motion picture feature. Ever since EG defined sex appeal as IT Hollywood has been seeking possessors of IT and endeavoring to get IT into its pictures." Cal York, "Studio News and Gossip," *Photoplay*, March 1927, 47. (Includes a photo of Bow looking Glynish.) EG says only GS, JG, RV, Vilma Bank, and Rex the horse possesses it. "As We Go to Press," *Photoplay*, March 1927, 6. "Sex Appeal Notes: Elinor Glyn will make her debut as an actress in 'It,'" *Photoplay*, April 1927, 10; "Studio News and Gossip," *Photoplay*, August 1927, 44; "Young Lochinvar Maynard," *Photoplay*, October 1927, 111; "As We Go to Press," *Photoplay*, January 1928, 10: "Famous players considering stellar possibilities of Gary Cooper now playing with Clara Bow in 'it.'" "Fighting the Sex Jinx," *Photoplay*, January 1927, 36.

29. Tricia Welsch, *Gloria Swanson: Ready for Her Close-Up* (Jackson: University of Mississippi Press, 2011), 198.

30. "IT," *Photoplay*, March 1927, 54.

31. EG, "In Defense of Clara Bow." "Elinor Glyn Rather Chary."

32. "Screen Notes," *New York Herald Tribune*, December 3, 1926; EG quoted in St. Johns, *Love, Laughter and Tears*, 229.

33. "My Life Story as Told to Adela Rogers St. Johns Pt. 3," *Photoplay*, April 1928, 125. Buddy Rogers quoted in Stenn, *Clara Bow*, 89.

34. All quotes, It (Paramount, 1927).

35. It (Paramount, 1927).

36. Whitney Williams "Under the Lights," *LAT*, Jan 16, 1927, J4.

37. Richard Watts Jr., "Saying Some Unkind Things about Madame Elinor Glyn," *New York Herald Tribune*, February 13, 1927; Harriette Underhill, "Elinor Glyn Explains 'It,'" February 7, 1927; "NEW FLAPPER MOVIE QUEEN," *Washington Post*, March 6, 1927; Robert F. Sisk, "Clara Bow Now Real Box Office Card," *Baltimore Sun*, May 27, 1927; "What 'Fans' Write to Stars," *NYT*, May 5, 1929.

38. Ivan St. Johns, "It Isn't Sex—It's Good Pictures: Elinor Glyn Gives a Convincing Analysis of What Makes Screen Success," *Photoplay*, March 1926, 36.

39. Harriette Underhill, "Red Hair," *New York Herald Tribune*, March 26, 1928; "Bow Scintillates as Gold-Digger," *Austin American*, March 11, 1928; "Clara Bow Appears in 'Red Hair' at Capitol Theater," *Hartford Courant*, April 29, 1928; "Clara Bow Stars in Gay Cinderella Comedy," *LAT*, December 2, 1928; "Clara Bow, Glyn, Produce Another 'Flaming Fillum,'" *Atlanta Constitution*, December 9, 1928; "'IT' GIRL IN GLYN STORY," *LAT*, December 14, 1928; "Mme. Glyn Has Fixed Opinions of Weekends," *Washington Post*, January 29, 1929; "The Flapper-De-Luxe of the Films," *Sporting and Dramatic News*, January 19, 1929; "Film Notables Make 'Red Hair' Great Picture," *The China Press*, February 13 1929; "What 'Fans' Write to Stars."

40. Fowler, *The Way She Looks Tonight*, 106–109.

41. On the film's box office, see Barnett and Weedon, *Elinor Glyn*, 115; "The Shadow Stage: Love's Blindness," *Photoplay*, March 1927, 53. "MANY OF FILMDOM'S PLUMS NOW ARE FALLING TO WOMEN," *Baltimore Sun*, December 25, 1927.

42. Zukor, *The Public Is Never Wrong*, 251. Michael Alexander, *Jazz Age Jews* (Princeton, NJ: Princeton University Press, 2001); Michael Rogin, *Black Face, White Noise: Jewish Immigrants and the Melting Pot* (Berkeley: University of California Press, 1998).

43. "Clara Now," *Kansas City Star*, November 16, 1933.

44. Mahar, *Women Filmmakers*; Stamp, *Lois Weber*; Gaines, *Pink-Slipped*; Cooper, *Universal Women*.

45. Weber quoted in Stamp, *Lois Weber*, 240.

46. Judith Mayne, *Directed by Dorothy Arzner* (Bloomington: Indiana University Press, 1994); Karen Ward Mahar, "True Womanhood in Hollywood: Gendered Business Strategies and the Rise and Fall of the Woman Filmmaker," *Enterprise & History* (2006): 75.

47. Barry quoted in Antonia Lant, with Ingrid Perez, eds., *Red Velvet Seat: Women's Writing on the First Fifty Years of Hollywood* (London: Verso, 2006), 26.
48. Marion quoted in Wendy Holliday, "Hollywood's Modern Woman: Screenwriting, Work, Culture and Feminism, 1910–1940," PhD diss., New York University, 1995, 391. *Film Weekly*, October 7, 1929; Beauchamp, *Without Lying Down*, 350, 354; On the shift in Thalberg's attitude, see Vieira, *Thalberg*, 140–144.

EPILOGUE: AFTERLIVES OF A TIGER QUEEN

1. Concern about Nell's tax troubles worried every lawyer who spoke to EG in the period and crescendoed over time. The archive at Reading is filled with letters, see particularly E.G.'s Income Tax in the US: Correspondence (1924–1929).
2. Ernest Freedman, "Elinor Glyn's Studio," *Times of India*, October 25, 1929, 16.
3. Quoted in Barnett and Weedon, *Elinor Glyn*, 159. For more details on her ventures directing in London see Barnett and Weedon, *Elinor Glyn*, 147–171. Lisa Stead, *Off to the Pictures: Cinema-going, Women's Writing and Movie Culture in Interwar Britain* (Edinburgh: Edinburgh University Press, 2016).
4. EG to Joseph Schenck, January 9, 1930, Box 20, Reading. Italics underlined in the original.
5. EG, *RA*, 333.
6. EG, "Human Vanity," October 17, 1939, Box 11, Reading.
7. This, of course, was the context for the picture on this book's cover. For more on the story, see Etherington-Smith and Pilcher, *It Girls*, 256.
8. LDG, *DI*, 1.
9. Beverley Nichols, *The Sweet and Twenties* (London: Weidenfeld and Nicolson, 1958), 35. Nichols, *The Unforgiving Minute*, 196.
10. EG, *RA*, 131.
11. Susan Sontag, "Notes on Camp" in *Partisan Review* 31 (1964): 517.
12. Beaton, "World of Elinor Glyn."
13. "Sex Symbol of Roaring 20s: Silent Movies 'It' Girl Clara Bow Dies at 60," *Atlanta Statesman*, September 27, 1965. Memory shared with the author, Susan Glyn. See Anthony Glyn to EG, Letter and reply (1929), Box 6, Reading; "The message of EG to the older Women of Britain," TS (1939), Box 11, Reading.
14. Beaton, "World of Elinor Glyn."

ILLUSTRATION CREDITS

INDEX

EG stands for Elinor Glyn. Page numbers in *italic* represents photos.